OXFORD WORLD'S CLASSICS

SYBIL

BENJAMIN DISRAELI, First Earl of Beaconsfield, was born in 1804 into a family of comfortably prosperous Jews, although he was baptized into the Anglican Church. He entered Lincoln's Inn in 1824, but his legal career was short-lived. He dabbled in journalism, and in his twenty-second year published his first novel, *Vivian Grey* (1826–7), to pay off his debts. In 1837 he entered Parliament as member for Maidstone, and in the next few years expressed his political and social views in fictional form in *Coningsby* (1844) and *Sybil* (1845). He was Prime Minister from February to December 1868 and from 1874 to 1880, and became the intimate friend of Queen Victoria. He died in 1881. He was the author not only of several novels, including *Tancred* (1847) and *Lothair* (1870), but also of political writings and a biography of Lord George Bentinck.

SHEILA M. SMITH, formerly Senior Lecturer in English at the University of Nottingham, is the author of *The Other Nation: The Poor in English Novels of the 1840s and 1850s*.

OXFORD WORLD'S CLASSICS

For over 100 years Oxford World's Classics have brought readers closer to the world's great literature. Now with over 700 titles—from the 4,000-year-old myths of Mesopotamia to the twentieth century's greatest novels—the series makes available lesser-known as well as celebrated writing.

The pocket-sized hardbacks of the early years contained introductions by Virginia Woolf, T. S. Eliot, Graham Greene, and other literary figures which enriched the experience of reading. Today the series is recognized for its fine scholarship and reliability in texts that span world literature, drama and poetry, religion, philosophy and politics. Each edition includes perceptive commentary and essential background information to meet the changing needs of readers.

OXFORD WORLD'S CLASSICS

BENJAMIN DISRAELI

Sybil

OR

The Two Nations

Edited with an Introduction and Notes by
SHEILA M. SMITH

OXFORD
UNIVERSITY PRESS

OXFORD

UNIVERSITY PRESS

Great Clarendon Street, Oxford OX2 6DP

Oxford University Press is a department of the University of Oxford.
It furthers the University's objective of excellence in research, scholarship,
and education by publishing worldwide in

Oxford New York

Auckland Bangkok Buenos Aires Cape Town Chennai
Dar es Salaam Delhi Hong Kong Istanbul Karachi Kolkata
Kuala Lumpur Madrid Melbourne Mexico City Mumbai Nairobi
São Paulo Shanghai Taipei Tokyo Toronto

Oxford is a registered trade mark of Oxford University Press
in the UK and in certain other countries

Published in the United States
by Oxford University Press Inc., New York

Introduction and Notes © Sheila M. Smith 1981

The moral rights of the author have been asserted

Database right Oxford University Press (maker)

First published as a World's Classics paperback 1981
Reissued as an Oxford World's Classics paperback 1998
Reissued 2008

British Library Cataloguing in Publication Data

Data available

Library of Congress Cataloging in Publication Data

Data available

ISBN 978-0-19-953905-5

4

Printed in Great Britain by
Clays Ltd, St Ives plc

CONTENTS

ACKNOWLEDGEMENTS

I AM GRATEFUL to the friends and colleagues who helped me elucidate Disraeli's references in *Sybil*, particularly Mr. John Bates, Dr. Thom Braun, Mr. W. R. Chalmers, Mr. George Cheshire, Professor K. Ingham, Mr. David Large, Mr. George Rowell, Dr. Michael Slater, Professor J. R. Vincent, Dr. Michael Watts, and Mr. David Young.

INTRODUCTION

The Times advertised *Sybil* as 'immediately ready' on 8 May
1845, and reviewed it on 13 May. Four days later Disraeli
received a letter from a young woman, Mrs. Baylis, who
described herself as 'a mechanic's wife' living in Sussex Terrace, a respectable, reasonably prosperous part of Camden
Town. She wrote of *Sybil*: 'Your writings *now* are for the great
body of the country, the People can feel, can understand, your
works . . . You set forth in stirring words in animated, striking,
and *truthful* description the real social condition of the country
the monstrous distinction betwixt Rich–Poor . . .'

I have already discussed the implications of this letter in *Mr.
Disraeli's Readers* (see Booklist p. xviii) but of interest here is
Mrs. Baylis's response to the novel's immediacy. Disraeli, a
practising politician, wrote it hurriedly to comment on contemporary and recently past events and to argue an acceptable
political creed offering hope for the future. The period covered
by the novel is 1837–44. Victoria became Queen in 1837, at a
time of national distress and disturbance. In the recurring
cycles of trade depression following the Napoleonic Wars
prices had fallen and wages had been cut. The people of the
rapidly increasing industrial towns, such as Manchester and
Birmingham, on which the country's wealth depended, had
lacked representation in Parliament. The Whig Reform Act
1832 provided for a more equitable distribution of seats, but
there was great disappointment that it extended the middle-
class rather than the working-class vote. Insufficient representation, falling wages, and the distress caused by the Poor Law
Amendment Act 1834 – an attempt to regulate the existing unsatisfactory poor laws by cutting down on outdoor relief and
forcing paupers to submit to the rigorous and inhuman regime
of the new workhouses – largely motivated the Chartists.
Chartism was a distinctively working-class movement which
began in the Working Men's Association, founded in 1836 by
William Lovett, and which aimed to secure, by every legal
method, equal political and social rights for all classes. The
Chartists believed that if the working class got the vote and if
working men were able to become MPs, working-class

wrongs would be righted. Their first National Petition to Parliament in 1839 (rejected) basically demanded universal male suffrage and the means to make it possible for a working man to be an MP.

It was not only factory-workers, then a small percentage of Britain's working-class population, who suffered low wages and bad living conditions. Agricultural labourers were among the last to receive material benefits from the new, expanding industrial system of nineteenth-century Britain, except in the areas where factories competed for available labour (see Harold Perkin: *The Origins of Modern English Society 1780–1880*, London, 1969, p. 147). In the south and east of the country wages were static and desperately low – in Wiltshire, for example, wages were 7s. a week in both 1770 and 1850. During the winter 1830–1 there were agricultural riots and rick burning, purportedly by the mysterious 'Captain Swing' (see E. J. Hobsbawm and George Rudé, *Captain Swing*, London, 1969, for a full treatment of the subject). The riots were quelled with great savagery, but poverty was so dire that ricks were burnt and farm-machines smashed each winter following, especially that of 1843–4. Aggravating the situation was the high price of bread due to the corn laws, which prevented cheap foreign wheat from being imported into the country. 1842, when the Home Secretary reported that almost 1,500,000 people in England and Wales were paupers receiving poor relief, has been described as 'probably the most distressed year of the whole nineteenth century' (see Steven Marcus, *Engels, Manchester, and the Working Class*, New York, 1974, p. 26 n and p. 87 n). After Parliament's rejection of the Chartists' second National Petition in 1842 there were riots and strikes in many parts of the country; also, it was the year of the 'plug riots' (described in *Sybil*, Book VI): Lancashire factory-workers demanded the restoration of the 1840 wage-level, and converged on Manchester (Disraeli's 'Mowbray') knocking out the plugs of the boilers in the mills and so depriving them of power and making them idle. Some working-class agitators and some middle-class observers (including Engels) thought it the beginning of the proletarian revolution. Eventually the factory operatives were forced to resume work without their demands being met; but it is important to remember that

Sybil was written at a time when revolution, on the French pattern, seemed possible in Britain.

When the novel was published Disraeli was forty, Tory MP for Shrewsbury in Peel's administration. He came of a family of comfortably prosperous Sephardim Jews, but his father, Isaac D'Israeli, a writer and scholar, had resigned from the Synagogue in 1817 and prudently had had his children baptized into the Anglican Church, so Benjamin's Jewish origins were no hindrance to his political ambitions. But first he started on a short-lived career as a lawyer; then he dabbled in journalism and accumulated debts. He wrote his first novel, *Vivian Grey* (1826–7), published anonymously, to pay them off. It is vigorous, satirical, and inventive, despite its wildly improbable plot and its equally improbable Byronic hero, who tries – and fails – to achieve power by political intrigue. From being acclaimed and eagerly read by London 'society', curious to identify the thinly disguised public figures in the book, it was vilified when the author was discovered to be an obscure young man, ignorant of London high life or politics. Later Disraeli was embarrassed by the novel and tried, unsuccessfully, to suppress it; but he revised it drastically for re-publication, attempting to eliminate its youthful brashness and ignorance of the world.

By 1845 Disraeli knew rather more about politics and the upper levels of London life. *Sybil* opens in Crockford's exclusive gambling club, St. James's Street, 'in a vast and golden saloon' where the young aristocrats are betting on the 1837 Derby and steadying their nerves with 'mystical combinations of French wines and German waters, flavoured with slices of Portugal fruits, and cooled with lumps of American ice'. Here are the details of luxurious living expected in a 'fashionable' or, to use Hazlitt's phrase, 'silver-fork' novel, popular after the publication of Robert Plumer Ward's *Tremaine* (1825). This genre was becoming unfashionable in 1845: Carlyle satirized it in *Sartor Resartus* (1833–4), and Dickens guyed it in *Nicholas Nickleby* (1838–9). But Disraeli, a flamboyant dandy like his friends Edward Bulwer and Count D'Orsay, enjoyed this kind of writing. He had already published several 'silver-fork' novels besides *Vivian Grey*: *The Young Duke* (1831), describing a wealthy young aristocrat's gradual acceptance of social responsibility; *Henrietta Temple* (1837), a semi-autobiographical love story; and *Venetia* (1837), a fictional account of the lives of Byron and Shelley. Delight in exotic scenes of aristocratic splendour is evident in all Disraeli's novels including the later ones: *Lothair* (1870), which was again concerned with contemporary events – Garibaldi's abortive attempt to liberate Italy in 1867, and the Marquess of Bute's conversion to Roman Catholicism in 1868; and his last complete novel, *Endymion* (1880), a nostalgic fairy tale of the political events of 1830–50. Although such scenes are sometimes almost as exaggerated as Daisy Ashford's high-life fantasies in *The Young Visiters*, from *Vivian Grey* onwards they are often spiced with satire and accompany keen interest in political intrigue and power. But they are given a much greater sense of purpose in *Coningsby* (1844), the novel immediately preceding *Sybil*. In both books Disraeli's knowledge of the London clubs and of the saloons and country houses of the great ladies of politics (such as the Tory Lady Jersey, the fictional Lady St. Julians) is used to express the nature of contemporary political life, not simply to indulge in daydreams of political power. Descriptions of English aristocratic life are the best and most substantial part of *Tancred* (1847), the extraordinary eulogy of Judaism as the fount of Christianity which completes Disraeli's trilogy of novels in the 1840s.

In the 1830s and 1840s an increasing number of writers and reformers attempted to inform middle-class readers and influence opinion concerning social distress accentuated by the Industrial Revolution. It was the time of the early Royal Commissions and Blue Books (Government Reports, so-called because they are bound in stiff blue paper) investigating labour conditions in factories, sanitation, and destitution both urban and rural. The literary counterparts of these enquiries were the novels 'with a purpose' which debated 'the Condition of England' and exposed social problems. The novel, the increasingly popular literary form, often available in cheap editions made possible by the newly invented steam printing press, was an excellent way of propagating ideas and ideologies. Anthony Trollope's mother, Frances, published *Michael Armstrong* (1840), a melodramatic account of child labour in the factories; in *Jessie Phillips* (1843) she attacked the 1834 Poor Law, as did Dickens in *Oliver Twist* (1837–8). Charlotte Elizabeth Tonna, in *Helen Fleetwood* (1841), exposed the miseries of the rural poor who came to look for work in the industrial town. In the General Preface to the collected edition of his novels (1870–1) Disraeli summarized the ideas embodied in the first two novels of his trilogy:

The derivation and character of political parties; the condition of the people which had been the consequence of them; the duties of the Church as a main remedial agency in our present state, were the three principal topics which I intended to treat, but I found they were too vast for the space I had allotted to myself. These were all launched in *Coningsby*; but the origin and condition of political parties, the first portion of the theme, was the only one completely handled in that work.

Next year, in *Sybil*, I considered the condition of the people.

The two novels express the Tory ideology formulated in Disraeli's *Vindication of the English Constitution* (1835), which attacked the Whigs and the Utilitarians and designated the Tory party 'the national party . . . It supports the institutions of the country, because they have been established for the common good, and because they secure the equality of civil rights, without which, whatever may be its name, no government can be free, and based upon which principle, every government, however it may be styled, is, in fact, a Democracy.' Obviously such thinking owes a debt to Burke, who argued that the state and its institutions are an organic growth, and is in opposition to Bentham, the father of Utilitarianism, who defined society as an aggregate of individuals.

Disraeli's philosophy of history – if his ideology merits that name – also has affinities with Cobbett's Radical Toryism and with Walter Scott's romantic Toryism. These ideas earned Disraeli the leadership of a small group of friends, all Tory MPs, known as 'Young England'. They appear in *Coningsby*. Coningsby himself is an idealized portrait of George Smythe, the brilliant and dissipated eldest son of Lord Strangford; Lord Henry Sydney is Lord John Manners, later the seventh Duke of Rutland; and Buckhurst is Alexander Baillie-Cochrane. Egremont, in *Sybil*, also owes a lot to Lord John Manners, although there is much of Disraeli himself in the character, especially in his attitude to Chartism. Young England was not a political party but a group of friends sharing political views. They were active for a very short period, from 1842 until 1846, when the alliance began to split up. They attacked the Utilitarians and yearned for an idealized feudal society in which Church and aristocracy combined to protect the people's rights. They criticized the 1834 Poor Law, attempted to improve working-class housing, supported Lord Ashley's factory reforms, and urged the importance of holidays (which they spelt 'holydays') for the people. Also, they argued that the Church had a responsibility for men's bodies as well as for their souls. (For a full account of Young England and Disraeli's association with it, see Robert Blake, *Disraeli*, London, 1966, pp. 167–89.) Like Pugin's Gothic architecture, the Oxford Movement, and the later Pre-Raphaelite Brotherhood, Young England was a romantic protest against the scientific, Utilitarian economics and politics of the time. They were guilty of many follies, including an uncritical adulation of the Stuarts, particularly Charles I ('Rightly was King Charles surnamed the Martyr; for he was the holocaust of direct taxation. Never yet did man lay down his heroic life for so great a cause: the cause of the Church and the cause of the Poor.' *Sybil*, Book IV, Chapter 6), and their dream of uniting aristocrat and working man was sometimes expressed in acutely embarrassing social functions and cricket matches. *Punch* mocked them; Dickens originally included satire on Young England in *The Chimes* (1844), and slyly ridiculed the cult of Charles I in poor Mr. Dick's obsession with that monarch's head in *David Copperfield* (1850). However, Young England genuinely desired reform, and Lord John Manners's journals show his determination to fulfil the responsibilities which he felt accompanied wealth and aristocratic position.

But Young England in 1844 were all, apart from Disraeli, youths in their twenties. Older than the rest and by far the most intelligent, Disraeli was ambitious, longing for power and the limelight. He was remarkable for his determination and resilience. He tried five times before he at last succeeded in getting into Parliament. Once there, his maiden speech was laughed to scorn. Undaunted, he shouted 'The time will come when you will hear me' – and it did. Such a man was not going to rest content with the leadership of a small Tory splinter

group. Disraeli bore a grudge against Peel who, not unreason-
ably, had refused to give him office in 1841. Although his
attitude towards Peel is amicable enough in *Coningsby*, he
criticizes Peel's Tamworth Manifesto of 1834 as 'an attempt
to construct a party without principles . . . There was indeed
considerable shouting about what they called Conservative
principles; but the awkward question naturally arose, what
will you conserve?' (*Coningsby*, Book II, Chapter 5.) The
criticism becomes sharper in *Sybil*. Cynicism, deviousness, and
political expediency characterize 'the Man in Downing Street',
the satiric portrait of Peel. In the earlier novel Coningsby
rejected the old-style, self-seeking Toryism of his grandfather
Lord Monmouth (based on the Marquess of Hertford, also the
model for Thackeray's Lord Steyne in *Vanity Fair*, 1848), as
Egremont rejects that of his brother, Lord Marney, in favour
of a new-style Toryism which yet has its roots in the past and
is based on an ideal union of Church, Monarch, and People.
This is Disraeli's political manifesto, as against Peel's. Like
Carlyle (see particularly *Chartism*, 1839, and *Past and Present*,
1843), Disraeli advocates a feudal hierarchy directed by
energetic, intelligent leaders who look to the future in that
they recognize the wonder and the potential of the Industrial
Revolution. Disraeli will have nothing of 'Gallic equality', no
English equivalent of the French Revolution. The people cannot lead, as Egremont explains to Sybil (Book IV, Chapter 15),
but they need a leader from the ranks of the true aristocracy. It
becomes plain in the novel that Disraeli feels himself to be one
of these aristocrats. After its publication, when Young England disintegrated, it became obvious that Disraeli aimed to
supplant Peel as leader of the Tory party.

In *Sybil* Disraeli explores and popularizes an idea which had
been current for some time – Cobbett and Carlyle, among
others, had expressed it – that Britain's increasing wealth had
divided it into the rich and the poor, the 'Two Nations' of the
novel's subtitle. Like Dickens's 'Boz' venturing into the unknown territory of the London poor, Egremont, the younger
son of an aristocratic family, ennobled through the spoliation
of the monasteries, learns something of working-class life
through his friendship with the Chartist leader Walter Gerard,
Gerard's daughter Sybil, and the Chartist journalist Stephen

Morley. Using his own experiences in brief visits to the northern industrial cities, drawing on Blue Book information and
on the Chartist leader Feargus O'Connor's file of correspondence for his newspaper the *Northern Star*, Disraeli crams a bewildering number of topics into the novel: Chartism and
Chartist riots, the iniquity of the truck system (payment of
workers in goods instead of in cash), female and child labour
in coal-mines, the growth of trades unions, the plight of the
handloom weavers, the agricultural depression, the insanitary
squalor of the agricultural labourers' existence. Although parts
of the novel are deliberately structured – for example the com-
parison between horse-racing and the jockeying for place in
political life made in the opening chapters, and the repeated
contrast between life lived by the rich and that experienced by
the poor as in the Deloraine House ball, with its political intrigues, followed by the Hyde Park scene of destitution in
which the crossing-sweepers aspire to be link-boys – it lacks
organization and some of the Blue Book facts are undigested.
It is held together only by Disraeli's voice, mostly using the
tones of Parliamentary debate: quiet sarcasm, fierce attack,
challenge, exhortation. In a sense, Disraeli himself is the most
important character in the novel, and its vigour proceeds
from his constant stream of ideas and wit. Its strength is the
evocation of the business of English politics – its passions, its
intrigues, its aspirations, its tedium. His creation of the agents
Tadpole and Taper, the Rosencrantz and Guildenstern of Tory
political life, would alone justify Disraeli's reputation as a
novelist. He is unable to create a community, as Elizabeth
Gaskell does in the Manchester scenes in *Mary Barton*, but he
competently assembles Wodgate from the Blue Books, as he
does the squalid rural town Marney, adding memories of his
own northern visits, and using the place as a foil for its selfish
landlord, Lord Marney, whose whining tone of self-justification
and complaint is perfectly caught. Generally, his characters are
pallid mouthpieces for ideas, such as Egremont, Gerard, and
Morley; or Blue Book facts galvanized into activity and improbable speech, such as Devilsdust and the inhabitants of
Mowbray; or theatrical tuppence-coloureds like Baptist
Hatton, with his aura of mystery, his gourmet breakfasts, and
his attendant cats. Sybil herself is an emblematic figure, the

emissary of a socially conscious Church. Presented in a series of static poses as the Ministering Angel or Lady Bountiful or Our Lady of Sorrows, like a stylized figure by a Nazarene painter, she first appears in the ruins of Marney Abbey (based on Fountains, beloved of contemporary engravers of the picturesque), which evoke Cobbett's pre-Reformation England and Pugin's humane Gothic church, which in *Contrasts* (1833) he set against the bleak Utilitarian workhouses. The ruins also suggest those in which Childe Harold found spiritual solace: both Egremont and Sybil are given to melancholy soul-searchings of the kind Byron made fashionable.

Disraeli's conviction that there is barbarism and savagery in the other 'Nation' of which his readers should take warning betrays him into the over-emphasis and exaggeration of which Dickens is sometimes guilty. He chooses to present the worst details of the worst trade in Wodgate, the town of locksmiths. But although he has no ability to tease out the complexity of a character or a situation, as does George Eliot for example, his freedom from moral earnestness and his ability to see more than one side of a question prevent his producing ludicrous ogres like Frances Trollope's factory-owner, Sir Matthew Dowling, in *Michael Armstrong*. 'Bishop' Hatton is grotesque, but he has vigour because, despite his brutality, his skill gives him an authority which England's effete aristocracy and indifferent clergy have forfeited.

Like most of the 'Condition of England' novels in the 1840s, *Sybil* is optimistic despite its note of warning. Although admitting injustices and imperfections, the energetic early Victorians could not countenance the idea of ultimate disaster and failure. The fear of revolution, evident in the description of the mob's attack on the tommy-shop or on Mowbray Castle, as it is in the riot-scenes in Dickens's *Barnaby Rudge* (1841) and Charles Kingsley's *Alton Locke* (1850), is countered by the final vision of hope for the future. England is to be saved by the nation's responsible youth, Disraeli obviously counting himself of the company despite his forty years. This is what his correspondent Mrs. Baylis, herself young and obviously idealistic, had responded to, although the 'truth' of Disraeli's descriptions is sometimes in doubt. The necessary secrecy with which trade union affairs were conducted (membership could cost a man his job) is reduced to melodrama and, despite the respect accorded to Gerard's and Morley's ideas, Chartism finally becomes a charade, at the mercy of the drunken egotist Hatton. Those hectic scenes at the end of the novel, which Disraeli tossed off in such haste for the publisher, illustrate the difficulty of reconciling an account of contemporary conditions with the demands of the novel, particularly a love-story with a happy ending. As contemporary reviewers pointed out, the plot does *not* unite the 'Two Nations'. Sybil is not a daughter of the people, who, we are told, are not worthy to provide a husband for her, but an aristocrat in disguise. This aristocracy is justified in its recognition of its social duties as well as its privileges, and therefore provides satisfactory leadership for the struggling people. That some of them were content that this should be so is clear from Mrs. Baylis's letter. But, as Robert Blake remarks in his biography of Disraeli, it is difficult to see how the union of Church, Throne, and People was to counteract the destitution described in the novel. Its vision does not spring from its factual observations, but is rather imposed upon them.

Disraeli was never a popular novelist like Dickens or Thackeray or Trollope. His novels had satisfactory rather than large sales, apart from *Lothair*, which attracted the curious because it was written by an ex-Prime Minister. He is an exotic among English novelists. Although he appreciated the increasing power of the middle class he did not share their attitudes. Even while admiring Trafford, the model factory-owner, he suggests that some of his work people were bored by the schooling he provided, and he describes the gaiety of the factory-workers as well as their hardships. To be properly understood Disraeli's novels should be approached by way of the eighteenth-century discursive novel, Byron's satiric narratives, and Thomas Love Peacock's witty conversation pieces. In such writing the domestic interior which Elizabeth Gaskell describes in *Mary Barton* is out of place. Disraeli's métier is wit which exposes the aristocrat or the politician:

Lord Marney, who was fond of chess, turned out Captain Grouse, and very gallantly proposed to finish his game with Miss Poinsett, which Miss Poinsett, who understood Lord Marney as well as he understood chess, took care speedily to lose, so that his lordship might encounter a champion worthy of him. (Book II, Chapter 6)

'People get into Parliament to get on; their aims are indefinite.' (Lady St. Julians, Book IV, Chapter 3)

'After all, it is only a turn-out. I cannot recast her Majesty's speech and bring in rebellion and closed mills, instead of loyalty and a good harvest.' (The 'gentleman in Downing Street', Book VI, Chapter 1)

Disraeli's scenes may sometimes be stagey, even ludicrous, as in the love-passages between Morley and Sybil (Book V, Chapter 4); his ideas may sometimes be outrageous or his interpretation of history preposterous; yet we are always aware of his sharp intelligence and lively mind. He has that inestimable virtue in a writer of fiction: he is never dull.

SHEILA M. SMITH

NOTE ON THE TEXT

The text of *Sybil* reproduced in this edition is that of Longmans' Collected and Revised Edition of Disraeli's Novels 1870–1, the most important collected edition of Disraeli's novels in the nineteenth century, overseen by the author. Unless mentioned in the Notes, the few alterations made to this text, such as corrections of misprints and occasional modernizations of spelling, have been effected silently.

SELECT BIBLIOGRAPHY

BIOGRAPHY, BACKGROUND, AND BIBLIOGRAPHY

Blake, Robert, *Disraeli* (Eyre & Spottiswoode, 1966).

Jerman, B. R., *The Young Disraeli* (Princeton University Press, 1960).

Maurois, André, *Disraeli: A Picture of the Victorian Age*, translated by Hamish Miles (John Lane, 1927).

Smith, Sheila M. (ed.), *Mr. Disraeli's Readers: Letters written to Benjamin Disraeli and his wife by nineteenth-century readers of 'Sybil; or the Two Nations'* (University of Nottingham, 1966).

Stewart, R. W., *Benjamin Disraeli: A list of writings by him, and writings about him, with notes* (Scarecrow, 1972).

STUDIES OF DISRAELI'S FICTION

Braun, Thom, *Disraeli the Novelist* (George Allen & Unwin, 1981).

Holloway, John, 'Disraeli' in *The Victorian Sage* (Macmillan, 1953).

Pritchett, V. S., 'Disraeli' in *The Living Novel* (Chatto and Windus, 1946).

Schwarz, Daniel R., *Disraeli's Fiction* (Macmillan, 1979).

VICTORIAN FICTION AND THE SOCIAL PROBLEM

Bodenheimer, Rosemarie, *The Politics of Story in Victorian Fiction* (Cornell University Press, 1988).

Brantlinger, Patrick, *The Spirit of Reform: British Literature and Politics, 1832–1867* (Harvard University Press, 1977).

Childers, Joseph W., *Novel Possibilities: Fiction and the Formation of Early Victorian Culture* (University of Pennsylvania Press, 1995).

Flint, Kate (ed.), *The Victorian Novelist: Social Problems and Social Change* (Croom Helm, 1987).

Gallagher, Catherine, *The Industrial Reformation of English Fiction: Social Discourse and Narrative Form, 1832–1867* (University of Chicago Press, 1985).

Smith, Sheila M., *The Other Nation: The Poor in English Novels of the 1840s and 1850s* (Oxford University Press, 1980).

SOME USEFUL ARTICLES ON *SYBIL*

Bivona, Daniel, 'Disraeli's Political Trilogy and the Antinomic Structure of Imperial Desire', *Novel*, 22 (1989), pp. 305–25.

Fido, Martin, '"From His Own Observation": Sources of Working Class Passages in Disraeli's *Sybil*', *Modern Languages Review*, 72 (1977), pp. 268–84.

Handwerk, Gary, 'Behind *Sybil*'s Veil: Disraeli's Mix of Ideological Messages', *Modern Languages Quarterly*, 49 (1988), pp. 321–41.

O'Kell, Robert, 'Two Nations, or One? Disraeli's Allegorical Romance', *Victorian Studies*, 30 (1987), pp. 211–34.

Yeazell, Ruth Bernard, 'Why Political Novels Have Heroines: *Sybil, Mary Barton*, and *Felix Holt*', *Novel*, 18 (1985), pp. 126–44.

SYBIL

OR

THE TWO NATIONS

*

The Commonalty murmured, and said, 'There never were so many Gentlemen, and so little Gentleness.'

BISHOP LATIMER

I would inscribe this work to one whose noble spirit and gentle nature ever prompt her to sympathise with the suffering; to one whose sweet voice has often encouraged, and whose taste and judgment have ever guided, its pages; the most severe of critics, but – a perfect Wife!

ADVERTISEMENT

(1845)

THE GENERAL READER whose attention has not been specially drawn to the subject which these volumes aim to illustrate – the Condition of the People – might suspect that the Writer had been tempted to some exaggeration in the scenes that he has drawn, and the impressions he has wished to convey. He thinks it therefore due to himself to state that the descriptions, generally, are written from his own observation; but while he hopes he has alleged nothing which is not true, he has found the absolute necessity of suppressing much that is genuine. For so little do we know of the state of our own country, that the air of improbability which the whole truth would inevitably throw over these pages, might deter some from their perusal.

GROSVENOR GATE:
May-Day, 1845.

BOOK I

*

CHAPTER I

'I'LL take the odds against Caravan.'

'In ponies?'

'Done.'

And Lord Milford, a young noble, entered in his book the bet which he had just made with Mr. Latour, a grey-headed member of the Jockey Club.

It was the eve of the Derby of 1837. In a vast and golden saloon, that in its decorations would have become, and in its splendour would not have disgraced, Versailles in the days of the grand monarch, were assembled many whose hearts beat at the thought of the morrow, and whose brains still laboured to control its fortunes to their advantage.

'They say that Caravan looks puffy,' lisped, in a low voice, a young man, lounging on the edge of a buhl table that had once belonged to a Mortemart, and dangling a rich cane with affected indifference, in order to conceal his anxiety from all, except the person whom he addressed.

'They are taking seven to two against him freely over the way,' was the reply. 'I believe it's all right.'

'Do you know I dreamed last night something about Mango?' continued the gentleman with the cane, and with a look of uneasy superstition.

His companion shook his head.

'Well,' continued the gentleman with the cane, 'I have no opinion of him. I betted Charles Egremont the odds against Mango this morning; he goes with us, you know. By-the-bye, who is our Fourth?'

'I thought of Milford,' was the reply in an under tone. 'What say you?'

'Milford is going with St. James and Punch Hughes.'

'Well, let us come in to supper, and we shall see some fellow we like.'

So saying, the companions, taking their course through more than one chamber, entered an apartment of less dimensions than the principal saloon, but not less sumptuous in its general appearance. The gleaming lustres poured a flood of soft yet brilliant light over a plateau glittering with gold plate, and fragrant with exotics embedded in vases of rare porcelain. The seats on each side of the table were occupied by persons consuming, with a heedless air, delicacies for which they had no appetite; while the conversation in general consisted of flying phrases referring to the impending event of the great day that had already dawned.

'Come from Lady St. Julians', Fitz?' said a youth of tender years, and whose fair visage was as downy and as blooming as the peach from which, with a languid air, he withdrew his lips to make this inquiry of the gentleman with the cane.

'Yes; why were not you there?'

'I never go anywhere,' replied the melancholy Cupid, 'everything bores me so.'

'Well, will you go to Epsom with us to-morrow, Alfred?' said Lord Fitzheron. 'I take Berners and Charles Egremont, and with you our party will be perfect.'

'I feel so cursed blasé!' exclaimed the boy in a tone of elegant anguish.

'I will give you a fillip, Alfred,' said Mr. Berners; 'do you all the good in the world.'

'Nothing can do me good,' said Alfred, throwing away his almost untasted peach; 'I should be quite content if anything could do me harm. Waiter, bring me a tumbler of Badminton.'

'And bring me one too,' sighed our Lord Eugene De Vere, who was a year older than Alfred Mountchesney, his companion and brother in listlessness. Both had exhausted life in their teens, and all that remained for them was to mourn, amid the ruins of their reminiscences, over the extinction of excitement.

'Well, Eugene, suppose you come with us,' said Lord Fitzheron.

'I think I shall go down to Hampton Court and play tennis,' said Lord Eugene. 'As it is the Derby, nobody will be there.'

'And I will go with you, Eugene,' said Alfred Mountchesney, 'and we will dine together afterwards at the Toy. Anything is better than dining in this infernal London.'

'Well, for my part,' said Mr. Berners, 'I do not like your

suburban dinners. You always get something you can't eat, and cursed bad wine.'

'I rather like bad wine,' said Mrs Mountchesney; 'one gets so bored with good wine.'

'Do you want the odds against Hybiscus, Berners?' said a guardsman, looking up from his book, which he had been intently studying.

'All I want is some supper, and as you are not using your place—'

'You shall have it. Oh! here's Milford, he will bet me them.'

And at this moment entered the room the young nobleman whom we have before mentioned, accompanied by an individual who was approaching perhaps the termination of his fifth lustre, but whose general air rather betokened even a less experienced time of life. Tall, with a well-proportioned figure and a graceful carriage, his countenance touched with a sensibility that at once engages the affections, Charles Egremont was not only admired by that sex whose approval generally secures men enemies among their fellows, but was at the same time the favourite of his own.

'Ah, Egremont! come and sit here,' exclaimed more than one banqueter.

'I saw you waltzing with the little Bertie, old fellow,' said Lord Fitzheron, 'and therefore did not stay to speak to you, as I thought we should meet here. I am to call for you, mind.'

'How shall we all feel this time to-morrow?' said Egremont, smiling.

'The happiest fellow at this moment must be Cockie Graves,' said Lord Milford. 'He can have no suspense. I have been looking over his book, and I defy him, whatever happens, not to lose.'

'Poor Cockie,' said Mr. Berners; 'he has asked me to dine with him at the Clarendon on Saturday.'

'Cockie is a very good Cockie,' said Lord Milford, 'and Caravan is a very good horse; and if any gentleman sportsman present wishes to give seven to two, I will take him to any amount.'

'My book is made up,' said Egremont: 'and I stand or fall by Caravan.'

'And I.'

'And I.'

'And I.'

'Well, mark my words,' said a fourth, rather solemnly, 'Rat-trap wins.'

'There is not a horse except Caravan,' said Lord Milford, 'fit for a borough stake.'

'You used to be all for Phosphorus, Egremont,' said Lord Eugene de Vere.

'Yes; but fortunately I have got out of that scrape. I owe Phip Dormer a good turn for that. I was the third man who knew he had gone lame.'

'And what are the odds against him now?'

'Oh! nominal; forty to one; what you please.'

'He won't run,' said Mr. Berners, 'John Day told me he had refused to ride him.'

'I believe Cockie Graves might win something if Phosphorus came in first,' said Lord Milford, laughing.

'How close it is to-night!' said Egremont. 'Waiter, give me some Seltzer water; and open another window; open them all.'

At this moment an influx of guests intimated that the assembly at Lady St. Julians' had broken up. Many at the table rose and yielded their places, clustering round the chimney-piece, or forming in various groups, and discussing the great question. Several of those who had recently entered were votaries of Rat-trap, the favourite, and quite prepared, from all the information that had reached them, to back their opinions valiantly. The conversation had now become general and animated, or rather there was a medley of voices in which little was distinguished except the names of horses and the amount of odds. In the midst of all this, waiters glided about, handing incomprehensible mixtures bearing aristocratic names; mystical combinations of French wines and German waters, flavoured with slices of Portugal fruits, and cooled with lumps of American ice, compositions which immortalized the creative genius of some high patrician name.

'By Jove! that's a flash,' exclaimed Lord Milford, as a blaze of lightning seemed to suffuse the chamber, and the beaming lustres turned white and ghastly in the glare.

The thunder rolled over the building. There was a dead

silence. Was it going to rain? Was it going to pour? Was the storm confined to the metropolis? Would it reach Epsom? A deluge, and the course would be a quagmire, and strength might baffle speed.

Another flash, another explosion, the hissing noise of rain. Lord Milford moved aside, and, jealous of the eye of another, read a letter from Chifney, and in a few minutes afterwards offered to take the odds against Pocket Hercules. Mr. Latour walked to the window, surveyed the heavens, sighed that there was not time to send his tiger from the door to Epsom, and get information whether the storm had reached the Surrey hills, for to-night's operations. It was too late. So he took a rusk and a glass of lemonade, and retired to rest with a cool head and a cooler heart.

The storm raged, the incessant flash played as it were round the burnished cornice of the chamber, and threw a lurid hue on the scenes of Watteau* and Boucher* that sparkled in the medallions over the lofty doors. The thunderbolts seemed to descend in clattering confusion upon the roof. Sometimes there was a moment of dead silence, broken only by the pattering of the rain in the street without, or the pattering of the dice in a chamber at hand. Then horses were backed, bets made, and there were loud and frequent calls for brimming goblets from hurrying waiters, distracted by the lightning and deafened by the peal. It seemed a scene and a supper where the marble guest of Juan* might have been expected; and, had he arrived, he would have found probably hearts as bold and spirits as reckless as he encountered in Andalusia.

CHAPTER 2

'WILL any one do anything about Hybiscus?' sang out a gentleman in the ring at Epsom. It was full of eager groups; round the betting post a swarming cluster, while the magic circle itself was surrounded by a host of horsemen shouting from their saddles the odds they were ready to receive or give, and the names of the horses they were prepared to back or to oppose.

'Will any one do anything about Hybiscus?'

'I'll bet you five to one,' said a tall, stiff Saxon peer, in a white great-coat.

'No; I'll take six.'

The tall, stiff peer in the white great-coat mused for a moment with his pencil at his lip, and then said, 'Well, I'll bet you six. What do you say about Mango?'

'Eleven to two against Mango,' called out a little hump-backed man in a shrill voice, but with the air of one who was master of his work.

'I should like to do a little business with you, Mr. Chippendale,' said Lord Milford, in a coaxing tone, 'but I must have six to one.'

'Eleven to two, and no mistake,' said this keeper of a second-rate gaming-house, who, known by the flattering appellation of Hump Chippendale, now turned with malignant abruptness from the heir-apparent of an English earldom.

'You shall have six to one, my Lord,' said Captain Spruce, a debonair personage, with a well-turned silk hat arranged a little aside, his coloured cravat tied with precision, his whiskers trimmed like a quickset hedge. Spruce, who had earned his title of Captain on the plains of Newmarket, which had witnessed for many a year his successful exploits, had a weakness for the aristocracy, who, knowing his graceful infirmity, patronized him with condescending dexterity, acknowledged his existence in Pall-Mall as well as at Tattersall's, and thus occasionally got a point more than the betting out of him. Hump Chippendale had none of these gentle failings; he was a democratic leg, who loved to fleece a noble, and thought all men were born equal; a consoling creed that was a hedge for his hump.

'Seven to four against the favourite; seven to two against Caravan; eleven to two against Mango. What about Benedict? Will any one do anything about Pocket Hercules? Thirty to one against Dardanelles.'

'Done.'

'Five-and-thirty ponies to one against Phosphorus,' shouted a little man vociferously and repeatedly.

'I will bet forty,' said Lord Milford. No answer; nothing done.

'Forty to one!' murmured Egremont, who stood against

Phosphorus. A little nervous, he said to the peer in the white great-coat, 'Don't you think that Phosphorus may, after all, have some chance?'

'I should be cursed sorry to be deep against him,' said the peer.

Egremont with a quivering lip walked away. He consulted his book; he meditated anxiously. Should he hedge? It was scarcely worth while to mar the symmetry of his winnings; he stood 'so well' by all the favourites; and for a horse at forty to one. No; he would trust his star, he would not hedge.

'Mr. Chippendale,' whispered the peer in the white great-coat, 'go and press Mr. Egremont about Phosphorus. I should not be surprised if you got a good thing.'

At this moment, a huge, broad-faced, rosy-gilled fellow, with one of those good-humoured yet cunning countenances that we meet occasionally north of the Trent, rode up to the ring on a square cob, and, dismounting, entered the circle. He was a carcase-butcher famous in Carnaby-market, and the prime counsellor of a distinguished nobleman, for whom privately he betted on commission. His secret service to-day was to bet against his noble employer's own horse, and so he at once sung out, 'Twenty to one against Man-trap.'

A young gentleman just launched into the world, and who, proud of his ancient and spreading acres, was now making his first book, seeing Man-trap marked eighteen to one on the cards, jumped eagerly at this bargain, while Lord Fitz-heron and Mr. Berners, who were at hand, and who in their days had found their names in the book of the carcase-butcher, and grown wise by it, interchanged a smile.

'Mr. Egremont will not take,' said Hump Chippendale to the peer in the white great-coat.

'You must have been too eager,' said his noble friend.

The ring is up; the last odds declared; all gallop away to the Warren. A few minutes, only a few minutes, and the event that for twelve months has been the pivot of so much calculation, of such subtle combinations, of such deep conspiracies, round which the thought and passion of the sporting world have hung like eagles, will be recorded in the fleeting tablets of the past. But what minutes! Count them by sensation, and not by calendars, and each moment is a day and the race a life.

Hogarth, in a coarse and yet animated sketch, has painted 'Before' and 'After.' A creative spirit of a higher vein might develop the simplicity of the idea with sublimer accessories. Pompeius before Pharsalia,* Harold before Hastings, Napoleon before Waterloo, might afford some striking contrasts to the immediate catastrophe of their fortunes. Finer still, the inspired mariner who has just discovered a new world; the sage who has revealed a new planet; and yet the 'Before' and 'After' of a first-rate English race, in the degree of its excitement, and sometimes in the tragic emotions of its close, may vie even with these.

They are saddling the horses; Caravan looks in great condition; and a scornful smile seems to play upon the handsome features of Pavis, as, in the becoming colours of his employer, he gracefully gallops his horse before his admiring supporters. Egremont, in the delight of an English patrician, scarcely saw Mango, and never even thought of Phosphorus; Phosphorus, who, by-the-bye, was the first horse that showed, with both his forelegs bandaged.

They are off!

As soon as they are well away, Chifney makes the running with Pocket Hercules. Up to the Rubbing House he is leading; this is the only point the eye can select. Higher up the hill, Caravan, Hybiscus, Benedict, Mahometan, Phosphorus, Michel Fell, and Rat-trap are with the grey, forming a front rank, and at the new ground the pace has told its fate, for half a dozen are already out of the race.

The summit is gained; the tactics alter; here Pavis brings up Caravan, with extraordinary severity; the pace round Tattenham corner terrific; Caravan leading, then Phosphorus a little above him, Mahometan, next, Hybiscus fourth, Rattrap looking badly. Wisdom, Benedict, and another handy. By this time Pocket Hercules has enough, and at the road the tailing grows at every stride. Here the favourite himself is hors de combat, as well as Dardanelles, and a crowd of lesser celebrities.

There are now but four left in the race, and of these, two, Hybiscus and Mahometan, are some lengths behind. Now it is neck and neck between Caravan and Phosphorus. At the stand, Caravan has decidedly the best; but just at the post,

Edwards, on Phosphorus, lifts the gallant little horse, and with an extraordinary effort contrives to shove him in by half a length.

'You look a little low, Charley,' said Lord Fitzheron, as, taking their lunch in their drag, he poured the champagne into the glass of Egremont.

'By Jove!' said Lord Milford, 'only think of Cockie Graves having gone and done it!'

CHAPTER 3

EGREMONT was the younger brother of an English earl, whose nobility, being of nearly three centuries' date, ranked him among our high and ancient peers, although its origin was more memorable than illustrious. The founder of the family had been a confidential domestic of one of the favourites of Henry VIII, and had contrived to be appointed one of the commissioners for 'visiting and taking the surrenders of divers religious houses.' It came to pass that divers of these religious houses surrendered themselves eventually to the use and benefit of honest Baldwin Greymount. The king was touched with the activity and zeal of his commissioner. Not one of them whose reports were so ample and satisfactory, who could baffle a wily prior with more dexterity, or control a proud abbot with more firmness. Nor were they well-digested reports alone that were transmitted to the sovereign: they came accompanied with many rare and curious articles, grateful to the taste of one who was not only a religious reformer but a dilettante; golden candlesticks and costly chalices; sometimes a jewelled pix; fantastic spoons and patens, rings for the fingers and the ear; occasionally a fair-written and blazoned manuscript: suitable offering to the royal scholar. Greymount was noticed; sent for; promoted in the household; knighted; might doubtless have been sworn of the council, and in due time have become a minister; but his was a discreet ambition, of an accumulative rather than an aspiring character. He served the king faithfully in all domestic matters that required an unimpressed, unscrupulous agent; fashioned his creed and conscience according to the royal model in all its freaks; seized the right moment to get sundry grants of abbey lands, and contrived in that dangerous age to save both his head and his estate.

The Greymount family having planted themselves in the land, faithful to the policy of the founder, avoided the public gaze during the troubled period that followed the reformation; and even during the more orderly reign ot Elizabeth, rather sought their increase in alliances than in court favour. But at the commencement of the seventeenth century, their abbey lands infinitely advanced in value, and their rental swollen by the prudent accumulation of more than seventy years, a Greymount, who was then a county member, was elevated to the peerage as Baron Marney. The heralds furnished his pedigree, and assured the world that, although the exalted rank and extensive possessions enjoyed at present by the Greymounts had their origin immediately in great territorial revolutions of a recent reign, it was not for a moment to be supposed that the remote ancestors of the Ecclesiastical Commissioner of 1530 were by any means obscure. On the contrary, it appeared that they were both Norman and baronial, their real name Egremont, which, in their patent of peerage, the family now resumed.

In the civil wars the Egremonts, pricked by their Norman blood, were cavaliers, and fought pretty well. But in 1688, alarmed at the prevalent impression that King James intended to insist on the restitution of the church estates to their original purposes, to wit, the education of the people and the maintenance of the poor, the Lord of Marney Abbey became a warm adherent of 'civil and religious liberty,' the cause for which Hampden had died in the field, and Russell* on the scaffold, and joined the other whig lords, and great lay impropriators, in calling over the Prince of Orange and a Dutch army, to vindicate those popular principles which, somehow or other, the people would never support. Profiting by this last pregnant circumstances, the lay abbot of Marney, also in this instance like the other whig lords, was careful to maintain, while he vindicated the cause of civil and religious liberty, a loyal and dutiful though secret correspondence with the court of St. Germains.*

The great deliverer King William III, to whom Lord

Marney was a systematic traitor, made the descendant of the
Ecclesiastical Commissioner of Henry VIII an English earl;
and from that time until the period of our history, though the
Marney family had never produced one individual eminent
for civil or military abilities, though the country was not indebted to them for a single statesman, orator, successful war-
rior, great lawyer, learned divine, eminent author, illustrious
man of science, they had contrived, if not to engross any great
share of public admiration and love, at least to monopolise no
contemptible portion of public money and public dignities.
During the seventy years of almost unbroken whig rule, from
the accession of the House of Hanover to the fall of Mr. Fox,*
Marney Abbey had furnished a never-failing crop of lord
privy seals, lord presidents, and lord lieutenants. The family
had had their due quota of garters and governments and
bishoprics; admirals without fleets, and generals who fought
only in America. They had glittered in great embassies with
clever secretaries at their elbow, and had once governed Ireland, when to govern Ireland was only to apportion the
public plunder to a corrupt senate.

Notwithstanding, however, this prolonged enjoyment of
undeserved prosperity, the lay abbots of Marney were not
content. Not that it was satiety which induced dissatisfaction.
The Egremonts could feed on. They wanted something more.
Not to be prime ministers or secretaries of state, for they were
a shrewd race who knew the length of their tether, and notwithstanding the encouraging example of his grace of Newcastle,* they could not resist the persuasion that some knowledge of the interests and resources of nations, some power
of expressing opinions with propriety, some degree of respect
for the public and for himself, were not altogether indispen-
sable qualifications, even under a Venetian constitution,* in
an individual who aspired to a post so eminent and responsible. Satisfied with the stars and mitres, and official seals,
which were periodically apportioned to them, the Marney
family did not aspire to the somewhat graceless office of being
their distributor. What they aimed at was promotion in their
order; and promotion to the highest class. They observed that
more than one of the other great 'civil and religious liberty'
families, the families who in one century plundered the church

to gain the property of the people and in another century
changed the dynasty to gain the power of the crown, had
their brows circled with the strawberry leaf. And why should
not this distinction be the high lot also of the descendants of
the old gentleman-usher of one of King Henry's plundering
vicar-generals? Why not? True it is, that a grateful sovereign
in our days has deemed such distinction the only reward for
half a hundred victories. True it is, that Nelson, after conquering the Mediterranean, died only a Viscount! But the
house of Marney had risen to high rank, counted themselves
ancient nobility; and turned up their noses at the Pratts and
the Smiths, the Jenkinsons and the Robinsons of our degenerate days; and never had done anything for the nation
or for their honours. And why should they now? It was unreasonable to expect it. Civil and religious liberty, that had
given them a broad estate and glittering coronet, to say nothing of half-a-dozen close seats in parliament, ought clearly
to make them dukes.

But the other great whig families who had obtained this
honour, and who had done something more for it than
spoliate their church and betray their king, set up their backs
against this claim of the Egremonts. The Egremonts had done
none of the work of the last hundred years of political mystification, during which a people without power or education
had been induced to believe themselves the freest and most
enlightened nation in the world, and had submitted to lavish
their blood and treasure, to see their industry crippled and
their labour mortgaged, in order to maintain an oligarchy,
that had neither ancient memories to soften nor present services to justify their unprecedented usurpation.

How had the Egremonts contributed to this prodigious result? Their family had furnished none of those artful orators
whose bewildering phrase had fascinated the public intelligence; none of those toilsome patricians whose assiduity in
affairs had convinced their unprivileged fellow-subjects that
government was a science, and administration an art, which
demanded the devotion of a peculiar class in the state for their
fulfilment and pursuit. The Egremonts had never said anything that was remembered, or done anything that could be
recalled. It was decided by the Great Revolution families,

that they should not be dukes. Infinite was the indignation of the lay abbot of Marney. He counted his boroughs, consulted his cousins, and muttered revenge. The opportunity soon offered for the gratification of his passion.

The situation of the Venetian party in the wane of the eighteenth century had become extremely critical. A young king was making often fruitless, but always energetic, struggles to emancipate his national royalty from the trammels of the factious dogeship. More than sixty years of a government of singular corruption had alienated all hearts from the oligarchy; never indeed much affected by the great body of the people. It could no longer be concealed that, by virtue of a plausible phrase, power had been transferred from the crown to a parliament, the members of which were appointed by a limited and exclusive class, who owned no responsibility to the country, who debated and voted in secret, and who were regularly paid by the small knot of great families that by this machinery had secured the permanent possession of the king's treasury. Whiggism was putrescent in the nostrils of the nation; we were probably on the eve of a bloodless yet important revolution; when Rockingham, a virtuous magnifico, alarmed and disgusted, resolved to revive something of the pristine purity and high-toned energy of the old whig connection, appealed to his 'new generation' from a degenerate age, arrayed under his banner the generous youth of the whig families, and was fortunate to enlist in the service the supreme genius of Edmund Burke.*

Burke effected for the whigs what Bolingbroke* in a preceding age had done for the tories: he restored the moral existence of the party. He taught them to recur to the ancient principles of their connection, and suffused those principles with all the delusive splendour of his imagination. He raised the tone of their public discourse; he breathed a high spirit into their public acts. It was in his power to do more for the whigs than St. John could do for his party. The oligarchy, who had found it convenient to attaint Bolingbroke for being the avowed minister of the English Prince with whom they were always in secret communication, when opinion forced them to consent to his restitution, had tacked to the amnesty a clause as cowardly as it was unconstitutional, and declared his incompetence to sit in the parliament of his country. Burke, on the contrary, fought the whig fight with a two-edged weapon: he was a great writer; as an orator he was transcendent. In a dearth of that public talent for the possession of which the whigs have generally been distinguished, Burke came forward and established them alike in the parliament and the country. And what was his reward? No sooner had a young and dissolute noble,* who, with some of the aspirations of a Caesar, oftener realized the conduct of a Catiline,* appeared on the stage, and after some inglorious tergiversation adopted their colours, than they transferred to him the command which had been won by wisdom and genius, vindicated by unrivalled knowledge, and adorned by accomplished eloquence. When the hour arrived for the triumph which he had prepared, he was not even admitted into the Cabinet,* virtually presided over by his graceless pupil, and who, in the profuse suggestions of his teeming converse, had found the principles and the information which were among the chief claims to public confidence of Mr. Fox.

Hard necessity made Mr. Burke submit to the yoke, but the humiliation could never be forgotten. Nemesis favours genius; the inevitable hour at length arrived. A voice like the Apocalypse sounded over England, and even echoed in all the courts of Europe. Burke poured forth the vials of his hoarded vengeance into the agitated heart of Christendom; he stimulated the panic of a world by the wild pictures of his inspired imagination; he dashed to the ground the rival who had robbed him of his hard-earned greatness; rent in twain the proud oligarchy* that had dared to use and to insult him; and, followed with servility by the haughtiest and the most timid of its members, amid the frantic exultations of his country, he placed his heel upon the neck of the ancient serpent.

Among the whig followers of Mr. Burke in this memorable defection, among the Devonshires and the Portlands, the Spencers and the Fitzwilliams, was the Earl of Marney, whom the whigs would not make a duke.

What was his chance of success from Mr. Pitt?*

If the history of England be ever written by one who has the knowledge and the courage, and both qualities are equally requisite for the undertaking, the world would be more

astonished then when reading the Roman annals by Niebuhr.*
Generally speaking, all the great events have been distorted,
most of the important causes concealed, some of the principal
characters never appear, and all who figure are so misunderstood and misrepresented, that the result is a complete mystification, and the perusal of the narrative about as profitable to
an Englishman as reading the Republic of Plato or the Utopia
of More, the pages of Gaudentio di Lucca* or the adventures
of Peter Wilkins.*

The influence of races in our early ages, of the Church in
our middle, and of parties in our modern history, are three
great moving and modifying powers, that must be pursued
and analyzed with an untiring, profound, and unimpassioned
spirit, before a guiding ray can be secured. A remarkable
feature of our written history is the absence in its pages of
some of the most influential personages. Not one man in a
thousand, for instance, has ever heard of Major Wildman:*
yet he was the soul of English politics in the most eventful
period of this kingdom, and one most interesting to this age,
from 1640 to 1688; and seemed more than once to hold the
balance which was to decide the permanent forms of our
government. But he was the leader of an unsuccessful party.
Even, comparatively speaking, in our own times, the same
mysterious oblivion is sometimes encouraged to creep over
personages of great social distinction as well as political importance.

The name of the second Pitt remains, fresh after forty years
of great events, a parliamentary beacon. He was the Chatterton* of politics; the 'marvellous boy.' Some have a vague impression that he was mysteriously moulded by his great father;
that he inherited the genius, the eloquence, the statecraft of
Chatham. His genius was of a different bent, his eloquence of
a different class, his statecraft of a different school. To understand Mr. Pitt, one must understand one of the suppressed
characters of English history, and that is Lord Shelburne.*

When the fine genius of the injured Bolingbroke, the only
peer of his period who was educated, and proscribed by the
oligarchy because they were afraid of his eloquence, 'the glory
of his order and the shame,' shut out from Parliament, found
vent in these writings which recalled to the English people

the inherent blessings of their old free monarchy, and painted in immortal hues his picture of a patriot king, the spirit that he raised at length touched the heart of Carteret, born a whig, yet sceptical of the advantages of that patrician constitution which made the Duke of Newcastle, the most incompetent of men, but the chosen leader of the Venetian party, virtually sovereign of England. Lord Carteret had many brilliant qualities: he was undaunted, enterprising, eloquent; had considerable knowledge of continental politics, was a great linguist, a master of public law; and, though he failed in his premature effort to terminate the dogeship of George II, he succeeded in maintaining a considerable though secondary position in public life. The young Shelburne married his daughter. Of him it is singular we know less than of his father-in-law, yet from the scattered traits some idea may be formed of the ablest and most accomplished minister of the eighteenth century. Lord Shelburne, influenced probably by the example and the traditionary precepts of his eminent father-in-law, appears early to have held himself aloof from the patrician connection, and entered public life as the follower of Bute in the first great effort of George III to rescue the sovereignty from what Lord Chatham called 'the Great Revolution families.' He became in time a member of Lord Chatham's last administration; one of the strangest and most unsuccessful efforts to aid the grandson of George II in his struggle for political emancipation. Lord Shelburne adopted from the first the Bolingbroke system; a real royalty, in lieu of the chief magistracy; a permanent alliance with France, instead of the whig scheme of viewing in that power the natural enemy of England; and, above all, a plan of commercial freedom, the germ of which may be found in the long-maligned negotiations of Utrecht, but which, in the instance of Lord Shelburne, were soon in time matured by all the economical science of Europe, in which he was a proficient. Lord Shelburne seems to have been of a reserved and somewhat astute disposition: deep and adroit, he was however brave and firm. His knowledge was extensive and even profound. He was a great linguist; he pursued both literary and scientific investigations; his house was frequented by men of letters, especially those distinguished by their political abilities or economical

attainments. He maintained the most extensive private correspondence of any public man of his time. The earliest and
most authentic information reached him from all courts and
quarters of Europe; and it was a common phrase, that the
minister of the day sent to him often for the important information which the cabinet could not itself command. Lord
Shelburne was the first great minister who comprehended the
rising importance of the middle class, and foresaw in its
future power a bulwark for the throne against 'the Great
Revolution families.' Of his qualities in council we have no
record; there is reason to believe that his administrative
ability was conscpicuous; his speeches prove that, if not supreme, he was eminent, in the art of parliamentary disputation,
while they show on all the questions discussed a richness and
variety of information, with which the speeches of no statesman of that age except Mr. Burke can compare.

Such was the man selected by George III as his champion
against the Venetian party, after the termination of the
American war. The prosecution of that war they had violently
opposed, though it had originated in their own policy. First
minister in the House of Lords, Shelburne entrusted the lead
in the House of Commons to his Chancellor of the Exchequer,
the youthful Pitt. The administration was brief, but it was not
inglorious. It obtained peace, and, for the first time since the
Revolution, introduced into modern debate the legitimate
principles on which commerce should be conducted. It fell
before the famous Coalition with which 'the Great Revolution families' commenced their fiercest and their last con-
tention for the patrician government of royal England.

In the heat of that great strife, the king, in the second
hazardous exercise of his prerogative, entrusted the perilous
command to Pitt. Why Lord Shelburne on that occasion was
set aside, will perhaps always remain a mysterious passage of
our political history, nor have we space on the present occasion to attempt to penetrate its motives. Perhaps the monarch,
with a sense of the rising sympathies of his people, was prescient of the magic power of youth in touching the heart of a
nation. Yet it would not be an unprofitable speculation, if for
a moment we pause to consider what might have been the
consequences to our country if Mr. Pitt had been content for

a season again to lead the Commons under Lord Shelburne, and to have secured for England the unrivalled knowledge and dexterity of that statesman in the conduct of our affairs during the confounding fortunes of the French revolution. Lord Shelburne was the only English minister competent to the place: he was the only public man who had the previous knowledge requisite to form accurate conclusions on such a conjecture; his remaining speeches on the subject attest the amplitude of his knowledge and the accuracy of his views; and in the rout of Jena, or the agony of Austerlitz, one cannot refrain from picturing the shade of Shelburne haunting the cabinet of Pitt, as the ghost of Canning is said occasionally to linger about the Speaker's chair, and smile sarcastically on the conscientious mediocrities who pilfered his hard-earned honours.

But, during the happier years of Mr. Pitt, the influence of the mind of Shelburne may be traced throughout his policy. It was Lansdowne House* that made Pitt acquainted with Dr. Price, a dissenting minister, whom Lord Shelburne, when at the head of affairs, courageously offered to make his private secretary, and who furnished Mr. Pitt, among other important suggestions, with his original plan of the sinking fund. The commercial treaties of '87 were struck in the same mint, and are notable as the first effort made by the English government to emancipate the country from the restrictive policy which had been introduced by the 'glorious revolution'; memorable epoch, that presented England at the same time with a corn-law and a public debt. But on no subject was the magnetic influence of the descendant of Sir William Petty* more decided, than in the resolution of his pupil to curb the power of the patrician party by an infusion from the middle classes into the government of the country. Hence the origin of Mr. Pitt's famous and long-misconceived plans of parliamentary reform. Was he sincere, is often asked by those who neither seek to discover the causes, nor are capable of calculating the effects of public transactions. Sincere! Why, he was struggling for his existence! And when, baffled, first by the Venetian party, and afterwards by the panic of Jacobinism, he was forced to forego his direct purpose, he still endeavoured partially to effect it by a circuitous process. He created a plebeian aristocracy and blended it with the patrician oligarchy. He made peers of second-rate squires and fat graziers. He caught them in the alloys of Lombard Street, and clutched them from the counting-houses of Cornhill. When Mr. Pitt, in an age of Bank restriction, declared that every man with an estate of ten thousand a-year had a right to be a peer, he sounded the knell of 'the cause for which Hampden had died on the field, and Sydney* on the scaffold.'

In ordinary times the pupil of Shelburne would have raised this country to a state of great material prosperity, and removed or avoided many of those anomalies which now perplex us; but he was not destined for ordinary times; and, though his capicity was vast and his spirit lofty, he had not that passionate and creative genius required by an age of revolution. The French outbreak was his evil daemon; he had not the means of calculating its effects upon Europe. He had but a meagre knowledge himself of continental politics: he was assisted by an inefficient diplomacy. His mind was lost in a convulsion of which he neither could comprehend the causes nor calculate the consequences; and, forced to act, he acted not only violently, but in exact opposition to the very system he was called into political existences to combat; he appealed to the fears, the prejudices, and the passions of a privileged class, revived the old policy of the oligarchy he had extinguished, and plunged into all the ruinous excesses of French war and Dutch finance.*

If it be a salutary principle in the investigation of historical transactions, to be careful in discriminating the cause from the pretext, there is scarcely any instance in which the application of this principle is more fertile in results, than in that of the Dutch invasion of 1688. The real cause of this invasion was financial. The Prince of Orange had found that the resources of Holland, however considerable, were inadequate to sustain him in his internecine rivalry with the great sovereign of France. In an authentic conversation which has descended to us, held by William at the Hague with one of the prime abettors of the invasion, the prince did not disguise his motives; he said, 'Nothing but such a constitution as you have in England can have the credit that is necessary to raise such sums as a great war requires.' The prince came, and used our constitution for his purpose: he introduced into England the system of Dutch finance. The principle of that system was to mortgage industry in order to protect property: abstractedly, nothing can be conceived more unjust; its practice in England has been equally injurious. In Holland, with a small population engaged in the same pursuits, in fact, a nation of bankers, the system was adapted to the circumstances which had created it. All shared in the present spoil, and therefore could endure the future burthen. And so to this day Holland is sustained, almost solely sustained, by the vast capital thus created which still lingers among its dykes. But applied to a country in which the circumstances were entirely different, to a considerable and rapidly-increasing population, where there was a numerous peasantry, a trading middle class struggling into existence, the system of Dutch finance, pursued more or less for nearly a century and a half, has ended in the degradation of a fettered and burthened multitude. Nor have the demoralizing consequences of the funding system on the more favoured classes been less decided. It has made debt a national habit; it has made credit the ruling power, not the exceptional auxiliary, of all transactions; it has introduced a loose, inexact, haphazard, and dishonest spirit in the conduct of both public and private life; a spirit dazzling and yet dastardly; reckless of consequences and yet shrinking from responsibility. And in the end, it has so over-stimulated the energies of the population to maintain the material engagements of the state, and of society at large, that the moral condition of the people has been entirely lost sight of.

A mortgaged aristocracy, a gambling foreign commerce, a home trade founded on a morbid competition, and a degraded people; these are great evils, but ought perhaps cheerfully to be encountered for the greater blessings of civil and religious liberty. Yet the first would seem in some degree to depend upon our Saxon mode of trial by our peers, upon the stipulations of the great Norman charters, upon the practice and the statute of Habeas Corpus, a principle native of our common law, but established by the Stuarts; nor in a careful perusal of the Bill of Rights, or in an impartial scrutiny of the subsequent legislation of those times, though some diminution of our political franchises must be confessed, is it easy to discover any increase of our civil privileges. To those, indeed, who believe that the English nation (at all times a religious and Catholic people, but who even in the days of the Plantagenets were anti-papal) were in any danger of again falling under the yoke of the Pope of Rome in the reign of James II, religious liberty was perhaps acceptable, though it took the shape of a discipline which at once anathematized a great portion of the nation, and virtually establishing Puritanism in Ireland, laid the foundation of those mischiefs which are now endangering the empire.

That the last of the Stuarts had any other object in his impolitic manœuvres than an impracticable scheme to blend the two Churches, there is now authority to disbelieve. He certainly was guilty of the offence of sending an envoy openly to Rome, who, by the bye, was received by the Pope with great discourtesy; and her Majesty Queen Victoria, whose Protestantism cannot be doubted, for it is one of her chief titles to our homage, has at this time a secret envoy at the same court; and that is the difference between them: both ministers doubtless working, however fruitlessly, for the same object, the termination of those terrible misconceptions, political and religious, that have occasioned so many martyrdoms, and so many crimes alike to sovereigns and to subjects.

If James II had really attempted to re-establish Popery in this country, the English people, who had no hand in his overthrow, would doubtless soon have stirred and secured their 'Catholic and Apostolic Church,' independent of any foreign dictation; the Church to which they still regularly profess their adherence; and, being a practical people, it is possible that they might have achieved their object and yet retained their native princes; under which circumstances we might have been saved from the triple blessings of Venetian politics, Dutch finance, and French wars: against which, in their happiest days, and with their happiest powers, struggled the three greatest of English statesmen, Bolingbroke, Shelburne, and, lastly, the son of Chatham.

We have endeavoured in another work, not we hope without something of the impartiality of the future, to sketch the character and career of his successors. From his death to 1825, the political history of England is a history of great events and little men. The rise of Mr. Canning, long kept down by the plebeian aristocracy of Mr. Pitt as an adventurer, had shaken parties to their centre. His rapid disappearance from the scene left both whigs and tories in a state of disorganisation. The distinctive principles of these connections were now difficult to trace. That period of public languor which intervenes between the breaking up of parties and the formation of factions now succeeded in England. An exhausted sensualist on the throne, who only demanded from his ministers repose, a voluptuous aristocracy, and a listless people, were content, in the absence of all public conviction and national passion, to consign the government of the country to a great man, whose decision relieved the sovereign, whose prejudices pleased the nobles, and whose achievements dazzled the multitude.

The DUKE OF WELLINGTON* brought to the post of first minister immortal fame; a quality of success which would almost seem to include all others. His public knowledge was such as might be expected from one whose conduct already formed an important portion of the history of his country. He had a personal and intimate acquaintance with the sovereigns and chief statesmen of Europe, a kind of information in which English ministers have generally been deficient, but without which the management of our external affairs must at the best be haphazard. He possessed administrative talents of the highest order.

The tone of the age, the temper of the country, the great qualities and the high character of the minister, indicated a long and prosperous administration. The only individual in his cabinet who, from a combination of circumstances rather than from any intellectual supremacy over his colleagues, was competent to be his rival, was content to be his successor. In his most aspiring moments. Mr. Peel,* in all probability, aimed at no higher reach; and with youth and the leadership of the House of Commons, one has no reason to be surprised at his moderation. The conviction that the duke's government would only cease with the termination of his public career was so general, that, the moment he was installed in office, the whigs smiled on him; political conciliation became

the slang of the day, and the fusion of parties the babble of
clubs and the tattle of boudoirs.

How comes it, then, that so great a man, in so great a
position, should have so signally failed; should have broken
up his government, wrecked his party, and so completely
annihilated his political position, that, even with his historical
reputation to sustain him, he can since only re-appear in the
councils of his sovereign in a subordinate, not to say equivocal, character?

With all those great qualities which will secure him a place
in our history not perhaps inferior even to Marlborough, the
Duke of Wellington has one deficiency which has been the
stumbling-block of his civil career. Bishop Burnet,* in speculating on the extraordinary influence of Lord Shaftesbury,*
and accounting how a statesman, so inconsistent in his conduct and so false to his confederates, should have so powerfully controlled his country, observes, 'HIS STRENGTH LAY
IN HIS KNOWLEDGE OF ENGLAND.'

Now that is exactly the kind of knowledge which the Duke
of Wellington never possessed.

When the king, finding that in Lord Goderich* he had a
minister who, instead of deciding, asked his royal master for
advice, sent for the Duke of Wellington to undertake the
government, a change in the carriage of his grace was perceived by some who had the opportunity to form an opinion
on such a subject. If one might venture to use such a word
in reference to such a man, we might remark, that the duke
had been somewhat daunted by the selection of Mr. Canning.*
It disappointed great hopes, it baffled great plans, and dispelled for a season the conviction that, it is believed, had been
long maturing in his grace's mind; that he was the man of the
age, that his military career had been only a preparation for a
civil course not less illustrious; and that it was reserved for
him to control for the rest of his life, undisputed, the destinies
of a country which was indebted to him in no slight degree
for its European pre-eminence. The death of Mr. Canning revived, the rout of Lord Goderich restored, these views.

Napoleon, at St. Helena, speculating in conversation on the
future career of his conqueror, asked, 'What will Wellington

do? After all he has done, he will not be content to be quiet. He will change the dynasty.'

Had the great exile been better acquainted with the real character of our Venetian constitution, he would have known that to govern England in 1820, it was not necessary to change its dynasty. But the Emperor, though wrong in the main, was right by the bye. It was clear that the energies which had twice entered Paris as a conqueror and had made kings and mediatised princes at Vienna, would not be content to subside into ermined insignificance. The duke commenced his political tactics early. The cabinet of Lord Liverpool,* especially during its latter term, was the hot-bed of many intrigues; but the obstacles were numerous, though the appointing fate, in which his grace believed, removed them. The disappearance of Lord Castlereagh* and Mr. Canning from the scene was alike unexpected. The Duke of Wellington was at length prime minister, and no individual ever occupied that post more conscious of its power, and more determined to exercise it.

This is not the occasion on which we shall attempt to do justice to a theme so instructive as the administration of his grace. Treated with impartiality and sufficient information, it would be an invaluable contribution to the stores of our political knowledge and national experience. Throughout its brief but eccentric and tumultuous annals we see continual proof, how important is that knowledge 'in which lay Lord Shaftesbury's strength.' In twenty-four months we find an aristocracy estranged, without a people being conciliated; while on two several occasions, first, the prejudices, and then the pretensions of the middle class, were alike treated with contumely. The public was astonished at hearing of statesmen of long parliamentary fame, men round whom the intelligence of the nation had gathered for years, if not with confidence, at least with interest, being expelled from the cabinet in a manner not unworthy of Colonel Joyce,* while their places were filled by second-rate soldiers, whose very names were unknown to the great body of the people, and who, under no circumstances, should have aspired beyond the government of a colony. This administration, which commenced in arrogance, ended in panic. There was an interval of perplexity, when occurred the most ludicrous instance extant of an attempt at coalition; subordinates were promoted while negotiations were still pending with their chiefs; and these negotiations, undertaken so crudely, were terminated in pique, in a manner which added to political disappointment personal offence. When even his parasites began to look gloomy, the duke had a specific that was to restore all, and, having allowed every element of power to escape his grasp, he believed he could balance everything by a beer bill. The growl of reform was heard, but it was not very fierce. There was yet time to save himself. His grace precipitated a revolution which might have been delayed for half a century, and never need have occurred in so aggravated a form. He rather fled than retired. He commenced his ministry like Brennus,* and finished it like the tall Gaul sent to murder the rival of Sylla,* but who dropped his weapon before the undaunted gaze of his intended victim.

Lord Marney was spared the pang of the catastrophe. Promoted to a high office in the household, and still hoping that, by the aid of his party, it was yet destined for him to achieve the hereditary purpose of his family, he died in the full faith of dukism; worshipping the duke, and believing that ultimately he should himself become a duke. It was under all the circumstances a euthanasia; he expired leaning as it were on his white wand and babbling of strawberry-leaves.*

CHAPTER 4

'My dear Charles,' said Lady Marney to Egremont, the morning after the Derby, as breakfasting with her in her boudoir, he detailed some of the circumstances of the race, 'we must forget your naughty horse. I sent you a little note this morning, because I wished to see you most particularly before you went out. Affairs,' continued Lady Marney, first looking round the chamber to see whether there were any fairy listening to her state secrets, 'affairs are critical.'

'No doubt of that,' thought Egremont, the horrid phantom of settling-day seeming to obtrude itself between his mother and himself; but, not knowing precisely at what she was driving, he merely sipped his tea, and innocently replied, 'Why?'

'There will be a dissolution,' said Lady Marney.

'What! are we coming in?'

Lady Marney shook her head.

'The present men will not better their majority,' said Egremont.

'I hope not,' said Lady Marney.

'Why you always said that, with another general election, we must come in, whoever dissolved.'

'But that was with the court in our favour,' rejoined Lady Marney, mournfully.

'What! has the king* changed?' said Egremont. 'I thought it was all right.'

'All was right,' said Lady Marney. 'These men would have been turned out again, had he only lived three months longer.'

'Lived!' exclaimed Egremont.

'Yes,' said Lady Marney; 'the king is dying.'

Slowly delivering himself of an ejaculation, Egremont leant back in his chair.

'He may live a month,' said Lady Marney; 'he cannot live two. It is the greatest of secrets; known at this moment only to four individuals, and I communicate it to you, my dear Charles, in that absolute confidence which I hope will always subsist between us, because it is an event that may greatly affect your career.'

'How so, my dear mother?'

'Marbury! I have settled with Mr. Tadpole that you shall stand for the old borough. With the government in our hands, as I had anticipated, at the general election success I think was certain: under the circumstances which we must encounter, the struggle will be more severe, but I think we shall do it: and it will be a happy day for me to have our own again, and to see you in Parliament, my dear child.'

'Well, my dear mother, I should like very much to be in Parliament, and particularly to sit for the old borough; but I fear the contest will be very expensive,' said Egremont, inquiringly.

'Oh! I have no doubt,' said Lady Marney, 'that we shall have some monster of the middle class, some tinker or tailor or candlestick-maker, with his long purse, preaching reform and practising corruption; exactly as the liberals did under Walpole: bribery was unknown in the time of the Stuarts; but we have a capital registration, Mr. Tadpole tells me. And a young candidate with the old name will tell,' said Lady Marney, with a smile: 'and I shall go down and canvass, and we must do what we can.'

'I have great faith in your canvassing,' said Egremont; 'but still at the same time, the powder and shot—'

'Are essential,' said Lady Marney, 'I know it, in these corrupt days; but Marney will of course supply those. It is the least he can do: regaining the family influence, and letting us hold up our heads again. I shall write to him the moment I am justified,' said Lady Marney, 'perhaps you will do so yourself, Charles.'

'Why, considering I have not seen my brother for two years, and we did not part on the best possible terms—'

'But that is all forgotten.'

'By your good offices, dear mother, who are always doing good: and yet,' continued Egremont, after a moment's pause, 'I am not disposed to write to Marney, especially to ask a favour.'

'Well, I will write,' said Lady Marney; 'though I cannot admit it as any favour. Perhaps it would be better that you should see him first. I cannot understand why he keeps so at the Abbey. I am sure I found it a melancholy place enough in my time. I wish you had gone down there, Charles, if it had been only for a few days.'

'Well, I did not, my dear mother, and I cannot go now. I shall trust to you. But are you quite sure that the king is going to die?'

'I repeat to you, it is certain,' replied Lady Marney, in a lowered voice, but decided tone; 'certain, certain, certain. My authority cannot be mistaken: but no consideration in the world must throw you off your guard at this moment; breathe not the shadow of what you know.'

At this moment a servant entered, and delivered a note to Lady Marney, who read it with an ironical smile. It was from Lady St. Julians, and ran thus

'Most confidential.

'My dearest Lady Marney. It is a false report; he is ill, but not dangerously; the hay fever; he always has it; nothing more; I will tell my authority when we meet; I dare not write it. It will satisfy you. I am going on with my quadrille.

'Most affectionately yours,
'A. St. J.'

'Poor woman! she is always wrong,' said Lady Marney, throwing the note to Egremont. 'Her quadrille will never take place, which is a pity, as it is to consist only of beauties and eldest sons. I suppose I must send her a line;' and she wrote:

'My dearest Lady St. Julians, How good of you to write to me, and send me such cheering news! I have no doubt you are right; you always are. I know he had the hay fever last year. How fortunate for your quadrille, and how charming it will be! Let me know if you hear anything further from your unmentionable quarter.

'Ever your affectionate
'C. M.'

CHAPTER 5

LORD MARNEY left several children; his heir was five years older than the next son, Charles, who at the period of his father's death was at Christchurch, and had just entered the last year of his minority. Attaining that age, he received the sum of fifteen thousand pounds, his portion, a third of which amount his expenditure had then already anticipated. Egremont had been brought up in the enjoyment of every comfort and every luxury that refinement could devise and wealth furnish. He was a favourite child. His parents emulated each other in pampering and indulging him. Every freak was pardoned, every whim was gratified. He might ride what horses he liked, and if he broke their knees, what in another would have been deemed a flagrant sin, was in him held only a proof of reckless spirit. If he were not a thoroughly selfish and altogether wilful person, but very much the reverse, it was not the fault of his parents, but rather the operation of a benignant nature that had bestowed on him a generous spirit and a tender heart, though accompanied with a dangerous susceptibility that made him the child and creature of impulse, and seemed to set at defiance even the course of time to engraft on his nature any quality of prudence. The tone of Eton during the days of Charles Egremont was not of the high character which at present distinguishes that community. It was the unforeseen eve of the great change, that, whatever was its purpose or have been its immediate results, at least gave the first shock to the pseudo-aristocracy of this country. Then all was blooming; sunshine and odour; not a breeze disturbing the meridian splendour. Then the world was not only made for a few, but a very few. One could almost tell upon one's fingers the happy families who could do anything, and might have everything. A schoolboy's ideas of the Church then were fat livings, and of the State rotten boroughs. To do nothing and get something formed a boy's ideal of a manly career. There was nothing in the lot, little in the temperament, of Charles Egremont, to make him an exception to the multitude. Gaily and securely he floated on the brilliant stream. Popular at school, idolized at home, the present had no cares, and the future secured him a family seat in Parliament the moment he entered life, and the inheritance of a glittering post at court in due time, as its legitimate consequence. Enjoyment, not ambition, seemed the principle of his existence. The contingency of a mitre, the certainty of rich preferment, would not reconcile him to the self-sacrifice which, to a certain degree, was required from a priest, even in those days of rampant Erastianism. He left the colonies as the spoil of his younger brothers; his own ideas of a profession being limited to a barrack in a London park varied by visits to Windsor. But there was time enough to think of these things. He had to enjoy Oxford as he had enjoyed Eton. Here his allowance from his father was extravagant, though greatly increased by tithes from his mother's pin-money. While he was pursuing his studies, hunting and boating, driving tandems, riding matches, tempering his energies in the crapulence of boyish banquets, and anticipating life, at the risk of expulsion, in a miserable mimicry of metropolitan dissipation, Dukism, that was supposed to be eternal, suddenly crashed.

The Reform Act has not placed the administration of our affairs in abler hands than conducted them previously to the passing of the measure, for the most efficient members of the present cabinet, with some few exceptions, and those attended by peculiar circumstances, were ministers before the Reform Act was contemplated. Nor has that memorable statute created a Parliament of a higher reputation for public qualities, such as politic ability, and popular eloquence, and national consideration, than was furnished by the old scheme. On the contrary, one house of Parliament has been irremediably degraded into the decaying position of a mere court of registry, possessing great privileges, on condition that it never exercises them; while the other chamber, that, at the first blush, and to the superficial, exhibits symptoms of almost unnatural vitality, engrossing in its orbit all the business of the country, assumes on a more studious inspection somewhat of the character of a select vestry, fulfilling municipal rather than imperial offices, and beleaguered by critical and clamorous millions, who cannot comprehend why a privileged and exclusive senate is requisite to perform functions which immediately concern all, which most personally comprehend, and which many in their civic spheres believe they could accomplish in a manner not less satisfactory, though certainly less ostentatious.

But if it have not furnished us with abler administrators or a more illustrious senate, the Reform Act may have exercised on the country at large a beneficial influence. Has it? Has it elevated the tone of the public mind? Has it cultured the popular sensibilities to noble and ennobling ends? Has it proposed to the people of England a higher test of national respect and confidence than the debasing qualification universally prevalent in this country since the fatal introduction of the system of Dutch finance? Who will pretend it? If a spirit of rapacious covetousness, desecrating all the humanities of life, has been the besetting sin of England for the last century and a half, since the passing of the Reform Act the altar of Mammon has blazed with triple worship. To acquire, to accumulate, to plunder each other by virtue of philosophic phrases, to propose a Utopia to consist only of WEALTH and TOIL, this has been the breathless business of enfranchised England for the last twelve years, until we are startled from our voracious strife by the wail of intolerable serfage.

Are we then to conclude, that the only effect of the Reform Act has been to create in this country another of those class interests which we now so loudly accuse as the obstacles to general amelioration? Not exactly that. The indirect influence of the Reform Act has been not inconsiderable, and may eventually lead to vast consequences. It set men a-thinking; it enlarged the horizon of political experience; it led the public mind to ponder somewhat on the circumstances of our national history; to pry into the beginnings of some social anomalies, which, they found, were not so ancient as they had been led to believe, and which had their origin in causes very different from what they had been educated to credit; and insensibly it created and prepared a popular intelligence to which one can appeal, no longer hopelessly, in an attempt to dispel the mysteries with which for nearly three centuries it has been the labour of party writers to involve a national history, and without the dispersion of which no political position can be understood and no social evil remedied.

The events of 1830* did not produce any change in the modes of thought and life of Charles Egremont. He took his political cue from his mother, who was his constant correspondent. Lady Marney was a distinguished 'states-woman,' as they called Lady Carlisle in Charles I's time, a great friend of Lady St. Julians, and one of the most eminent and impassioned votaries of Dukism. Her first impression on the overthrow of her hero was astonishment at the impertinence of his adversaries, mingled with some lofty pity for their silly ambition and short-lived career. She existed for a week in the delightful expectation of his grace being sent for again, and informed every one in confidence, that 'these people could not form a cabinet.' When the tocsin of peace, reform, and retrenchment sounded, she smiled bitterly; was sorry for poor Lord Grey,* of whom she had thought better, and gave them a year, adding, with consoling malice, 'that it would be another Canning affair.' At length came the Reform Bill itself, and no one laughed more heartily than Lady Marney; not even the House of Commons to whom it was presented.

The bill was thrown out, and Lady Marney gave a grand

ball to celebrate the event, and to compensate the London shopkeepers for the loss of their projected franchise. Lady Marney was preparing to resume her duties at court, when, to her great surprise, the firing of cannon announced the dissolution of Parliament. She turned pale; she was too much in the secrets of Tadpole and Taper to be deceived as to the consequences; she sank into her chair, and denounced Lord Grey as a traitor to his order.

Lady Marney, who for six months had been writing to her son at Oxford the most charming letters, full of fun, quizzing the whole Cabinet, now announced to Egremont that a revolution was inevitable, that all property would be instantly confiscated, the poor deluded king led to the block or sent over to Hanover at the best, and the whole of the nobility and principal gentry, and every one who possessed anything, guillotined without remorse.

Whether his friends were immediately to resume power, or whether their estates ultimately were to be confiscated, the practical conclusion to Charles Egremont appeared to be the same. '*Carpe diem.*' He therefore pursued his career at Oxford unchanged, and entered life in the year 1833, a younger son with extravagant tastes and expensive habits, with a reputation for lively talents though uncultivated, for his acquisitions at Eton had been quite puerile, and subsequently he had not become a student, – with many manly accomplishments, and with a mien and visage that at once took the fancy and enlisted the affections. Indeed, a physiologist would hardly have inferred from the countenance and structure of Egremont the career he had pursued, or the character which attached to him. The general cast and expression of his features when in repose was pensive: an air of refinement distinguished his well-moulded brow; his mouth breathed sympathy, and his rich brown eye gleamed with tenderness. The sweetness of his voice in speaking was in harmony with this organisation.

Two years passed in the most refined circles of our society exercised a beneficial influence on the general tone of Egremont, and may be said to have finished his education. He had the good sense and the good taste not to permit his predilection for sports to degenerate into slang; he yielded himself to the delicate and profitable authority of woman, and, as ever happens, it softened his manners and brightened his wit. He was fortunate in having a clever mother, and he appreciated this inestimable possession. Lady Marney had great knowledge of society, and some acquaintance with human nature, which she fancied she had fathomed to its centre; she piqued herself upon her tact, and indeed she was very quick, but she was so energetic that her art did not always conceal itself; very worldly, she was nevertheless not devoid of impulse; she was animated, and would have been extremely agreeable, if she had not restlessly aspired to wit; and would certainly have exercised much more influence in society, if she had not been so anxious to show it. Nevertheless, still with many personal charms, a frank and yet, if need be, a finished manner, a quick brain, a lively tongue, a buoyant spirit, and a great social position, Lady Marney was universally and extremely popular; and adored by her children, for she was a mother most affectionate and true.

When Egremont was four-and-twenty, he fell in love; a real passion. He had fluttered like others from flower to flower, and like others had often fancied the last perfume the sweetest, and then had flown away. But now he was entirely captivated. The divinity was a new beauty; the whole world raving of her. Egremont also advanced. The Lady Arabella was not only beautiful: she was clever, fascinating. Her presence was inspiration; at least for Egremont. She condescended to be pleased by him; she signalised him by her notice; their names were mentioned together. Egremont indulged in flattering dreams. He regretted he had not pursued a profession; he regretted he had impaired his slender patrimony: thought of love in a cottage, and renting a manor; thought of living a good deal with his mother, and a little with his brother; thought of the law and the church; thought once of New Zealand. The favourite of nature and of fashion, this was the first time in the life of Egremont that he had been made conscious that there was something in his position which, with all its superficial brilliancy, might prepare for him, when youth had fled and the blaze of society grown dim, a drear and bitter lot.

He was roused from his reveries by a painful change in the

demeanour of his adored. The mother of the Lady Arabella was alarmed. She liked her daughter to be admired even by younger sons, when they were distinguished, but only at a distance. Mr. Egremont's name had been mentioned too often. It had appeared coupled with her daughter's, even in a Sunday paper. The most decisive measures were requisite, and they were taken. Still smiling when they met, still kind when they conversed, it seemed by some magic dexterity which even baffled Egremont, that their meetings every day grew rarer, and their opportunities for conversation less frequent. At the end of the season, the Lady Arabella selected from a crowd of admirers equally qualified, a young peer of great estate, and of the 'old nobility,' a circumstance which, as her grandfather had only been an East India director,* was very gratifying to the bride.

This unfortunate passion of Charles Egremont, with its mortifying circumstances and consequences, was just that earliest shock in one's life which occurs to all of us; which first makes us think. We have all experienced that disheartening catastrophe when the illusions first vanish; and our balked imagination, or our mortified vanity, first intimates to us that we are neither infalliable nor irresistible. Happily 'tis the season of youth for which the first lessons of experience are destined; and, bitter and intolerable as is the first blight of our fresh feelings, the sanguine impulse of early life bears us along. Our first scrape generally leads to our first travel. Disappointment requires change of air; desperation, change of scene. Egremont quitted his country, never to return to it again; and returned to it after a year and a-half's absence a much wiser man. Having left England in a serious mood, and having already tasted with tolerable freedom of the pleasures and frivolities of life, he was not in an inapt humour to observe, to enquire, and to reflect. The new objects that surrounded him excited his intelligence; he met, which indeed is the principal advantage of travel, remarkable men, whose conversation opened his mind. His mind was worth opening. Energies began to stir of which he had not been conscious; awakened curiosity led him to investigate and to read; he discovered that, when he imagined his education was completed, it had in fact not commenced; and that, although he had been

at a public school and a university, he in fact knew nothing.
To be conscious that you are ignorant is a great step to knowledge. Before an emancipated intellect and an expanding intelligence, the great system of exclusive manners and exclusive feelings in which he had been born and nurtured, began
to tremble; the native generosity of his heart recoiled at a re-
currence to that arrogant and frigid life, alike devoid of sympathy and real grandeur.

In the early spring of 1837, Egremont re-entered the world,
where he had once sparkled, and which he had once conceived
to comprise within its circle all that could interest or occupy
man. His mother, delighted at finding him again under her
roof, had removed some long-standing coolness between him
and his elder brother; his former acquaintance greeted him
with cordiality, and introduced him to the new heroes who
had sprung up during the season of his absence. Apparently
Egremont was not disinclined to pursue, though without
eagerness, the same career that had originally engaged him.
He frequented assemblies, and lingered in clubs; rode in the
park, and lounged at the opera. But there was this difference
in his existence before and since his travels: he was now conscious he wanted an object; and was ever musing over action,
though as yet ignorant how to act. Perhaps it was this want
of being roused that led him, it may be for distraction, again
to the turf. It was a pursuit that seemed to him more real than
the life of saloons, full of affectation, perverted ideas, and
factitious passions. Whatever might be the impulse, Egremont however was certainly not slightly interested in the
Derby; and, though by no means uninstructed in the mysteries of the turf, had felt such confidence in his information,
that, with his usual ardour, he had backed to a considerable
amount the horse that ought to have won, but which nevertheless only ran second.

CHAPTER 6

NOTWITHSTANDING the confidence of Lady St. Julians and
her unrivalled information, the health of the king did not improve: but still it was the hay fever, only the hay fever. An

admission had been allowed to creep into the Court Circular, that 'his majesty has been slightly indisposed within the last few days;' but then it was soon followed by a positive assurance, that his majesty's favourite and long-matured resolution to give a state banquet to the knights of the four orders* was immediately to be carried into effect. Lady St. Julians had the first information of this important circumstance; it confirmed her original conviction; she determined to go on with her quadrille. Egremont, with something interesting at stake himself, was staggered by this announcement, and by Lady St. Julians' unshaken faith. He consulted his mother. Lady Marney shook her head. 'Poor woman!' said Lady Marney, 'she is always wrong. I know,' continued her ladyship, placing her finger to her lip, 'that Prince Esterhazy has been pressing his long-postponed investiture as a Grand Cross,* in order that he may dine at this very banquet; and it has been announced to him that it is impossible, the king's health will not admit of it. When a simple investiture is impossible, a state banquet to the four orders is very probable. No,' said Lady Marney with a sigh; 'it is a great blow for all of us, but it is no use shutting our eyes to the fact. The poor dear king will never show again.'

And about a week after this there appeared the first bulletin. From that instant, though the gullish multitude studied the daily reports with grave interest, their hopes and speculations and arrangements changing with each phrase, for the initiated there was no suspense. All knew that it was over; and Lady St. Julians, giving up her quadrille, began to look about for seats in parliament for her sons.

'What a happiness it is to have a clever mother!' exclaimed Egremont, as he pondered over the returns of his election agent. Lady Marney, duly warned of the impending catastrophe, was experiencing all the advantages of prior information. It delighted her to meet Lady St. Julians driving distractedly about town, calling at clubs, closeted with red-tapers, making ingenious combinations that would not work, by means of which some one of her sons was to stand in coalition with some rich parvenu; to pay none of the expenses and yet to come in first. And all this time, Lady Marney, serene and smiling, had the daily pleasure of assuring Lady St. Julians what a relief it was to her that Charles had fixed on his place. It had been arranged indeed these weeks past; 'but then, you know,' concluded Lady Marney in the sweetest voice and with a blandishing glance, 'I never did believe in that hay fever.'

In the meantime the impending event changed the whole aspect of the political world. The king dying before the new registration was the greatest blow to pseudo-toryism since his majesty, calling for a hackney coach, went down and dissolved parliament in 1831.* It was calculated by the Tadpoles and Tapers that a dissolution by Sir Robert, after the registration of 1837, would give him a clear majority, not too great a one, but large enough; a manageable majority; some five-and-twenty or thirty men, who with a probable peerage or two dangling in the distance, half-a-dozen positive baronetcies, the Customs for their constituents, and Court balls for their wives, might be induced to save the state. O! England, glorious and ancient realm, the fortunes of thy polity are indeed strange! The wisdom of the Saxons, Norman valour, the statecraft of the Tudors, the national sympathies of the Stuarts, the spirit of the latter Guelphs struggling against their enslaved sovereignty, these are the high qualities, that for a thousand years have secured thy national development. And now all thy memorial dynasties end in the huckstering rule of some thirty unknown and anonymous jobbers! The Thirty at Athens* were at least tyrants. They were marked men. But the obscure majority, who, under our present constitution, are destined to govern England, are as secret as a Venetian conclave.* Yet on their dark voices all depends. Would you promote or prevent some great measure that may affect the destinies of unborn millions, and the future character of the people: take, for example, a system of national education: the minister must apportion the plunder to the illiterate clan, the scum that floats on the surface of a party; or hold out the prospect of honours, which are only honourable when in their transmission they impart and receive lustre; when they are the meed of public virtue and public services, and the distinction of worth and of genius. It is impossible that the system of the Thirty can long endure in an age of inquiry and agitated spirit like the present. Such a system may suit the balanced interests and the periodical and alternate command of rival oligarchical connections; but it can subsist only by the subordination of the sovereign and the degradation of the multitude; and cannot accord with an age, whose genius will soon confess that Power and the People are both divine.

'He can't last ten days,' said a whig secretary of the treasury with a triumphant glance at Mr. Taper as they met in Pall Mall; 'you're out for our lives.'

'Don't you make too sure for yourselves,' rejoined in despair the dismayed Taper. 'It does not follow that because we are out, that you are in.'

'How do you mean?'

'There is such a person as Lord Durham* in the world,' said Mr. Taper very solemnly.

'Pish,' said the secretary.

'You may pish,' said Mr. Taper, 'but, if we have a radical government, as I believe and hope, they will not be able to get up the steam as they did in '31; and what with church and corn together, and the Queen Dowager, we may go to the country with as good a cry as some other persons.'

'I will back Melbourne against the field, now,' said the secretary.

'Lord Durham dined at Kensington on Thursday,' said Taper, 'and not a whig present.'

'Ay; Durham talks very fine at dinner,' said the secretary, 'but he has no real go in him. When there is a Prince of Wales, Lord Melbourne means to make Durham governor to the heir apparent, and that will keep him quiet.'

'What do you hear?' said Mr. Tadpole, joining them; 'I am told he has quite rallied.'

'Don't you flatter yourself,' said the secretary.

'Well, we shall hear what they say on the hustings,' said Tadpole, looking boldly.

'Who's afraid!' said the secretary. 'No, no, my dear fellow, you are dead beat; the stake is worth playing for, and don't suppose we are such flats as to lose the race for want of jockeying. Your humbugging registration will never do against a new reign. Our great men mean to shell out, I tell you; we have got Croucher; we will denounce the Carlton* and corruption all over the kingdom; and if that won't do, we will swear till we are black in the face, that the King of Hanover is engaged in a plot to dethrone our young Queen:' and the triumphant secretary wished the worthy pair good morning.

'They certainly have a good cry,' said Taper, mournfully.

'After all, the registration might be better,' said Tadpole 'but still it is a good one.'

The daily bulletins became more significant; the crisis was evidently at hand. A dissolution of Parliament at any time must occasion great excitement; combined with a new reign, it inflames the passions of every class of the community. Even the poor begin to hope; the old, wholesome superstition that the sovereign can exercise power, still lingers; and the suffering multitude are fain to believe that its remedial character may be about to be revealed in their instance. As for the aristocracy in a new reign, they are all in a flutter. A bewildering vision of coronets, stars, and ribbons; smiles, and places at Court; haunts their noontide speculations and their midnight dreams. Then we must not forget the numberless instances in which the coming event is deemed to supply the long-sought opportunity of distinction, or the long-dreaded cause of utter discomfiture; the hundreds, the thousands, who mean to get into parliament, the units who dread getting out. What a crashing change from lounging in St. James' Street to sauntering on Boulogne pier; or, after dining at Brooks'* and supping at Crockford's,* to be saved from destruction by the friendly interposition that sends you in an official capacity to the marsupial sympathies of Sydney or Swan River!*

Now is the time for the men to come forward who have claims; claims for spending their money, which nobody asked them to do, but which of course they only did for the sake of the party. They never wrote for their party, or spoke for their party, or gave their party any other vote than their own; but they urge their claims, to something; a commissionership of anything, or a consulship anywhere; if no place to be had, they are ready to take it out in dignities. They once looked to the privy council, but would now be content with an hereditary honour; if they can have neither, they will take a clerkship in the treasury for a younger son. Perhaps they may get that in time; at present they go away growling with a gaugership; or having with desperate dexterity at length contrived to transform a tidewaiter into a landwaiter. But there is nothing like asking, except refusing.

Hark! it tolls! All is over. The great bell of the metropolitan cathedral announces the death of the last son of George III who probably will ever reign in England. He was a good man: with feelings and sympathies; deficient in culture rather than ability; with a sense of duty; and with something of the conception of what should be the character of an English monarch. Peace to his manes! We are summoned to a different scene.

In a palace in a garden,* not in a haughty keep, proud with the fame but dark with the violence of ages; not in a regal pile, bright with the splendour, but soiled with the intrigues, of courts and factions; in a palace in a garden, meet scene for youth, and innocence, and beauty, came a voice that told the maiden that she must ascend her throne!

The council of England is summoned for the first time within her bowers. There are assembled the prelates and captains and chief men of her realm; the priests of the religion that consoles, the heroes of the sword that has conquered, the votaries of the craft that has decided the fate of empires; men grey with thought, and fame, and age; who are the stewards of divine mysteries, who have toiled in secret cabinets, who have encountered in battle the hosts of Europe, who have struggled in the less merciful strife of aspiring senates; men too, some of them, lords of a thousand vassals and chief proprietors of provinces, yet not one of them whose heart does not at this moment tremble as he awaits the first presence of the maiden who must now ascend her throne.

A hum of half-suppressed conversation which would attempt to conceal the excitement, which some of the greatest of them have since acknowledged, fills that brilliant assemblage; that sea of plumes, and glittering stars, and gorgeous dresses. Hush! the portals open; she comes; the silence is as deep as that of a noontide forest. Attended for a moment by her royal mother and the ladies of her court, who bow and then retire, VICTORIA ascends her throne; a girl, alone, and for the first time, amid an assemblage of men.

In a sweet and thrilling voice, and with a composed mien

which indicates rather the absorbing sense of august duty than an absence of emotion, THE QUEEN announces her accession to the throne of her ancestors, and her humble hope that divine Providence will guard over the fulfilment of her lofty trust.

The prelates and captains and chief men of her realm then advance to the throne, and, kneeling before her, pledge their troth, and take the sacred oaths of allegiance and supremacy.

Allegiance to one who rules over the land that the great Macedonian could not conquer; and over a continent of which even Columbus never dreamed: to the Queen of every sea, and of nations in every zone.

It is not of these that I would speak; but of a nation nearer her footstool, and which at this moment looks to her with anxiety, with affection, perhaps with hope. Fair and serene, she has the blood and beauty of the Saxon. Will it be her proud destiny at length to bear relief to suffering millions, and, with that soft hand which might inspire troubadours and guerdon knights, break the last links in the chain of Saxon thraldom?

END OF THE FIRST BOOK

BOOK II

*

CHAPTER I

THE building which was still called MARNEY ABBEY, though remote from the site of the ancient monastery, was an extensive structure raised at the latter end of the reign of James I, and in the stately and picturesque style of that age. Placed on a noble elevation in the centre of an extensive and well-wooded park, it presented a front with two projecting wings of equal dimensions with the centre, so that the form of the building was that of a quadrangle, less one of its sides. Its ancient lattices had been removed, and the present windows, though convenient, accorded little with the structure; the old entrance door in the centre of the building, however, still remained, a wondrous specimen of fantastic carving: Ionic columns of black oak, with a profusion of fruits and flowers, and heads of stags, and sylvans. The whole of the building was crowned with a considerable pediment of what seemed at the first glance fanciful open work, but which, examined more nearly, offered in gigantic letters the motto of the house of Marney. The portal opened to a hall, such as is now rarely found; with the dais, the screen, the gallery, and the buttery-hatch all perfect, and all of carved black oak. Modern luxury, and the refined taste of the lady of the late lord, had made Marney Abbey as remarkable for its comfort and pleasantness of accommodation as for its ancient state and splendour. The apartments were in general furnished with all the cheerful ease and brilliancy of the modern mansion of a noble, but the grand gallery of the seventeenth century was still preserved, and was used on great occasions as the chief reception-room. You ascended the principal staircase to reach it through a long corridor. It occupied the whole length of one of the wings; was one hundred feet long, and forty-five feet broad, its walls hung with a collection of choice pictures rich in history; while the Axminster carpets, the cabinets, carved tables, and variety of easy chairs, ingeniously grouped, imparted even to this palatian chamber a lively and habitable air.

Lord Marney was several years the senior of Charles Egremont, yet still a young man. He was handsome; there was indeed a general resemblance between the brothers, though the expression of their countenances was entirely different; of the same height and air, and throughout the features a certain family cast: but there the likeness ceased. The countenance of Lord Marney bespoke the character of his mind; cynical, devoid of sentiment, arrogant, literal, hard. He had no imagination, had exhausted his slight native feeling; but he was acute, disputatious, and firm even to obstinacy. Though his early education had been imperfect, he had subsequently read a good deal, especially in French literature. He had formed his mind by Helvetius,* whose system he deemed irrefutable, and in whom alone he had faith. Armed with the principles of his great master, he believed he could pass through existence in adamantine armour, and always gave you in the business of life the idea of a man who was conscious you were trying to take him in, and rather respected you for it, but the working of whose cold unkind eye defied you.

There never had been excessive cordiality between the brothers even in their boyish days, and shortly after Egremont's entrance into life they had become estranged. They were to meet now for the first time since Egremont's return from the continent. Their mother had arranged their reconciliation. They were to meet as if no misunderstanding had ever existed between them; it was specially stipulated by Lord Marney, that there was to be no 'scene.' Apprised of Egremont's impending arrival, Lord Marney was careful to be detained late that day at petty sessions, and entered the room only a few minutes before dinner was announced, where he found Egremont not only with the countess and a young lady who was staying with her, but with additional bail against any ebullition of sentiment in the shape of the vicar of Marney, and a ceratin Captain Grouse, who was a kind of aide-de-camp of the earl; killed birds and carved them; played billiards with him and lost; had, indeed, every accomplishment that could please woman or ease man; could sing, dance, draw, make artificial flies, break horses, exercise a supervision over stewards and bailiffs, and make everybody comfortable by taking everything on his own shoulders.

Lady Marney had received Egremont in a manner which expressed the extreme satisfaction she experienced at finding him once more beneath his brother's roof. When he arrived, indeed, he would have preferred to have been shown at once to his rooms, but a message immediately delivered expressed the wish of his sister-in-law at once to see him. She received him alone and with great warmth. She was beautiful, and soft as May; a glowing yet delicate face; rich brown hair, and large blue eyes; not yet a mother, but with something of the dignity of the matron blending with the lingering timidity of the girl.

Egremont was glad to join his sister-in-law again in the drawing-room before dinner. He seated himself by her side, and in answer to her enquiries was giving her some narrative of his travels; the vicar, who was low church, was shaking his head at Lady Marney's young friend, who was enlarging on the excellence of Mr. Paget's tales;* while Captain Grouse, in a stiff white neckcloth, tight pantaloons, to show his celebrated legs, transparent stockings and polished shoes, was throwing himself into attitudes in the background, and, with a zeal amounting almost to enthusiasm, teaching Lady Marney's spaniel to beg, when the door opened and Lord Marney entered, but, as if to make security doubly sure, not alone. He was accompanied by a neighbour and brother magistrate, Sir Vavasour Firebrace, a baronet of the earliest batch, and a gentleman of great family and great estate.

'Well, Charles!'

'How are you, George?'

And the brothers shook hands.

'Tis the English way; and if they had been inclined to fall into each other's arms, they would not probably have done more.

In a few minutes it was announced that dinner was served, and so, secured from a scene, having a fair appetite, and surrounded by dishes that could agreeably satisfy it, a kind of vague fraternal sentiment began to stir the breast of Lord Marney: he really was glad to see his brother again; remembered the days when they rode their ponies and played cricket; his voice softened, his eyes sparkled, and he at length exclaimed, 'Do you know, old fellow, it makes me quite happy to see you here again? Suppose we take a glass of wine.'

The softer heart and more susceptible spirit of Egremont were well calculated to respond to this ebullition of feeling, however slight; and truly it was for many reasons not without considerable emotion, that he found himself once more at Marney. He sat by the side of his gentle sister-in-law, who seemed pleased by the unwonted cordiality of her husband, and anxious by many kind offices to second every indication of good feeling on his part. Captain Grouse was assiduous; the vicar was of the deferential breed, agreed with Lady Marney on the importance of infant schools, but recalled his opinion when Lord Marney expressed his imperious hope that no infant schools would ever be found in his neighbourhood. Sir Vavasour was more than middle-aged, comely, very gentle-manlike, but with an air occasionally of absence which hardly agreed with his frank and somewhat hearty idiosyncrasy, his clear brow, florid complexion, and blue eye. But Lord Marney talked a good deal, though chiefly dogmatical or argumenta-tive. It was rather difficult for him to find a sufficient stock of opposition, but he lay in wait and seized every opening with wonderful alacrity. Even Captain Grouse could not escape him: if driven to extremity, Lord Marney would even ques-tion his principles on fly-making. Captain Grouse gave up, but not too soon; he was well aware that his noble friend's passion for controversy was equal to his love of conquest. As for Lady Marney, it was evident that, with no inconsider-able talents, and with an intelligence richly cultivated, the controversial genius of her husband had completely cowed her conversational charms. She never advanced a proposition that he did not immediately bristle up, and she could only evade the encounter by a graceful submission. As for the vicar, a frequent guest, he would fain have taken refuge in silence, but the earl, especially when alone, would what he called 'draw him out,' and the game once unearthed, with so skilled a pack there was but little fear of a bad run. When all were reduced to silence, Lord Marney, relinquishing contro-versy, assumed the positive. He eulogised the new poor-law, which he declared would be the salvation of the country, pro-vided it was 'carried out' in the spirit in which it was de-veloped in the Marney Union; but then he would add that there was no district except their union in which it was

properly observed. He was tremendously fierce against allotments,* and analysed the system with merciless sarcasm. Indeed, he had no inconsiderable acquaintance with the doctrines of the economists, and was rather inclined to carry
them into practice in every instance, except that of the landed
proprietary, which he clearly proved 'stood upon different
grounds' from those of any other 'interest.' There was nothing he hated so much as a poacher, except a lease; though
perhaps, in the catalogue of his aversions, we ought to
give the preference to his anti-ecclesiastical prejudice; this
amounted even to acrimony. Though there was no man
breathing who was possessed with such a strong repugnance
to subscriptions of any kind, it delighted Lord Marney to see
his name among the contributors to all sectarian institutions.
The vicar of Marney, who had been presented by himself,
was his model of a priest: he left everybody alone. Under the
influence of Lady Marney, the worthy vicar had once warmed
up into some ebullition of very low church zeal; there was
some talk of an evening lecture, the schools were to be re-
modelled, certain tracts were actually distributed. But Lord
Marney soon stopped all this. 'No priestcraft at Marney,' said
this gentle proprietor of abbey lands.

'I wanted very much to come and canvass for you,' said
Lady Marney to Egremont, 'but George did not like it.'

'The less the family interfered the better,' said Lord Marney;
'and for my part, I was very much alarmed when I heard my
mother had gone down.'

'Oh! my mother did wonders,' said Egremont; 'we should
have been beaten without her. Indeed, to tell the truth, I quite
gave up the thing the moment they started their man. Before
that we were on velvet; but the instant he appeared everything was changed, and I found some of my warmest supporters members of his committee.'

'You had a formidable opponent, Lord Marney told me,'
said Sir Vavasour. 'Who was he?'

'Oh! a dreadful man! A Scotchman, richer than Croesus,
one McDruggy, fresh from Canton, with a million of opium
in each pocket, denouncing corruption, and bellowing free
trade.'

'But they do not care much for free trade in the old borough?' said Lord Marney.

'No, it was a mistake,' said Egremont; 'and the cry was changed the moment my opponent was on the ground. Then all the town was placarded with "Vote for McDruggy and our young Queen," as if he had coalesced with her Majesty.'

'My mother must have been in despair,' said Lord Marney.

'We issued our placard instantly of "Vote for our young Queen and Egremont," which was at least more modest, and turned out more popular.'

'That I am sure was my mother,' said Lord Marney.

'No,' said Egremont; 'it was the effusion of a far more experienced mind. My mother was in hourly communication with head-quarters, and Mr. Taper sent down the cry by express.'

'Peel, in or out, will support the Poor-Law,' said Lord Marney, rather audaciously, as he reseated himself after the ladies had retired. 'He must;' and he looked at his brother, whose return had in a great degree been secured by crying that Poor-Law down.

'It is impossible,' said Charles, fresh from the hustings, and speaking from the card of Taper; for the condition of the people was a subject of which he knew nothing.

'He will carry it out,' said Lord Marney, 'you'll see, or the land will not support him.'

'I wish,' said Sir Vavasour, 'we could manage some modification about out-door relief.'

'Modification!' said Lord Marney; 'why, there has been nothing but modification. What we want is stringency.'

'The people will never bear it,' said Egremont; 'there must be some change.'

'You cannot go back to the abuses of the old system,' said Captain Grouse, making, as he thought, a safe observation.

'Better go back to the old system than modify the new,' said Lord Marney.

'I wish the people would take to it a little more,' said Sir Vavasour; 'they certainly do not like it in our parish.'

'The people are very contented here, eh, Slimsey?' said Lord Marney.

'Very,' said the vicar.

Hereupon a conversation took place, principally sustained by the earl and the baronet, which developed all the resources of the great parochial mind. Dietaries, bastardy, gaol regulations, game laws, were amply discussed; and Lord Marney wound up with a declaration of the means by which the country might be saved, and which seemed principally to consist of high prices and low church.

'If the sovereign could only know her best friends,' said Sir Vavasour, with a sigh.

Lord Marney seemed to get uneasy.

'And avoid the fatal mistakes of her predecessor,' continued the baronet.

'Charles, another glass of claret,' said the earl.

'She might yet rally round the throne a body of men—'

'Then we will go to the ladies,' said the earl, abruptly disturbing his guest.

CHAPTER 2

THERE was music as they re-entered the drawing-room. Sir Vavasour attached himself to Egremont.

'It is a great pleasure for me to see you again, Mr. Egremont,' said the worthy baronet. 'Your father was my earliest and kindest friend. I remember you at Firebrace, a very little boy. Happy to see you again, sir, in so eminent a position; a legislator – one of our legislators. It gave me a sincere satisfaction to observe your return.'

'You are very kind, Sir Vavasour.'

'But it is a responsible position,' continued the baronet. 'Think you they'll stand? A majority, I suppose, they have; but, I conclude, in time, Sir Robert will have it in time. We must not be in a hurry; "the more haste" – you know the rest. The country is decidedly conservative. All that we want now is a strong government, that will put all things to rights. If the poor king had lived—'

'He would have sent these men to the right-about,' said Egremont, a young politician, proud of his secret intelligence.

'Ah! the poor king!' said Sir Vavasour, shaking his head.

'He was entirely with us,' said Egremont.

'Poor man!' said Sir Vavasour.

'You think it was too late, then?' said his companion.

'You are a young man entering political life,' said the baronet, taking Egremont kindly by the arm, and leading him to a sofa; 'everything depends on the first step. You have a great opportunity. Nothing can be done by a mere individual. The most powerful body in this country wants a champion.'

'But you can depend on Peel?' said Egremont.

'He is one of us; we ought to be able to depend on him. But I have spoken to him for an hour, and could get nothing out of him.'

'He is cautious; but depend upon it, he will stand or fall by the land.'

'I am not thinking of the land,' said Sir Vavasour; 'of something much more important; with all the influence of the land, and a great deal more besides; of an order of men who are ready to rally round the throne, and are, indeed, if justice were done to them, its natural and hereditary champions. Egremont looked perplexity. 'I am speaking,' added Sir Vavasour in a solemn voice, 'I am speaking of the baronets!'

'The baronets! And what do they want?'

'Their rights; their long-withheld rights. The poor king was with us. He has frequently expressed to me and other deputies his determination to do us justice; but he was not a strong-minded man,' said Sir Vavasour, with a sigh; 'and in these revolutionary and levelling times he had a hard task, perhaps. And the peers, who are our brethren, they were, I fear, against us. But, in spite of the ministers and in spite of the peers, had the poor king lived we should at least have had the badge,' added Sir Vavasour, mournfully.

'The badge!'

'It would have satisfied Sir Grosvenor le Draughte,' said Sir Vavasour; 'and he had a strong party with him; he was for compromise, but d—— him, his father was only an accoucheur.'

'And you wanted more?' inquired Egremont, with a demure look.

'All, or nothing,' said Sir Vavasour: 'principle is ever my

motto, no expediency. I made a speech to the order at the
Clarendon; there were four hundred of us; the feeling was
very strong.'

'A powerful party,' said Egremont.

'And a military order, sir, if properly understood. What
could stand against us? The Reform Bill could never have
passed if the baronets had been organized.'

'I have no doubt you could bring us in now,' said Egremont.

'That is exactly what I told Sir Robert. I want him to be
brought in by his own order. It would be a grand thing.'

'There is nothing like *esprit de corps*,' said Egremont.

'And such a body!' exclaimed Sir Vavasour, with animation.
'Picture us for a moment, to yourself, going down in procession to Westminster, for example, to hold a chapter. Five or
six hundred baronets in dark green costume, – the appropriate
dress of *equites aurati*; each not only with his badge, but with
his collar of SS; belted and scarfed; his star glittering; his
pennon flying; his hat white, with a plume of white feathers;
of course the sword and the gilt spurs. In our hand, the
thumb-ring and signet not forgotten, we hold our coronet of
two balls!'

Egremont stared with irrepressible astonishment at the excited being, who unconsciously pressed his companion's arm
as he drew this rapid sketch of the glories so unconstitutionally
withheld from him.

'A magnificent spectacle!' said Egremont.

'Evidently the body destined to save this country,' eagerly
continued Sir Vavasour. 'Blending all sympathies; the crown
of which they are the peculiar champions; the nobles of
whom they are the popular branch; the people who recognize
in them their natural leaders. But the picture is not complete.
We should be accompanied by an equal number of gallant
knights, our elder sons, who, the moment they come of age,
have the right to claim knighthood of their sovereign, while
their mothers and wives, no longer degraded to the nomen-
clature of a sheriff's lady, but resuming their legal or analogical
dignities, and styled the "honourable baronetess," with her
coronet and robe, or the "honourable knightess," with her
golden collar of SS, and chaplet or cap of dignity, may either

accompany the procession, or, ranged in galleries in a becoming situation, rain influence from above.'

'I am all for their going in the procession,' said Egremont.

'The point is not so clear,' said Sir Vavasour, solemnly; 'and indeed, although we have been firm in defining our rightful claims in our petitions, as for "honorary epithets, secondary titles, personal decorations, and augmented heraldic bearings," I am not clear, if the government evinced a disposition for a liberal settlement of the question, I would not urge a too stringent adherence to every point. For instance, I am prepared myself, great as would be the sacrifice, even to renounce the claim of secondary titles for our eldest sons, if, for instance, they would secure us our coronet.'

'Fie, fie, Sir Vavasour,' said Egremont, seriously; 'remember principle: no expediency, no compromise.'

'You are right,' said the baronet, colouring a little; 'and do you know, Mr. Egremont, you are the only individual I have yet met out of the order, who has taken a sensible view of this great question, which, after all, is the question of the day.'

CHAPTER 3

THE situation of the rural town of Marney* was one of the most delightful easily to be imagined. In a spreading dale, contiguous to the margin of a clear and lively stream, surrounded by meadows and gardens, and backed by lofty hills, undulating and richly wooded, the traveller on the opposite heights of the dale would often stop to admire the merry prospect that recalled to him the traditional epithet of his country.

Beautiful illusion! For behind that laughing landscape, penury and disease fed upon the vitals of a miserable population.

The contrast between the interior of the town and its external aspect was as striking as it was full of pain. With the exception of the dull high street, which had the usual characteristics of a small agricultural market town, some sombre mansions, a dingy inn, and a petty bourse, Marney mainly consisted of a variety of narrow and crowded lanes formed by cottages built of rubble, or unhewn stones without cement,

and, from age or badness of the material, looking as if they
could scarcely hold together. The gaping chinks admitted
every blast; the leaning chimneys had lost half their original
height; the rotten rafters were evidently misplaced; while in
many instances the thatch, yawning in some parts to admit
the wind and wet, and in all utterly unfit for its original purpose of giving protection from the weather, looked more like
the top of a dunghill than a cottage. Before the doors of these
dwellings, and often surrounding them, ran open drains full
of animal and vegetable refuse, decomposing into disease, or
sometimes in their imperfect course filling foul pits or spreading into stagnant pools, while a concentrated solution of every
species of dissolving filth was allowed to soak through, and
thoroughly impregnate, the walls and ground adjoining.

These wretched tenements seldom consisted of more than
two rooms, in one of which the whole family, however numerous, were obliged to sleep, without distinction of age, or sex,
or suffering. With the water streaming down the walls, the
light distinguished through the roof, with no hearth even in
winter, the virtuous mother in the sacred pangs of childbirth
gives forth another victim to our thoughtless civilisation;
surrounded by three generations whose inevitable presence is
more painful than her suffering in that hour of travail; while
the father of her coming child, in another corner of the sordid
chamber, lies stricken by that typhus which his contaminating
dwelling has breathed into his veins, and for whose next prey
is perhaps destined his new-born child. These swarming walls
had neither windows nor doors sufficient to keep out the
weather, or admit the sun, or supply the means of ventilation;
the humid and putrid roof of thatch exhaling malaria like all
other decaying vegetable matter. The dwelling-rooms were
neither boarded nor paved; and whether it were that some
were situate in low and damp places, occasionally flooded by
the river, and usually much below the level of the road; or
that the springs, as was often the case, would burst through
the mud floor; the ground was at no time better than so much
clay, while sometimes you might see little channels cut from
the centre under the doorways to carry off the water, the door
itself removed from its hinges; a resting-place for infancy in
its deluged home. These hovels were in many instances not

provided with the commonest conveniences of the rudest police; contiguous to every door might be observed the dung-heap on which every kind of filth was accumulated, for the purpose of being disposed of for manure, so that, when the poor man opened his narrow habitation in the hope of re-freshing it with the breeze of summer, he was met with a mix-ture of gases from reeking dunghills.

This town of Marney was a metropolis of agricultural labour, for the proprietors of the neighbourhood having for the last half-century acted on the system of destroying the cottages on their estates, in order to become exempted from the maintenance of the population, the expelled people had flocked to Marney, where, during the war, a manufactory had afforded them some relief, though its wheels had long ceased to disturb the waters of the Mar.

Deprived of this resource, they had again gradually spread themselves over that land which had, as it were, rejected them; and obtained from its churlish breast a niggardly subsistence. Their re-entrance into the surrounding parishes was viewed with great suspicion; their renewed settlement opposed by every ingenious contrivance. Those who availed themselves of their labour were careful that they should not become dwellers on the soil; and though, from the excessive com-petition, there were few districts in the kingdom where the rate of wages was more depressed, those who were fortunate enough to obtain the scant remuneration had, in addition to their toil, to endure, each morn and even, a weary journey before they could reach the scene of their labour, or return to the squalid hovel which profaned the name of home. To that home, over which malaria hovered, and round whose shiver-ing hearth were clustered other guests besides the exhausted family of toil, Fever, in every form, pale Consumption, ex-hausting Synochus,* and trembling Ague, returned, after cul-tivating the broad fields of merry England,* the bold British peasant,* returned to encounter the worst of diseases, with a frame the least qualified to oppose them; a frame that, sub-dued by toil, was never sustained by animal food; drenched by the tempest, could not change its dripping rags; and was indebted for its scanty fuel to the windfalls of the woods.

The eyes of this unhappy race might have been raised to

the solitary spire that sprang up in the midst of them, the
bearer of present consolation, the harbinger of future equality;
but Holy Church at Marney had forgotten her sacred mission.
We have introduced the reader to the vicar, an orderly man,
who deemed he did his duty if he preached each week two
sermons, and enforced humility on his congregation, and
gratitude for the blessings of this life. The high street and
some neighbouring gentry were the staple of his hearers.
Lord and Lady Marney, attended by Captain Grouse, came
every Sunday morning, with commendable regularity, and
were ushered into the invisible interior of a vast pew, that
occupied half of the gallery, was lined with crimson damask,
and furnished with easy chairs, and, for those who chose
them, well-padded stools of prayer. The people of Marney
took refuge in conventicles, which abounded; little plain
buildings of pale brick, with the names painted on them of
Sion, Bethel, Bethesda; names of a distant land, and the language of a persecuted and ancient race; yet such is the mysterious power of their divine quality, breathing consolation
in the nineteenth century to the harassed forms and the har-
rowed souls of a Saxon peasantry.

But however devoted to his flock might have been the
Vicar of Marney, his exertions for their well-being, under any
circumstances, must have been mainly limited to spiritual consolation. Married, and a father, he received for his labours the
small tithes of the parish, which secured to him an income by
no means equal to that of a superior banker's clerk, or the
cook of a great loanmonger. The great tithes of Marney,
which might be counted by thousands, swelled the vast rental
which was drawn from this district by the fortunate earls that
bore its name.

The morning after the arrival of Egremont at the Abbey,
an unusual stir might have been observed in the high street of
the town. Round the portico of the Green Dragon hotel and
commercial inn, a knot of principal personages, the chief lawyer, the brewer, the vicar himself, and several of those easy
quidnuncs who abound in country towns, and who rank
under the designation of retired gentlemen, were in close and
earnest converse. In a short time, a servant on horseback, in
the Abbey livery, galloped up to the portico, and delivered a

letter to the vicar. The excitement apparently had now greatly increased. On the opposite side of the way to the important group, a knot, in larger numbers, but deficient in quality, had formed themselves, and remained transfixed with gaping mouths and a curious, not to say alarmed air. The head constable walked up to the door of the Green Dragon, and, though he did not presume to join the principal group, was evidently in attendance, if required. The clock struck eleven; a cart had stopped to watch events, and a gentleman's coachman riding home with a led horse.

'Here they are!' said the brewer.

'Lord Marney himself,' said the lawyer.

'And Sir Vavasour Firebrace, I declare! I wonder how he came here,' said a retired gentleman, who had been a tallow-chandler on Holborn Hill.

The vicar took off his hat, and all uncovered. Lord Marney and his brother magistrate rode briskly up to the inn, and rapidly dismounted.

'Well, Snigford,' said his lordship, in a peremptory tone, 'this is a pretty business; I'll have this stopped directly.'

Fortunate man, if he succeeded in doing so! The torch of the incendiary had for the first time been introduced into the parish of Marney; and last night the primest stacks of the Abbey farm had blazed, a beacon to the agitated neighbourhood.

CHAPTER 4

'It is not so much the fire, sir,' said Mr. Bingley, of the Abbey farm, to Egremont, 'but the temper of the people that alarms me. Do you know, sir, there were two or three score of them here, and, except my own farm-servants, not one of them would lend a helping hand to put out the flames, though, with water so near, they might have been of great service.'

'You told my brother, Lord Marney, this?'

'Oh! it's Mr. Charles I'm speaking to! My service to you, sir; I'm glad to see you in these parts again. It's a long time that we have had that pleasure, sir. Travelling in foreign parts, as I have heard say?'

'Something of that; but very glad to find myself at home once more, Mr. Bingley, though very sorry to have such a welcome as a blazing rick at the Abbey farm.'

'Well, do you know, Mr. Charles, between ourselves,' and Mr. Bingley lowered his tone and looked around him, 'things is very bad here; I can't make out, for my part, what has become of the country. 'Tayn't the same land to live in as it was when you used to come to our moor coursing, with the old lord; you remember that, I be sure, Mr. Charles?'

''Tis not easy to forget good sport, Mr. Bingley. With your permission, I will put my horse up here for half an hour. I have a fancy to stroll to the ruins.'

'You wunna find them much changed,' said the farmer, smiling. 'They have seen a deal of different things in their time! But you will taste our ale, Mr. Charles?'

'When I return.'

But the hospitable Bingley would take no denial, and as his companion waived on the present occasion entering his house, for the sun had been some time declining, the farmer, calling one of his labourers to take Egremont's horse, hastened into the house to fill the brimming cup.

'And what do you think of this fire?' said Egremont to the hind.

'I think 'tis hard times for the poor, sir.'

'But rick-burning will not make the times easier, my good man.'

The man made no reply, but with a dogged look led away the horse to his stable.

About half a mile from Marney the dale narrowed, and the river took a winding course. It ran through meads, soft and vivid with luxuriant vegetation, bounded on either side by rich hanging woods, save where occasionally a quarry broke the verdant bosom of the heights with its rugged and tawny form. Fair stone and plenteous timber, and the current of fresh waters, combined, with the silent and secluded scene screened from every harsh and angry wind, to form the sacred spot that in old days Holy Church loved to hallow with its beauteous and enduring structures. Even the stranger, therefore, when he had left the town about two miles behind him, and had heard the farm and mill which he had since passed called the Abbey farm and the Abbey mill, might have been prepared for the grateful vision of some monastic remains. As for Egremont, he had been almost born amid the ruins of Marney Abbey; its solemn relics were associated with his first and freshest fancies; every footstep was as familiar to him as it could have been to one of the old monks; yet never without emotion could he behold these unrivalled remains of one of the greatest of the great religious houses of the North.

Over a space of not less than ten acres might still be observed the fragments of the great Abbey; these were, towards their limit, in general moss-grown and mouldering memorials that told where once rose the offices, and spread the terraced gardens, of the old proprietors; here might still be traced the dwelling of the lord abbot; and there, still more distinctly, because built on a greater scale and of materials still more intended for perpetuity, the capacious hospital, a name that did not then denote the dwelling of disease, but a place where all the rights of hospitality were practised; where the traveller, from the proud baron to the lonely pilgrim, asked the shelter and the succour that never were denied, and at whose gate, called the Portal of the Poor, the peasants on the Abbey lands, if in want, might appeal each morn and night for raiment and for food.

But it was in the centre of this tract of ruins, occupying a space of not less than two acres, that, with a strength which had defied time, and with a beauty which had at last turned away the wrath of man, still rose, if not in perfect, yet admirable, form and state, one of the noblest achievements of Christian art, the Abbey church. The summer vault was now its only roof, and all that remained of its gorgeous windows was the vastness of their arched symmetry, and some wreathed relics of their fantastic framework, but the rest was uninjured.

From the west window, looking over the transept chapel of the Virgin, still adorned with pillars of marble and alabaster, the eye wandered down the nave to the great orient light, a length of nearly three hundred feet, through a gorgeous avenue of unshaken walls and columns that clustered to the skies. On each side of the Lady's chapel rose a tower. One, which was of great antiquity, being of that style which is commonly called Norman, short, and thick, and square, did not mount much above the height of the western front; but the other tower was of a character very different. It was tall and light, and of a Gothic style most pure and graceful; the stone of which it was built, of a bright and even sparkling colour, and looking as if it were hewn but yesterday. At first, its turreted crest seemed injured; but the truth is, it was unfinished; the workmen were busied on this very tower the day that Baldwin Greymount came as the king's commissioner to enquire into the conduct of this religious house. The abbots loved to memorize their reigns by some public work, which should add to the beauty of their buildings or the convenience of their subjects; and the last of the ecclesiastical lords of Marney, a man of fine taste, and a skilful architect, was raising this new belfry for his brethren, when the stern decree arrived that the bells should no more sound. And the hymn was no more to be chaunted in the Lady's chapel; and the candles were no more to be lit on the high altar; and the gate of the poor was to be closed for ever; and the wanderer was no more to find a home.

The body of the church was in many parts overgrown with brambles, and in all covered with a rank vegetation. It had been a sultry day, and the blaze of the meridian heat still inflamed the air; the kine, for shelter rather than for sustenance, had wandered through some broken arches, and were lying in the shadow of the nave. This desecration of a spot once sacred, still beautiful and solemn, jarred on the feelings of Egremont. He sighed, and turning away, followed a path that after a few paces led him into the cloister garden. This was a considerable quadrangle, once surrounding the garden of the monks; but all that remained of that fair pleasaunce was a solitary yew in its centre, which seemed the oldest tree that could well live, and was, according to tradition, more ancient than the most venerable walls of the Abbey. Round this quadrangle were the refectory, the library, and the kitchen, and above them the cells and dormitory of the brethren. An imperfect staircase, not without danger, led to these unroofed chambers; but Egremont, familiar with the way, did not hesitate to pursue it, so that he soon found himself on an elevation overlooking the garden, while further on extended the vast cloisters of the monks, and adjoining was a cemetery, that had once been enclosed, and communicated with the cloister garden.

It was one of those summer days that are so still, that they seem as it were a holiday of Nature. The weary winds were sleeping in some grateful cavern, and the sunbeams basking on some fervent knoll; the river floated with a drowsy unconscious course; there was no wave in the grass, no stir in the branches.

A silence so profound amid these solemn ruins offered the perfection of solitude; and there was that stirring in the mind of Egremont which rendered him far from indisposed for this loneliness.

The slight words that he had exchanged with the farmer and the hind had left him musing. Why was England not the same land as in the days of his light-hearted youth? Why were these hard times for the poor? He stood among the ruins that, as the farmer had well observed, had seen many changes: changes of creeds, of dynasties, of laws, of manners. New orders of men had arisen in the country, new sources of wealth had opened, new dispositions of power to which that wealth had necessarily led. His own house, his own order, had established themselves on the ruins of that great body, the emblems of whose ancient magnificence and strength surrounded him. And now his order was in turn menaced. And the People, the millions of Toil on whose unconscious energies during these changeful centuries all rested, what changes had these centuries brought to them? Had their advance in the national scale borne a due relation to that progress of their rulers, which had accumulated in the treasuries of a limited class the riches of the world, and made their possessors boast that they were the first of nations; the most powerful and the most free, the most enlightened, the most moral, and the most religious? Were there any rick-burners in the times of the lord abbots? And if not, why not? And why should the stacks of the Earls of Marney be destroyed, and those of the abbots of Marney spared?

Brooding over these suggestions, some voices disturbed him, and, looking round, he observed in the cemetery two men: one was standing beside a tomb, which his companion was apparently examining.

The first was of lofty stature, and, though dressed with simplicity, had nothing sordid in his appearance. His garments gave no clue to his position in life; they might have been worn by a squire or by his gamekeeper; a dark velveteen dress and leathern gaiters. As Egremont caught his form, he threw his broad-brimmed country hat upon the ground, and showed a frank and manly countenance. His complexion might in youth have been ruddy, but time and time's attendants, thought and passion, had paled it; his chestnut hair, faded, but not grey, still clustered over a noble brow; his features were regular and handsome, a well-formed nose, the square mouth and its white teeth, and the clear grey eye, which befitted such an idiosyncrasy. His time of vigorous manhood, for he was nearer forty than fifty years of age, perhaps better suited his athletic form than the more supple and graceful season of youth.

Stretching his powerful arms in the air, and delivering himself of an exclamation which denoted his weariness, and which had broken the silence, he expressed to his companion his determination to rest himself under the shade of the yew in the contiguous garden, and, inviting his friend to follow him, he took up his hat and moved away.

There was something in the appearance of the stranger that interested Egremont; and, waiting till he had established himself in his pleasant resting-place. Egremont descended into the cloister garden and determined to address him.

CHAPTER 5

'You lean against an ancient trunk,' said Egremont, carelessly advancing to the stranger, who looked up at him without any expression of surprise, and then replied, 'They say 'tis the trunk beneath whose branches the monks encamped when they came to this valley to raise their building. It was their house, till with the wood and stone around them, their labour and their fine art, they piled up their abbey. And then they were driven out of it, and it came to this. Poor men! poor men!'

'They would hardly have forfeited their resting-place had they deserved to retain it,' said Egremont.

'They were rich. I thought it was poverty that was a crime,' replied the stranger, in a tone of simplicity.

'But they had committed other crimes.'

'It may be so; we are very frail. But their history has been written by their enemies; they were condemned without a hearing; the people rose oftentimes in their behalf; and their property was divided among those on whose reports it was forfeited.'

'At any rate, it was a forfeiture which gave life to the community,' said Egremont; 'the lands are held by active men and not by drones.'

'A drone is one who does not labour,' said the stranger; 'whether he wear a cowl or a coronet, 'tis the same to me. Somebody I suppose must own the land; though I have heard say that this individual tenure is not a necessity; but, however this may be, I am not one who would object to the lord, provided he were a gentle one. All agree that the Monastics were easy landlords; their rents were low; they granted leases in those days. Their tenants, too, might renew their term before their tenure ran out: so they were men of spirit and property. There were yeomen then, sir: the country was not divided into two classes, masters and slaves; there was some resting-place between luxury and misery. Comfort was an English habit then, not merely an English word.'

'And do you really think they were easier landlords than our present ones?' said Egremont, inquiringly.

'Human nature would tell us that, even if history did not confess it. The Monastics could possess no private property; they could save no money; they could bequeath nothing. They lived, received, and expended in common. The monastery, too, was a proprietor that never died and never wasted. The farmer had a deathless landlord then; not a harsh guardian, or a grinding mortgagee, or a dilatory master in chancery: all was certain; the manor had not to dread a change of lords, or the oaks to tremble at the axe of the squandering heir. How proud we are still in England of an old family, though, God knows, 'tis rare to see one now. Yet the people

like to say, We held under him, and his father and his grandfather before him: they know that such a tenure is a benefit.
The abbot was ever the same. The monks were, in short, in
every district a point of refuge for all who needed succour,
counsel, and protection; a body of individuals having no
cares of their own, with wisdom to guide the inexperienced,
with wealth to relieve the suffering, and often with power to
protect the oppressed.'

'You plead their cause with feeling,' said Egremont, not
unmoved.

'It is my own; they were the sons of the people, like myself.'

'I had thought rather these monasteries were the resort of
the younger branches of the aristocracy,' said Egremont.

'Instead of the pension list,' replied his companion, smiling,
but not with bitterness. 'Well, if we must have an aristocracy,
I would rather that its younger branches should be monks
and nuns than colonels without regiments, or housekeepers
of royal palaces that exist only in name. Besides, see what advantage to a minister if the unendowed artsiocracy were thus
provided for now. He need not, like a minister in these days,
entrust the conduct of public affairs to individuals notoriously
incompetent, appoint to the command of expeditions generals
who never saw a field, make governors of colonies out of men
who never could govern themselves, or find an ambassador
in a broken dandy or a blasted favourite. It is true that many
of the monks and nuns were persons of noble birth. Why
should they not have been? The aristocracy had their share;
no more. They, like all other classes, were benefited by the
monasteries: but the list of the mitred abbots, when they were
suppressed, shows that the great majority of the heads of
houses were of the people.'

'Well, whatever difference of opinion may exist on these
points,' said Egremont, 'there is one on which there can be
no controversy: the monks were great architects.'

'Ah! there it is,' said the stranger, in a tone of plaintiveness;
'if the world but only knew what they had lost! I am sure that
not the faintest idea is generally prevalent of the appearance
of England before and since the dissolution. Why, sir, in
England and Wales alone, there were of these institutions of
different sizes, I mean monasteries, and chantries and chapels,

and great hospitals, considerably upwards of three thousand; all of them fair buildings, many of them of exquisite beauty. There were on an average in every shire at least twenty structures such as this was; in this great county double that number: establishments that were as vast and as magnificent and as beautiful as your Belvoirs and your Chatsworths, your Wentworths and your Stowes.* Try to imagine the effect of thirty or forty Chatsworths in this county, the proprietors of which were never absent. You complain enough now of absentees. The monks were never non-resident. They expended their revenue among those whose labour had produced it. These holy men, too, built and planted, as they did everything else, for posterity: their churches were cathedrals; their schools colleges; their halls and libraries the muniment rooms of kingdoms; their woods and waters, their farms and gardens, were laid out and disposed on a scale and in a spirit that are now extinct; they made the country beautiful, and the people proud of their country.'

'Yet if the monks were such public benefactors, why did not the people rise in their favour?'

'They did, but too late. They struggled for a century, but they struggled against property, and they were beat. As long as the monks existed, the people, when aggrieved, had property on their side. And now 'tis all over,' said the stranger; 'and travellers come and stare at these ruins, and think themselves very wise to moralise over time. They are the children of violence, not of time. It is war that created these ruins, civil war, of all our civil wars the most inhuman, for it was waged with the unresisting. The monasteries were taken by storm, they were sacked, gutted, battered with warlike instruments, blown up with gunpowder; you may see the marks of the blast against the new tower here. Never was such a plunder. The whole face of the country for a century was that of a land recently invaded by a ruthless enemy; it was worse than the Norman conquest; nor has England ever lost this character of ravage. I don't know whether the union workhouses will remove it. They are building something for the people at last. After an experiment of three centuries, your gaols being full, and your treadmills losing something of their virtue, you have given us a substitute for the monasteries.'*

'You lament the old faith,' said Egremont, in a tone of respect.

'I am not viewing the question as one of faith,' said the stranger. 'It is not as a matter of religion, but as a matter of right, that I am considering it: as a matter, I should say, of private right and public happiness. You might have changed, if you thought fit, the religion of the abbots as you changed the religion of the bishops: but you had no right to deprive men of their property, and property moreover which, under their administration, so mainly contributed to the welfare of the community.'

'As for community,' said a voice which proceeded neither from Egremont nor the stranger, 'with the monasteries expired the only type that we ever had in England of such an intercourse. There is no community in England; there is aggregation, but aggregation under circumstances which make it rather a dissociating than a uniting principle.'

It was a still voice that uttered these words, yet one of a peculiar character; one of those voices that instantly arrest attention: gentle and yet solemn, earnest yet unimpassioned. With a step as whispering as his tone; the man who had been kneeling by the tomb had unobserved joined his associate and Egremont. He hardly reached the middle height; his form slender, but well-proportioned; his pale countenance, slightly marked with the small-pox, was redeemed from absolute ugliness by a highly intellectual brow, and large dark eyes that indicated deep sensibility and great quickness of apprehension. Though young, he was already a little bald; he was dressed entirely in black; the fairness of his linen, the neatness of his beard, his gloves much worn, yet carefully mended, intimated that his faded garments were the result of necessity rather than of negligence.

'You also lament the dissolution of these bodies,' said Egremont.

'There is so much to lament in the world in which we live.' said the younger of the strangers, 'that I can spare no pang for the past.'

'Yet you approve of the principle of their society; you prefer it, you say, to our existing life.'

'Yes; I prefer association to gregariousness.'

'That is a distinction,' said Egremont, musingly.

'It is a community of purpose that constitutes society,' continued the younger stranger; 'without that, men may be drawn into contiguity, but they still continue virtually isolated.'

'And is that their condition in cities?'

'It is their condition everywhere; but in cities that condition is aggravated. A density of population implies a severer struggle for existence, and a consequent repulsion of elements brought into too close contact. In great cities men are brought together by the desire of gain. They are not in a state of co-operation, but of isolation, as to the making of fortunes; and for all the rest they are careless of neighbours. Christianity teaches us to love our neighbour as ourself; modern society acknowledges no neighbour.'

'Well, we live in strange times,' said Egremont, struck by the observation of his companion, and relieving a perplexed spirit by an ordinary exclamation, which often denotes that the mind is more stirred than it cares to acknowledge, or at the moment is able to express.

'When the infant begins to walk, it also thinks that it lives in strange times,' said his companion.

'Your inference?' asked Egremont.

'That society, still in its infancy, is beginning to feel its way.'

'This is a new reign,' said Egremont, 'perhaps it is a new era.'

'I think so,' said the younger stranger.

'I hope so,' said the elder one.

'Well, society may be in its infancy,' said Egremont, slightly smiling; 'but, say what you like, our Queen reigns over the greatest nation that ever existed.'

'Which nation?' asked the younger stranger, 'for she reigns over two.'

The stranger paused; Egremont was silent, but looked inquiringly.

'Yes,' resumed the younger stranger after a moment's interval. 'Two nations; between whom there is no intercourse and no sympathy; who are as ignorant of each other's habits, thoughts, and feelings, as if they were dwellers in different

zones, or inhabitants of different planets; who are formed by
a different breeding, are fed by a different food, are ordered
by different manners, and are not governed by the same laws.'

'You speak of—' said Egremont, hesitatingly.

'THE RICH AND THE POOR.'

At this moment a sudden flush of rosy light, suffusing the
grey ruins, indicated that the sun had just fallen; and, through
a vacant arch that overlooked them, alone in the resplendent
sky, glittered the twilight star. The hour, the scene, the solemn
stillness and the softening beauty, repressed controversy, induced even silence. The last words of the stranger lingered in
the ear of Egremont; his musing spirit was teeming with
many thoughts, many emotions; when from the Lady's chapel
there rose the evening hymn to the Virgin. A single voice;
but tones of almost supernatural sweetness; tender and solemn
yet flexible and thrilling.

Egremont started from his reverie. He would have spoken,
but he perceived that the elder of the strangers had risen from
his resting-place, and, with downcast eyes and crossed arms,
was on his knees. The other remained standing in his former
posture.

The divine melody ceased; the elder stranger rose; the
words were on the lips of Egremont, that would have asked
some explanation of this sweet and holy mystery, when, in the
vacant and star-lit arch on which his glance was fixed, he beheld a female form. She was apparently in the habit of a
Religious, yet scarcely could be a nun, for her veil if, indeed
it were a veil, had fallen on her shoulders, and revealed her
thick tresses of long fair hair. The blush of deep emotion
lingered on a countenance which, though extremely young,
was impressed with a character of almost divine majesty;
while her dark eyes and long dark lashes, contrasting with the
brightness of her complexion and the luxuriance of her radiant
locks, combined to produce a beauty as rare as it is choice;
and so strange, that Egremont might for a moment have been
pardoned for believing her a seraph, who had lighted on this
sphere, or the fair phantom of some saint haunting the sacred
ruins of her desecrated fane.

CHAPTER 6

'I UNDERSTAND, then,' said Lord Marney to his brother, as on the evening of the same day they were seated together in the drawing-room, in close converse, 'I understand, then, that you have in fact paid nothing, and that my mother will give you a thousand pounds. That won't go very far.'

'It will hardly pay for the chairing,' said Egremont; 'the restoration of the family influence was celebrated on so great a scale.'

'The family influence must be supported,' said Lord Marney 'and my mother will give you a thousand pounds; as I said, that will not do much for you, but I like her spirit. Contests are expensive things, yet I quite approve of what you have done, especially as you won. It is a great thing in these ten-pound days* to win your first contest, and shows powers of calculation which I respect. Everything in this world is calculation; there is no such thing as luck, depend upon it; and if you go on calculating with equal exactness, you must succeed in life. Now, the question is, what is to be done with your election bills?'

'Exactly.'

'You want to know what I will do for you, or rather what I can do for you; that is the point. My inclination of course is to do everything for you; but when I calculate my resources, I may find that they are not equal to my inclination.'

'I am sure, George, you will do everything, and more than everything, you ought.'

'I am extremely pleased about this thousand pounds of my mother, Charles.'

'Most admirable of her! But she always is so generous!'

'Her jointure has been most regularly paid,' continued Lord Marney. 'Always be exact in your payments, Charles. There is no end to the good it produces. Now, if I had not been so regular in paying my mother her jointure, she would not in all probability have been able to give you this thousand pounds, and therefore, to a certain extent, you are indebted for this thousand pounds to me.'

Egremont drew up a little, but said nothing.

'I am obliged to pay my mother her jointure, whether ricks are burnt or not,' said Lord Marney. 'It's very hard, don't you think so?'

'But these ricks were Bingley's!'

'But he was not insured, and he will want some reduction in his rent, and if I do not see fit to allow it him, which I probably shall not, for he ought to have calculated on these things, I have ricks of my own, and they may be burnt any night.'

'But you, of course, are insured?'

'No, I am not, I calculate 'tis better to run the risk.'

'I wonder why ricks are burnt now, and were not in old days,' said Egremont.

'Because there is a surplus population in the kingdom,' said Lord Marney, 'and no rural police in the county.'

'You were speaking of the election, George,' said Egremont, not without reluctance, yet anxious, as the ice had been broken, to bring the matter to a result. Lord Marney, before the election, had written, in reply to his mother consulting him on the step, a letter with which she was delighted, but which Egremont at the time could have wished to have been more explicit. However, in the excitement attendant on a first contest, and influenced by the person whose judgment always swayed, and, in the present case, was peculiarly entitled to sway him, he stifled his scruples, and persuaded himself that he was a candidate, not only with the sanction but at the instance of his brother. 'You were speaking of the election, George,' said Egremont.

'About the election, Charles. Well, the long and short of it is this: that I wish to see you comfortable. To be harassed about money is one of the most disagreeable incidents of life. It ruffles the temper, lowers the spirits, disturbs the rest, and finally breaks up one's health. Always, if you possibly can, keep square. And if by any chance you do find yourself in a scrape, come to me. There is nothing under those circumstances like the advice of a cool-headed friend.'

'As valuable as the assistance of a cold-hearted one,' thought Egremont, who did not fancy too much the tone of this conversation.

'But there is one thing of which you must particularly beware,' continued Lord Marney, 'there is one thing worse even than getting into difficulties – patching them up. The patching-up system is fatal; it is sure to break down; you never get clear. Now, what I want to do for you, Charles, is to put you right altogether. I want to see you square and more than square, in a position which will for ever guarantee you from any annoyance of this kind.'

'He is a good fellow, after all,' thought Egremont.

'That thousand pounds of my mother was very apropos,' said Lord Marney; 'I suppose it was a sop that will keep them all right till we have made our arrangements.'

'Oh! there is no pressure of that kind,' said Egremont; 'if I see my way, and write to them, of course they will be quite satisfied.'

'Excellent,' said Lord Marney; 'and nothing could be more convenient to me, for, between ourselves, my balances are very low at this moment. The awful expenditure of keeping up this place! And then such terrible incumbrances as I came to!'

'Incumbrances, George! Why, I thought you had not any. There was not a single mortgage.'

'No mortgages; they are nothing; you find them, you get used to them, and you calculate accordingly. You quite forget the portions for younger children.'

'Yes; but you had plenty of ready money for them.'

'I had to pay them though,' said Lord Marney. 'Had I not I might have bought Grimblethorpe with the money; such an opportunity will never occur again.'

'But you talked of incumbrances,' said Egremont.

'Ah! my dear fellow,' said Lord Marney, 'you don't know what it is to have to keep up an estate like this; and very lucky for you. It is not the easy life you dream of. There are buildings; I am ruined in buildings; our poor dear father thought he left me Marney without an incumbrance; why there was not a barn on the whole estate that was weather-proof; not a farm-house that was not half in ruins. What I have spent in buildings! And draining! Though I make my own tiles, draining, my dear fellow, is a something of which you have not the least idea!'

'Well,' said Egremont, anxious to bring his brother back

to the point, 'you think, then, I had better write to them and
say—'

'Ah! now for your business,' said Lord Marney. 'Now I
will tell you what I can do for you. I was speaking to Arabella
about it last night; she quite approves my idea. You remember the De Mowbrays? Well, we are going to stay at Mowbray Castle, and you are to go with us. It is the first time they
have received company since their great loss. Ah! you were
abroad at the time, and so you are behindhand. Lord Mowbray's only son, Fitz-Warene, you remember him a deuced
clever fellow, he died about a year ago, in Greece, of a fever.
Never was such a blow! His two sisters, Lady Joan and Lady
Maud, are looked upon as the greatest heiresses in the kingdom: but I know Mowbray well; he will make an eldest son
of his eldest daughter. She will have it all; she is one of
Arabella's dearest friends, and you are to marry her.'

Egremont stared at his brother, who patted him on the
back with an expression of unusual kindness, adding, 'You
have no idea what a load this has taken off my mind, my dear
Charles; so great has my anxiety always been about you, particularly of late. To see you lord of Mowbray Castle will
realize my fondest hopes. That is a position fit for a man, and
I know none more worthy of it than yourself, though I am
your brother who say so. Now let us come and speak to
Arabella about it.'

So saying, Lord Marney, followed somewhat reluctantly by
his brother, advanced to the other end of the drawing-room,
where his wife was employed with her embroidery-frame, and
seated next to her young friend, Miss Poinsett, who was
playing chess with Captain Grouse, a member of the chess
club, and one of the most capital performers extant.

'Well, Arabella,' said Lord Marney, 'it is all settled; Charles
agrees with me about going to Mowbray Castle, and I think
the sooner we go the better. What do you think of the day
after to-morrow? That will suit me exactly, and therefore I
think we had better fix on it. We will consider it settled.'

Lady Marney looked embarrassed, and a little distressed.
Nothing could be more unexpected by her than this proposition; nothing more inconvenient than the arrangement. It
was true that Lady Joan Fitz-Warene had invited them to

Mowbray, and she had some vague intention, some day or other, of deliberating whether they should avail themselves of this kindness; but to decide upon going, and upon going instantly, without the least consultation, the least enquiry as to the suitableness of the arrangement, the visit of Miss Poinsett abruptly and ungraciously terminated, for example – all this was vexatious, distressing: a mode of management which out of the simplest incidents of domestic life contrived to extract some degree of perplexity and annoyance.

'Do not you think, George,' said Lady Marney, 'that we had better talk it over a little?'

'Not at all,' said Lord Marney; 'Charles will go, and it quite suits me, and therefore what necessity for any consultation?'

'Oh! if you and Charles like to go, certainly,' said Lady Marney, in a hesitating tone; 'only I shall be very sorry to lose your society.'

'How do you mean lose our society, Arabella? Of course you must go with us. I particularly want you to go. You are Lady Joan's most intimate friend; I believe there is no one she likes so much.'

'I cannot go the day after to-morrow,' said Lady Marney. speaking in a whisper, and looking volumes of deprecation.

'I cannot help it,' said Lord Marney; 'you should have told me this before. I wrote to Mowbray to-day, that we should be with him the day after to-morrow, and stay a week.'

'But you never mentioned it to me,' said Lady Marney, slightly blushing and speaking in a tone of gentle reproach.

'I should like to know when I am to find time to mention the contents of every letter I write,' said Lord Marney, 'particularly with all the vexatious business I have had on my hands to-day. But so it is; the more one tries to save you trouble, the more discontented you get.'

'No, not discontented, George.'

'I do not know what you call discontented: but when a man has made every possible arrangement to please you and everybody, and all his plans are to be set aside, merely because the day he has fixed on does not exactly suit your fancy, if that be not discontent, I should like very much to know what is, Arabella.'

Lady Marney did not reply. Always sacrificed, always yielding, the moment she attempted to express an opinion, she ever seemed to assume the position, not of the injured, but the injurer.

Arabella was a woman of abilities, which she had cultivated. She had excellent sense, and possessed many admirable qualities; she was far from being devoid of sensibility; but her sweet temper shrank from controversy, and nature had not endowed her with a spirit which could direct and control. She yielded without a struggle to the arbitrary will and unreasonable caprice of a husband who was scarcely her equal in intellect and far her inferior in all the genial qualities of our nature, but who governed her by his iron selfishness.

Lady Marney absolutely had no will of her own. A hard, exact, literal, bustling, acute being environed her existence; directed, planned, settled everything. Her life was a series of petty sacrifices and balked enjoyments. If her carriage were at the door, she was never certain that she should not have to send it away; if she had asked some friends to her house, the chances were she would have to put them off; if she were reading a novel, Lord Marney asked her to copy a letter; if she were going to the opera, she found that Lord Marney had got seats for her and some friend in the House of Lords, and seemed expecting the strongest expressions of delight and gratitude from her for his unasked and inconvenient kindness. Lady Marney had struggled against this tyranny in the earlier days of their union. Innocent, inexperienced Lady Marney! As if it were possible for a wife to contend against a selfish husband, at once sharp-witted and blunt-hearted! She had appealed to him, she had even reproached him; she had wept, once she had knelt. But Lord Marney looked upon these demonstrations as the disordered sensibility of a girl unused to the marriage state, and ignorant of the wise authority of husbands, of which he deemed himself a model. And so, after a due course of initiation, Lady Marney, invisible for days, plunged in remorseful reveries in the mysteries of her boudoir, and her lord dining at a club, and going to the minor theatres; the countess was broken in.

Lord Marney, who was fond of chess, turned out Captain Grouse, and gallantly proposed to finish his game with Miss Poinsett, which Miss Poinsett, who understood Lord Marney as well as he understood chess, took care speedily to lose, so that his lordship might encounter a champion worthy of him. Egremont, seated by his sister-in-law, and anxious by kind words to soothe the irritation which he had observed with pain his brother create, entered into easy talk, and after some time, said, 'I find you have been good enough to mould my destiny.'

Lady Marney looked a little surprised, and then said, 'How so?'

'You have decided on, I hear, the most important step of my life.'

'Indeed you perplex me.'

'Lady Joan Fitz-Warene, your friend—'

The countess blushed; the name was a clue which she could follow, but Egremont nevertheless suspected that the idea had never previously occurred to her. Lady Joan she described as not beautiful; certainly not beautiful; nobody would consider her beautiful, many would, indeed, think her quite the reverse; and yet she had a look, one particular look, when, according to Lady Marney, she was more than beautiful. But she was very clever, very indeed, something quite extraordinary.

'Accomplished?'

'Oh! far beyond that; I have heard even men say that no one knew so much.'

'A regular blue?'

'Oh! no; not at all a blue; not that kind of knowledge. But languages and learned books; Arabic, and Hebrew, and old manuscripts. And then she has an observatory, and was the first person who discovered the comet. Dr. Buckland* swears by her; and she corresponds with Arago.'*

'And her sister, is she the same?'

'Lady Maud: she is very religious. I do not know her so well.'

'Is she pretty?'

'Some people admire her much.'

'I never was at Mowbray. What sort of a place is it?'

'Oh! it is very grand,' said Lady Marney; 'but, like all places in the manufacturing districts, very disagreeable. You never have a clear sky. Your toilette table is covered with blacks; the deer in the park seem as if they had bathed in a lake of Indian ink; and as for the sheep, you expect to see chimney-sweeps for the shepherds.'

'And do you really mean to go on Thursday?' said Egremont: 'I think we had better put it off.'

'We must go,' said Lady Marney, with a sort of sigh, and shaking her head.

'Let me speak to Marney.'

'Oh! no. We must go. I am annoyed about this dear little Poinsett: she has been to stay with me so very often, and she has been here only three days. When she comes in again, I wish you would ask her to sing, Charles.'

Soon the dear little Poinsett was singing, much gratified by being invited to the instrument by Mr. Egremont, who for a few minutes hung over her, and then, evidently under the influence of her tones, walked up and down the room, and only speaking to beg that she would continue her charming performances. Lady Marney was engrossed with her embroidery; her lord and the captain with their game.

And what was Egremont thinking of? Of Mowbray, be you sure. And of Lady Joan or Lady Maud? Not exactly. Mowbray was the name of the town to which the strangers he had met with in the Abbey were bound. It was the only piece of information that he had been able to obtain of them; and that casually.

When the fair vision of the starlit arch, about to descend to her two companions, perceived that they were in conversation with a stranger, she hesitated, and in a moment withdrew. Then the elder of the travellers, exchanging a glance with his friend, bade good even to Egremont.

'Our way perhaps lies the same?' said Egremont.

'I should deem not,' said the stranger, 'nor are we alone.'

'And we must be stirring, for we have far to go,' said he who was dressed in black.

'My journey is brief,' said Egremont, making a desperate effort to invite communication; 'and I am on horseback!'

'And we on foot,' said the elder; 'nor shall we stop till we reach Mowbray;' and, with a slight salute, they left Egremont alone. There was something in the manner of the elder stranger which repressed the possibility of Egremont following him. Leaving then the cloister garden in another direction, he speculated on meeting them outside the Abbey. He passed through the Lady's chapel. The beautiful Religious was not there. He gained the west front; no one was visible. He took a rapid survey of each side of the Abbey; not a being to be recognized. He fancied they must have advanced towards the Abbey farm; yet they might have proceeded further on in the dale. Perplexed, he lost time. Finally he proceeded towards the farm, but did not overtake them; reached it, but learned nothing of them; and arrived at his brother's full of a strange yet sweet perplexity.

CHAPTER 7

IN a commercial country like England, every half century develops some new and vast source of public wealth, which brings into national notice a new and powerful class. A couple of centuries ago, a Turkey Merchant was the great creator of wealth; the West India Planter followed him. In the middle of the last century appeared the Nabob. These characters in their zenith in turn merged in the land, and became English aristocrats; while, the Levant decaying, the West Indies exhausted, and Hindostan plundered, the breeds died away, and now exist only in our English comedies, from Wycherly and Congreve to Cumberland* and Morton.* The expenditure of the revolutionary was produced the Loanmonger, who succeeded the Nabob; and the application of science to industry developed the Manufacturer, who in turn aspires to be 'large acred,' and always will, so long as we have a territorial constitution; a better security for the preponderance of the landed interest than any corn-law, fixed or fluctuating.

Of all these characters, the one that on the whole made the largest fortunes in the most rapid manner, and we do not forget the marvels of the Waterloo loan, or the miracles of Manchester during the Continental blockade, was the Anglo-East-Indian about the time that Hastings* was first appointed to the great viceroyalty. It was not unusual for men in positions so obscure that their names had never reached the public in this country, and who yet had not been absent from their native land for a longer period than the siege of Troy, to return with their million.

One of the most fortunate of this class of obscure adventurers was a certain John Warren. A few years before the breaking out of the American war, he was a waiter at a celebrated club in St. James' Street; a quick, yet steady young fellow; assiduous, discreet, and very civil. In this capacity, he pleased a gentleman who was just appointed to the government of Madras, and who wanted a valet. Warren, though prudent, was adventurous; and accepted the opening which he believed fortune offered him. He was prescient. The voyage in those days was an affair of six months. During this period, Warren still more ingratiated himself with his master. He wrote a good hand, and his master a very bad one. He had a natural talent for accounts; a kind of information which was useful to his employer. He arrived at Madras, no longer a valet, but a private secretary.

His master went out to make a fortune; but he was indolent, and had indeed none of the qualities for success, except his great position. Warren had every quality but that. The basis of the confederacy therefore was intelligible; it was founded on mutual interests and cemented by reciprocal assistance. The governor granted monopolies to the secretary, who apportioned a due share to his sleeping partner. There appeared one of those dearths not unusual in Hindostan; the population of the famished province cried out for rice; the stores of which, diminished by nature, had for months mysteriously disappeared. A provident administration it seems had invested the public revenue in its benevolent purchase; the misery was so excessive that even pestilence was anticipated, when the great forestallers came to the rescue of the people over whose destinies they presided; and at the same time fed, and pocketed, millions.

This was the great stroke of the financial genius of Warren. He was satisfied. He longed once more to see St. James' Street, and to become a member of the club where he had once been a waiter. But he was the spoiled child of fortune, who would not so easily spare him. The governor died, and had appointed his secretary his sole executor. Not that his Excellency particularly trusted his agent, but he dared not confide the knowledge of his affairs to any other individual. The estate was so complicated, that Warren offered the heirs a good round sum for his quittance, and to take the settlement upon himself. India so distant, and Chancery so near, the heirs accepted the proposition. Winding up this estate, Warren avenged the cause of plundered provinces; and the House of Commons, itself with Burke and Francis at its head, could scarcely have mulcted the late governor more severely.

A Mr. Warren, of whom no one had ever heard except that he was a Nabob, had recently returned from India, and purchased a large estate in the north of England; was returned to Parliament one of the representatives of a close borough which he had also purchased; a quiet, gentlemanlike, middle-aged man, with no decided political opinions; and, as parties were then getting equal, of course much courted. The throes of Lord North's administration* were commencing. The minister asked the new member to dine with him, and found the new member singularly free from all party prejudices. Mr. Warren was one of those members who announced their determination to listen to the debates and to be governed by the arguments. All complimented him, all spoke to him. Mr. Fox declared that he was a most superior man; Mr. Burke said that these were the men who could alone save the country. Mrs. Crewe* asked him to supper; he was caressed by the most brilliant of duchesses.

At length there arrived one of those fierce trials of strength, which precede the fall of a minister, but which sometimes, from peculiar circumstances, as in the instances of Walpole and Lord North, are not immediate in their results. How would Warren vote? was the great question. He would listen to the arguments. Burke was full of confidence that he should catch Warren. The day before the debate there was a levée, which Mr. Warren attended. The sovereign stopped him, spoke to him, smiled on him, asked him many questions: about himself, the House of Commons, how he liked it, how he liked England. There was a flutter in the circle; a new favourite at court.

The debate came off, the division took place. Mr. Warren voted for the minister. Burke denounced him; the king made him a baronet.

Sir John Warren made a great alliance, at least for him; he married the daughter of an Irish earl; became one of the king's friends; supported Lord Shelburne, threw over Lord Shelburne, had the tact early to discover that Mr. Pitt was the man to stick to, stuck to him. Sir John Warren bought another estate, and picked up another borough. He was fast becoming a personage. Throughout the Indian debates he kept himself quiet; once indeed in vindication of Mr. Hastings, whom he greatly admired, he ventured to correct Mr. Francis on a point of fact with which he was personally acquainted. He thought that it was safe, but he never spoke again. He knew not the resources of vindictive genius or the powers of a malignant imagination. Burke owed the Nabob a turn for the vote which had gained him a baronetcy. The orator seized the opportunity, and alarmed the secret conscience of the Indian adventurer by his dark allusions and his fatal familiarity with the subject.

Another estate, however, and another borough were some consolation for this little misadventure; and in time the French Revolution, to Sir John's great relief, turned the public attention for ever from Indian affairs. The Nabob, from the faithful adherent of Mr. Pitt, had become even his personal friend. The wits, indeed, had discovered that he had been a waiter; and endless were the epigrams of Fitzpatrick and the jokes of Hare; but Mr. Pitt cared nothing about the origin of his supporters. On the contrary, Sir John was exactly the individual from whom the minister meant to carve out his plebeian aristocracy; and, using his friend as a feeler before he ventured on his greater operations, the Nabob one morning was transformed into an Irish baron.

The new Baron figured in his patent as Lord Fitz-Warene, his Norman origin and descent from the old barons of this name having been discovered at Herald's College. This was a rich harvest for Fitzpatrick and Hare; but the public gets accustomed to everything, and has an easy habit of faith. The new Baron cared nothing for ridicule, for he was working for posterity. He was compensated for every annoyance by the remembrance that the St. James' Street waiter was ennobled, and by his determination that his children should rank still higher in the proud peerage of his country. So he obtained the royal permission to resume the surname and arms of his ancestors, as well as their title.

There was an ill-natured story set afloat, that Sir John owed this promotion to having lent money to the minister; but this was a calumny. Mr. Pitt never borrowed money of his friends. Once, indeed, to save his library, he took a thousand pounds from an individual on whom he had conferred high rank and immense promotion: and this individual, who had the minister's bound when Mr. Pitt died, insisted on his right, and actually extracted the 1,000*l.* from the insolvent estate of his magnificent patron. But Mr. Pitt always preferred a usurer to a friend; and to the last day of his life borrowed money at fifty per cent.

The Nabob departed this life before the minister, but he lived long enough to realise his most aspiring dream. Two years before his death, the Irish baron was quietly converted into an English peer; and without exciting any attention, all the squibs of Fitzpatrick, all the jokes of Hare, quite forgotten, the waiter of the St. James' Street club took his seat in the most natural manner possible in the House of Lords.

The great estate of the late Lord Fitz-Warene was situate at Mowbray, a village which principally belonged to him, and near which he had raised a Gothic castle, worthy of his Norman name and ancestry. Mowbray was one of those places which, during the long war, had expanded from an almost unknown village to a large and flourishing manufacturing town; a circumstance which, as Lady Marney observed, might have somewhat deteriorated the atmosphere of the splendid castle, but which had nevertheless trebled the vast rental of its lord. He who had succeeded to his father was Altamont Belvidere, named after his mother's family, Fitz-Warene, Lord Fitz-Warene. He was not deficient in abilities, though he had not his father's talents, but he was over-educated for his intellect; a common misfortune. The new Lord Fitz-Warene was the most aristocratic of breathing beings. He most fully, entirely, and absolutely believed in his pedigree; his coat of arms was emblazoned on every window, embroidered on every chair, carved in every corner. Shortly after his father's death, he was united to the daughter of a ducal house, by whom he had a son and two daughters, christened by names which the ancient records of the Fitz-Warenes authorised. His son, who gave promise of abilities which might have rendered the family really distinguished, was Valence; his daughters, Joan and Maud. All that seemed wanting to the glory of the house was a great distinction, of which a rich peer, with six seats in the House of Commons,* could not ultimately despair. Lord Fitz-Warene aspired to rank among the earls of England. But the successors of Mr. Pitt were strong; they thought the Fitz-Warenes had already been too rapidly advanced; it was whispered that the king did not like the new man; that his majesty thought him pompous, full of pretence, in short, a fool. But though the successors of Mr. Pitt managed to govern the country for twenty years, and were generally very strong, in such an interval of time, however good their management or great their luck, there were inevitably occasions when they found themselves in difficulties, when it was necessary to conciliate the lukewarm or to reward the devoted. Lord Fitz-Warene well understood how to avail himself of these occasions; it was astonishing how conscientious and scrupulous he became during Walcheren expeditions,* Manchester massacres,* Queen's trials.* Every scrape of the government was a step in the ladder to the great boroughmonger. The old king too had disappeared from the stage; and the tawdry grandeur of the great Norman peer rather suited George the Fourth. He was rather a favourite at the Cottage;* they wanted his six votes for Canning;* he made his terms; and one of the means by which we got a man of genius for a minister was elevating Lord Fitz-Warene in the peerage, by the style and title of Earl de Mowbray of Mowbray Castle.

CHAPTER 8

WE must now for a while return to the strangers of the Abbey ruins. When the two men had joined the beautiful Religious, whose apparition had so startled Egremont, they all three quitted the Abbey by a way which led them by the back of the cloister garden, and so on by the bank of the river for about a hundred yards, when they turned up the winding glen of a dried-up tributary stream. At the head of the glen, at which they soon arrived, was a beer-shop, screened by some huge elms from the winds that blew over the vast moor, which, except in the direction of Mardale, now extended as far as the eye could reach. Here the companions stopped, the beautiful Religious seated herself on a stone bench beneath the trees, while the elder stranger, calling out to the inmate of the house to apprise him of his return, himself proceeded to a neighbouring shed, whence he brought forth a small rough pony, with a rude saddle, but one evidently intended for a female rider.

'It is well,' said the taller of the men, 'that I am not a member of a temperance society like you, Stephen, or it would be difficult to reward this good man for his care of our steed. I will take a cup of the drink of Saxon kings.' Then leading up the pony to the Religious, he placed her on its back with gentleness and much natural grace, saying at the same time in a subdued tone, 'And you; shall I bring you a glass of nature's wine?'

'I have drunk of the spring of the Holy Abbey,' said the Religious, 'and none other must touch my lips this eve.'

'Come, our course must be brisk,' said the elder of the men, as he gave up his glass to their host and led off the pony, Stephen walking on the other side.

Though the sun had fallen, the twilight was still glowing, and even on this wide expanse the air was still. The vast and undulating surface of the brown and purple moor, varied occasionally by some fantastic rocks, gleamed in the shifting light. Hesperus was the only star that yet was visible, and seemed to move before them and lead them on their journey.

'I hope,' said the Religious, turning to the elder stranger, 'if ever we regain our right, my father, and that we ever can, save by the interposition of divine will, seems to me clearly impossible, that you will never forget how bitter it is to be driven from the soil; and that you will bring back the people to the land.'

'I would pursue our right for no other cause,' said the father. 'After centuries of sorrow and degradation, it should never be said that we had no sympathy with the sad and the oppressed.'

'After centuries of sorrow and degradation,' said Stephen,

'let it not be said that you acquire your right only to create a baron or a squire.'

'Nay, thou shalt have thy way, Stephen,' said his companion, smiling, 'if ever the good hour come. As many acres as thou choosest for thy new Jerusalem.'

'Call it what you will, Walter,' replied Stephen; 'but if I ever gain the opportunity of fully carrying the principle of association into practice, I will sing "Nunc me dimittes." '

' "Nunc me dimittes," ' burst forth the Religious, in a voice of thrilling melody, and she pursued for some minutes the divine canticle. Her companions gazed on her with an air of affectionate reverence as she sang; each instant the stars becoming brighter, the wide moor assuming a darker hue.

'Now, tell me, Stephen,' said the Religious, turning her head and looking round with a smile, 'think you not it would be a fairer lot to hide this night at some kind monastery, then to be hastening now to that least picturesque of all creations, a railway station?'

'The railways will do as much for mankind as the monasteries did,' said Stephen.

'Had it not been for the railway, we should never have made our visit to Marney Abbey,' said the elder of the travellers.

'Nor seen its last abbot's tomb,' said the Religious. 'When I marked your name upon the stone, my father, – woe is me, but I felt sad indeed, that it was reserved for our blood to surrender to ruthless men that holy trust.'

'He never surrendered,' said her father. 'He was tortured and hanged.'

'He is with the communion of saints,' said the Religious.

'I would I could see a communion of Men,' said Stephen, 'and then there would be no more violence, for there would be no more plunder.'

'You must regain our lands for us, Stephen,' said the Religious; 'promise me, my father, that I shall raise a holy house for pious women, if that ever hap.'

'We will not forget our ancient faith,' said her father, 'the only old thing that has not left us.'

'I cannot understand,' said Stephen, 'why you should ever have lost sight of these papers, Walter.'

'You see, friend, they were never in my possession; they were never mine when I saw them. They were my father's; and he was jealous of all interference. He was a small yeoman, who had risen in the war time, well-to-do in the world, but always hankering after the old tradition that the lands were ours. This Hatton got hold of him; he did his work well, I have heard; – certain it is, my father spared nothing. It is twenty-five years come Martinmas since he brought his writ of right; and though baffled, he was not beaten. But then he died; his affairs were in great confusion; he had mortgaged his land for his writ, and the war prices were gone. There were debts that could not be paid. I had no capital for a farm. I would not sink to be a labourer on the soil that had once been our own. I had just married; it was needful to make a great exertion. I had heard much of the high wages of this new industry; I left the land.'

'And the papers?'

'I never thought of them, or thought of them with disgust, as the cause of my ruin. Then when you came the other day, and showed me in the book that the last Abbot of Marney was a Walter Gerard, the old feeling stirred again; and I could not help telling you that my fathers fought at Azincourt, though I was only the overlooker at Mr. Trafford's mill.'

'A good old name of the good old faith,' said the Religious; 'and a blessing be on it!'

'We have cause to bless it,' said Gerard. 'I thought it then something to serve a gentleman; and as for my daughter, she, by their goodness, was brought up in holy walls, which have made her what she is.'

'Nature made her what she is,' said Stephen, in a low voice, and speaking not without emotion. Then he continued, in a louder and brisker tone, 'But this Hatton; you know nothing of his whereabouts?'

'Never heard of him since. I had indeed, about a year after my father's death, cause to enquire after him; but he had quitted Mowbray, and none could give me tidings of him. He had lived, I believe, on our law-suit, and vanished with our hopes.'

After this there was silence; each was occupied with his

thoughts, while the influence of the soft night and starry hour induced to contemplation.

'I hear the murmur of the train,' said the Religious.

' 'Tis the up-train,' said her father. 'We have yet a quarter of an hour; we shall be in good time.'

So saying, he guided the pony to where some lights indicated the station of the railway, which here crossed the moor. There was just time to return the pony to the person at the station from whom it had been borrowed, and obtain their tickets, when the bell of the down-train sounded, and in a few minutes the Religious and her companions were on their way to Mowbray, whither a course of two hours carried them.

In was two hours to midnight when they arrived at Mowbray station, which was about a quarter of a mile from the town. Labour had long ceased; a beautiful heaven, clear and serene, canopied the city of smoke and toil; in all directions rose the columns of the factories, dark and defined in the purple sky; a glittering star sometimes hovering by the crest of their tall and tapering forms.

The travellers proceeded in the direction of a suburb, and approached the high wall of an extensive garden. The moon rose as they reached it, tipped the trees with light, and revealed a lofty and centre portal, by the side of it a wicket, at which Gerard rang. The wicket was quickly opened.

'I fear, holy sister,' said the Religious, 'that I am even later than I promised.'

'Those that come in our Lady's name are ever welcome,' was the reply.

'Sister Marion,' said Gerard to the portress, 'we have been to visit a holy place.'

'All places are holy with holy thoughts, my brother.'

'Dear father, good night,' said the Religious; 'the blessings of all the saints be on thee; and on thee, Stephen, though thou dost not kneel to them!'

'Good night, mine own child,' said Gerard.

'I could believe in saints when I am with thee,' murmured Stephen. 'Good night, – SYBIL.'

CHAPTER 9

WHEN Gerard and his friend quitted the convent they proceeded at a brisk pace into the heart of the town. The streets were nearly empty; and, with the exception of some occasional burst of brawl or merriment from a beer-shop, all was still. The chief street of Mowbray, called Castle Street, after the ruins of the old baronial stronghold in its neighbourhood, was as significant of the present civilisation of this community as the haughty keep had been of its ancient dependence. The dimensions of Castle Street were not unworthy of the metropolis: it traversed a great portion of the town, and was proportionately wide; its broad pavements and its blazing gaslights indicated its modern order and prosperity; while on each side of the street rose huge warehouses, not as beautiful as the palaces of Venice, but in their way not less remarkable; magnificent shops; and, here and there, though rarely, some ancient factory built among the fields in the infancy of Mowbray by some mill-owner not sufficiently prophetic of the future, or sufficiently confident in the energy and enterprise of his fellow-citizens, to foresee that the scene of his labours would be the future eyesore of a flourishing posterity.

Pursuing their course along Castle Street for about a quarter of a mile, Gerard and Stephen turned down a street which intersected it, and so on, though a variety of ways and winding lanes, till they arrived at an open portion of the town, a district where streets and squares, and even rows, disappeared, and where the tall chimneys and bulky barrack-looking buildings that rose in all directions, clustering yet isolated, announced that they were in the principal scene of the industry of Mowbray. Crossing this open ground, they gained a suburb but one of a very different kind from that in which was situate the convent where they had parted with Sybil. This one was populous, noisy, and lighted. It was Saturday night; the streets were thronged; an infinite population kept swarming to and from the close courts and pestilential cul-de-sacs that continually communicated with the streets by narrow archways, like the entrance of hives, so low that you were obliged to stoop for admission; while, ascending to these same streets from their dank and dismal dwellings by narrow flights of steps, the subterraneous nation of the cellars poured forth to enjoy the coolness of the summer night, and market for the day of rest. The bright and lively shops were crowded; and groups of purchasers were gathered round the stalls, that, by the aid of glaring lamps and flaunting lanterns, displayed their wares.

'Come, come, it's a prime place,' said a jolly-looking woman, who was presiding at a stall which, though considerably thinned by previous purchasers, still offered many temptations to many who could not purchase.

'And so it is, widow,' said a little pale man, wistfully.

'Come, come, it's getting late, and your wife's ill; you're a good soul, we'll say fi'pence a pound, and I'll throw you the scrag end in for love.'

'No butcher's meat to-morrow for us, widow,' said the man.

'And why not, neighbour? With your wages, you ought to live like a prize-fighter, or the Mayor of Mowbray at least.'

'Wages!' said the man: 'I wish you may get 'em. Those villains, Shuffle and Screw, have sarved me with another bate ticket;* and a pretty figure too.'

'Oh! the carnal monsters!' exclaimed the widow. 'If their day don't come, the bloody-minded knaves!'

'And for small cops,* too! Small cops be hanged! Am I the man to send up a bad-bottomed cop,* Widow Carey?'

'You sent up for snicks!* I have known you man and boy, John Hill, these twenty summers, and never heard a word against you till you got into Shuffle and Screw's mill. Oh! they are a bad yarn, John.'

'They do us all, widow. They pretends to give the same wages as the rest, and works it out in fines. You can't come, and you can't go, but there's a fine; you're never paid wages but there's a bate ticket. I've heard they keep their whole establishment on factory fines.'

'Soul alive, but these Shuffle and Screw are rotten, snickey,* bad yards,' said Mistress Carey. 'Now, ma'am, if you please; fi'pence ha'penny; no, ma'am, we've no weal left. Weal, indeed! you look very like a soul as feeds on weal,' continued Mrs. Carey in an undertone as her declining customer moved away. 'Well, it gets late,' said the widow, 'and if you like to take this scrag end home to your wife, neighbour Hill, we can talk of the rest next Saturday. And what's your will, sir?' said the widow, with a stern expression, to a youth who now stopped at her stall.

He was about sixteen, with a lithe figure, and a handsome, faded, impudent face. His long, loose, white trousers gave him height; he had no waistcoat, but a pink silk handkerchief was twisted carelessly round his neck, and fastened with a large pin, which, whatever were its materials, had unquestionably a gorgeous appearance. A loose frock-coat of a coarse white cloth, and fastened by one button round his waist, completed his habiliments, with the addition of the covering to his head, a high-crowned dark-brown hat, which relieved his complexion, and heightened the effect of his mischievous blue eye.

'Well, you need not be so fierce, Mother Carey,' said the youth, with an affected air of deprecation.

'Don't mother me,' said the jolly widow, with a kindling eye; 'go to your own mother, who is dying in a back cellar without a winder, while you've got lodgings in a two-pair.'

'Dying! she's only drunk,' said the youth.

'And if she is only drunk,' rejoined Mrs. Carey, in a passion, 'what makes her drink but toil? working from five o'clock in the morning to seven o'clock at night, and for the like of such as you.'

'That's a good one,' said the youth. 'I should like to know what my mother ever did for me, but give me treacle and laudanum when I was a baby to stop my tongue and fill my stomach; by the token of which, as my gal says, she stunted the growth of the prettiest figure in all Mowbray.' And here the youth drew himself up, and thrust his hands in the side pockets of his pea-jacket.

'Well, I never!' said Mrs. Carey. 'No; I never heard a thing like that!'

'What, not when you cut up the jackass and sold it for veal cutlets, mother?'

'Hold your tongue, Mr. Imperence,' said the widow. 'It's very well known you're no Christian, and who'll believe what you say?'

'It's very well known that I'm a man what pays his way,'

said the boy, 'and don't keep a huckster's stall to sell carrion by starlight; but live in a two-pair, if you please, and has a wife and family, or as good.'

'Oh! you aggravating imp!' exclaimed the widow, in despair, unable to wreak her vengeance on one who kept in a secure position, and whose movements were as nimble as his words.

'Why, Madam Carey, what has Dandy Mick done to thee?' said a good-humoured voice. It came from one of two factory girls who were passing her stall, and stopped. They were gaily dressed, a light handkerchief tied under the chin, their hair scrupulously arranged; they wore coral necklaces and earrings of gold.

'Ah! is it you, my child?' said the widow, who was a good-hearted creature. 'The dandy has been giving me some of his imperence.'

'But I meant nothing, dame,' said Mick. 'It was fun; only fun.'

'Well, let it pass,' said Mrs. Carey. 'And where have you been this long time, my child? And who's your friend?' she added, in a lower tone.

'Well, I have left Mr. Trafford's mill,' said the girl.

'That's a bad job,' said Mrs. Carey; 'for those Traffords are kind to their people. It's a great thing for a young person to be in their mill.'

'So it is,' said the girl; 'but then it was so dull. I can't stand a country life, Mrs. Carey. I must have company.'

'Well, I do love a bit of gossip myself,' said Mrs. Carey, with great frankness.

'And then I'm no scholar,' said the girl, 'and never could take to learning. And those Traffords had so many schools.'

'Learning is better than house and land,' said Mrs. Carey. 'though I'm no scholar myself; but then in my time things was different. But young persons—'

'Yes,' said Mick; 'I don't think I could get through the day if it wurno' for our Institute.'

'And what's that?' asked Mrs. Carey, with a sneer.

'The Shoddy-Court Literary and Scientific, to be sure,' said Mick; 'we have got fifty members, and take in three London papers; one "Northern Star" and two "Moral Worlds." '*

'And where are you now, child?' continued the widow to the girl.

'I am at Wiggins and Webster's,' said the girl; 'and this in my partner. We keep house together; we have a very nice room in Arbour Court, No. 7, high up; it's very airy. If you will take a dish of tea with us to-morrow, we expect some friends.'

'I take it kindly,' said Mrs. Carey; 'and so you keep house together! All the children keep house in these days. Times is changed indeed!'

'And we shall be happy to see you, Mick; and Julia, if you are not engaged,' continued the girl; and she looked at her friend, a pretty demure girl who, immediately said, but in a somewhat faltering tone, 'Oh! that we shall.'

'And what are you going to do now, Caroline?' said Mick.

'Well, we had no thoughts; but I said to Harriet, as it is a fine night, let us walk about as long as we can, and then to-morrow we will lie in bed till afternoon.'

'That's all well eno' in winter-time, with plenty of baccy,' said Mick, 'but at this season of the year I must have life. The moment I came out I bathed in the river, and then went home and dressed,' he added in a satisfied tone; 'and now I am going to the Temple. I'll tell you what, Julia has been pricked to-day with a shuttle; 'tis not much, but she can't go out: I'll stand treat, and take you and your friend to the Temple.'

'Well, that's delight,' said Caroline. 'There's no one does the handsome thing like you, Dandy Mick, and I always say so. Oh! I love the Temple! 'Tis so genteel! I was speaking of it to Harriet last night; she never was there. I proposed to go with her, but two girls alone, you understand me. One does not like to be seen in these places, as if one kept no company.'

'Very true,' said Mick; 'and now we'll be off. Goodnight, widow.'

'You'll remember us to-morrow evening,' said Caroline.

'To-morrow evening! The Temple!' murmured Mrs. Carey to herself. 'I think the world is turned upside downwards in these parts. A brat like Mick Radley to live in a two-pair, with a wife and family, or as good, as he says; and this girl asks me to take a dish of tea with her and keeps house! Fathers and mothers goes for nothing,' continued Mrs. Carey, as she took a very long pinch of snuff, and deeply mused. ' 'Tis the children gets the wages,' she added after a profound pause, 'and there it is.'

CHAPTER 10

IN the meantime Gerard and Stephen stopped before a tall, thin, stuccoed house, balustraded and friezed, very much lighted both within and without, and from the sounds that issued from it, and the persons who retired and entered, evidently a locality of great resort and bustle. A sign, bearing the title of the Cat and Fiddle, indicated that it was a place of public entertainment, and kept by one who owned the legal name of John Trottman, though that was but a vulgar appellation, lost in his well-earned and far-famed title of Chaffing Jack.

The companions entered the spacious premises; and, making their way to the crowded bar, Stephen, with a glance serious but which indicated intimacy, caught the eye of a comely lady, who presided over the mysteries, and said in a low voice, 'Is he here?'

'In the Temple, Mr. Morley, asking for you and your friend more than once. I think you had better go up. I know he wishes to see you.'

Stephen whispered to Gerard, and after a moment's pause he asked the fair president for a couple of tickets, for each of which he paid threepence; a sum, however, according to the printed declaration of the voucher, convertible into potential liquid refreshments, no great compensation to a very strict member of the Temperance Society of Mowbray.

A handsome staircase with bright brass banisters led them to an ample landing-place, on which opened a door, now closed, and by which sat a boy who collected the tickets of those who would enter it. The portal was of considerable dimensions and of architectural pretension; it was painted of a bright green colour, the panels gilt. Within the pediment, described in letters of flaming gas you read, 'THE TEMPLE OF THE MUSES.'*

Gerard and Morley entered an apartment very long and sufficiently lofty, though rather narrow for such proportions. The ceiling was even richly decorated; the walls were painted, and by a brush of no inconsiderable power. Each panel represented some well-known scene from Shakespeare, Byron, or Scott; King Richard, Mazeppa,* the Lady of the Lake, were easily recognised: in one panel, Hubert menaced Arthur; here Haidee rescued Juan; and there Jeanie Deans curtsied before the Queen. The room was very full; some three or four hundred persons were seated in different groups at different tables, eating, drinking, talking, laughing, and even smoking; for, notwithstanding the pictures and the gilding, it was found impossible to forbid, though there were efforts to discourage, this practice, in the Temple of the Muses. Nothing, however, could be more decorous than the general conduct of the company, though they consisted principally of factory people. The waiters flew about with as much agility as if they were serving nobles. In general the noise was great, though not disagreeable; sometimes a bell rang, and there was comparative silence, while a curtain drew up at the farther end of the room, opposite to the entrance, where there was a theatre, the stage raised at a due elevation, and adorned with side scenes, from which issued a lady in a fancy dress, who sang a favourite ballad; or a gentleman elaborated habited in a farmer's costume of the old comedy, a bob-wig, silver buttons and buckles, and blue stockings, and who favoured the company with that melancholy effusion called a comic song. Some nights there was music on the stage; a young lady in a white robe with a golden harp, and attended by a gentleman in black mustachios. This was when the principal harpiste of the King of Saxony and his first fiddler happened to be passing through Mowbray, merely by accident, or on a tour of pleasure and instruction, to witness the famous scenes of British industry. Otherwise the audience of the Cat and Fiddle, we mean the Temple of the Muses, were fain to be content with four Bohemian brothers, or an equal number of Swiss sisters. The most popular amusements, however, were the 'Thespian recitations,' by amateurs, or novices who wished to become professional. They tried their metal on an audience which could be critical.

A sharp waiter, with a keen eye on the entering guests, immediately saluted Gerard and his friend, with profuse offers of hospitality, insisting that they wanted much refreshment; that they were both hungry and thirsty; that, if not hungry, they should order something to drink that would give them an appetite; if not inclined to quaff, something to eat that would make them athirst. In the midst of these embarrassing attentions, he was pushed aside by his master with, 'There, go; hands wanted at the upper end; two American gentlemen from Lowell* singing out for sherry cobler,* don't know what it is; give them our bar-mixture; if they complain, say it's the Mowbray slap-bang, and no mistake. Must have a name, Mr. Morley; name's everything; made the fortune of the Temple; if I had called it the Saloon, it never would have filled, and perhaps the magistrates never have granted a licence.'

The speaker was a portly man, who had passed the maturity of manhood, but active as Harlequin. He had a well-favoured countenance; fair, good-humoured, but sly. He was dressed like the head butler of the London Tavern, and was particular as to his white waistcoats and black silk stockings, punctilious as to his knee-buckles, proud of his diamond pin; that is to say, when he officiated at the Temple.

'Your mistress told us we should find you here,' said Stephen, 'and that you wished to see us.'

'Plenty to tell you,' said their host, putting his finger to his nose. 'If information *is* wanted in this part of the world, I flatter myself – Come, Master Gerard, here's a table; what shall I call for? glass of the Mowbray slap-bang? No better; the receipt has been in our family these fifty years. Mr. Morley I know won't join us. Did you say a cup of tea, Mr. Morley? Water, only water; well, that's strange. Boy, alive there! do you hear me call? Water wanted, glass of water for the Secretary of the Mowbray Temperance and Teetotal. Sing it out. I like titled company. Brush!'

'And so you can give us some information about this—'

'Be back directly,' exclaimed their host, darting off with a swift precision that carried him through a labyrinth of tables without the slightest inconvenience to their occupiers. 'Beg pardon. Mr. Morley,' he said, sliding again into his chair; 'but saw one of the American gentlemen brandishing his bowie-knife against one of my waiters; called him Colonel; quieted him directly; a man of his rank brawling with a help; oh! no; not to be thought of; no squabbling here; licence in danger.'

'You were saying—' resumed Morley.

'Ah! yes, about that man Hatton; remember him perfectly well; a matter of twenty, or it may be nineteen years since he bolted. Queer fellow; lived upon nothing; only drank water; no temperance and teetotal then, so no excuse. Beg pardon, Mr. Morley; no offence, I hope; can't bear whims; but respectable societies, if they don't drink, they make speeches, hire your rooms, leads to business.'

'And this Hatton?' said Gerard.

'Ah! a queer fellow; lent him a one-pound note; never saw it again; always remember it; last one-pound note I had. He offered me an old book instead; not in my way; took a china jar for my wife. He kept a curiosity-shop; always prowling about the country, picking up old books and hunting after old monuments; called himself an antiquarian; queer fellow, that Hatton.'

'And you have heard of him since?' said Gerard rather impatiently.

'Not a word,' said their host; 'never knew any one who had.'

'I thought you had something to tell us about him,' said Stephen.

'So I have: I can put you in the way of getting hold of him and anything else. I haven't lived in Mowbray man and boy for fifty years; seen it a village, and now a great town full of first-rate institutions and establishments like this,' added their host, surveying the Temple with a glance of admiring complacency; 'I say I haven't lived here all this time and talked to the people for nothing.'

'Well, we are all attention,' said Gerard, with a smile.

'Hush!' said their host as a bell sounded, and he jumped up. 'Now ladies, now gentlemen, if you please; silence if you please, for a song from a Polish lady. The Signora sings English like a new-born babe;' and the curtain drew up amid the hushed voices of the company and the restrained clatter of their knives and forks and glasses.

The Polish lady sang 'Cherry Ripe' to the infinite satisfaction of her audience. Young Mowbray indeed, in the shape of Dandy Mick, and some of his followers and admirers, insisted on an encore. The lady, as she retired, curtseyed like a prima donna; but the host continued on his legs for some time, throwing open his coat and bowing to his guests, who expressed by their applause how much they approved his enterprise. At length he resumed his seat. 'It's almost too much,' he exclaimed; 'the enthusiasm of these people. I believe they look upon me as a father.'

'And you think you have some clue to this Hatton?' resumed Stephen.

'They say he has no relations,' said their host.

'I have heard as much.'

'Another glass of the bar-mixture, Master Gerard. What did we call it? Oh! the bricks and beans; the Mowbray bricks and beans; known by that name in the time of my grandfather. No more! No use asking Mr. Morley, I know. Water! well, I must say; and yet, in an official capacity, drinking water is not so unnatural.'

'And Hatton,' said Gerard; 'they say he has no relations.'

'They do, and they say wrong. He has a relation; he has a brother; and I can put you in the way of finding him.'

'Well, that looks like business,' said Gerard; 'and where may he be?'

'Not here,' said their host; 'he never put his foot in the Temple, to my knowledge; and lives in a place where they have as much idea of popular institutions as any Turks or heathen you ever heard of.'

'And where might we find him?' said Stephen.

'What's that?' said their host, jumping up and looking around him. 'Here, boys, brush about. The American gentleman is a-whittling his name on that new mahogany table. Take him the printed list of rules, stuck up in a public place, under a great coat, and fine him five shillings for damaging the furniture. If he resists, he has paid for his liquor, call in the police; X Z, No. 5, is in the bar, taking tea with your mistress. Now brush.'

'And this place is—'

'In the land of mines and minerals,' said their host, 'about ten miles from ——. He works in metals on his own account. You have heard of a place called Hell-house Yard? well, he lives there; and his name is Simon.'

'And does he keep up any communication with his brother, think you?' said Gerard.

'Nay, I know no more, at least at present,' said their host. 'The secretary asked me about a person absent without leave for twenty years, and who was said to have no relations. I found you one, and a very near one. You are at the station, and you have got your ticket. The American gentleman's violent. Here's the police. I must take a high tone.' And with these words Chaffing Jack quitted them.

In the meantime we must not forget Dandy Mick and his two young friends, whom he had so generously offered to treat to the Temple.

'Well, what do you think of it?' asked Caroline of Harriet, in a whisper, as they entered the splendid apartment.

'It's just what I thought the Queen lived in,' said Harriet; 'but, indeed, I'm all of a flutter.'

'Well, don't look as if you were,' said her friend.

'Come along, gals,' said Mick; 'who's afraid? Here, we'll sit down at this table. Now what shall we have? Here, waiter; I say, waiter!'

'Yes, sir; yes, sir.'

'Well, why don't you come when I call?' said Mick, with a consequential air. 'I have been hallooing these ten minutes. Couple of glasses of bar-mixture for these ladies, and a go of gin for myself. And I say, waiter, stop, stop, don't be in such a deuced hurry; do you think folks can drink without eating? sausages for three; and, damme, take care they are not burnt.'

'Yes, sir; directly, directly.'

'That's the way to talk to these fellows,' said Mick, with a self-satisfied air, and perfectly repaid by the admiring gaze of his companions.

'It's pretty, Miss Harriett,' said Mick, looking up at the ceiling with a careless, *nil admirari* glance.

'Oh! it is beautiful,' said Harriet.

'You never were here before; it's the only place. That's the

Lady of the Lake,' he added, pointing to a picture; 'I've seen her at the Circus, with real water.'

The hissing sausages, crowning a pile of mashed potatoes, were placed before them; the delicate rummers* of the Mowbray slap-bang for the girls; the more masculine pewter measure for their friend.

'Are the plates very hot?' said Mick.

'Very, sir.'

'Hot plates half the battle,' said Mick.

'Now, Caroline; here, Miss Harriet; don't take away your plate, wait for the mash; they mash their taters here very elegant.'

It was a happy and a merry party. Mick delighted to help his guests, and to drink their healths.

'Well,' said he, when the waiter had cleared away their plates, and left them to their less substantial luxuries – 'Well,' said Mick, sipping a renewed glass of gin-twist, and leaning back in his chair, 'say what they please, there's nothing like life.'

'At the Traffords',' said Caroline, 'the greatest fun we ever had was a singing-class.'

'I pity them poor devils in the country,' said Mick; 'we got some of them at Collinson's, come from Suffolk, they say; what they call hagricultural labourers; a very queer lot indeed.'

'Ah! them's the himmigrants,' said Caroline; 'they're sold out of slavery, and sent down by Pickford's van into the labour market to bring down our wages.'

'We'll teach them a trick or two before they do that,' urged Mick. 'Where are you, Miss Harriet?'

'I am at Wiggins and Webster's, sir.'

'Where they clean machinery during meal-time; that won't do,' said Mick. 'I see one of your partners coming in,' said Mick, making many signals to a person who soon joined them. 'Well, Devilsdust, how are you?'

This was the familiar appellation of a young gentleman who really had no other, baptismal or patrimonial. About a fortnight after his mother had introduced him into the world, she returned to her factory, and put her infant out to nurse; that is to say, paid threepence a week to an old woman, who takes charge of these new-born babes for the day, and gives them back at night to their mothers as they hurriedly return from the scene of their labour to the dungeon or the den, which is still by courtesy called 'home.' The expense is not great; laudanum and treacle, administered in the shape of some popular elixir, affords these innocents a brief taste of the sweets of existence, and, keeping them quiet, prepares them for the silence of their impending grave. Infanticide is practised as extensively and as legally in England as it is on the banks of the Ganges; a circumstance which apparently has not yet engaged the attention of the Society for the Propagation of the Gospel in Foreign Parts.* But the vital principle is an impulse from an immortal Artist, and sometimes baffles, even in its tenderest phasis, the machinations of society for its extinction. There are infants that will defy even starvation and poison, unnatural mothers and demon nurses. Such was the nameless one of whom we speak. We cannot say he thrived; but he would not die. So, at two years of age, his mother being lost sight of, and the weekly payment having ceased, he was sent out in the street to 'play,' in order to be run over. Even this expedient failed. The youngest and the feeblest of the band of victims, Juggernaut* spared him to Moloch.* All his companions were disposed of. Three months 'play' in the streets got rid of this tender company, shoeless, half-naked, and uncombed, whose age varied from two to five years. Some were crushed, some were lost, some caught cold and fevers, crept back to their garret or their cellars, were dosed with Godfrey's cordial,* and died in peace. The nameless one would not disappear. He always got out of the way of the carts and horses, and never lost his own. They gave him no food; he foraged for himself, and shared with the dogs the garbage of the streets. But still he lived; stunted and pale, he defied even the fatal fever which was the only habitant of his cellar that never quitted it. And slumbering at night on a bed of mouldering straw, his only protection against the plashy surface of his den, with a dung-heap at his head, and a cesspool at his feet, he still clung to the only roof which shielded him from the tempest.

At length, when the nameless one had completed his fifth year, the pest which never quitted the nest of cellars of which he was a citizen, raged in the quarter with such intensity, that

the extinction of its swarming population was menaced. The
haunt of this child was peculiarly visited. All the children
gradually sickened except himself; and one night when he returned home he found the old woman herself dead, and surrounded only by corpses. The child before this had slept on
the same bed of straw with a corpse, but then there were also
breathing beings for his companions. A night passed only
with corpses seemed to him in itself a kind of death. He stole
out of the cellar, quitted the quarter of pestilence, and after
much wandering lay down near the door of a factory. Fortune
had guided him. Soon after break of day, he was awakened by
the sound of the factory bell, and found assembled a crowd
of men, women, and children. The door opened, they entered,
the child accompanied them. The roll was called; his un-
authorised appearance noticed; he was questioned; his acute-
ness excited attention. A child was wanting in the Wadding
Hole, a place for the manufacture of waste and damaged
cotton, the refuse of the mills, which is here worked up into
counterpanes and coverlets. The nameless one was preferred
to the vacant post, received even a salary, more than that, a
name; for as he had none, he was christened on the spot
DEVILSDUST.*

Devilsdust had entered life so early, that at seventeen he
combined the experience of manhood with the divine energy
of youth. He was a first-rate workman, and received high
wages; he had availed himself of the advantages of the factory
school; he soon learnt to read and write with facility, and at
the moment of our history was the leading spirit of the
Shoddy-court Literary and Scientific Institute. His great
friend, his only intimate, was Dandy Mick. The apparent contrariety of their qualities and structure perhaps led to this. It
is indeed the most assured basis of friendship. Devilsdust was
dark and melancholy, ambitious and discontented, full of
thought, and with powers of patience and perseverance that
alone amounted to genius. Mick was as brilliant as his complexion; gay, irritable, evanescent, and unstable. Mick enjoyed
life; his friend only endured it; yet Mick was always complaining of the lowness of his wages, and the greatness of his
toil; while Devilsdust never murmured, but read and pon-

dered on the rights of labour, and sighed to vindicate his order.

'I have some thoughts of joining the Total Abstinence,' said Devilsdust; 'ever since I read Stephen Morley's address, it has been in my mind. We shall never get our rights till we leave off consuming exciseable articles; and the best thing to begin with is liquors.'

'Well, I could do without liquors myself,' said Caroline. 'If I was a lady, I would never drink anything except fresh milk from the cow.'

'Tea for my money,' said Harriet; 'I must say there's nothing I grudge for good tea. Now I keep house, I mean always to drink the best.'

'Well, you have not yet taken the pledge, Dusty,' said Mick; 'and so suppose we order a go of gin, and talk this matter of temperance over.'

Devilsdust was manageable in little things, especially by Mick: he acceded, and seated himself at their table.

'I suppose you have heard this last dodge of Shuffle and Screw, Dusty?' said Mick.

'What's that?'

'Every man had his key given him this evening; half-a-crown a week round deducted from wages for rent. Jim Plastow told them he lodged with his father, and didn't want a house; upon which they said he must let it.'

'Their day will come,' said Devilsdust, thoughtfully. 'I really think that those Shuffles and Screws are worse even than Truck and Trett. You knew where you were with those fellows; it was five-and-twenty per cent. off wages, and very bad stuff for your money. But as for Shuffle and Screw, what with their fines and their keys, a man never knows what he has to spend. Come,' he added, filling his glass, 'let's have a toast: Confusion to Capital.'

'That's your sort,' said Mick. 'Come, Caroline; drink to your partner's toast, Miss Harriet. Money's the root of all evil, which nobody can deny. We'll have the rights of labour yet; the ten-hour bill,* no fines, and no individuals admitted to any work who have not completed their sixteenth year.'

'No, fifteen,' said Caroline, eagerly.

S.T.N.—6

'The people won't bear their grievances much longer,' said Devilsdust.

'I think one of the greatest grievances the people have,' said Caroline, 'is the beaks serving notice of Chaffing Jack to shut up the Temple on Sunday nights.'

'It is infamous,' said Mick; 'ayn't we to have no recreation? One might as well live in Suffolk, where the immigrants come from, and where they are obliged to burn ricks to pass the time.'

'As for the rights of labour,' said Harriet, 'the people goes for nothing with this machinery.'

'And you have opened your mouth to say a very sensible thing, Miss Harriet,' said Mick; 'but if I were Lord Paramount for eight and forty hours, I'd soon settle that question. Wouldn't I fire a broadside into their "double deckers?" The battle of Navarino* at Mowbray fair, with fourteen squibs from the admiral's ship going off at the same time, should be nothing to it.'

'Labour may be weak, but capital is weaker,' said Devilsdust. 'Their capital is all paper.'

'I tell you what,' said Mick, with a knowing look, and in a lowered tone, 'the only thing, my hearties, that can save this here nation is a ——— good strike.'*

CHAPTER II

'YOUR lordship's dinner is served,' announced the groom of the chambers to Lord de Mowbray; and the noble lord led our Lady Marney. The rest followed. Egremont found himself seated next to Lady Maud Fitz-Warene, the younger daughter of the earl. Nearly opposite to him was Lady Joan.

The ladies Fitz-Warene were sandy girls, somewhat tall, with rather good figures, and a grand air; the eldest ugly, the second rather pretty; and yet both very much alike. They had both great conversational powers, though in different ways. Lady Joan was doctrinal; Lady Maud inquisitive: the first often imparted information which you did not previously possess; the other suggested ideas which were often before in your own mind, but lay tranquil and unobserved till called

into life and notice by her fanciful and vivacious tongue. Both
of them were endowed with a remarkable self-possession; but
Lady Joan wanted softness, and Lady Maud repose.

This was the result of the rapid observation of Egremont,
who was, however, experienced in the world and quick in his
detection of manner and of character.

The dinner was stately, as becomes the high nobility. There
were many guests, yet the table seemed only a gorgeous spot
in the capacious chamber. The side tables were laden with
silver vases and golden shields arranged on shelves of crimson velvet. The walls were covered with Fitz-Warenes, De
Mowbrays, and De Veres. The attendants glided about without noise, and with the precision of military discipline. They
watched your wants, they anticipated your wishes, and they
supplied all you desired with a lofty air of pompous devotion.

'You came by the railroad?' inquired Lord de Mowbray
mournfully, of Lady Marney.

'From Marham; about ten miles from us,' replied her ladyship.

'A great revolution!'

'Isn't it?'

'I fear it has a dangerous tendency to equality,' said his lordship, shaking his head: 'I suppose Lord Marney gives them
all the opposition in his power.'

'There is nobody so violent against railroads as George,'
said Lady Marney. 'I cannot tell you what he does not do!
He organised the whole of our division against the Marham
line!'

'I rather counted on him,' said Lord de Mowbray, 'to
assist me in resisting this joint branch here; but I was surprised to learn he had consented.'

'Not until the compensation was settled,' innocently remarked Lady Marney; 'George never opposes them after that.
He gave up all opposition to the Marham line when they
agreed to his terms.'

'And yet,' said Lord de Mowbray, 'I think if Lord Marney
would take a different view of the case, and look to the moral
consequences, he would hesitate. Equality, Lady Marney,
equality is not our *métier*. If we nobles do not make a stand
against the levelling spirit of the age, I am at a loss to know

who will fight the battle. You may depend upon it that these railroads are very dangerous things.'

'I have no doubt of it. I suppose you have heard of Lady Vanilla's trip from Birmingham? Have you not, indeed? She came up with Lady Laura, and two of the most gentlemanlike men sitting opposite her; never met, she says, two more intelligent men. She begged one of them at Wolverhampton to change seats with her, and he was most politely willing to comply with her wishes, only it was necessary that his companion should move at the same time, for they were chained together! Two gentlemen, sent to town for picking a pocket at Shrewsbury races.'

'A countess and a felon! So much for public conveyances,' said Lord Mowbray. 'But Lady Vanilla is one of those who will talk with everybody.'

'She is very amusing, though,' said Lady Marney.

'I dare say she is,' said Lord de Mowbray; 'but believe me, my dear Lady Marney, in these times especially, a countess has something else to do than be amusing.'

'You think, as property has its duties as well as its rights, rank has its bores as well as its pleasures.'

Lord Mowbray mused.

'How do you do, Mr. Jermyn?' said a lively little lady with sparkling beady black eyes, and a yellow complexion, though with good features: 'when did you arrive in the north? I have been fighting your battles finely since I saw you,' she added, shaking her head rather with an expression of admonition than of sympathy.

'You are always fighting one's battles, Lady Firebrace; it is very kind of you. If it were not for you, we should none of us know how much we are all abused,' replied Mr. Jermyn, a young M.P.

'They say you gave the most radical pledges,' said Lady Firebrace eagerly, and not without malice. 'I heard Lord Muddlebrains say that if he had had the least idea of your principles, you would not have had his influence.'

'Muddlebrains can't command a single vote,' said Mr. Jermyn. 'He is a political humbug, the greatest of all humbugs; a man who swaggers about London clubs and consults solemnly about his influence, and in the country is a nonentity.'

'Well, that can't be said of Lord Clarinel,' rejoined Lady Firebrace.

'And have you been defending me against Lord Clarinel's attacks?' inquired Mr. Jermyn.

'No; but I am going to Wemsbury, and then I have no doubt I shall have the opportunity.'

'I am going to Wemsbury myself,' said Mr. Jermyn.

'And what does Lord Clarinel think of your pledge about the pension list?' said Lady Firebrace, daunted but malignant.

'He never told me,' said Mr. Jermyn.

'I believe you did not pledge yourself to the ballot?' inquired Lady Firebrace with an affected air of inquisitiveness.

'It is a subject that requires some reflection,' said Mr. Jermyn. 'I must consult some profound politician like Lady Firebrace. By-the-bye, you told my mother that the conservatives would have a majority of fifteen. Do you think they will have so much?' said Mrs. Jermyn with an innocent air, it now being notorious that the whig administration had a majority of double that amount.

'I said Mr. Tadpole gave us a majority of fifteen,' said Lady Firebrace. 'I knew he was in error: because I had happened to see Lord Melbourne's own list, made up to the last hour; and which gave the government a majority of sixty. It was only shown to three members of the cabinet.' she added, in a tone of triumphant mystery.

Lady Firebrace, a great stateswoman among the tories, was proud of an admirer who was a member of the whig cabinet. She was rather an agreeable guest in a country house, with her extensive correspondence, and her bulletins from both sides. Tadpole, flattered by her notice, and charmed with female society that talked his own slang, and entered with affected enthusiasm into all his petty plots and barren machinations, was vigilant in his communications; while her whig cavalier, an easy individual, who always made love by talking or writing politics, abandoned himself without reserve, and instructed Lady Firebrace regularly after every council. Taper* looked grave at this connection between Tadpole and Lady Firebrace; and whenever an election was lost, or a division stuck in the mud, he gave the cue with a nod and monosyllable, and the conservative pack that infests clubs, chattering on subjects of which it is impossible they can know anything, instantly began barking and yelping, denouncing traitors, and wondering how the leaders could be so led by the nose and not see that which was flagrant to the whole world. If, on the other hand, the advantage seemed to go with the Carlton Club, or the opposition benches, then it was the whig and liberal hounds who howled and moaned, explaining everything by the indiscretion, infatuation, treason of Lord Viscount Masque, and appealing to the initiated world of idiots around them, whether any party could ever succeed, hampered by such men, and influenced by such means.

The best of the joke was, that all this time Lord Masque and Tadpole were two old foxes, neither of whom conveyed to Lady Firebrace a single circumstance but with the wish, intention, and malice aforethought, that it should be communicated to his rival.

'I must get you to interest Lord de Mowbray in our cause,' said Sir Vavasour Firebrace, in an insinuating voice, to his neighbour, Lady Joan; 'I have sent him a large packet of documents. You know, he is one of us; still one of us. Once a baronet, always a baronet. The dignity merges, but does not cease; and happy as I am to see one covered with high honours who is in every way so worthy of them, still I confess to you it is not so much as Earl de Mowbray that your worthy father interests me, as in his undoubted character and capacity of Sir Altamont Fitz-Warene, baronet.'

'You have the data on which you move, I suppose, well digested,' said Lady Joan, attentive, but not interested.

'The case is clear; so far as equity is concerned, irresistible; indeed the late king pledged himself to a certain point, But if you would do me the favour of reading our memorial.'

The proposition is not one adapted to our present civilisation,' said Lady Joan. 'A baronetcy has become the distinction of the middle class; a physician, our physician for example, is a baronet; and I dare say some of our tradesmen; brewers, or people of that class. An attempt to elevate them into an order of nobility, however inferior, would partake, in some degree, of the ridiculous.'

'And has the duke escaped his gout this year?' inquired Lord Marney of Lady de Mowbray.

'A slight touch; I never knew my father so well. I expect you will meet him here. We look for him daily.'

'I shall be delighted; I hope he will come to Marney in October. I keep the blue ribbon cover for him.'*

'What you suggest is very just,' said Egremont to Lady Maud. 'If we only, in our own spheres, made the exertion, the general effect would be great. Marney Abbey, for instance, I believe one of the finest of our monastic remains, that indeed is not disputed, diminished yearly to repair barns; the cattle browsing in the nave; all this might be prevented. If my brother would not consent to preserve or to restore, still any member of the family, even I, without expense, only with a little zeal as you say, might prevent mischief, might stop at least demolition.'

'If this movement in the church had only revived a taste for Christian architecture,'* said Lady Maud, 'it would not have been barren, and it has done so much more! But I am surprised that old families can be so dead to our national art; so full of our ancestors, their exploits, their mind, Indeed you and I have no excuse for such indifference, Mr. Egremont.'

'And I do not think I shall ever again he justly accused of it,' replied Egremont, 'you plead its cause so effectively. to tell you the truth, I have been thinking of late about these things; monasteries and so on; the influence of the old church system on the happiness and comfort of the People.'

'And on the tone of the Nobles; do not you think so?' said Lady Maud. 'I know it is the fashion to deride the crusades but do not you think they had their origin in a great impulse, and, in a certain sense, led to great results? Pardon me if I speak with emphasis, but I never can forget I am a daughter of the first Crusaders.'

'The tone of society is certainly lower than of yore,' said Egremont. 'It is easy to say we view the past through a fallacious medium. We have, however, ample evidence that men feel less deeply than of old, and act with less devotion. But how far is this occasioned by the modern position of our church? That is the question.'

'You must speak to Mr. St. Lys about that,' said Lady Maud. 'Do you know him?' she added in a lower tone.

'No; is he here?'

'Next to mamma.'

And, looking in that direction, on the left hand of Lady Mowbray, Egremont beheld a gentleman in the last year of his youth, if youth according to the scale of Hippocrates cease at thirty-five. He was distinguished by that beauty of the noble English blood, of which in these days few types remain; the Norman tempered by the Saxon; the fire of conquest softened by integrity; and a serene, though inflexible habit of mind. The chains of convention, an external life grown out of all proportion with that of the heart and mind, have destroyed this dignified beauty. There is no longer in fact an aristocracy in England, for the superiority of the animal man is an essential quality of aristocracy. But that it once existed, any collection of portraits from the sixteenth century will show.

Aubrey St. Lys was a younger son of the most ancient Norman family in England. The Conqueror had given them the moderate estate on which they now lived, and which, in spite of so many civil conflicts and religious changes, they had handed down to each other, from generation to generation, for eight centuries. Aubrey St. Lys was the vicar of Mowbray. He had been the college tutor of the late Lord Fitz-Warene, whose mind he had formed, whose bright abilities he had cultivated, who adored him. To that connection he owed the slight preferment which he possessed, but which was all he desired. A bishopric would not have tempted him from his peculiar charge.

In the centre of the town of Mowbray, teeming with its toiling thousands, there rose a building which might vie with many of the cathedrals of our land. Beautiful its solemn towers, its sculptured western front; beautiful its columned aisles and lofty nave; its sparkling shrine and delicate chantry; most beautiful the streaming glories of its vast orient light!

This magnificent temple, built by the monks of Mowbray, and once connected with their famous house, of which not a trace now remained, had in time become the parish church of an obscure village, whose population could not have filled one of its side chapels. These strange vicissitudes of ecclesiastical buildings are not singular in the north of England.

Mowbray Church remained for centuries the wonder of passing peasants, and the glory of county histories. But there is a magic in beautiful buildings which exercises an irresistible influence over the mind of man. One of the reasons urged for the destruction of the monasteries after the dispersion of their inhabitants, was the pernicious influence of their solemn and stately forms on the memories and imagination of those that beheld them. It was impossible to connect systematic crime with the creators of such divine fabrics. And so it was with Mowbray Church. When manufactures were introduced into this district, which abounded with all the qualities necessary for their successful pursuit, to Mowbray, offering equal though not superior advantages to other positions, was accorded the preference, 'because it possessed such a beautiful church.' The lingering genius of the monks of Mowbray hovered round the spot which they had adorned, and sanctified, and loved; and thus they had indirectly become the authors of its present greatness and prosperity.

Unhappily, for a long season the vicars of Mowbray had been little conscious of their mission. An immense population gathered round the sacred citadel and gradually spread on all sides of it for miles. But the parish church for a long time remained the only one at Mowbray when the population of the town exceeded that of some European capitals. And even in the parish church the frigid spell of Erastian self-complacency fatally prevailed. A scanty congregation gathered together for form, and as much influenced by party as higher sentiments. Going to church was held more genteel than going to meeting. The principal tradesmen of the neighbouring great houses deemed it more 'aristocratic;' using a favourite and hackneyed epithet, which only expressed their own servility. About the time the Church Commission issued, the congregation of Mowbray was approaching zero. There was an idea afloat for a time of making it the seat of a new bishopric; the cathedral was ready; another instance of the influence of fine art. But there was no residence for the projected prelate, and a jobbing bishop on the commission was afraid that he might have to contribute to building one. So the idea died away; and the living having become vacant at this moment, instead of a bishop, Mowbray received an humble vicar in the shape of Aubrey St. Lys, who came among a hundred thousand heathen to preach 'the Unknown God.'

CHAPTER 12

'AND how do you find the people about you, Marney?' said Lord de Mowbray, seating himself on a sofa by his guest.

'All very well, my lord,' replied the earl, who ever treated Lord de Mowbray with a certain degree of ceremony, especially when the descendant of the Crusaders affected the familiar. There was something of a Puck-like malignity in the temperament of Lord Marney, which exhibited itself in a remarkable talent for mortifying persons in a small way: by a gesture, an expression, a look, cloaked, too, very often with all the character of profound deference. The old nobility of Spain delighted to address each other only by their names, when in the presence of a spic-and-span grandee; calling each other, 'Infantado,' 'Sidonia,' 'Ossuna,' and then turning round with the most distinguished consideration, and appealing to the Most Noble Marquis of Ensenada.

'They begin to get a little uneasy here,' said Lord de Mowbray.

'We have nothing to complain of,' said Lord Marney. 'We continue reducing the rates, and as long as we do that the country must improve. The workhouse test tells. We had the other day a case of incendiarism, which frightened some people; but I inquired into it, and am quite satisfied it originated in purely accidental circumstances; at least nothing to do with wages. I ought to be a judge, for it was on my own property.'

'And what is the rate of wages in your part of the world, Lord Marney?' enquired Mr. St. Lys, who was standing by.

'Oh! good enough: not like your manufacturing districts; but people who work in the open air instead of a furnace can't expect, and don't require such. They get their eight shillings a week; at least generally.'

'Eight shillings a week!' said Mr. St. Lys. 'Can a labouring man with a family, perhaps of eight children, live on eight shillings a week?'

'Oh! as for that,' said Lord Marney, 'they get more than that, because there is beer-money allowed, at least to a great extent among us, though I for one do not approve of the practice, and that makes nearly a shilling per week additional; and then some of them have potato grounds, though I am entirely opposed to that system.'

'And yet,' said Mr. St. Lys, 'how they contrive to live is to me marvellous.'

'Oh! as for that,' said Lord Marney, 'I have generally found the higher the wages the worse the workman. They only spend their money in the beer-shops. *They* are the curse of this country.'

'But what is a poor man to do,' said Mr. St. Lys, 'after his day's work, if he returns to his own roof and finds no home; his fire extinguished, his food unprepared; the partner of his life, wearied with labour in the field or the factory, still absent, or perhaps in bed from exhaustion, or because she has returned wet to the skin, and has no change of raiment for her relief? We have removed woman from her sphere; we may have reduced wages by her introduction into the market of labour; but under these circumstances what we call domestic life is a condition impossible to be realised for the people of this country; and we must not therefore be surprised that they seek solace or rather refuge in the beer-shop.'

Lord Marney looked up at Mr. St. Lys with a stare of high-bred impertinence, and then carelessly observed, without directing his words to him, 'They may say what they like, but it is all an affair of population.'

'I would rather believe that it is an affair of resources,' said Mr. St. Lys; 'not what is the amount of our population, but what is the amount of our resources for their maintenance.'

'It comes to the same thing,' said Lord Marney. 'Nothing can put this country right but emigration on a great scale; and as the government do not choose to undertake it, I have commenced it for my own defence on a small scale. I will take care that the population of my parishes is not increased. I build no cottages, and I destroy all I can; and I am not ashamed or afraid to say so.'

'You have declared war to the cottage, then,' said Mr. St. Lys, smiling. 'It is not at the first sound so startling a cry as war to the castle.'

'But you think it may lead to it?' said Lord de Mowbray.

'I love not to be a prophet of evil,' said Mr. St. Lys.

Lord Marney rose from his seat and addressed Lady Fire-brace, whose husband in another part of the room had caught Mr. Jermyn, and was opening his mind on 'the question of the day;' Lady Maud, followed by Egremont, approached Mr. St. Lys, and said. 'Mr. Egremont has a great feeling for Christian architecture, Mr. St. Lys, and wishes particularly to visit our church, of which we are so proud.' And in a few moments they were seated together, and engaged in conversation.

Lord de Mowbray placed himself by the side of Lady Marney who, was seated by his countess.

'Oh! how I envy you at Marney!' he exclaimed. 'No manufactures, no smoke; living in the midst of a beautiful park, and surrounded by a contented peasantry!'

'It is very delightful,' said Lady Marney, 'but then we are so dull; we have really no neighbourhood.'

'I think that such an advantage,' said Lady de Mowbray; 'I must say I like my friends from London. I never know what to say to the people here. Excellent people, the very best people in the world; the way they behaved to poor dear Fitz-Warene, when they wanted him to stand for the county, I never can forget; but then they do not know the people we know, or do the things we do; and when you have gone through the routine of county questions, and exhausted the weather and all the winds, I am positively, my dear Lady Marney, *aux abois*, and then they think you are proud, when really one is only stupid.'

'I am fond of work,' said Lady Marney, 'and I talk to them always about it.'

'Ah! you are fortunate, I never could work; and Joan and Maud, they neither of them work. Maud did embroider a banner once for her brother; it is in the hall. I think it beautiful: but somehow or other she never cultivated her talent.'

'For all that has occurred, or may occur,' said Mr. St. Lys to Egremont, 'I blame only the church. The church deserted the people; and from that moment the church has been in danger, and the people degraded. Formerly religion undertook to satisfy the noble wants of human nature, and by its festivals relieved the painful weariness of toil. The day of rest was consecrated, if not always to elevated thoughts, at least to sweet and noble sentiments. The church convened to its solemnities, under its splendid and almost celestial roofs, amid the finest monuments of art that human hands have raised, the whole Christian population; for there, in the presence of God, all were brethren. It shared equally among all its prayer, its incense, and its music; its sacred instructions, and the highest enjoyments that the arts could afford.'

'You believe, then, in the efficacy of forms and ceremonies?'

'What you call forms and ceremonies represent the divinest instincts of our nature. Push your aversion to forms and ceremonies to a legitimate conclusion, and you would prefer kneeling in a barn rather than in a cathedral. Your tenets would strike at the very existence of all art, which is essentially spiritual.'

'I am not speaking abstractedly,' said Egremont, 'but rather with reference to the indirect connection of these forms and ceremonies with another church. The people of this country associate them with an enthralling superstition and a foreign dominion.'

'With Rome,' said Mr. St. Lys; 'yet forms and ceremonies existed before Rome.'

'But practically,' said Egremont, 'has not their revival in our service at the present day a tendency to restore the Romish system in this country?'

'It is difficult to ascertain what may be the practical effect of certain circumstances among the uninformed,' said Mr. St. Lys. 'The Church of Rome is to be respected as the only Hebræo-christian church extant; all other churches established by the Hebrew apostles have disappeared, but Rome remains; and we must never permit the exaggerated position which it assumed in the middle centuries to make us forget its early and apostolical character, when it was fresh from Palestine, and as it were fragrant from Paradise. The Church of Rome is sustained by apostolical succession; but apostolical succession is not an institution complete in itself; it is a part of a whole; if it be not part of a whole it has no foundation. The apostles succeeded the prophets. Our Master announced himself as the last of the prophets. They in their turn were the heirs of the patriarchs: men who were in direct communication with the Most High. To men not less favoured than the apostles, the revelation of the priestly character was made, and those forms and ceremonies ordained which the Church of Rome has never relinquished. But Rome did not invent them: upon their practice, the duty of all congregations, we cannot consent to her founding a claim to supremacy. For would you maintain then that the church did not exist in the time of the prophets? Was Moses then not a churchman? And Aaron, was he not a high priest? Ay! greater than any pope or prelate, whether he be at Rome or at Lambeth.

'In all these church discussions, we are apt to forget that the second Testament is avowedly only a supplement. Jehovah-Jesus came to complete the "law and the prophets." Christianity is completed Judaism, or it is nothing. Christianity is incomprehensible without Judaism, as Judaism is incomplete without Christianity. What has Rome to do with its completion; what with its commencement? The law was not thundered forth from the Capitolian mount; the divine atonement was not fulfilled upon Mons Sacer. No; the order of our priesthood comes directly from Jehovah; and the forms and ceremonies of His church are the regulations of His supreme intelligence. Rome indeed boasts that the authenticity of the second Testament depends upon the recognition of her infallibility. The authenticity of the second Testament depends upon its congruity with the first. Did Rome preserve that? I recognise in the church an institution thoroughly, sincerely catholic: adapted to all climes, and to all ages. I do not bow to the necessity of a visible head in a defined locality; but were I to seek for such, it would not be at Rome. I cannot discover in its history, however memorable, any testimony of a mission so sublime. When Omnipotence deigned to be incarnate, the Ineffable Word did not select a Roman frame. The prophets were not Romans; the apostles were not Romans; she who was blessed above all women, I never heard she was a Roman maiden. No, I should look to a land more distant than Italy, to a city more sacred even than Rome.'

CHAPTER 13

It was a cloudy, glimmering dawn. A cold withering east wind blew through the silent streets of Mowbray. The sounds of the night had died away, the voices of the day had not commenced. There reigned a stillness complete and absorbing.

Suddenly there is a voice, there is movement. The first footstep of the new week of toil is heard. A man muffled up in a thick coat, and bearing in his hand what would seem at the first glance to be a shepherd's crook, only its handle is much longer, appears upon the pavement. He touches a number of windows with great quickness as he moves rapidly along. A rattling noise sounds upon each pane. The use of the long handle of his instrument becomes apparent as he proceeds, enabling him as it does to reach the upper windows of the dwellings whose inmates he has to rouse. Those inmates are the factory girls, who subscribe in districts to engage these heralds of the dawn; and by a strict observance of whose citation they can alone escape the dreaded fine that awaits those who have not arrived at the door of the factory before the bell ceases to sound.

The sentry in question, quitting the streets, and stooping through one of the small archways that we have before noticed, entered a court. Here lodged a multitude of his employers; and the long crook, as it were by some sleight of hand, seemed sounding on both sides, and at many windows at the same moment. Arrived at the end of the court, he was about to touch the window of the upper story of the last tenement, when that window opened, and a man, pale and careworn, and in a melancholy voice, spoke to him.

'Simmons,' said the man, 'you need not rouse this story any more; my daughter has left us.'

'Has she left Webster's?'

'No; but she has left us. She has long murmured at her hard lot; working like a slave, and not for herself. And she has gone, as they all go, to keep house for herself.'

'That's a bad business,' said the watchman, in a tone not devoid of sympathy.

'Almost as bad as for parents to live on their children's wages,' replied the man mournfully.

'And how is your good woman?'

'As poorly as needs be. Harriet has never been home since Friday night. She owes you nothing?'

'Not a halfpenny. She was as regular as a little bee, and always paid every Monday morning. I am sorry she has left you, neighbour.'

'The Lord's will be done. It's hard times for such as us,' said the man; and, leaving the window open, he retired into his room.

It was a single chamber of which he was the tenant. In the centre, placed so as to gain the best light which the gloomy situation could afford, was a loom. In two corners of the room were mattresses placed on the floor, a check curtain, hung upon a string, if necessary, concealing them. On one was his sick wife; on the other, three young children: two girls, the eldest about eight years of age; between them their baby brother. An iron kettle was by the hearth, and on the mantelpiece some candles, a few lucifer matches, two tin mugs, a paper of salt, and an iron spoon. In a farther part, close to the wall, was a heavy table or dresser; this was a fixture, as well as the form which was fastened by it.

The man seated himself at his loom; he commenced his daily task.

'Twelve hours of daily labour, at the rate of one penny each hour; and even this labour is mortgaged! How is this to end? Is it rather not ended?' And he looked around him at his mugs, a paper of salt, and an iron spoon. In a farther part, chamber without resources: no food, no fuel, no furniture and four human beings dependent on him, and lying in their wretched beds, because they had no clothes. 'I cannot sell my loom,' he continued, 'at the price of old firewood, and it cost me gold. It is not vice that has brought me to this, nor indolence, nor imprudence. I was born to labour, and I was ready to labour. I loved my loom, and my loom loved me. It gave me a cottage in my native village, surrounded by a garden of whose claims on my solicitude it was not jealous. There was time for both. It gave me for a wife the maiden that I had ever loved; and it gathered my children round my hearth with plenteousness and peace. I was content: I sought no other lot. It is not adversity that makes me look back upon the past with tenderness.

'Then why am I here? Why am I, and six hundred thousand subjects of the Queen, honest, loyal, and industrious, why are we, after manfully struggling for years, and each year sinking lower in the scale, why are we driven from our innocent and happy homes, our country cottages that we loved, first to bide in close towns without comforts and gradually to crouch into cellars, or find a squalid lair like this, without even the common necessaries of existence; first the ordinary conveniences of life, then raiment, and at length food, vanishing from us.

'It is that the Capitalist has found a slave that has supplanted the labour and ingenuity of man. Once he was an artisan: at the best, he now only watches machines; and even that occupation slips from his grasp to the woman and the child. The capitalist flourishes, he amasses immense wealth; we sink, lower and lower; lower than the beasts of burthen; for they are fed better than we are, cared for more. And it is just, for according to the present system they are more precious. And yet they tell us that the interests of Capital and of Labour are identical.

'If a society that has been created by labour suddenly becomes independent of it, that society is bound to maintain the race whose only property is labour, out of the proceeds of that other property, which has not ceased to be productive.

'When the class of the Nobility were supplanted in France, they did not amount in number to one-third of us Hand-loom weavers; yet all Europe went to war to avenge their wrongs, every state subscribed to maintain them in their adversity, and when they were restored to their own country their own land supplied them with an immense indemnity. Who cares for us? Yet we have lost our estates. Who raises a voice for us? Yet we are at least as innocent as the nobility of France. We sink among no sighs except our own. And if they give us sympathy, what then? Sympathy is the solace of the Poor; but for the Rich there is compensation.'

'Is that Harriet?' said his wife, moving in her bed.

The Hand-loom weaver was recalled from his reverie to the urgent misery that surrounded him.

'No!' he replied in a quick hoarse voice, 'it is not Harriet.'

'Why does not Harriet come?'

'She will come no more!' replied the weaver; 'I told you so last night: she can bear this place no longer; and I am not surprised.'

'How are we to get food, then?' rejoined his wife; 'you ought not to have let her leave us. You do nothing, Warner. You get no wages yourself; and you have let the girl escape.'

'I will escape myself if you say that again,' said the weaver: 'I have been up these three hours finishing this piece, which ought to have been taken home on Saturday night.'

'But you have been paid for it beforehand. You get nothing for your work. A penny an hour! What sort of work is it that brings a penny an hour?'

'Work that you have often admired, Mary; and has before this gained a prize. But if you don't like the work,' said the man, quitting his loom, 'let it alone. There was enough yet owing on this piece to have allowed us to break our fast. However, no matter; we must starve sooner or later. Let us begin at once.'

'No, no, Philip! work. Let us break our fast, come what may.'

'Twit me no more, then,' said the weaver, resuming his seat, 'or I throw the shuttle for the last time.'

'I will not taunt you,' said his wife in a kinder tone. 'I was wrong; I am sorry; but I am very ill. It is not for myself I speak; I want not to eat; I have no appetite; my lips are so very parched. But the children, the children went supperless to bed, and they will wake soon.'

'Mother, we ayn't asleep,' said the elder girl.

'No, we ayn't asleep, mother,' said her sister; 'we heard all that you said to father.'

'And baby?'

'He sleeps still.'

'I shiver very much!' said the mother. 'It's a cold day. Pray shut the window, Warner. I see the drops upon the pane; it is raining. I wonder if the persons below would lend us one block of coal.'

'We have borrowed too often,' said Warner.

'I wish there were no such thing as coal in the land,' said his wife, 'and then the engines would not be able to work; and we should have our rights again.'

'Amen!' said Warner.

'Don't you think, Warner,' said his wife, 'that you could sell that piece to some other person, and owe Barber for the money he advanced?'

'No!' said her husband, fiercely. 'I'll go straight.'

'And let your children starve,' said his wife, 'when you could get five or six shillings at once. But so it always was with you. Why did not you go to the machines years ago like other men, and so get used to them?'

'I should have been supplanted by this time,' said Warner, 'by a girl or a woman! It would have been just as bad!'

'Why there was your friend, Walter Gerard; he was the same as you, and yet now he gets two pound a week; at least I have often heard you say so.'

'Walter Gerard is a man of great parts,' said Warner, 'and might have been a master himself by this time had he cared.'

'And why did he not?'

'He had no wife and children,' said Warner; 'he was not so blessed.'

The baby woke and began to cry.

'Ah! my child!' exclaimed the mother. 'That wicked Harriet! Here, Amelia, I have a morsel of crust here. I saved it yesterday for baby; moisten it in water, and tie it up in this piece of calico: he will suck it; it will keep him quiet; I can bear anything but his cry.'

'I shall have finished my job by noon,' said Warner; 'and then, please God, we shall break our fast.'

'It is yet two hours to noon,' said his wife. 'And Barber always keeps you so long! I cannot bear that Barber: I dare say he will not advance you money again, as you did not bring the job home on Saturday night. If I were you, Philip, I would go and sell the piece unfinished at once to one of the cheap shops.'

'I have gone straight all my life,' said Warner.

'And much good it has done you,' said his wife.

'My poor Amelia! How she shivers! I think the sun never touches this house. It is, indeed, a most wretched place.'

'It will not annoy you long, Mary,' said her husband: 'I can pay no more rent; and I only wonder they have not been here already to take the week.'

'And where are we to go?' said the wife.

'To a place which certainly the sun never touches,' said her husband, with a kind of malice in his misery – 'to a cellar.'

'Oh! why was I ever born?' exclaimed his wife. 'And yet I was so happy once! And it is not our fault. I cannot make it out, Warner, why you should not get two pounds a week like Walter Gerard.'

'Bah!' said the husband.

'You said he had no family,' continued his wife. 'I thought he had a daughter.'

'But she is no burthen to him. The sister of Mr. Trafford is the Superior of the convent here, and she took Sybil when her mother died, and brought her up.'

'Oh! then she is a nun?'

'Not yet; but I dare say it will end in it.'

'Well, I think I would even sooner starve,' said his wife, 'than my children should be nuns.'

At this moment there was a knocking at the door. Warner descended from his loom, and opened it.

'Lives Philip Warner here?' enquired a clear voice of peculiar sweetness.

'My name is Warner.'

'I come from Walter Gerard,' continued the voice. 'Your letter reached him only last night. The girl at whose house your daughter left it has quitted this week past Mr. Trafford's factory.'

'Pray enter.'

And there entered Sybil.

CHAPTER 14

'YOUR wife is ill?' said Sybil.

'Very!' replied Warner's wife. 'Our daughter has behaved infamously to us. She has quitted us without saying by your leave or with your leave. And her wages were almost the only thing left to us; for Philip is not like Walter Gerard, you see: he cannot earn two pounds a week, though why he cannot I never could understand.'

'Hush, hush, wife!' said Warner. 'I speak, I apprehend, to Gerard's daughter?'

'Just so.'

'Ah! this is good and kind; this is like old times, for Walter Gerard was my friend, when I was not exactly as I am now.'

'He tells me so: he sent a messenger to me last night to visit you this morning. Your letter reached him only yesterday.'

'Harriet was to give it to Caroline,' said the wife. 'That's the girl who has done all the mischief and inveigled her away. And she has left Trafford's works, has she? Then I will be bound she and Harriet are keeping house together.'

'You suffer?' said Sybil, moving to the bed-side of the woman. 'Give me your hand,' she added in a soft sweet tone. ' 'Tis hot.'

'I feel very cold,' said the woman. 'Warner would have the window open, till the rain came in.'

'And you, I fear, are wet,' said Warner, addressing Sybil, and interrupting his wife.

'Very slightly. And you have no fire. Ah! I have brought some things for you, but not fuel.'

'If he would only ask the person down stairs,' said his wife, 'for a block of coal; I tell him, neighbours could hardly refuse; but he never will do anything; he says he has asked too often.'

'I will ask,' said Sybil. 'But first, I have a companion without,' she added, 'who bears a basket for you. Come in, Harold.'

The baby began to cry the moment a large dog entered the room; a young bloodhound of the ancient breed, such as are now found but in a few old halls and granges in the north of

England. Sybil untied the basket, and gave a piece of sugar
to the screaming infant. Her glance was sweeter even than
her remedy; the infant stared at her with his large blue eyes,
for an instant astonished, and then he smiled.

'Oh! beautiful child!' exclaimed Sybil; and she took the
babe up from the mattress and embraced it.

'You are an angel from heaven,' exclaimed the mother,
'and you may well say beautiful. And only to think of that
infamous girl, Harriet, to desert us all in this way!'

Sybil drew forth the contents of the convent basket, and
called Warner's attention to them. 'Now,' she said, 'arrange
all this as I tell you, and I will go down stairs and speak to
them below as you wish. Harold, rest there;' and the dog laid
himself down in the remotest corner.

'And is that Gerard's daughter?' said the weaver's wife.

'Only think what it is to gain two pounds a week, and
bring up your daughters in that way, instead of such shame-
less husseys as our Harriet! But with such wages one can do
anything. What have you there, Warner? Is that tea? Oh! I
should like some tea. I do think tea would do me some good.
I have quite a longing for it. Run down, Warner, and ask
them to let us have a kettle of hot water. It is better than all
the fire in the world. Amelia, my dear, do you see what they
have sent us? Plenty to eat. Tell Maria all about it. You are
good girls; you will never be like that infamous Harriet. When
you earn wages you will give them to your poor mother and
baby, won't you?'

'Yes, mother,' said Amelia.

'And father, too,' said Maria.

'And father, too,' said the wife. 'He has been a very good
father to you all; and I never can understand why one who
works so hard should earn so little; but I believe it is the
fault of those machines. The police ought to put them down,
and then everybody would be comfortable.'

Sybil and Warner re-entered; the fire was lit, the tea made,
the meal partaken of. An air of comfort, even of enjoyment,
was diffused over this chamber, but a few minutes back so
desolate and unhappy.

'Well,' said the wife, raising herself a little up in her bed,

'I feel as if that dish of tea had saved my life. Amelia, have you had any tea? And Maria? You see what it is to be good, girls; the Lord will never desert you. The day is fast coming when that Harriet will know what the want of a dish of tea is, with all her fine wages. And I am sure,' she added, addressing Sybil, 'what we all owe to you is not to be told. Your father well deserves his good fortune, with such a daughter.'

'My father's fortunes are not much better than his neighbours,', said Sybil, 'but his wants are few; and who should sympathise with the poor but the poor? Alas! none else can. Besides, it is the Superior of our convent that has sent you this meal. What my father can do for you I have told your husband. 'Tis little; but with the favour of Heaven it may avail. When the people support the people the Divine blessing will not be wanting.'

'I am sure the Divine blessing will never be wanting to you,' said Warner, in a voice of emotion.

There was silence; the querulous spirit of the wife was subdued by the tone of Sybil; she revolved in her mind the present and the past; the children pursued their ungrudged and unusual meal; the daughter of Gerard, that she might not interfere with their occupation, walked to the window and surveyed the chink of troubled sky which was visible in the court. The wind blew in gusts; the rain beat against the glass. Soon after this, there was another knock at the door. Harold started from his repose, and growled. Warner rose, and saying, 'They have come for the rent. Thank God, I am ready,' advanced and opened the door. Two men offered with courtesy to enter.

'We are strangers,' said he who took the lead, 'but would not be such. I speak to Warner?'

'My name.'

'And I am your spiritual pastor, if to be the vicar of Mowbray entitles me to that description.'

'Mr. St. Lys.'

'The same. One of the most valued of my flock, and the most influential person in this district, has been speaking much of you to me this morning. You are working for him. He did not hear of you on Saturday night; he feared you were ill. Mr. Barber spoke to me of your distress, as well as of your good character. I came to express to you my respect and my sympathy, and to offer you my assistance.'

'You are most good, sir, and Mr. Barber too; and indeed, an hour ago, we were in as great straits—'

'And are now, sir,' exclaimed his wife, interrupting him. 'I have been in this bed a week, and may never rise from it again; the children have no clothes; they are pawned; everything is pawned; this morning we had neither fuel nor food. And we thought you had come for the rent, which we cannot pay. If it had not been for a dish of tea which was charitably given me this morning by a person almost as poor as ourselves, that is to say, they live by labour, though their wages are much higher, as high as two pounds a week, though how that can be I never shall understand, when my husband is working twelve hours a day, and gaining only a penny an hour; if it had not been for this I should have been a corpse; and yet he says we were in straits, merely because Walter Gerard's daughter, who I willingly grant is an angel from heaven for all the good she has done us, has stepped in to our aid. But the poor supporting the poor, as she well says, what good can come from that?'

During this ebullition, Mr. St. Lys had surveyed the apartment and recognised Sybil.

'Sister,' he said, when the wife of Warner had ceased, 'this is not the first time we have met under the roof of sorrow.'

Sybil bent in silence, and moved as if she were about to retire; the wind and rain came dashing against the window. The companion of Mr. St. Lys, who was clad in a rough great coat, and was shaking the wet off an oilskin hat known by the name of a 'south-wester,' advanced and said to her, 'It is but a squall, but a severe one; I would recommend you to stay for a few minutes.'

She received this remark with courtesy, but did not reply.

'I think,' continued the companion of Mr. St. Lys, 'that this is not the first time also that we have met?'

'I cannot recall our meeting before,' said Sybil.

'And yet it was not many days past; though the sky was so different, that it would almost make one believe it was in another land and another clime.'

Sybil looked at him as if for explanation.

'It was at Marney Abbey,' said the companion of Mr. St. Lys.

'I was there; and I remember when about to rejoin my companions, they were not alone.'

'And you disappeared, very suddenly I thought; for I left the ruins almost at the same moment as your friends, yet I never saw any of you again.'

'We took our course; a very rugged one; you perhaps pursued a more even way.'

'Was it your first visit to Marney?'

'My first and my last. There was no place I more desired to see; no place of which the vision made me so sad.'

'The glory has departed,' said Egremont, mournfully.

'It is not that,' said Sybil; 'I was prepared for decay, but not for such absolute desecration. The Abbey seems a quarry for materials to repair farm-houses; and the nave a cattle gate. What people they must be – that family of sacrilege who hold these lands!'

'Hem!' said Egremont. 'They certainly do not appear to have much feeling for ecclesiastical art.'

'And for little else, as we were told,' said Sybil. 'There was a fire at the Abbey farm the day we were there, and, from all that reached us, it would appear the people were as little tended as the Abbey walls.'

'They have some difficulty perhaps in employing their population in those parts.'

'You know the country?'

'Not at all; I was travelling in the neighbourhood, and made a diversion for the sake of seeing an abbey of which I had heard so much.'

'Yes; it was the greatest of the Northern Houses. But they told me the people were most wretched round the Abbey; nor do I think there is any other cause for their misery, than the hard hearts of the family that have got the lands.'

'You feel deeply for the people!' said Egremont, looking at her earnestly.

Sybil returned him a glance expressive of some astonishment, and then said, 'And do not you? Your presence here assures me of it.'

'I humbly follow one who would comfort the unhappy.'

'The charity of Mr. St. Lys is known to all.'

'And you – you, too, are a ministering angel.'

'There is no merit in my conduct, for there is no sacrifice. When I remember what this English people once was; the truest, the freest, and the bravest, the best-natured and the best-looking, the happiest and most religious race upon the surface of this globe; and think of them now, with all their crimes and all their slavish sufferings, their soured spirits and their stunted forms; their lives without enjoyment, and their deaths without hope; I may well feel for them, even if I were not the daughter of their blood.'

And that blood mantled to her cheek as she ceased to speak, and her dark eye gleamed with emotion, and an expression of pride and courage hovered on her brow. Egremont caught her glance and withdrew his own; his heart was troubled.

St. Lys, who had been in conference with the weaver, left him and went to the bedside of his wife. Warner advanced to Sybil, and expressed his feelings for her father, his sense of her goodness. She, observing that the squall seemed to have ceased, bade him farewell, and calling Harold, quitted the chamber.

CHAPTER 15

'WHERE have you been all the morning, Charles?' said Lord Marney, coming into his brother's dressing-room a few minutes before dinner: 'Arabella had made the nicest little riding party for you and Lady Joan, and you were to be found nowhere. If you go on in this way, there is no use in having affectionate relations, or anything else.'

'I have been walking about Mowbray. One should see a factory once in one's life.'

'I don't see the necessity,' said Lord Marney; 'I never saw one, and never intend. Though, to be sure, when I hear the rents that Mowbray gets for his land in this neighbourhood, I must say I wish the worsted works had answered at Marney. And if it had not been for our poor dear father, they would.'

'Our family have always been against manufactories, rail-roads – everything,' said Egremont.

'Railroads are very good things, with high compensation,'

said Lord Marney: 'and manufactories not so bad, with high rents; but, after all, these are enterprises for the canaille, and I hate them in my heart.'

'But they employ the people, George.'

'The people do not want employment; it is the greatest mistake in the world; all this employment is a stimulus to population. Never mind that; what I came in for is, to tell you that both Arabella and myself think you talk too much to Lady Maud.'

'I like her the best.'

'What has that to do with it, my dear fellow? Business is business. Old Mowbray will make an elder son out of his elder daughter. The affair is settled; I know it from the best authority. Talking to Lady Maud is insanity. It is all the same for her if Fitz-Warene had never died. And then that great event, which ought to be the foundation of your fortune, would be perfectly thrown away. Lady Maud, at the best, is nothing more than twenty thousand pounds and a fat living. Besides, she is engaged to that parson fellow, St. Lys.'

'St. Lys told me to-day that nothing would ever induce him to marry. He would practise celibacy, though he would not enjoin it.'

'Enjoin fiddle-stick! How came you to be talking to such a sanctified impostor; and, I believe, with all his fine phrases, a complete radical. I tell you what, Charles, you must really make way with Lady Joan. The grandfather has come to-day, the old duke. Quite a family party. It looks so well. Never was such a golden opportunity. And you must be sharp too. That little Jermyn, with his brown eyes and his white hands, has not come down here, in the month of August, with no sport of any kind, for nothing.'

'I shall set Lady Firebrace at him.'

'She is quite your friend, and a very sensible woman too, Charles, and an ally not to be despised. Lady Joan has a high opinion of her. There's the bell. Well, I shall tell Arabella that you mean to put up the steam, and Lady Firebrace shall keep Jermyn off. And perhaps it is as well you did not seem too eager at first. Mowbray Castle, my dear fellow, in spite of its manufactories, is not to be despised. And with a little firmness, you could keep the people out of your park. Mowbray

could do it, only he has no pluck. He is afraid people would
say he was the son of a footman.'

The duke, who was the father of the Countess de Mowbray,
was also lord-lieutenant of the county. Although advanced in
years, he was still extremely handsome, with the most winning
manners; full of amenity and grace. He had been a roué in his
youth, but seemed now the perfect representative of a benignant and virtuous old age. He was universally popular; admired by young men, adored by young ladies. Lord de Mowbray paid him the most distinguished consideration. It was
genuine. However maliciously the origin of his own father
might be represented, nobody could deprive him of that great
fact, his father-in-law; a duke, a duke of a great house who
had intermarried for generations with great houses, one of
the old nobility, and something even loftier.

The county of which his grace was lord-lieutenant was
proud of its nobility; and certainly with Marney Abbey at
one end, and Mowbray Castle at the other, it had just cause;
but both these illustrious houses yielded in importance,
though not in possessions, to the great peer who was the
governor of the province.

A French actress, clever as French actresses always are, had
persuaded, once upon a time, an easy-tempered monarch of
this realm, that the paternity of her coming babe was a distinction of which his majesty might be proud. His majesty did
not much believe her; but he was a sensible man, and never
disputed a point with a woman; so when the babe was born,
and proved a boy, he christened him with his name; and elevated him to the peerage in his cradle by the title of Duke of
Fitz-Aquitaine and Marquis of Gascony.

An estate the royal father could not endow him with, for
he had spent all his money, mortgaged all his resources, and
was obliged to run in debt himself for the jewels of the rest
of his mistresses; but he did his best for the young peer, as
became an affectionate father or a fond lover. His majesty
made him, when he arrived at man's estate, the hereditary
keeper of a palace which he possessed in the north of England;
and this secured his grace a castle and a park. He could wave
his flag and kill his deer; and if he had only possessed an
estate, he would have been as well off as if he had helped to

conquer the realm with King William, or plundered the
church for King Harry. A revenue must, however, be found
for the Duke of Fitz-Aquitaine, and it was furnished without
the interference of Parliament, but with a financial dexterity
worthy of that assembly, to whom and not to our sovereigns
we are obliged for the public debt. The king granted the duke
and his heirs for ever a pension on the post-office, a light tax
upon coals shipped to London, and a tithe of all the shrimps
caught on the southern coast. This last source of revenue became in time, with the development of watering-places, extremely prolific. And so, what with the foreign courts and
colonies for the younger sons, it was thus contrived very re-
spectably to maintain the hereditary dignity of this great peer.

The present Duke of Fitz-Aquitaine had supported the
Reform Bill, but had been shocked by the Appropriation
clause;* very much admired Lord Stanley,* and was apt to
observe that, if that nobleman had been the leader of the conservative party, he hardly knew what he might not have done
himself. But the duke was an old whig, had lived with old
whigs all his life, feared revolution, but still more the necessity
of taking his name out of Brooks's, where he had looked in
every day or night since he came of age. So, not approving of
what was going on, yet not caring to desert his friends, he
withdrew, as the phrase runs, from public life; that is to say,
was rarely in his seat; did not continue to Lord Melbourne
the proxy* that had been entrusted to Lord Grey; and made
tory magistrates in his county, though a whig lord-lieutenant.

When forces were numbered, and speculations on the future
indulged in by the Tadpoles and Tapers, the name of the
Duke of Fitz-Aquitaine was mentioned with a knowing look,
and in a mysterious tone. Nothing more was necessary between Tadpole and Taper; but, if some hack *in statu pupillari*
happened to be present at the conference, and the gentle
novice, greedy for party tattle, and full of admiring reverence
for the two great hierophants of petty mysteries before him,
ventured to intimate his anxiety for initiation, the secret was
entrusted to him, 'that all was right there; that his grace only
watched his opportunity; that he was heartily sick of the present men; indeed, would have gone over with Lord Stanley
in 1835,* had he not had a fit of the gout, which prevented

him from coming up from the north; and though, to be sure, his son and brother did vote against the Speaker, still that was a mistake; if a letter had been sent, which was not written, they would have voted the other way, and perhaps Sir Robert might have been in at the present moment.'

The Duke of Fitz-Aquitaine was the great staple of Lady Firebrace's correspondence with Mr. Tadpole. 'Woman's mission' took the shape, to her intelligence, of getting over his grace to the conservatives. She was much assisted in these endeavours by the information which she so dexterously acquired from the innocent and incautious Lord Masque.

Egremont was seated at dinner to-day by the side of Lady Joan. Unconsciously to himself, this had been arranged by Lady Marney. The action of woman on our destiny is unceasing. Egremont was scarcely in a happy mood for conversation. He was pensive, inclined to be absent; his thoughts, indeed, were of other things and persons than those around him. Lady Joan, however, only required a listener; she did not make inquiries like Lady Maud, or impart her own impressions by suggesting them as your own. Lady Joan gave Egremont an account of the Aztec cities, of which she had been reading that morning, and of the several historical theories which their discovery had suggested; then she imparted her own, which differed from all, but which seemed clearly the right one. Mexico led to Egypt. Lady Joan was as familiar with the Pharaohs as with the Caciques of the new world. The phonetic system was despatched by the way. Then came Champollion; then Paris; then all its celebrities, literary and especially scientific; then came the letter from Arago received that morning; and the letter from Dr. Buckland expected to-morrow. She was delighted that one had written; wondered why the other had not. Finally, before the ladies had retired, she had invited Egremont to join Lady Marney in a visit to her observatory, where they were to behold a comet which she had been the first to detect.

Lady Firebrace, next to the duke, indulged in mysterious fiddle-faddle as to the state of parties. She, too, had her correspondents, and her letters received or awaited. Tadpole said this; Lord Masque, on the contrary, said that: the truth lay, perhaps, between them; some result, developed by the clear intelligence of Lady Firebrace, acting on the data with which they supplied her. The duke listened with calm excitement to the transcendental revelations of his Egeria. Nothing appeared to be concealed from her; the inmost mind of the sovereign; there was not a royal prejudice that was not mapped in her secret inventory; the cabinets of the whigs, and the clubs of the tories, she had the 'open sesame' to all of them. Sir Somebody did not want office, though he pretended to; and Lord Nobody did want office, though he pretended he did not. One great man thought the pear was not ripe; another that it was quite rotten; but then the first was coming on the stage, and the other was going off. In estimating the accuracy of a political opinion, one should take into consideration the standing of the opinionist.

At the right moment, and when she was sure she was not overheard, Lady Firebrace played her trump card, the pack having been previously cut by Mr. Tadpole.

'And whom do you think Sir Robert would send to Ireland?' and she looked up in the face of the Duke of Fitz-Aquitaine.

'I suppose the person he sent before,' said his grace.

Lady Firebrace shook her head.

'Lord Haddington will not go to Ireland again,' replied her ladyship, mysteriously; 'mark me. And Lord de Grey does not like to go; and if he did, there are objections. And the Duke of Northumberland, he will not go. And who else is there? We must have a nobleman of the highest rank for Ireland; one who has not mixed himself up with Irish questions; who had always been in old days for emancipation; a conservative, not an Orangeman. You understand. That is the person Sir Robert will send, and whom Sir Robert wants.'

'He will have some difficulty in finding such a person,' said the duke. 'If, indeed, the blundering affair of 1834 had not occurred, and things had taken their legitimate course, and we had seen a man like Lord Stanley, for instance, at the head of affairs, or leading a great party, why then indeed your friends the conservatives, for every sensible man must be a conservative, in the right sense of the word, would have stood in a very different position; but now—,' and his grace shook his head.

'Sir Robert will never consent to form a government again without Lord Stanley,' said Lady Firebrace.

'Perhaps not,' said the duke.

'Do you know whose name I have heard mentioned in a certain quarter as the person Sir Robert would wish to see in Ireland?' continued Lady Firebrace.

His grace lent his ear.

'The Duke of Fitz-Aquitaine,' said Lady Firebrace.

'Quite impossible,' said the duke. 'I am no party man; if I be anything, I am a supporter of the government. True it is, I do not like the way they are going on, and I disapprove of all their measures; but we must stand by our friends, Lady Firebrace. To be sure, if the country were in danger, and the Queen personally appealed to one, and the conservative party were really a conservative party, and not an old crazy faction, vamped up, and whitewashed into decency, one might pause and consider. But I am free to confess I must see things in a very different condition from what they are at present, before I could be called upon to take that step. I must see men like Lord Stanley—'

'I know what you are going to say, my dear Duke of Fitz-Aquitaine. I tell you again, Lord Stanley is with us heart and soul; and before long I feel persuaded I shall see your grace in the Castle of Dublin.'

'I am too old; at least, I am afraid so,' said the Duke of Fitz-Aquitaine, with a relenting smile.

CHAPTER 16

ABOUT three miles before it reaches the town, the river Mowe undulates through a plain. The scene, though not very picturesque, has a glad and sparkling character. A stone bridge unites the opposite banks by three arches of good proportion; the land about consists of meads of a vivid colour, or vegetable gardens to supply the neighbouring population, and whose various hues give life and lightness to the level ground. The immediate boundaries of the plain on either side are chiefly woods; above the crest of which in one direction expands the brown bosom of a moor. The cottages which are sprinkled about this scene, being built of stone, and on an ample scale, contribute to the idea of comfort and plenty which, with a serene sky and on a soft summer day, the traveller willingly associates with it.

Such were the sky and season in which Egremont emerged on this scene, a few days after the incidents recorded in our last chapter. He had been fishing in the park of Mowbray, and had followed the rivulet through many windings until, quitting the enclosed domain, it had forced its way through some craggy underwood at the bottom of the hilly moors we have noticed, and, finally entering the plain, lost itself in the waters of the greater stream.

Good sport had not awaited Egremont. Truth to say, his rod had played in a careless hand. He had taken it, though an adept in the craft when in the mood, rather as an excuse to be alone than a means to be amused. There are seasons in life when solitude is a necessity; and such a one had now descended on the spirit of the brother of Lord Marney.

The form of Sybil Gerard was stamped upon his brain. It blended with all his thoughts; it haunted every object. Who was this girl, unlike all women whom he had yet encountered, who spoke with such sweet seriousness of things of such vast import, but which had never crossed his mind, and with a kind of mournful majesty bewailed the degradation of her race? The daughter of the lowly, yet proud of her birth. Not a noble lady in the land who could boast a mien more complete, and none of them thus gifted, who possessed withal the fascinating simplicity that pervaded every gesture and accent of the daughter of Gerard.

Yes! the daughter of Gerard; the daughter of a workman at a factory. It had not been difficult, after the departure of Sybil, to extract this information from the garrulous wife of the weaver. And that father, – he was not unknown to Egremont. His proud form and generous countenance were still fresh in the mind's eye of our friend. Not less so his thoughtful speech; full of knowledge and meditation and earnest feeling! How much that he had spoken still echoed in the heart and rung in the brooding ear of Egremont. And his friend, too, that pale man with those glittering eyes, who, without affection, without pedantry, with artlessness on the contrary, and a degree of earnest singleness, had glanced like a master of philosophy at the loftiest principles of political science, was he too a workman? And are these then THE PEOPLE? If so, thought Egremont, would that I lived more among them! Compared with their converse, the tattle of our saloons has in it something humiliating. It is not merely that it is deficient in warmth, and depth, and breadth; that it is always discussing persons instead of principles, and cloaking its want of thought in mimetic dogmas, and its want of feeling in superficial raillery; it is not merely that it has neither imagination, nor fancy, nor sentiment, nor feeling, nor knowledge to recommend it; but it appears to me, even as regards manner and expression, inferior in refinement and phraseology; in short, trivial, uninteresting, stupid, really vulgar.

It seemed to Egremont that, from the day he met these persons in the Abbey ruins, the horizon of his experience had insensibly expanded; more than that, there were streaks of light breaking in the distance, which already gave a new aspect to much that was known, and which perhaps was ultimately destined to reveal much that was now utterly obscure. He could not resist the conviction that, from the time in question, his sympathies had become more lively and more extended; that a masculine impulse had been given to his mind; that he was inclined to view public questions in a light very different from that in which he had surveyed them a few weeks back, when on the hustings of his borough.

Revolving these things, he emerged, as we have stated, into the plain of the Mowe, and, guiding his path by the course of the river, he arrived at the bridge which a fancy tempted him to cross. In its centre was a man gazing on the waters below and leaning over the parapet. His footstep roused the loiterer, who looked round; and Egremont saw that it was Walter Gerard.

Gerard returned his salute, and said, 'Early hours on Saturday afternoon make us all saunterers;' and then, as their way was the same, they walked on together. It seemed that Gerard's cottage was near at hand, and, having inquired after Egremont's sport, and receiving for a reply a present of a brace of trout, – the only one, by-the-bye, that was in Egremont's basket, – he could scarcely do less than invite his companion to rest himself.

'There is my home,' said Gerard, pointing to a cottage recently built, and in a pleasing style. Its materials were of a fawn-coloured stone, common in the Mowbray quarries. A scarlet creeper clustered round one side of its ample porch; its windows were large, mullioned, and neatly latticed; it stood in the midst of a garden of no mean dimensions, but every bed and nook of which teemed with cultivation; flowers and vegetables both abounded, while an orchard rich with the promise of many fruits – ripe pears and famous pippins of the north and plums of every shape and hue – screened the dwelling from that wind against which the woods that formed its background were no protection.

'And you are well lodged! Your gardens does you honour.'

'I'll be honest enough to own I have no claim to the credit,' said Gerard. 'I am but a lazy chiel.'

They entered the cottage where a hale old woman greeted them.

'She was too old to be his wife, and too young to be my mother,' said Gerard, smiling; 'but she is a good creature, and has looked after me many a long day. Come, dame,' he said, 'thou'lt bring us a cup of tea,' 'tis a good evening beverage,' he added, turning to Egremont, 'and what I ever take at this time. And if you care to light a pipe, you will find a companion.'

'I have renounced tobacco,' said Egremont; 'tobacco is the tomb of love,' and they entered a neatly-furnished chamber, having that habitable look which the best room of a farm-house too often wants. Instead of the cast-off furniture of other establishments, at the same time dingy and tawdry, mock rosewood chairs and tarnished mahogany tables, it contained an oaken table, some cottage chairs made of beechwood, and a Dutch clock. But what surprised Egremont was the appearance of several shelves well lined with volumes. Their contents too on closer inspection were remarkable. They indicated a student of a high order. Egremont read the titles of works which he only knew by fame, but which treated of the loftiest and most subtle questions of social and political philosophy. As he was throwing his eye over them, his companion said, 'Ah! I see you think me as great a scholar as I am a gardener; but with as little justice: these books are not mine.'

'To whomsoever they belong,' said Egremont, 'if we are to judge from his collection, he has a tolerably strong head.'

'Ay, ay,' said Gerard, 'the world will hear of him yet, though he was only a workman, and the son of a workman. He has not been at your schools and your colleges, but he can write his mother tongue, as Shakespeare and Cobbett wrote it; and you must do that, if you wish to influence the people.'

'And might I ask his name,' said Egremont.

'Stephen Morley, my friend.'

'The person I saw with you at Marney Abbey?'

'The same.'

'And he lives with you.'

'Why, we kept house together, if you could call it so. Stephen does not give much trouble in that way. He only drinks water and only eats herbs and fruits. He is the gardener,' added Gerard, smiling. 'I don't know how we shall fare when he leaves me.'

'And is he going to leave you?'

'Why, in a manner he has gone. He has taken a cottage about a quarter of a mile up dale, and only left his books here, because he is going into ——shire in a day or two, on some business, that maybe will take him a week or so. The books are safer here you see for the present, for Stephen lives alone, and is a good deal away, for he edits a paper at Mowbray, and that must be looked after. He is to be my gardener still. I promised him that. Well done, dame,' said Gerard, as the old woman entered; 'I hope, for the honour of the house, a good brew. Now, comrade, sit down: it will do you good after your long stroll. You should eat your own trout if you would wait?'

'By no means. You will miss your friend, I should think?'

'We shall see a good deal of him, I doubt not, what with the garden and neighbourhood and so on; besides, in a manner, he is master of his own time. His work is not like ours; and though the pull on the brain is sometimes great, I have often wished I had a talent that way. It's a drear life to do the same thing every day at the same hour. But I never could express my ideas except with my tongue; and there I feel tolerably at home.'

'It will be a pity to see this room without these books,' said Egremont, encouraging conversation on domestic subjects.

'So it will,' said Gerard. 'I have got very few of my own. But my daughter will be able to fill the shelves in time, I warrant.'

'Your daughter; she is coming to live with you?'

'Yes; that is the reason why Stephen quits us. He only remained here until Sybil could keep my house, and that happy day is at hand.'

'That is a great compensation for the loss of your friend,' said Egremont.

'And yet she talks of flitting,' said Gerard, in rather a melancholy tone. 'She hankers after the cloister. She has passed a still, sweet life in the convent here; the Superior is the sister of my employer and a very saint on earth; and Sybil knows nothing of the real world except its sufferings. No matter,' he added more cheerfully; 'I would not have her take the veil rashly, but, if I lose her, it may be for the best. For the married life of a woman of our class, in the present condition of our country, is a lease of woe,' he added, shaking his head, 'slaves, and the slaves of slaves! Even woman's spirit cannot stand against it; and it can bear up against more than we can master.'

'Your daughter is not made for the common cares of life,' said Egremont.

'We'll not talk of them, said Gerard. 'Sybil has an English heart, and that's not easily broken. And you, comrade, you are a traveller in these parts, eh?'

'A kind of traveller; something in the way of your friend Morley – connected with the press.'

'Indeed! a reporter, eh? I thought you had something about you a little more knowing than we provincials.'

'Yes; a reporter. They want information in London as to the real state of the country, and this time of the year, Parliament not sitting—'

'Ah; I understand, a flying commission and a summer tour.

Well, I often wish I were a penman; but I never could do it. I'll read any day as long as you like, but that writing I could never manage. My friend Morley is a powerful hand at it. His journal circulates a good deal about here; and if, as I often tell him, he would only sink his high-flying philosophy and stick to old English politics, he might make a property of it. You'll like to know him?'

'Much.'

'And what first took you to the press, if I may ask?'

'Why – my father was a gentleman,' said Egremont in a hesitating tone, 'and I was a younger son.'

'Ah!' said Gerard, 'that is as bad as being a woman.'

'I had no patrimony,' continued Egremont, 'and I was obliged to work; I had no head I believe for the law; the church was not exactly in my way; and as for the army, how was I to advance without money or connexions! I had had some education, and so I thought I would turn it to account.'

'Wisely done! you are one of the working classes, and will enlist I hope in the great struggle against the drones. The natural friends of the people are younger sons, though they are generally enlisted against us. The more fools they; to devote their energies to the maintenance of a system which is founded on selfishness and which leads to fraud; and of which they are the first victims. But every man thinks he will be an exception.'

'And yet,' said Egremont, 'a great family, rooted in the land, has been deemed to be an element of political strength.'

'I'll tell you what,' said Gerard, 'there is a great family in this country, and rooted in it, of which we have heard much less than they deserved, but of which I suspect we shall very soon hear enough to make us all think a bit.'

'In this county?'

'Ay; in this county and every other one: I mean the PEOPLE.'

'Ah!' said Egremont, 'that family has existed for a long time.'

'But it has taken to increase rapidly of late, my friend – how may I call you?'

'They call me Franklin.'

'A good English name of a good English class that has disappeared. Well, Mr. Franklin, be sure of this, that the Population Returns of this country are very instructive reading.'

'I can conceive so.'

'I became a man when the bad times were beginning,' said Gerard; 'I have passed through many doleful years. I was a Franklin's son myself, and we had lived on this island at least no worse for a longer time than I care to recollect, as little as what I am now. But that's nothing; I am not thinking of myself. I am prosperous in a fashion; it is the serfs I live among of whom I am thinking. Well, I have heard, in the course of years, of some specifics for this constant degradation of the people; some thing or some person that was to put all right; and for my part, I was not unready to support any proposal or follow any leader. There was reform, and there was paper money, and no machinery, and a thousand other remedies; and there were demagogues of all kinds, some as base as myself, and some with blood in their veins almost as costly as flows in those of our great neighbour here, Earl de Mowbray, and I have always heard that was very choice: but I will frankly own to you, I never had much faith in any of these proposals or proposers; still they were a change, and that is something. But I have been persuaded of late that there is something going on in this country of more efficacy; a remedial power, as I believe, and irresistible; but whether remedial or not, at any rate a power that will mar all or cure all. You apprehend me?' I speak of the annual arrival of more than three hundred thousand strangers in this island. How will you feed them? How will you clothe them? How will you house them? They have given up butcher's meat; must they give up bread? And as for raiment and shelter, the rags of the kingdom are exhausted, and your sinks and cellars already swarm like rabbit warrens.'

' 'Tis an awful consideration,' said Egremont, musing.

'Awful,' said Gerard; ' 'tis the most solemn thing since the deluge. What kingdom can stand against it? Why, go to your history, you're a scholar, and see the fall of the great Roman empire; what was that? Every now and then, there came two or three hundred thousand strangers out of the forests, and crossed the mountains and rivers. They come to us every year, and in greater numbers. What are your invasions of the barbarous nations, your Goths and Visigoths, your Lombards and Huns, to our Population Returns!'

END OF THE SECOND BOOK

BOOK III

*

THE last rays of the sun, contending with clouds of smoke that drifted across the country, partially illumined a peculiar landscape. Far as the eye could reach, and the region was level, except where a range of limestone hills formed its distant limit, a wilderness of cottages, or tenements that were hardly entitled to a higher name, were scattered for many miles over the land; some detached, some connected in little rows, some clustering in groups, yet rarely forming continuous streets, but interspersed with blazing furnaces, heaps of burning coal, and piles of smouldering ironstone; while forges and engine chimneys roared and puffed in all directions, and indicated the frequent presence of the mouth of the mine, and the bank of the coal-pit. Notwithstanding the whole country might be compared to a vast rabbit warren, it was nevertheless intersected with canals, crossing each other at various levels; and though the subterranean operations were prosecuted with so much avidity that it was not uncommon to observe whole rows of houses awry, from the shifting and hollow nature of the land, still, intermingled with heaps of mineral refuse, or of metallic dross, patches of the surface might here and there be recognised, covered, as if in mockery, with grass and corn, looking very much like those gentlemen's sons that we used to read of in our youth, stolen by the chimneysweeps, and giving some intimations of their breeding beneath their grimy livery. But a tree or a shrub, such an existence was unknown in this dingy rather than dreary region.

It was the twilight hour; the hour at which in southern climes the peasant kneels before the sunset image of the blessed Hebrew maiden; when caravans halt in their long course over vast deserts, and the turbaned traveller, bending in the sand, pays his homage to the sacred stone and the sacred city; the hour, not less holy, that announces the cessation of English toil, and sends forth the miner and the collier to breathe the air of earth, and gaze on the light of heaven.

They came forth: the mine delivers its gang and the pit its bondsmen; the forge is silent and the engine is still. The plain is covered with the swarming multitude: bands of stalwart men, broad-chested and muscular, wet with toil, and black as the children of the tropics; troops of youth, alas! of both sexes, though neither their raiment nor their language indicates the difference; all are clad in male attire; and oaths that man might shudder at, issue from lips born to breathe words of sweetness. Yet these are to be, some are, the mothers of England! But can we wonder at the hideous coarseness of their language, when we remember the savage rudeness of their lives? Naked to the waist, an iron chain fastened to a belt of leather* runs between their legs clad in canvas trousers, while on hands and feet an English girl, for twelve, sometimes for sixteen hours a day, hauls and hurries tubs of coals up subterranean roads, dark, precipitous, and plashy; circumstances that seem to have escaped the notice of the Society for the Abolition of Negro Slavery.* Those worthy gentlemen too appear to have been singularly unconscious of the sufferings of the little trappers, which was remarkable, as many of them were in their own employ.

See, too, these emerge from the bowels of the earth! Infants of four and five years of age, many of them girls, pretty and still soft and timid; entrusted with the fulfilment of responsible duties, and the nature of which entails on them the necessity of being the earliest to enter the mine and the latest to leave it. Their labour indeed is not severe, for that would be impossible, but it is passed in darkness and in solitude. They endure that punishment which philosophical philanthropy has invented for the direst criminals,* and which those criminals deem more terrible than the death for which it is substituted. Hour after hour elapses, and all that reminds the infant trappers of the world they have quitted and that which they have joined, is the passage of the coal-waggons for which they open the air-doors of the galleries, and on keeping which doors constantly closed, except at this moment of passage, the safety of the mine and the lives of the persons employed in it entirely depend.

Sir Joshua, a man of genius and a courtly artist, struck by the seraphic countenance of Lady Alice Gordon, when a child of very tender years, painted the celestial visage in various attitudes on the same canvas, and styled the group of heavenly faces guardian angels!*

We would say to some great master of the pencil, Mr. Landseer,* or Mr. Etty,* go thou to the little trappers and do likewise!

A small party of miners approached a house of more pretension than the generality of the dwellings, and announcing its character by a flagrant sign of the Rising Sun. They entered it as men accustomed, and were greeted with smiles and many civil words from the lady at the bar, who enquired cheerfully what the gentlemen would have. They soon found themselves seated in the tap, and, though it was not entirely unoccupied, in their accustomed places; for there seemed a general understanding that they enjoyed a prescriptive right.

With hunches of white bread in their black hands, and grinning with their sable countenances and ivory teeth, they really looked like a gang of negroes at a revel.

The cups of ale circulated, the pipes were lighted, the preliminary puffs achieved. There was at length silence, when he who seemed their leader, and who filled a sort of president's seat, took his pipe from his mouth, and then uttering the first complete sentence that had yet been expressed aloud, thus delivered himself.

'The fact is, we are tommied to death.'

'You never spoke a truer word, Master Nixon,' said one of his companions.

'It's gospel, every word of it,' said another.

'And the point is,' continued Master Nixon, 'what are we for to do?'

'Ay, surely,' said a collier, 'that's the marrow.'

'Ay, ay,' agreed several; 'there it is.'

'The question is,' said Nixon, looking round with a magisterial air,' 'what *is* wages? I say, 'tayn't sugar, 'tayn't tea, 'tayn't bacon. I don't think 'tis candles; but of this I be sure, 'tayn't waistcoats.'

Here there was a general groan.

'Comrades,' continued Nixon, 'you know what has happened; you know as how Juggins applied for his balance after his tommy-book was paid up, and that incarnate nigger Diggs has made him take two waistcoats. Now the question rises, what is a collier to do with waistcoats? Pawn 'em I s'pose to Diggs' son-in-law, next door to his father's shop, and sell the ticket for sixpence. Now, there's the question; keep to the question; the question is waistcoats and tommy: first waistcoats, and then tommy.'

'I have been making a pound a-week these two months past,' said another, 'but, as I'm a sinner saved, I have never seen the young Queen's picture* yet.'

'And I have been obliged to pay the doctor for my poor wife in tommy,' said another. ' "Doctor," I said, says I, "I blush to do it, but all I have got is tommy, and what shall it be, bacon or cheese?" "Cheese at tenpence a pound," says he, "which I buy for my servants at sixpence! Never mind," says he, for he is a thorough Christian. "I'll take the tommy as I find it." '

'Juggins has got his rent to pay, and is afeard of the bums,'* said Nixon; 'and he has got two waistcoats!'

'Besides,' said another, 'Diggs' tommy is only open once a-week, and if you're not there in time, you go over for another seven days. And it's such a distance, and he keeps a body there such a time; it's always a day's work for my poor woman; she can't do nothing after it, what with the waiting, and the standing, and the cussing of Master Joseph Diggs; for he do swear at the women, when they rush in for the first turn, most fearful.'

'They do say he's a shocking little dog.'*

'Master Joseph is wery wiolent, but there is no one like old Diggs for grabbing a bit of one's wages. He do so love it! And then he says you never need be at no loss for nothing; you can find everything under my roof. I should like to know who is to mend our shoes. Has Gaffer Diggs a cobbler's stall?'

'Or sell us a penn'orth of potatoes,' said another. 'Or a ha'porth of milk.'

'No; and so to get them one is obliged to go and sell some tommy, and much one gets for it. Bacon at ninepence a-pound at Diggs', which you may get at a huckster's for sixpence; and therefore the huckster can't be expected to give you more than fourpence-halfpenny, by which token the tommy in our field just cuts our wages atween the navel.'

'And that's as true as if you heard it in church, Master Waghorn.'

'This Diggs seems to be an oppressor of the people,' said a voice from a distant corner of the room.

Master Nixon looked around, smoked, puffed, and then said, 'I should think he wor; as bloody-a-hearted butty[1] as ever jingled.'

'But what business has a butty to keep a shop?' inquired the stranger. 'The law touches him.'

'I should like to know who would touch the law,' said Nixon; 'not I for one. Them tommy-shops is very delicate things; they won't stand no handling, I can tell you that.'

'But he cannot force you to take goods,' said the stranger; 'he must pay you in current coin of the realm, if you demand it.'

'They only pay us once in five weeks,' said a collier; 'and how is a man to live meanwhile. And suppose we were to make shift for a month or five weeks, and have all our money coming, and have no tommy out of the shop, what would the butty say to me? He would say, "Do you want e'er a note this time?" and if I was to say, "No," then he would say, "You've no call to go down to work any more here." And that's what I call forsation.'

'Ay, ay,' said another collier; 'ask for the young Queen's picture, and you would soon have to put your shirt on, and go up the shaft.'

'It's them long reckonings that force us to the tommy-shops,' said another collier; 'and if a butty turns you away because you won't take no tommy, you're a marked man in every field about.'

'There's wuss things as tommy,' said a collier who had hitherto been silent, 'and that's these here butties. What's going on in the pit is known only to God Almighty and the colliers. I have been a consistent methodist for many years, strived to do well, and all the harm I have ever done to the

[1] A Butty in the mining districts is a middleman; a Doggy is his manager. The Butty generally keeps a Tommy or a Truck shop, and pays the wages of his labourers in goods. When miners and colliers strike, they term it 'going to play.' [Author's note.]

butties was to tell them that their deeds would not stand on the day of judgment.'

'They are deeds of darkness surely; for many's the morn we work for nothing, by one excuse or another, and many's the good stint that they undermeasure. And many's the cup of their ale that you must drink before they will give you any work. If the Queen would do something for us poor men, it would be a blessed job.'

'There ayn't no black tyrant on this earth like a butty, surely,' said a collier; 'and there's no redress for poor men.'

'But why do not you state your grievances to the landlords and lessees?' said the stranger.

'I take it you be a stranger in these parts, sir,' said Master Nixon, following up this remark by an enormous puff. He was the oracle of his circle, and there was silence whenever he was inclined to address them, which was not too often, though when he spoke, his words, as his followers often observed, were a regular ten-yard coal.*

'I take it you be a stranger in these parts, sir, or else you would know that it's as easy for a miner to speak to a main-master, as it is for me to pick coal with this here clay.* Sir, there's a gulf atween 'em. I went into the pit when I was five year old, and I counts forty year in the service come Martin-mas, and a very good age, sir, for a man that does his work, and I knows what I'm speaking about. In forty year, sir, a man sees a pretty deal, 'specially when he don't move out of the same spot and keeps his 'tention. I've been at play, sir, several times in forty year, and have seen as great stick-outs as ever happened in this country. I've seen the people at play for weeks together, and so clammed* that I never tasted no-thing but a potato and a little salt for more than a fortnight. Talk of tommy, that was hard fare, but we were holding out for our rights, and that's sauce for any gander. And I'll tell you what, sir, that I never knew the people play yet, but if a word had passed atween them and the main-masters afore-hand, it might not have been settled; but you can't get at them any way. Atween the poor man and the gentleman there never was no connection, and that's the wital mischief of this country.'

'It's a very true word, Master Nixon, and by this token

that when we went to play in '28, and the masters said they would meet us; what did they do but walk about the ground and speak to the butties. The butties has their ear.'

'We never want no soldiers here if the masters would speak with the men; but the sight of a pitman is pison to a gentleman, and if we go up to speak with 'em, they always run away.'

'It's the butties,' said Nixon; 'they're wusser nor tommy.'

'The people will never have their rights,' said the stranger, 'until they learn their power. Suppose, instead of sticking out and playing, fifty of your families were to live under one roof. You would live better than you live now; you would feed more fully, and be lodged and clothed more comfortably, and you might save half the amount of your wages; you would become capitalists; you might yourselves hire your mines and pits from the owners, and pay them a better rent than they now obtain, and yet yourselves gain more and work less.'

'Sir,' said Mr. Nixon, taking his pipe from his mouth, and sending forth a volume of smoke, 'you speak like a book.'

'It is the principle of association,' said the stranger; 'the want of the age.'

'Sir,' said Mr. Nixon, 'this here age wants a great deal, but what it principally wants is to have its wages paid in the current coin of the realm.'

Soon after this there were symptoms of empty mugs and exhausted pipes, and the party began to stir. The stranger addressing Nixon, inquired of him what was their present distance from Wodgate.

'Wodgate!' exclaimed Mr. Nixon with an unconscious air.

'The gentleman means Hell-house Yard,' said one of his companions.

'I'm at home,' said Mr. Nixon, 'but 'tis the first time I ever heard Hell-house Yard called Wodgate.'

'It's called so in joggraphy,' said Juggins.

'But you bayn't going to Hell-house Yard this time of night!' said Mr. Nixon. 'I'd as soon think of going down the pit with the windlass turned by lushy* Bob.'

' 'Tayn't a journey for Christians,' said Juggins.

'They're a very queer lot even in sunshine,' said another.

'And how far is it?' asked the stranger.

'I walked there once in three hours,' said a collier, 'but that was to the wake. If you want to see divils carnal, there's your time of day. They're no less than heathens, I be sure. I'd be sorry to see even our butty among them, for he is a sort of a Christian when he has taken a glass of ale.'

CHAPTER 2

Two days after the visit of Egremont to the cottage of Walter Gerard, the visit of the Marney family to Mowbray terminated, and they returned to the Abbey.

There is something mournful in the breaking up of an agreeable party, and few are the roofs in which one has sojourned, which are quitted without some feeling of depression. The sudden cessation of all those sources of excitement which pervade a gay and well-arranged mansion in the country unstrings the nervous system. For a week or so, we have done nothing which was not agreeable, and heard nothing which was not pleasant. Our self-love has been respected; there has been a total cessation of petty cares; all the enjoyment of an establishment without any of its solicitude. We have beheld civilisation only in its favoured aspect, and tasted only the sunny side of the fruit. Sometimes there are associations with our visit of a still sweeter and softer character, but on these we need not dwell: glances that cannot be forgotten, and tones that linger in the ear; sentiment that subdues the soul, and flirtation that agitates the fancy. No matter, whatever may be the cause, one too often drives away from a country-house rather hipped.* The specific would be immediately to drive to another, and it is a favourite remedy. But sometimes it is not in our power; sometimes, for instance, we must return to our household gods in the shape of a nursery; and though this was not the form assumed by the penates of Lord Marney, his presence, the presence of an individual so important and so indefatigable, was still required. His lordship had passed his time at Mowbray to his satisfaction. He had had his own way in everything. His selfishness had not received a single shock. He had laid down the law and it had not been questioned. He had dogmatised and impugned, and his assertions had passed current, and his doctrines had been accepted as orthodox. Lord de Mowbray suited him; he liked the consideration of so great a personage. Lord Marney also really liked pomp, a curious table, and a luxurious life; but he liked them under any roof rather than his own. Not that he was what is commonly called a Screw,* that is to say, he was not a mere screw; but he was acute and malicious; saw everybody's worth and position at a glance; could not bear to expend his choice wines and costly viands on hangers-on and toad-eaters, though at the same time no man encouraged and required hangers-on and toad-eaters more. Lord Marney had all the petty social vices, and none of those petty social weaknesses which soften their harshness or their hideousness. To receive a prince of the blood, or a great peer, he would spare nothing. Had he to fulfil any of the public duties of his station, his performance would baffle criticism. But he enjoyed making the Vicar of Marney or Captain Grouse drink some claret that was on the wane, or praise a bottle of Burgundy that he knew was pricked.*

Little things affect little minds. Lord Marney rose in no very good humour; he was kept at the station, which aggravated his spleen. During his journey on the railroad he spoke little, and though he more than once laboured to get up a controversy he was unable, for Lady Marney, who rather dreaded her dull home, and was not yet in a tone of mind that could hail the presence of the little Poinsett as full compensation for the brilliant circle of Mowbray, replied in amiable monosyllables, and Egremont himself in austere ones, for he was musing over Sybil Gerard and a thousand things as wild and sweet.

Everything went wrong this day. Even Captain Grouse was not at the Abbey to welcome them back. He was playing in a cricket match, Marney against Marham. Nothing else would have induced him to be absent. So it happened that the three fellow-travellers had to dine together, utterly weary of themselves and of each other. Captain Grouse was never more wanted; he would have amused Lord Marney, relieved his wife and brother, reported all that had been said and done in their neighbourhood during their absence, introduced a new tone, and effected a happy diversion. Leaving Mowbray, detained at the station, Grouse away, some disagreeable letters, or letters which an ill-humoured man chooses to esteem dis-agreeable, seemed to announce a climax. Lord Marney ordered the dinner to be served in the small dining-room, which was contiguous to a saloon in which Lady Marney, when they were alone, generally passed the evening.

The dinner was silent and sombre; happily it was also short. Lord Marney tasted several dishes, ate of none; found fault with his own claret, though the butler had given him a choice bottle; praised Lord Mowbray's, wondered where he got it, 'all the wines at Mowbray were good;' then for the twentieth time wondered what could have induced Grouse to fix the cricket match the day he returned home, though he chose to forget that he had never communicated to Grouse even the probable day on which he might be expected.

As for Egremont, it must be admitted that he was scarcely in a more contented mood than his brother, though he had not such insufficient cause for his dark humours. In quitting Mowbray, he had quitted something else than merely an agreeable circle: enough had happened in that visit to stir up the deep recesses of his heart, and to prompt him to investi-gate in an unusual spirit the cause and attributes of his posi-tion. He had found a letter on his return to the Abbey, not calculated to dispel these somewhat morbid feelings; a letter from his agent, urging the settlement of his election accounts, the primary cause of his visit to his brother.

Lady Marney left the dining-room; the brothers were alone. Lord Marney filled a bumper, which he drank off rapidly, pushed the bottle to his brother, and then said again, 'What a cursed bore it is that Grouse is not here!'

'Well, I cannot say, George, that I particularly miss the pre-sence of Captain Grouse,' said his brother.

Lord Marney looked at Egremont pugnaciously, and then observed, 'Grouse is a capital fellow; one is never dull when Grouse is here.'

'Well, for my part,' said Egremont, 'I do not much admire that amusement which is dependent on the efforts of hangers-on.'

'Grouse is no more a hanger-on than any one else,' said Lord Marney, rather fiercely.

'Perhaps not,' said Egremont quietly; 'I am no judge of such sort of people.'

'I should like to know what you are a judge of; certainly not of making yourself agreeable to young ladies. Arabella cannot be particularly charmed with the result of your visit to Mowbray, as far as Lady Joan is concerned, Arabella's most intimate friend, by-the-by. If for no other reason, you ought to have paid her more attention.'

'I cannot pay attention unless I am attracted,' said Egremont; 'I have not the ever-ready talent of your friend, Captain Grouse.'

'I do not know what you mean by my friend Captain Grouse. Captain Grouse is no more my friend than your friend. One must have people about the house to do a thousand things which one cannot do one's self, and which one cannot trust to servants, and Grouse does all this capitally.'

'Exactly; he is just what I said, a capital hanger-on if you like, but still a hanger-on.'

'Well, and what then? Suppose he is a hanger-on; may I not have hangers-on as well as any other man?'

'Of course you may; but I am not bound to regret their absence.'

'Who said you were? But I will regret their absence, if I choose. And I regret the absence of Grouse, regret it very much; and if he did happen to be inextricably engaged in this unfortunate match, I say, and you may contradict me, if you please, that he ought to have taken care that Slimsy dined here, to tell me all that had happened.'

'I am very glad he omitted to do so,' said Egremont; 'I prefer Grouse to Slimsy.'

'I dare say you do,' said Lord Marney, filling his glass and looking very black; 'you would like, I have no doubt, to see a fine gentleman-saint, like your friend Mr. St. Lys, at Marney, preaching in cottages, filling the people with discontent, lecturing me about low wages, soliciting plots of ground for new churches, and inveigling Arabella into subscriptions to painted windows.'

'I certainly should like to see a man like Aubrey St. Lys at Marney,' said Egremont quietly, but rather doggedly.

'And if he were here, I would soon see who should be master,' said Lord Marney; 'I would not succumb like Mowbray. One might as well have a jesuit in the house at once.'

'I dare say St. Lys would care very little about entering your house,' said Egremont. 'I know it was with great reluctance that he ever came to Mowbray Castle.'

'I dare say; very great reluctance indeed. And very reluctant he was, I make no doubt, to sit next to Lady Maud. I wonder he does not fly higher, and preach to Lady Joan; but she is too sensible a woman for such fanatical tricks.'

'St. Lys thinks it his duty to enter all societies. That is the reason why he goes to Mowbray Castle, as well as to the squalid courts and cellars of the town. He takes care that those who are clad in purple and fine linen shall know the state of their neighbours. They cannot at least plead ignorance for the non-fulfilment of their duty. Before St. Lys' time, the family at Mowbray Castle might as well have not existed, so far as benefiting their miserable vicinage. It would be well perhaps for other districts not less wretched, and for other families as high and favoured as the Mowbrays, if there were a Mr. St. Lys on the spot instead of a Mr. Slimsey.'

'I suppose that is meant for a cut,' said Lord Marney; 'but I wish the people were as well off in every part of the country as they are on my estate. They get here their eight shillings a-week, always at least seven, and every hand is at this moment in employ, except a parcel of scoundrels who prefer wood-stealing and poaching, and who would prefer wood-stealing and poaching if you gave them double the wages. The rate of wages is nothing: certainty is the thing; and every man at Marney may be sure of his seven shillings a week for at least nine months in the year; and for the other three, they can go to the House,* and a very proper place for them; it is heated with hot air, and has every comfort. Even Marney Abbey is not heated with hot air. I have often thought of it; it makes me mad sometimes to think of those lazy, pampered menials passing their lives with their backs to a great roaring fire; but I am afraid of the flues.'

'I wonder, talking of fires, that you are not more afraid of burning ricks,' said Egremont.

'It's an infernal lie,' said Lord Marney, very violently.

'What is ?' said Egremont.

'That there is any incendiarism in this neighbourhood.'

'Why, there was a fire the day after I came.'

'That had nothing to do with wages; it was an accident. I examined into it myself; so did Grouse, so did Slimsey; I sent them about everywhere. I told them I was sure the fire was purely accidental, and to go and see about it; and they came back, and agreed that it was purely accidental.'

'I dare say they did,' said Egremont; 'but no one has discovered the accident.'

'For my part, I believe it was spontaneous combustion,'* said Lord Marney.

'That is a satisfactory solution,' said Egremont; 'but for my part, the fire being a fact, and it being painfully notorious that the people of Marney—'

'Well, sir, the people of Marney?' said his lordship, fiercely.

'Are without question the most miserable population in the county—'

'Did Mr. St. Lys tell you that?' interrupted Lord Marney, white with rage.

'No, not Mr. St. Lys, but one better acquainted with the neighbourhood.'

'I'll know your informant's name,' said Lord Marney, with energy.

'My informant was a woman,' said Egremont.

'Lady Maud, I suppose; second-hand from Mr. St. Lys.'

'My informant was a woman, and one of the people', said Egremont.

'Some poacher's drab! I don't care what women say, high or low, they always exaggerate.'

'The misery of a family who live upon seven or even eight shillings a-week can scarcely be exaggerated.'

'What should you know about it? Did you ever live on seven or eight shillings a-week? What can you know about the people, who pass your time at London clubs or in fine country houses? I suppose you want the people to live as they do at a house dinner at Boodle's.* I say that a family can live well on seven shillings a-week, and on eight shillings very well indeed. The poor are well off, at least the agricultural poor, very well off indeed. Their incomes are certain, that is a great point, and they have no cares, no anxieties; they always have a resource, they always have the House. People without cares do not require so much food as those whose life entails anxieties. See how long they live! Compare the rate of mortality among them with that of the manufacturing districts. Incendiarism indeed! If there had been a proper rural police, such a thing as incendiarism would never have been heard of!'

There was a pause. Lord Marney dashed off another bumper; Egremont sipped his wine. At length he said, 'This argument made me forget the principal reason, George, why I am glad that we are alone together to-day. I am sorry to bore you, but I am bored myself deucedly. I find a letter from my agent. These election accounts must be settled.'

'Why, I thought they were settled.'

'How do you mean?'

'I thought my mother had given you a thousand pounds.'

'No doubt of that, but that was long ago disposed of.'

'In my opinion quite enough for a seat in these times. Instead of paying to get into Parliament, a man ought to be paid for entering it.'

'There may be a good deal in what you say,' said Egremont; 'but it is too late to take that view of the business. The expense has been incurred and must be met.'

'I don't see that,' said Lord Marney; 'we have paid one thousand pounds and there is a balance unsettled. When was there ever a contest without a balance being unsettled? I remember hearing my father often say that when he stood for this county, our grandfather paid more than a hundred thousand pounds, and yet I know to this day there are accounts unsettled. Regularly every year I receive anonymous letters threatening me with fearful punishment if I don't pay one hundred and fifty pounds for a breakfast at the Jolly Tinkers.'

'You jest: the matter indeed requires a serious vein. I wish these accounts to be settled at once.'

'And I should like to know where the funds are to come from! I have none. The quantity of barns I am building now is something tremendous! Then this rage for draining; it would dry up any purse. What think you of two million tiles this year? And rents, to keep up which we are making these awful sacrifices; they are merely nominal, or soon will be. They never will be satisfied till they have touched the land. That is clear to me. I am prepared for a reduction of five-and-twenty per cent.; if the corn-laws are touched it can't be less than that. My mother ought to take it into consideration and reduce her jointure accordingly. But I dare say she will not; people are so selfish; particularly as she has given you this thousand pounds, which in fact after all comes out of my pocket.'

'All this you have said to me before. What does it mean? I fought this battle at the instigation of the family, from no feeling of my own. You are the head of the family, and you were consulted on the step. Unless I had concluded that it was with your sanction, I certainly should not have made my appearance on the hustings.'

'I am glad you did, though,' said Lord Marney; 'Parliament is a great point for our class; in these days especially, more even than in the old time. I was truly rejoiced at your success, and it mortified the whigs about us confoundedly. Some people thought there was only one family in the world to have their Richmond or their Malton.* Getting you in for the old borough was really a coup.'

'Well, now to retain our interest,' said Egremont, 'quick payment of our expenses is the most efficient way, believe me.'

'You have got six years, perhaps seven,' said Lord Marney, 'and long before that I hope to find you the husband of Lady Joan Fitz-Warene.'

'I do not wish to connect the two contingencies,' said Egremont, firmly.

'They are inseparable,' said Lord Marney.

'What do you mean?'

'I mean that I think this pedantic acquittance of an electioneering account is in the highest degree ridiculous, and that I cannot interfere in it. The legal expenses are, you say, paid; and if they were not, I should feel myself bound, as the head of the family, to defray them, but I can go no further. I cannot bring myself to sanction an expenditure for certainly unnecessary, perhaps, and I much fear it, for illegal and immoral purposes.'

'That really is your determination?'

'After the most mature reflection, prompted by a sincere solicitude for your benefit.'

'Well, George, I have often suspected it, but now I feel

quite persuaded, that you are really the greatest humbug that ever existed.'

'Abuse is not argument. Mr. Egremont.'

'You are beneath abuse, as you are beneath every sentiment but one, which I entirely feel;' and Egremont rose from the table.

'You may thank your own obstinacy and conceit,' said Lord Marney. 'I took you to Mowbray Castle, and the cards were in your own hands if you chose to play them.'

'You have interfered with me once before on such a subject, Lord Marney,' said Egremont, with a kindling eye, and a cheek pallid with rage.

'You had better not say that again,' said Lord Marney, in a tone of menace.

'Why not?' asked Egremont, fiercely. 'Who and what are you to dare to address me thus?'

'I am your elder brother, sir, whose relationship to you is your only claim to the consideration of society.'

'A curse on the society that has fashioned such claims,' said Egremont, in a heightened tone: 'claims founded in selfishness, cruelty, and fraud, and leading to demoralization, misery, and crime.'

'Claims which I will make you respect, at least in this house, sir,' said Lord Marney, springing from his chair.

'Touch me at your peril!' exclaimed Egremont, 'and I will forget you are my mother's son, and cleave you to the ground. You have been the blight of my life; you stole from me my bride, and now you would rob me of my honour.'

'Liar and villain!' exclaimed Lord Marney, darting forward; but at this moment his wife rushed into the apartment, and clung to him. 'For Heaven's sake,' she exclaimed, 'what is all this? George, Charles, dearest George!'

'Let me go, Arabella.'

'Let him come on.'

But Lady Marney gave a piercing shriek, and held out her arms to keep the brothers apart. A sound was heard at the other door; there was nothing in the world that Lord Marney dreaded so much as that his servants should witness a domestic scene. He sprang forward to the door, to prevent any one

entering; partially opening it, he said Lady Marney was un-
well and desired her maid; returning, he found Arabella insensible on the ground, and Egremont vanished!

CHAPTER 3

IT was a wet morning; there had been a heavy rain since
dawn, which, impelled by a gusty south-wester, came driving
on a crowd of women and girls who were assembled before
the door of a still closed shop. Some protected themselves
with umbrellas; some sought shelter beneath a row of old
elms that grew alongside the canal that fronted the house.
Notwithstanding the weather, the clack of tongues was incessant.

'I thought I saw the wicket of the yard gates open,' said a
woman.

'So did I,' said her neighbour, 'but it was shut again immediately.'

'It was only Master Joseph,' said a third. 'He likes to see
us getting wet through.'

'If they would only let us into the yard, and get under one
of the workshop sheds, as they do at Simmon's,' said another.

'You may well say Simmon's, Mrs. Page; I only wish my
master served in his field.'

'I have been here since half-past four, Mrs. Grigsby, with
this chilt at my breast all the time. It's three miles for me here,
and the same back, and unless I get the first turn, how are
my poor boys to find their dinner ready when they come out
of the pit?'

'A very true word, Mrs. Page; and by this token, that last
Thursday, I was here by half-past eleven, certainly afore noon,
having only called at my mother-in-law's in the way, and it
was eight o'clock before I got home. Ah! it's cruel work, is
the tommy-shop.'

'How d'ye do, neighbour Prance?' said a comely dame,
with a large white basket. 'And how's your good man? They
was saying at Belfy's he had changed his service. I hear
there's a new butty in Mr. Parker's field; but the old doggy
kept on; so I always thought; he was always a favourite, and

they do say measured the stints* very fair. And what do you
hear bacon is in town? They do tell me only sixpence, and
real home-cured. I wonder Diggs has the face to be selling
still at ninepence, and so very green! I think I see Dame
Toddles; how wonderful she do wear! What are you doing
here, little dear; very young to fetch tommy; keeping place
for mother, eh! that's a good girl; she'd do well to be here
soon, for I think the strike's on eight. Diggs is sticking it on
yellow soap very terrible. What do you think – Ah! the doors
are going to open. No – a false alarm.'

'How fare you, neighbour?' said a pale young woman,
carrying an infant to the comely dame. 'Here's an awful
crowd, surely. The women will be fighting and tearing to get
in, I guess. I be much afeard.'

'Well, "first come, first served." all the world over,' said
the comely dame. 'And you must put a good heart on the
business, and tie your bonnet. I dare guess there are not much
less than two hundred here. It's grand tommy-day, you know.
And for my part, I don't care so much for a good squeedge;
one sees so many faces one knows.'

'The cheese here at sixpence is pretty tidy,' said a crone to
her companion; 'but you may get as good in town for fourpence.'

'What I complain is the weights,' replied her companion.
'I weighed my pound of butter bought last tommy-day and
it was two penny pieces too light. Indeed! I have been, in
my time, to all the shops about here, for the lads or their
father, but never knew tommy so bad as this. I have two
children at home ill from their flour; I have been very poorly
myself; one is used to a little white clay, but when they lay it
on thick, it's very grave.'

'Are your girls in the pit?'

'No; we strive to keep them out, and my man has gone
scores of days on bread and water for that purpose; and if
we were not forced to take so much tommy, one might
manage; but tommy will beat anything. Health first, and
honesty afterwards, that's my say.'

'Well, for my part,' said the crone, 'meat's my grievance:
all the best bits go to the butties, and the pieces with bone
in are chopped off for the colliers' wives.'

'Dame, when will the door open?' asked a little pale-faced boy. 'I have been here all this morn, and never broke my fast.'

'And what do you want, chilt?'

'I want a loaf for mother; but I don't feel I shall ever get home again, I'm all in a way so dizzy.'

'Liza Gray,' said a woman with black beady eyes, and a red nose, speaking in a sharp voice, and rushing up to a pretty slatternly woman in a straw bonnet, with a dirty fine ribbon, and a babe at her breast; 'you know the person I'm looking for.'

'Well, Mrs. Mullins, and how do you do?' she replied, in a sweet sawney* tone.

'How do you do, indeed! How are people to do in these bad times?'

'They is indeed hard, Mrs. Mullins. If you could see my tommy-book! How I wish I knew figures! Made up as of last Thursday night by that little devil, Master Joe Diggs. He has stuck it in here, and stuck it in there, till it makes one all of a maze. I'm sure I never had the things; and my man is out of all patience, and says I can no more keep house than a natural born.'

'My man is a-wanting to see your man,' said Mrs Mullins, with a flashing eye: 'and you know what about.'

'And very natural, too,' said Liza Gray; 'but how are we to pay the money we owe him with such a tommy-book as this, good neighbour Mullins?'

'We're as poor as our neighbours, Mrs. Gray; and if we are not paid, we must borrow. It's a scarlet shame to go to the spout* because money lent to a friend is not to be found. You had it in your need, Liza Gray, and we want it in our need; and have it I will, Liza Gray.'

'Hush, hush!' said Liza Gray; 'don't wake the little 'un, for she is very fretful.'

'I will have the five shillings, or I will have as good,' said Mrs. Mullins.

'Hush, hush, neighbour; now, I'll tell you, – you shall have it; but yet a little time. This is great tommy-day, and settles our reckoning for five weeks; but my man may have a draw after to-morrow, and he shall draw five shillings, and give you half.'

'And the other half?' said Mrs. Mullins.

'Ah! the other half,' said Liza Gray, with a sigh. 'Well, then, we shall have a death in our family soon: this poor babe can't struggle on much longer. It belongs to two burial clubs: that will be three pounds from each, and after the drink and the funeral, there will be enough to pay all our debts and put us all square.'

The door of Mr. Diggs' tommy-shop opened. The rush was like the advance into the pit of a theatre when the drama existed; pushing, squeezing, fighting, tearing, shrieking. On a high seat, guarded by rails from all contact, sat Mr. Diggs, senior, with a bland smile on his sanctified countenance, a pen behind his ear, and recommending his constrained customers in honeyed tones to be patient and orderly. Behind the substantial counter, which was an impregnable fortification, was his popular son, Master Joseph; a short, ill-favoured cur, with a spirit of vulgar oppression and malicious mischief stamped on his visage. His black, greasy lank hair, his pug nose, his coarse red face, and his projecting tusks, contrasted with the mild and lengthened countenance of his father, who looked very much like a wolf in sheep's clothing.

For the first five minutes Master Joseph Diggs did nothing but blaspheme and swear at his customers, occasionally leaning over the counter and cuffing the women in the van or lugging some girl by the hair.

'I was first, Master Joseph,' said a woman, eagerly.

'No; I was,' said another.

'I was here,' said the first, 'as the clock struck four, and seated myself on the steps, because I must be home early; my husband is hurt in the knee.'

'If you were first, you shall be helped last,' said Master Joseph, 'to reward you for your pains;' and he began taking the orders of the other woman.

'Oh! Lord have mercy on me!' said the disappointed woman; 'and I got up in the middle of the night for this!'

'More fool you! And what you came for I am sure I don't know,' said Master Joseph; 'for you have a pretty long figure against you, I can tell you that.'

'I declare most solemnly—' said the woman.

'Don't make a brawling here,' said Master Joseph, 'or I'll

jump over this here counter and knock you down, like no-think. What did you say, woman? are you deaf? what did you say? how much best tea do you want?'

'I don't want any, sir.'

'You never want best tea; you must take three ounces of best tea, or you shan't have nothing. If you say another word, I'll put you down four. You tall gal, what's your name, you keep back there, or I'll fetch you such a cut as 'll keep you at home till next reckoning. Cuss you, you old fool, do you think I am to be kept all day while you are mumbling here? Who's pushing on there? I see you, Mrs. Page. Won't there be a black mark against you! Oh! it's Mrs. Prance, is it? Father, put down Mrs. Prance for a peck of flour. I'll have order here. You think the last bacon a little too fat: oh! you do, ma'am, do you? I'll take care you shan't complain in future; I likes to please my customers. There's a very nice flitch hanging up in the engine-room; the men wanted some rust for the machinery; you shall have a slice of that; and we'll say tenpence a pound, high-dried, and wery lean; will that satisfy you?

'Order there, order; you cussed women, order, or I'll be among you. And if I just do jump over this here counter, won't I let fly right and left! Speak out, you idiot! do you think I can hear your muttering in this Babel? Cuss them; I'll keep them quiet:' and so he took up a yard measure, and, leaning over the counter hit right and left.

'Oh! you little monster!' exclaimed a woman, 'you have put out my babby's eye.'

There was a murmur; almost a groan. 'Whose baby's hurt?' asked Master Joseph, in a softened tone.

'Mine, sir,' said an indignant voice; 'Mary Church.'

'Oh! Mary Church, is it!' said the malicious imp; 'then I'll put Mary Church down for half a pound of best arrowroot; that's the nicest thing in the world for babbies, and will cure you of bringing your cussed monkeys here, as if you all thought our shop was a hinfant school.

'Where's your book, Susan Travers? Left at home! Then you may go and fetch it. No books, no tommy. You are Jones' wife, are you? Ticket for three and sixpence out of eighteen shillings wages. Is this the only ticket you have

brought? There's your money; and you may tell your husband he need not take his coat off again to go down our
shaft. He must think us cussed fools! Tell him I hope he has
got plenty of money to travel into Wales, for he won't have
no work in England again, or my name ayn't Diggs. Who's
pushing there? I'll be among you; I'll close the shop. If I do
get hold of some of you cussed women, you shan't forget it.
If anybody will tell me who is pushing there, they shall have
their bacon for sevenpence. Will nobody have bacon for
sevenpence? Leagued together, eh? Then everybody shall
have their bacon for tenpence. Two can play at that. Push
again, and I'll be among you,' said the infuriated little tyrant.
But the waving of the multitude, impatient and annoyed by
the weather, was not to be stilled; the movement could not
be regulated; the shop was in commotion; and Master Joseph
Diggs, losing all patience, jumped on the counter, and amid
the shrieks of the women, sprang into the crowd. Two women
fainted; others cried for their bonnets; others bemoaned their
aprons; nothing, however, deterred Diggs, who kicked and
cuffed and cursed in every quarter, and gave none. At last
there was a general scream of horror, and a cry of 'a boy
killed!'

The senior Diggs, who from his eminence had hitherto
viewed the scene with unruffled complacency; who, in fact,
derived from these not unusual exhibitions the same agreeable excitement which a Roman emperor might have received
from the combats of the circus; began to think that affairs
were growing serious, and rose to counsel order and enforce
amiable dispositions. Even Master Joseph was quelled by that
mild voice, which would have become Augustus. It appeared
to be quite true that a boy was dead. It was the little boy who,
sent to get a loaf for his mother, had complained before the
shop was opened of his fainting energies. He had fallen in the
fray, and it was thought, to use the phrase of the comely
dame who tried to rescue him, 'that he was quite smothered.'

They carried him out of the shop; the perspiration poured
off him; he had no pulse. He had no friends there. 'I'll stand
by the body,' said the comely dame, 'though I lose my turn.'

At this moment, Stephen Morley, for the reader has doubtless discovered that the stranger who held colloquy with the

colliers was the friend of Walter Gerard, arrived at the tommy-shop, which was about half-way between the house where he had passed the night and Wodgate. He stopped, inquired, and being a man of science and some skill, decided, after examining the poor boy, that life was not extinct. Taking the elder Diggs aside, he said, 'I am the editor of the Mowbray Phalanx; I will not speak to you before these people; but I tell you fairly you and your son have been represented to me as oppressors of the people. Will it be my lot to report this death and comment on it? I trust not. There is yet time and hope.'

'What is to be done, sir?' inquired the alarmed Mr. Diggs; 'a fellow-creature in this condition—'

'Don't talk, but act,' said Morley. 'There is no time to be lost. The boy must be taken upstairs and put to bed; a warm bed, in one of your best rooms, with every comfort. I am pressed for business, but I will wait and watch over him till the crisis is passed. Come, let you and I take him in our arms, and carry him upstairs through your private door. Every minute is precious.' And so saying, Morley and the elder Diggs entered the house.

CHAPTER 4

WODGATE,* or Wogate, as it was called on the map, was a district that in old days had been consecrated to Woden, and which appeared destined through successive ages to retain its heathen character. At the beginning of the revolutionary war, Wodgate was a sort of squatting district of the great mining region to which it was contiguous, a place where adventurers in the industry which was rapidly developing settled themselves; for though the great veins of coal and ironstone cropped up, as they phrase it, before they reached this bare and barren land, and it was thus deficient in those mineral and metallic treasures which had enriched its neighbourhood, Wodgate had advantages of its own, and of a kind which touch the fancy of the lawless. It was land without an owner; no one claimed any manorial right over it; they could build cottages without paying rent. It was a district recognised by no parish; so there were no tithes, and no meddlesome supervision. It abounded in fuel which cost nothing, for though the

veins were not worth working as a source of mining profit,
the soil of Wodgate was similar in its superficial character to
that of the country around. So a population gathered, and
rapidly increased, in the ugliest spot in England, to which
neither Nature nor art had contributed a single charm; where
a tree could not be seen, a flower was unknown, where there
was neither belfry nor steeple, nor a single sight or sound that
could soften the heart or humanize the mind.

Whatever may have been the cause, whether, as not un-
likely, the original squatters brought with them some traditionary skill, or whether their isolated and unchequered existence concentrated their energies on their craft, the fact is
certain, that the inhabitants of Wodgate early acquired a celebrity as skilful workmen. This reputation so much increased,
and in time spread so far, that, for more than a quarter of a
century, both in their skill and the economy of their labour,
they have been unmatched throughout the country. As manufacturers of ironmongery, they carry the palm from the whole
district; as founders of brass and workers of steel, they fear
none; while, as nailers and locksmiths, their fame has spread
even to the European markets, whither their most skilful
workmen have frequently been invited.

Invited in vain! No wages can tempt the Wodgate man from
his native home, that squatters' seat which soon assumed the
form of a large village, and then in turn soon expanded into a
town, and at the present moment numbers its population by
swarming thousands, lodged in the most miserable tenements
in the most hideous burgh in the ugliest country in the world.

But it has its enduring spell. Notwithstanding the spread of
its civic prosperity, it has lost none of the characteristics of its
original society; on the contrary, it has zealously preserved
them. There are no landlords, head-lessees, main-masters, or
butties in Wodgate. No church there has yet raised its spire;
and, as if the jealous spirit of Woden still haunted his ancient
temple, even the conventicle scarcely dares show its humble
front in some obscure corner. There is no municipality, no
magistrate; there are no local acts, no vestries, no schools of
any kind. The streets are never cleaned; every man lights his
own house; nor does any one know anything except his
business.

More than this, at Wodgate a factory or large establishment of any kind is unknown. Here Labour reigns supreme. Its division indeed is favoured by their manners, but the interference or influence of mere capital is instantly resisted. The business of Wodgate is carried on by master workmen in their own houses, each of whom possesses an unlimited number of what they call apprentices, by whom their affairs are principally conducted, and whom they treat as the Mamlouks* treated the Egyptians.

These master workmen indeed form a powerful aristocracy, nor is it possible to conceive one apparently more oppressive. They are ruthless tyrants; they habitually inflict upon their subjects punishments more grievous than the slave population of our colonies were ever visited with; not content with beating them with sticks or flogging them with knotted ropes, they are in the habit of felling them with hammers, or cutting their heads open with a file or lock. The most usual punishment, however, or rather stimulus to increase exertion, is to pull an apprentice's ears till they run with blood. These youths, too, are worked for sixteen and even twenty hours a day; they are often sold by one master to another; they are fed on carrion, and they sleep in lofts or cellars: yet, whether it be that they are hardened by brutality, and really unconscious of their degradation and unusual sufferings, or whether they are supported by the belief that their day to be masters and oppressors will surely arrive, the aristocracy of Wodgate is by no means so unpopular as the aristocracy of most other places.

In the first place, it is a real aristocracy; it is privileged, but it does something for its privileges. It is distinguished from the main body not merely by name. It is the most knowing class at Wodgate; it possesses indeed in its way complete knowledge; and it imparts in its manner a certain quantity of it to those whom it guides. Thus it is an aristocracy that leads, and therefore a fact. Moreover, the social system of Wodgate is not an unvarying course of infinite toil. Their plan is to work hard, but not always. They seldom exceed four days of labour in the week. On Sunday the masters begin to drink; for the apprentices there is dog-fighting without any stint. On Monday and Tuesday the whole population of Wodgate is

drunk; of all stations, ages, and sexes; even babes who should
be at the breast; for they are drammed with Godfrey's Cordial.
Here is relaxation, excitement; if less vice otherwise than
might be at first anticipated we must remember that excesses
are checked by poverty of blood and constant exhaustion.
Scanty food and hard labour are in their way, if not exactly
moralists, a tolerably good police.

There are no others at Wodgate to preach or to control.
It is not that the people are immoral, for immorality implies
some forethought; or ignorant, for ignorance is relative; but
they are animals; unconscious; their minds a blank; and their
worst actions only the impulse of a gross or savage instinct.
There are many in this town who are ignorant of their very
names; very few who can spell them. It is rare that you meet
with a young person who knows his own age; rarer to find
the boy who has seen a book, or the girl who has seen a
flower. Ask them the name of their sovereign, and they will
give you an unmeaning stare; ask them the name of their religion, and they will laugh: who rules them on earth, or who
can save them in heaven, are alike mysteries to them.

Such was the population with whom Morley was about to
mingle. Wodgate had the appearance of a vast squalid suburb.
As you advanced, leaving behind you long lines of little
dingy tenements, with infants lying about the road, you expected every moment to emerge into some streets, and encounter buildings bearing some correspondence, in their size
and comfort, to the considerable population swarming and
busied around you. Nothing of the kind. There were no
public buildings of any sort; no churches, chapels, town-hall,
institute, theatre; and the principal streets in the heart of the
town in which were situate the coarse and grimy shops,
though formed by houses of a greater elevation than the preceding, were equally narrow, and if possible more dirty. At
every fourth or fifth house, alleys seldom above a yard wide,
and streaming with filth, opened out of the street. These were
crowded with dwellings of various size, while from the principal court often branched out a number of smaller alleys, or
rather narrow passages, than which nothing can be conceived
more close and squalid and obscure. Here, during the days of
business, the sound of the hammer and the file never ceased,

amid gutters of abomination, and piles of foulness, and stagnant pools of filth; reservoirs of leprosy and plague, whose exhalations were sufficient to taint the atmosphere of the whole kingdom, and fill the country with fever and pestilence.

A lank and haggard youth, ricketty, smoke-dried, and black with his craft, was sitting on the threshold of a miserable hovel, and working at the file. Behind him stood a stunted and meagre girl, with a back like a grasshopper; a deformity occasioned by the displacement of the bladebone, and prevalent among the girls of Wodgate from the cramping posture of their usual toil. Her long melancholy visage and vacant stare at Morley, as he passed, attracted his notice, and it occurring to him that the opportunity was convenient to inquire something of the individual of whom he was in search, he stopped and addressed the workman.

'Do you happen to know, friend, a person here or hereabouts by name Hatton?'

'Hatton!' said the youth, looking up with a grin, yet still continuing his labour, 'I should think I did!'

'Well, that's fortunate; you can tell me something about him?'

'Do you see this here?' said the youth, still grinning, and, letting the file drop from his distorted and knotty hand, he pointed to a deep scar that crossed his forehead: 'he did that.'

'An accident?'

'Very like. An accident that often happened. I should like to have a crown for every time he has cut my head open. He cut it open once with a key, and twice with a lock; he knocked the corner of a lock into my head twice, once with a bolt, and once with a shut; you know what that is; the thing what runs into the staple. He hit me on the head with a hammer once. That was a blow! I fell away that time. When I came to, master had stopped the blood with some fur off his hat. I had to go on with my work immediately; master said I should do my stint if I worked till twelve o'clock at night. Many's the ash stick he has broken on my body; sometimes the weals remained on me for a week; he cut my eyelid open once with a nutstick; cut a regular hole in it, and it bled all over the files I was working at. He has pulled my ears sometimes that I thought they must come off in his hand. But all this was a mere nothin' to this here cut; that was serious; and if I hadn't got thro' that, they do say there must have been a crowner's quest; though I think that gammon, for old Tugsford did for one of his prentices, and the body was never found. And now you ask me if I know Hatton? I should think I did!' And the lank, haggard youth laughed merrily, as if he had been recounting a series of the happiest adventures.

'But is there no redress for such iniquitous oppression?' said Morley, who had listened with astonishment to this complacent statement. 'Is there no magistrate to apply to?'

'No, no,' said the filer, with an air of obvious pride; we don't have no magistrates at Wodgate. We've got a constable, and there was a prentice, who, coz his master laid it on only with a sear rod, went over to Ramborough and got a warrant. He fetched the summons himself, and give it to the constable, but he never served it. That's why they has a constable here.'

'I am sorry,' said Morley, 'that I have affairs with such a wretch as this Hatton.'

'You'll find him a wery hearty sort of man,' said the filer, 'if he don't hap to be in drink. He's a little robustious then, but take him all in all for a master, you may go further and fare worse.'

'What! this monster!'

'Lord bless you! it's his way, that's all; we be a queer set here; but he has his pints. Give him a lock to make, and you won't have your box picked; he's wery lib'ral too in the wittals. Never had horse-flesh the whole time I was with him; they has nothin' else at Tugsford's; never had no sick cow except when meat was very dear. He always put his face agin still-born calves; he used to say he liked his boys to have meat what was born alive, and killed alive. By which token there never was any sheep what had bust in the head sold in our court. And then sometimes he would give us a treat of fish, when it had been four or five days in town, and not sold. No, give the devil his due, say I. There never was no want for anything at meals with the Bishop, except time to eat them in.'

'And why do you call him the Bishop?'

'That's his name and authority; for he's the governor here over all of us. And it has always been so that Wodgate has been governed by a bishop; because, as we have no church,

we will have as good. And by this token that this day se'n-
night, the day my time was up, he married me to this here
young lady. She is of the Baptist school religion, and wanted
us to be tied by her clergyman, but all the lads that served
their time with me were married by the Bishop, and many a
more, and I saw no call to do no otherwise. So he sprinkled
some salt over a gridiron, read 'Our Father' backwards, and
wrote our name in a book: and we were spliced; but I didn't
do it rashly, did I, Suky, by the token that we had kept company for two years, and there isn't a gal in all Wodgate what
handles a file like Sue.'

'And what is your name, my good fellow?'

'They call me Tummas, but I ayn't got no second name;
but now I am married I mean to take my wife's, for she has
been baptized, and so has got two.'

'Yes, sir,' said the girl with the vacant face and the back
like a grasshopper; 'I be a reg'lar born Christian and my
mother afore me, and that's what few gals in the Yard can
say. Thomas will take to it himself when work is slack; and
he believes now in our Lord and Saviour Pontius Pilate, who
was crucified to save our sins; and in Moses, Goliath, and the
rest of the Apostles.'

'Ah! me,' thought Morley, 'and could not they spare one
Missionary from Tahiti for their fellow countrymen at Wodgate!'

CHAPTER 5

THE summer twilight had faded into sweet night; the young
and star-attended moon glittered like a sickle in the deep
purple sky; of all the luminous host Hesperus alone was
visible; and a breeze, that bore the last embrace of the flowers
by the sun, moved languidly and fitfully over the still and
odorous earth.

The moonbeam fell upon the roof and garden of Gerard.
It suffused the cottage with its brilliant light, except where
the dark depth of the embowered porch defied its entry. All
around the beds of flowers and herbs spread sparkling and
defined. You could trace the minutest walk; almost distin-

guish every leaf. Now and then there came a breath, and the
sweet-peas murmured in their sleep; or the roses rustled, as
if they were afraid they were about to be roused from their
lightsome dreams. Farther on the fruit trees caught the splendour of the night; and looked like a troop of sultanas taking
their garden air, when the eye of man could not profane them,
and laden with jewels. There were apples that rivalled rubies;
pears of topaz tint; a whole paraphernalia of plums, some
purple as the amethyst, others blue and brilliant as the sapphire;
an emerald here, and now a golden drop that gleamed like
the yellow diamond of Gengis Khan.

Within, was the scene less fair? A single lamp shed over
the chamber a soft and sufficient light. The library of Stephen
Morley had been removed, but the place of his volumes had
been partly supplied, for the shelves were far from being
empty. Their contents were of no ordinary character: many
volumes of devotion, some of church history, one or two on
ecclesiastical art, several works of our elder dramatists, some
good reprints of our chronicles, and many folios of church
music, which last indeed amounted to a remarkable collection.
There was no musical instrument of any kind, however, in
the room, and the only change in its furniture, since we last
visited the room of Gerard, was the presence of a long-backed
chair of antique form, beautifully embroidered, and a portrait
of a female saint over the mantel-piece. As for Gerard himself,
he sat with his head leaning on his arm, which rested on the
table, while he listened with great interest to a book which
was read to him by his daughter, at whose feet lay the fiery
and faithful bloodhound.

'So you see, my father,' said Sybil with animation and,
dropping her book, which, however, her hand did not relinquish, 'even then all was not lost. The stout earl retired
beyond the Trent, and years and reigns elapsed before this
part of the island accepted their laws and customs.'

'I see,' said her father, 'and yet I cannot help wishing that
Harold——' Here the hound, hearing his name, suddenly rose
and looked at Gerard, who, smiling, patted him and said, 'We
were not talking of thee, good sir, but of thy great namesake;
but ne'er mind, a live dog they say is worth a dead king.'

'Ah! why have we not such a man now,' said Sybil, 'to

protect the people! Were I a prince I know no career that I should deem so great.'

'But Stephen says no,' said Gerard: 'he says that these great men have never made use of us but as tools; and that the people never can have their rights until they produce competent champions from their own order.'

'But then Stephen does not want to recall the past,' said Sybil with a kind of sigh; 'he wishes to create the future.'

'The past is a dream,' said Gerard.

'And what is the future?' inquired Sybil.

'Alack! I know not; but I often wish the battle of Hastings were to be fought over again, and I was going to have a hand in it.'

'Ah! my father,' said Sybil with a mournful smile, 'there is ever your fatal specific of physical force. Even Stephen is against physical force, with all his odd fancies.'

'All very true,' said Gerard, smiling with good nature; 'but all the same when I was coming home a few days ago, and stopped awhile on the bridge and chanced to see myself in the stream, I could not help fancying that my Maker had fashioned these limbs rather to hold a lance or draw a bow that to supervise a shuttle or a spindle.'

'Yet with the shuttle and the spindle we may redeem our race,' said Sybil with animation, 'if we could only form the minds that move those peaceful weapons. Oh! my father, I will believe that moral power is irresistible, or where are we to look for hope?'

Gerard shook his head with his habitual sweet good-tempered smile. 'Ah!' said he, 'what can we do; they have got the land, and the land governs the people. The Normans knew that, Sybil, as you just read. If indeed we had our rights, one might do something; but I don't know; I dare say if I had our land again, I should be as bad as the rest.'

'Oh! no, my father,' exclaimed Sybil with energy, 'never, never! Your thoughts would be as princely as your lot. What a leader of the people you would make!'

Harold sprang up suddenly and growled.

'Hush!' said Gerard; 'some one knocks:' and he rose and left the room. Sybil heard voices and broken sentences: 'You'll excuse me:' 'I take it kindly:' 'So we are neighbours.'

And then her father returned, ushering in a person, and saying, 'Here is my friend Mr. Franklin, that I was speaking of, Sybil, who is going to be our neighbour; down, Harold, down!' and he presented to his daughter the companion of Mr. St. Lys in that visit to the hand-loom weaver when she had herself met the vicar of Mowbray.

Sybil rose, and letting her book drop gently on the table, received Egremont with composure and native grace. It is civilisation that makes us awkward, for it gives us an uncertain position. Perplexed, we take refuge in pretence; and embarrassed, we seek a resource in affectation. The Bedouin and the Red Indian never lose their presence of mind; and the wife of a peasant, when you enter her cottage, often greets you with a propriety of mien which favourably contrasts with your reception by some grand dame in some grand assembly, meeting her guests alternately with a caricature of courtesy or an exaggeration of supercilious self-control.

'I dare say,' said Egremont, bowing to Sybil, 'you have seen our poor friend the weaver since we met there.'

'The day I quitted Mowbray,' said Sybil. 'They are not without friends.'

'Ah! you have met my daughter before.'

'On a mission of grace,' said Egremont.

'And I suppose you found the town not very pleasant, Mr. Franklin,' returned Gerard.

'No; I could not stand it, the nights were so close. Besides, I have a great accumulation of notes, and I fancied I could reduce them into a report more efficiently in comparative seclusion. So I have got a room near here, with a little garden, not so pretty as yours; but still a garden is something; and if I want any additional information, why, after all, Mowbray is only a walk.'

'You say well, and have done wisely. Besides, you have such late hours in London, and hard work. Some country air will do you all the good in the world. That gallery must be tiresome. Do you use shorthand?'

'A sort of shorthand of my own,' said Egremont. 'I trust a good deal to my memory.'

'Ah! you are young. My daughter also has a wonderful

memory. For my own part, there are many things which I am not sorry to forget.'

'You see I took you at your word, neighbour,' said Egremont. 'When one has been at work the whole day one feels a little lonely towards night.'

'Very true; and I dare say you find desk work sometimes dull; I never could make anything of it myself. I can manage a book well enough, if it be well written, and on points I care for; but I would sooner listen than read any time,' said Gerard. 'Indeed I should be right glad to see the minstrel and the storyteller going their rounds again. It would be easy after a day's work, when one has not, as I have now, a good child to read to me.'

'This volume?' said Egremont, drawing his chair to the table, and looking at Sybil, who intimated assent by a nod.

'Ah! it's a fine book,' said Gerard, 'though on a sad subject,'

'The History of the Conquest of England by the Normans,' said Egremont, reading the title page, on which also was written, 'Ursula Trafford to Sybil Gerard.'

'You know it?' said Sybil.

'Only by fame.'

'Perhaps the subject may not interest you so much as it does us,' said Sybil.

'It must interest all, and all alike,' said her father; 'for we are divided between the conquerors and the conquered.'

'But do not you think,' said Egremont, 'that such a distinction has long ceased to exist?'

'In what degree?' asked Gerard. 'Many circumstances of oppression have doubtless gradually disappeared; but that has arisen from the change of manners, not from any political recognition of their injustice. The same course of time which has removed many enormities, more shocking, however, to our modern feelings than to those who devised and endured them, has simultaneously removed many alleviating circumstances. If the mere baron's grasp be not so ruthless, the champion we found in the church is no longer so ready. The spirit of Conquest has adapted itself to the changing circumstances of ages, and, however its results vary in form, in degree they are much the same.'

'But how do they show themselves?'

'In many circumstances, which concern many classes; but I speak of those which touch my own order; and therefore I say at once, in the degradation of the people.'

'But are the people so degraded?'

'There is more serfdom in England now than at any time since the Conquest. I speak of what passes under my daily eyes when I say, that those who labour can as little choose or change their masters now, as when they were born thralls. There are great bodies of the working classes of this country nearer the condition of brutes than they have been at any time since the Conquest. Indeed I see nothing to distinguish them from brutes, except that their morals are inferior. Incest and infanticide are as common among them as among the lower animals. The domestic principle wanes weaker and weaker every year in England; nor can we wonder at it, when there is no comfort to cheer and no sentiment to hallow the Home.'

'I was reading a work the other day,' said Egremont, 'that statistically proved that the general condition of the people was much better at this moment than it had been at any known period of history.'

'Ah! yes, I know that style of speculation,' said Gerard; 'your gentleman who reminds you that a working man now has a pair of cotton stockings, and that Harry the Eighth himself was not as well off. At any rate, the condition of classes must be judged of by the age, and by their relation with each other. One need not dwell on that. I deny the premises. I deny that the condition of the main body is better now than at any other period of our history; that it is as good as it has been at several. I say, for instance, the people were better clothed, better lodged, and better fed just before the War of the Roses than they are at this moment. We know how an English peasant lived in those times: he ate fish every day, he never drank water, was well housed, and clothed in stout woollens. Nor are the Chronicles necessary to tell us this. The Acts of Parliament from the Plantagenets to the Tudors, teach us alike the price of provisions and the rate of wages; and we see in a moment that the wages of those days brought as much sustenance and comfort as a reasonable man could desire.'

'I know how deeply you feel upon this subject,' said Egremont, turning to Sybil.

'Indeed it is the only subject that ever engages my thought,' she replied, 'except one.'

'And that one?'

'Is to see the people once more kneel before our blessed Lady,' replied Sybil.

'Look at the average term of life,' said Gerard, coming unintentionally to the relief of Egremont, who was a little embarrassed. 'The average term of life in this district among the working classes is seventeen. What think you of that? Of the infants born in Mowbray, more than a moiety die before the age of five.'

'And yet,' said Egremont, 'in old days they had terrible pestilences.'

'But they touched all alike,' said Gerard. 'We have more pestilence now in England than we ever had, but it only reaches the poor. You never hear of it. Why, Typhus alone takes every year from the dwellings of the artisan and peasant a population equal to that of the whole county of Westmoreland. This goes on every year, but the representatives of the conquerors are not touched; it is the descendants of the conquered alone who are the victims.'

'It sometimes seems to me,' said Sybil despondingly, 'that nothing short of the descent of angels can save the people of this kingdom.'

'I sometimes think I hear a little bird,' said Gerard, 'who sings that the long frost may yet break up. I have a friend, him of whom I was speaking to you the other day, who has his remedies.'

'But Stephen Morley does not believe in angels,' said Sybil with a sigh; 'and I have no faith in his plan.'

'He believes that God will help those who help themselves,' said Gerard.

'And I believe,' said Sybil, 'that those only can help themselves whom God helps.'

All this time Egremont was sitting at the table, with a book in his hand, gazing fitfully and occasionally with an air of absence on its title-page, whereon was written the name of its owner, Suddenly he said 'Sybil.'

'Yes,' said the daughter of Gerard, with an air of some astonishment.

'I beg your pardon,' said Egremont blushing; 'I was reading your name. I thought I was reading it to myself. Sybil Gerard! What a beautiful name is Sybil!'

'My mother's name,' said Gerard; 'and my grandame's name, and a name, I believe, that has been about our hearth as long as our race; and that's a very long time indeed.' he added, smiling, 'for we were tall men in King John's reign, as I have heard say.'

'Yours is indeed an old family.'

'Ay, we have some English blood in our veins, though peasants and the sons of peasants. But there was one of us who drew a bow at Azincourt; and I have heard greater things, but I believe they are old wives' tales.'

'At least we have nothing left,' said Sybil, 'but our old faith; and that we have clung to through good report and evil report.'

'And now,' said Gerard, 'I rise with the lark, good neighbour Franklin; but before you go, Sybil will sing to us a requiem that I love: it stills the spirit before we sink into the slumber which may this night be death, and which one day must be.'

CHAPTER 6

A BLOOM was spread over the morning sky. A soft golden light bathed with its fresh beam the bosom of the valley, except where a delicate haze, rather than a mist, still partially lingered over the river, which yet occasionally gleamed and sparkled in the sunshine. A sort of shadowy lustre suffused the landscape, which, though distinct, was mitigated in all its features: the distant woods, the clumps of tall trees that rose about the old grey bridge, the cottage chimneys that sent their smoke into the blue still air, amid their clustering orchards and gardens of flowers and herbs.

Ah! what is there so fresh and joyous as a summer morn! that spring time of the day, when the brain is bright, and the heart is brave; the season of daring and of hope; the renovating hour!

Forth from his cottage room came the brother of Lord Marney, to feel the vigorous bliss of life amid sunshiny gardens and the voices of bees and birds.

'Ah! this is delicious!' he felt. 'This is existence! Thank God I am here; that I have quitted for ever that formal and heartless Marney. Were it not for my mother I would remain Mr. Franklin for ever. Would I were indeed a journalist; provided I always had a mission to the vale of Mowbray. Or anything, so that I were ever here. As companions, independently of everything else, they are superior to any that I have been used to. Why do these persons interest me? They feel and they think: two habits that have quite gone out of fashion, if ever they existed, among my friends. And that polish of manners, that studied and factitious refinement, which is to compensate for the heartlessness of the stupidity we are doomed to; is my host of last night deficient in that refinement? If he do want our conventional discipline, he has a native breeding which far excels it. I observe no word or action which is not prompted by that fine feeling which is the sure source of good taste. This Gerard appears to me a real genuine man; full of knowledge worked out by his own head; with large yet wholesome sympathies; and a deuced deal better educated than Lord de Mowbray or my brother; and they do occasionally turn over a book, which is not the habit of our set.

'And his daughter; ay, his daughter! There is something almost sublime about that young girl, yet strangely sweet withal; a tone so lofty combined with such simplicity is very rare. For there is no affection of enthusiasm about her; nothing exaggerated, nothing rhapsodical. Her dark eyes and lustrous face, and the solemn sweetness of her thrilling voice, they haunt me; they have haunted me from the first moment I encountered her like a spirit amid the ruins of our abbey. And I am one of "the family of sacrilege." If she knew that! And I am one of the conquering class she denounces. If also she knew that! Ah! there is much to know! Above all, the future. Away! the tree of knowledge is the tree of death. I will have no thought that is not as bright and lovely as this morn.'

He went forth from his little garden, and strolled along the road in the direction of the cottage of Gerard, which was about three quarters of a mile distant. You might see almost as far; the sunshiny road a little winding and rising a very slight ascent. The cottage itself was hid by its trees. While Egremont was still musing of one who lived under that roof, he beheld in the distance Sybil.

She was springing along with a quick and airy step. Her black dress displayed her undulating and elastic figure. Her little foot bounded from the earth with a merry air. A long rosary hung at her side; and her head was partly covered with a hood which descended just over her shoulders. She seemed gay, for Harold kept running before her with a frolicsome air, and then, returning to his mistress, danced about her, and almost overpowered her with his gambols.

'I salute thee, holy sister,' said Egremont.

'Oh! is not this a merry morn!' she exclaimed, with a bright and happy face.

'I feel it as you. And whither do you go?'

'I go to the convent; I pay my first visit to our Superior since I left them.'

'Not very long ago,' said Egremont, with a smile, and turning with her.

'It seems so,' said Sybil.

They walked on together; Sybil, glad as the hour, noticing a thousand cheerful sights, speaking to her dog in her ringing voice, as he gambolled before them, or seized her garments in his mouth, and ever and anon bounded away and then returned, looking up in his mistress's face to inquire whether he had been wanted in his absence.

'What a pity it is that your father's way each morning lies up the valley,' said Egremont; 'he would be your companion to Mowbray.'

'Ah! but I am so happy that he has not to work in a town,' said Sybil. 'He is not made to be cooped up in a hot factory in a smoky street. At least he labours among the woods and waters. And the Traffords are such good people! So kind to him and to all.'

'You love your father very much.'

She looked at him a little surprised; and then her sweet serious face broke into a smile, and she said, 'And is that strange?'

'I think not,' said Egremont; 'I am inclined to love him myself.'

'Ah! you win my heart,' said Sybil, 'when you praise him. I think that is the real reason why I like Stephen; for otherwise he is always saying something with which I cannot agree, which I disapprove; and yet he is so good to my father!'

'You speak of Mr. Morley—'

'Oh! we don't call him "Mr.," ' said Sybil, slightly laughing.

'I mean Stephen Morley,' said Egremont, recalling his position, 'whom I met in Marney Abbey. He is very clever, is he not?'

'He is a great writer and a great student; and what he is he has made himself. I hear, too, that you follow the same pursuit,' said Sybil.

'But I am not a great writer or a great student,' said Egremont.

'Whatever you be, I trust,' said Sybil, in a more serious tone, 'that you will never employ the talents that God has given you against the People.'

'I have come here to learn something of their condition,' said Egremont. 'That is not to be done in a great city like London. We all of us live too much in a circle. You will assist me. 'I am sure,' added Egremont; 'your spirit will animate me. You told me last night that there was no other subject, except one, which ever occupied your thoughts.'

'Yes,' said Sybil, 'I have lived under two roofs, only two roofs; and each has given me a great idea; the Convent and the Cottage. One has taught me the degradation of my faith, the other of my race. You should not wonder, therefore, that my heart is concentrated on the Church and the People.'

'But there are other ideas,' said Egremont, 'that might equally be entitled to your thought.'

'I feel these are enough,' said Sybil; 'too great, as it is, for my brain.'

CHAPTER 7

At the end of a court in Wodgate, of rather larger dimensions
than usual in that town, was a high and many-windowed
house, of several stories in height, which had been added to it
at intervals. It was in a most dilapidated state; the principal
part occupied as a nail-workshop, where a great number of
heavy iron machines were working in every room on each
floor; the building itself in so shattered a condition that every
part of it creaked and vibrated with their motion. The flooring
was so broken that in many places one could look down
through the gaping and rotten planks, while the upper floors
from time to time had been shored up with props.

This was the Palace of the Bishop of Wodgate, and there,
with his arms bare and black, he worked at those locks, which
defied any skeleton key that was not made by himself. He was a
short, thickset man, powerfully made, with brawny arms dis-
proportionately short even for his height, and with a countenance, as far as one could judge of a face so disfigured by grimy
toil, rather brutal than savage. His choice apprentices, full of
admiration and terror, worked about him; lank and haggard
youths, who never for an instant dared to raise their dingy faces
and lack-lustre eyes from their ceaseless labour. On each side
of their master, seated on a stool higher than the rest, was an
urchin of not more than four or five years of age, serious and
demure, and as if proud of his eminent position, and working
incessantly at his little file: these were two sons of the bishop.

'Now, boys,' said the bishop, in a hoarse, harsh voice,
'steady, there; steady. There's a file what don't sing; can't
deceive my ear; I know all their voices. Don't let me find that
'un out, or I won't walk into him, won't I? Ayn't you lucky,
boys, to have reg'lar work like this, and the best of prog!* It
worn't my lot, I can tell you that. Give me that shut, you there,
Scubbynose, can't you move? Look sharp, or I won't move
you, won't I? Steady, steady! All right! That's music. Where
will you hear music like twenty files all working at once! You
ought to be happy, boys, oughtn't you? Won't there be a treat
of fish after this, that's all! Hulloa, there, you red-haired
varmint, what are you looking after? Three boys looking

about them; what's all this? won't I be among you?' and he sprang forward and seized the luckless ears of the first apprentice he could get hold of, and wrung them till the blood spouted forth.

'Please, bishop,' sang out the boy, 'it worn't my fault. Here's a man what want's you.'

'Who wants me?' said the bishop, looking round, and he caught the figure of Morley, who had just entered the shop.

'Well, what's your will? Locks or nails?'

'Neither,' said Morley; 'I wish to see a man named Hatton.'

'Well, you see a man named Hatton,' said the bishop; 'and now what do you want of him?'

'I should like to say a word to you alone,' said Morley.

'Hem! I should like to know who is to finish this lock, and to look after my boys! If it's an order, let's have it at once.'

'It is not an order,' said Morley.

'Then I don't want to hear nothing about it,' said the bishop.

'It's about family matters,' said Morley.

'Ah!' said Hatton, eagerly, 'what, do you come from him?'

'It may be,' said Morley.

Upon this the bishop, looking up to the ceiling of the room in which there were several large chinks, began calling out lustily to some unseen person above, and immediately was replied to in a shrill voice of objurgation, demanding in peremptory words, interlarded with many oaths, what he wanted. His reply called down his unseen correspondent, who soon entered his workshop. It was the awful presence of Mrs. Hatton; a tall bearded virago, with a file in her hand, for that seemed the distinctive arm of the house, and eyes flashing with unbridled power.

'Look after the boys,' said Hatton, 'for I have business.'

'Won't I?' said Mrs. Hatton; and a thrill of terror pervaded the assembly. All the files moved in regular melody; no one dared to raise his face; even her two young children looked still more serious and demure. Not that any being present flattered himself for an instant that the most sedulous attention on his part could prevent an outbreak; all that each aspired to, and wildly hoped, was that he might not be the victim singled out to have his head cut open, or his eye knocked out, or his ears half pulled off by the being who was the terror not only of the workshop, but of Wodgate itself; their bishop's gentle wife.

In the meantime, that worthy, taking Morley into a room where there were no machines at work except those made of iron, said, 'Well, what have you brought me?'

'In the first place,' said Morley, 'I would speak to you of your brother.'

'I concluded that,' said Hatton, 'when you spoke of family matters bringing you here; he is the only relation I have in this world, and therefore it must be of him.'

'It is of him,' said Morley.

'Has he sent anything?'

'Hem!' said Morley, who was by nature a diplomatist, and instantly comprehended his position, being himself pumped when he came to pump; but he resolved not to precipitate the affair. 'How late it is since you heard from him?' he asked.

'Why, I suppose you know,' said Hatton; 'I heard as usual.'

'From his usual place?' inquired Morley.

'I wish you would tell me where that is,' said Hatton, eagerly.

'Why, he writes to you?'

'Blank letters; never had a line except once, and that is more than twelve year ago. He sends me a twenty-pound note every Christmas; and that is all I know about him.'

'Then he is rich, and well to do in the world?' said Morley.

'Why, don't you know?' said Hatton; 'I thought you came from him!'

'I came about him. I wished to know whether he were alive, and that you have been able to inform me: and where he was; and that you have not been able to inform me.'

'Why, you're a regular muff!' said the bishop.

CHAPTER 8

A FEW days after his morning walk with Sybil, it was agreed that Egremont should visit Mr. Trafford's factory, which he had expressed a great desire to inspect. Gerard always left his cottage at break of dawn, and as Sybil had not yet paid her accustomed visit to her friend and patron, who was the employer of her father, it was arranged that Egremont should accompany her at a later and more convenient hour in the morning, and then that they should all return together.

The factory was about a mile distant from their cottage, which belonged indeed to Mr. Trafford, and had been built by him. He was the younger son of a family that had for centuries been planted in the land, but who, not satisfied with the factitious consideration with which society compensates the junior members of a territorial house for their entailed poverty, had availed himself of some opportunities that offered themselves, and had devoted his energies to those new sources of wealth that were unknown to his ancestors. His operations at first had been extremely limited, like his fortunes; but with a small capital though his profits were not considerable, he at least gained experience. With gentle blood in his veins, and old English feelings, he imbibed, at an early period of his career, a correct conception of the relations which should subsist between the employer and the employed. He felt that between them there should be other ties than the payment and the receipt of wages.

A distant and childless relative, who made him a visit, pleased with his energy and enterprise, and touched by the development of his social views, left him a considerable sum, at a moment, too, when a great opening was offered to manufacturing capital and skill. Trafford, schooled in rigid fortunes, and formed by struggle, if not by adversity, was ripe for the occasion, and equal to it. He became very opulent, and he lost no time in carrying into life and being the plans which he had brooded over in the years when his good thoughts were limited to dreams. On the banks of his native Mowe he had built a factory, which was now one of the marvels of the district; one might almost say, of the country; a single room, spreading over nearly two acres, and holding more than two thousand workpeople. The roof of groined arches, lighted by ventilating domes at the height of eighteen feet, was supported by hollow cast-iron columns, through which the drainage of the roof was effected. The height of the ordinary rooms in which the workpeople in manufactories are engaged, is not more than from nine to eleven feet; and these are built in stories, the heat and effluvia of the lower rooms communicated to those above, and the difficulty of ventilation insurmountable. At Mr. Trafford's, by an ingenious process, not unlike that which is practised in the House of Commons, the ventilation was also carried on from below, so that the whole building was kept at a steady temperature, and little susceptible to atmospheric influence. The physical advantages of thus carrying on the whole work in one chamber are great: in the improved health of the people, the security against dangerous accidents to women and youth, and the reduced fatigue resulting from not having to ascend and descend, and carry materials to the higher rooms. But the moral advantages resulting from superior inspection and general observation are not less important: the child works under the eye of the parent, the parent under that of the superior workman; the inspector or employer at a glance can behold all.

When the workpeople of Mr. Trafford left his factory they were not forgotten. Deeply had he pondered on the influence of the employer on the health and content of his workpeople. He knew well that the domestic virtues are dependent in the existence of a home, and one of his first efforts had been to build a village where every family might be well lodged. Though he was the principal proprietor, and proud of that character, he nevertheless encouraged his workmen to purchase the fee: there were some who had saved sufficient money to effect this; proud of their house and their little garden, and of the horticultural society, where its produce permitted them to be annual competitors. In every street there was a well: behind the factory were the public baths; the schools were under the direction of the perpetual curate of the church, which Mr. Trafford, though a Roman Catholic, had raised and endowed. In the midst of this village, surrounded by beautiful gardens, which gave an impulse to the horticulture of the community, was the house of Trafford himself, who comprehended his position too well to withdraw himself with vulgar exclusiveness from his real dependents, but recognised the baronial principle, reviving in a new form, and adapted to the softer manners and more ingenious circumstances of the times.

And what was the influence of such an employer and such a system of employment on the morals and manners of the employed? Great; infinitely beneficial. The connection of a

labourer with his place of work, whether agricultural or manufacturing, is itself a vast advantage. Proximity to the employer
brings cleanliness and order, because it brings observation and
encouragement. In the settlement of Trafford crime was positively unknown, and offences were slight. There was not a
single person in the village of a reprobate character. The men
were well clad; the women had a blooming cheek; drunken-
ness was unknown; while the moral condition of the softer sex
was proportionately elevated.

The vast form of the spreading factory, the roofs and gardens of the village, the Tudor chimneys of the house of
Trafford, the spire of the gothic church, with the sparkling
river and the sylvan background, came rather suddenly on the
sight of Egremont. They were indeed in the pretty village-
street before he was aware he was about to enter it. Some
beautiful children rushed out of a cottage and flew to Sybil,
crying out, 'the queen, the queen;' one clinging to her dress,
another seizing her arm, and a third, too small to struggle,
pouting out its lips to be embraced.

'My subjects,' said Sybil laughing, as she greeted them all;
and then they ran away to announce to others that their queen
had arrived.

Others came; beautiful and young. As Sybil and Egremont
walked along, the race too tender for labour seemed to spring
out of every cottage to greet 'their queen.' Her visits had been
rare of late, but they were never forgotten; they formed epochs
in the village annals of the children, some of whom knew only
by tradition the golden age when Sybil Gerard lived at the
great house, and daily glanced like a spirit among their homes,
smiling and met with smiles, blessing and ever blessed.

'And here,' she said to Egremont, 'I must bid you good
bye; and this little boy,' touching gently on his head a serious
urchin who had never left her side for a moment, proud of his
position, and holding tight her hand with all his strength, 'this
little boy shall be your guide. It is not a hundred yards. Now,
Pierce, you must take Mr. Franklin to the factory, and ask for
Mr. Gerard.' And she went her way.

They had not separated five minutes, when the sound of
whirling wheels caught the ear of Egremont, and, looking
round, he saw a cavalcade of great pretension rapidly ap-

proaching; dames and cavaliers on horseback; a brilliant equipage, postilions and four horses; a crowd of grooms. Egremont stood aside. The horsemen and horsewomen caracoled gaily by him; proudly swept on the sparkling barouche; the saucy grooms pranced in his face. Their masters and mistresses were not strangers to him: he recognised with some dismay the liveries, and then the arms of Lord de Mowbray, and caught the cold, proud countenance of Lady Joan, and the flexible visage of Lady Maud, both on horseback, and surrounded by admiring cavaliers.

Egremont flattered himself that he had not been recognised, and, dismissing his little guide, instead of proceeding to the factory, he sauntered away in an opposite direction, and made a visit to the church.

The wife of Trafford embraced Sybil, and then embraced her again. She seemed as happy as the children of the village, that the joy of her roof, as of so many others, had returned to them, though only for a few hours. Her husband she said had just quitted the house; he was obliged to go to the factory to receive a great and distinguished party who were expected this morning, having written to him several days before for permission to view the works. 'We expect them to lunch here afterwards,' said Mrs. Trafford, a refined woman, but unused to society, and who rather trembled at the ceremony; 'Oh! do stay with me, Sybil, to receive them.'

This intimation so much alarmed Sybil that she rose as soon as was practicable; and saying that she had some visits to make in the village, she promised to return when Mrs. Trafford was less engaged.

An hour elapsed; there was a loud ring at the hall-door, the great and distinguished party had arrived. Mrs. Trafford prepared for the interview, and looked a little frightened as the doors opened, and her husband ushered in and presented to her Lord and Lady de Mowbray, their daughters, Lady Firebrace, Mr. Jermyn, who still lingered at the castle, and Mr. Alfred Mountchesney and Lord Milford, who were mere passing guests, on their way to Scotland, but reconnoitering the heiresses in their course.

Lord de Mowbray was profuse of praise and compliments. His lordship was apt to be too civil. The breed would come out sometimes. To-day he was quite the coffee-house waiter. He praised everything: the machinery, the workmen, the cotton manufactured and the cotton raw, even the smoke. But Mrs. Trafford would not have the smoke defended, and his lordship gave up the smoke, but only to please her. As for Lady de Mowbray, she was as usual courteous and condescending, with a kind of smouldering smile on her fair aquiline face, that seemed half pleasure and half surprise at the strange people she was among. Lady Joan was haughty and scientific, approved of much, but principally of the system of ventilation, of which she asked several questions which greatly perplexed Mrs. Trafford, who slightly blushed, and looked at her husband for relief, but he was engaged with Lady Maud, who was full of enthusiasm, entered into everything with the zest of sympathy, identified herself with the factory system almost as much as she had done with the crusades, and longed to teach in singing schools, found public gardens, and bid fountains flow and sparkle for the people.

'I think the works were wonderful,' said Lord Milford, as he was cutting a pasty; 'and indeed, Mrs. Trafford, everything here is charming; but what I have most admired at your place, is a young girl we met; the most beautiful I think I ever saw.'

'With the most beautiful dog,' said Mr. Mountchesney.

'Oh! that must have been Sybil!' exclaimed Mrs. Trafford.

'And who is Sybil?' asked Lady Maud. 'That is one of our family names. We all thought her quite beautiful.'

'She is a child of the house,' said Mrs. Trafford, 'or rather was, for I am sorry to say she has long quitted us.'

'Is she a nun?' asked Lord Milford, 'for her vestments had a conventual air.'

'She has just left your convent at Mowbray,' said Mr. Trafford, addressing his answer to Lady Maud, 'and rather against her will. She clings to the dress she was accustomed to there.'

'And now she resides with you?'

'No; I should be happy if she did. I might almost say she was brought up under this roof. She lives now with her father.'

'And who is so fortunate as to be her father?' inquired Mr. Mountchesney.

'Her father is the inspector of my works; the person who accompanied us over them this morning.'

'What! that handsome man I so much admired,' said Lady Maud, 'so very aristocratic-looking. Papa,' she said, addressing herself to Lord de Mowbray, 'the inspector of Mr. Trafford's works we are speaking of, that aristocratic-looking person that I observed to you, he is the father of the beautiful girl.'

'He seemed a very intelligent person,' said Lord de Mowbray, with many smiles.

'Yes,' said Mr. Trafford; 'he has great talents and great integrity. I would trust him with anything and to any amount. All I wish,' he added, with a smile and in a lower tone to Lady de Mowbray, 'all I wish is, that he was not quite so fond of politics.'

'Is he very violent?' inquired her ladyship, in a sugary tone.

'Too violent,' said Mr. Trafford; 'and wild in his ideas.'

'And yet I suppose,' said Lord Milford, 'he must be very well off?'

'Why I must say for him it is not selfishness that makes him a malcontent,' said Mr. Trafford; 'he bemoans the condition of the people.'

'If we are to judge of the condition of the people by what we see here,' said Lord de Mowbray, 'there is little to lament in it. But I fear these are instances not so common as we could wish. You must have been at a great outlay, Mr. Trafford?'

'Why,' said Mr. Trafford, 'for my part, I have always considered that there was nothing so expensive as a vicious population. I hope I had other objects in view in what I have done than a pecuniary compensation. They say we all have our hobbies; and it was ever mine to improve the condition of my workpeople, to see what good tenements, and good schools, and just wages paid in a fair manner, and the encouragement of civilizing pursuits, would do to elevate their character. I should find an ample reward in the moral tone and material happiness of this community; but really viewing it in a pecuniary point of view, the investment of capital has been one of the most profitable I ever made; and I would not, I assure you, for double its amount, exchange my workpeople for the promiscuous assemblage engaged in other factories.'

'The influence of the atmosphere on the condition of the

labourer is a subject which deserves investigation,' said Lady Joan to Mr. Jermyn, who stared and bowed.

'And you do not feel alarmed at having a person of such violent opinions as your inspector at the head of your establishment?' said Lady Firebrace to Mr. Trafford, who smiled a negative.

'What is the name of the intelligent individual who accompanied us?' inquired Lord de Mowbray.

'His name is Gerard,' said Mr. Trafford.

'I believe a common name in these parts,' said Lord de Mowbray, looking a little confused.

'Not very,' said Mr. Trafford; ' 'tis an old name, and the stock has spread; but all Gerards claim a common lineage, I believe, and my inspector has gentle blood, they say, in his veins.'

'He looks as if he had,' said Lady Maud.

'All persons with good names affect good blood,' said Lord de Mowbray; and then turning to Mrs. Trafford he overwhelmed her with elaborate courtesies of phrase; praised everything again: first generally and then in detail; the factory, which he seemed to prefer to his castle; the house, which he seemed to prefer even to the factory; the gardens, from which he anticipated even greater gratification than from the house. And this led to an expression of a hope that he would visit them. And so in due time the luncheon was achieved. Mrs. Trafford looked at her guests, there was a rustling and a stir, and everybody was to go and see the gardens that Lord de Mowbray had so much praised.

'I am all for looking after the beautiful Nun,' said Mr. Mountchesney to Lord Milford.

'I think I shall ask the respectable manufacturer to introduce me to her,' replied his lordship.

In the meantime Egremont had joined Gerard at the factory.

'You should have come sooner,' said Gerard, 'and then you might have gone round with the fine folks. We have had a grand party here from the castle.'

'So I perceived,' said Egremont, 'and withdrew.'

'Ah! they were not in your way, eh?' he said in a mocking smile. 'Well, they were very condescending; at least for such great people. An earl! Earl de Mowbray; I suppose he came

over with William the Conqueror. Mr. Trafford makes a show
of the place, and it amuses their visitors, I dare say, like anything else that's strange. There were some young gentlemen
with them, who did not seem to know much about anything.
I thought I had a right to be amused too; and I must say I liked
very much to see one of them looking at the machinery
through his eye-glass. There was one very venturesome chap:
I thought he was going to catch hold of the fly-wheel, but I
gave him a spin which I believe, saved his life, though he did
rather stare. He was a lord.'

'They are great heiresses, his daughters, they say at Mowbray,' said Egremont.

'I dare say,' said Gerard. 'A year ago this earl had a son, an
only son, and then his daughters were not great heiresses. But
the son died, and now it's their turn. And perhaps some day it
will be somebody else's turn. If you want to understand the
ups and downs of life, there's nothing like the parchment of an
estate. Now master, now man! He who served in the hall now
lords in it; and very often the baseborn change their liveries
for coronets, while gentle blood has nothing left but – dreams;
eh, Master Franklin?'

'It seems you know the history of this Lord de Mowbray?'

'Why a man learns a good many things in his time; and
living in these parts, there are few secrets of the notables. He
has had the title to his broad acres questioned before this time,
my friend.'

'Indeed!'

'Yes; I could not help thinking of that to-day,' said Gerard,
'when he questioned me with his mincing voice and pulled
the wool with his cursed white hands and showed it to his
dame, who touched it with her little finger; and his daughters
who tossed their heads like peahens, Lady Joan and Lady
Maud. Lady Joan and Lady Maud!' repeated Gerard in a voice
of bitter sarcasm. 'I did not care for the rest; but I could not
stand that Lady Joan and that Lady Maud. I wonder if my
Sybil saw them.'

In the meantime, Sybil had been sent for by Mrs. Trafford.
She had inferred from the message that the guests had departed, and her animated cheek showed the eagerness with
which she had responded to the call. Bounding along with a

gladness of the heart which lent additional lustre to her transcendent brightness, she suddenly found herself surrounded in the garden by Lady Maud and her friends. The daughter of Lord de Mowbray, who could conceive nothing but humility as the cause of her alarmed look, attempted to re-assure her by condescending volubility, turning often to her friends and praising in admiring interrogatories Sybil's beauty.

'And we took advantage of your absence,' said Lady Maud in a tone of amiable artlessness, 'to find out all about you. And what a pity we did not know you when you were at the convent, because then you might have been constantly at the castle; indeed I should have insisted on it. But still I hear we are neighbours; you must promise to pay me a visit you must indeed. Is not she beautiful?' she added in a lower but still distinct voice to her friend. 'Do you know I think there is so much beauty among the lower order.'

Mr. Mountchesney and Lord Milford poured forth several insipid compliments, accompanied with some speaking looks which they flattered themselves could not be misconstrued. Sybil said not a word, but answered each flood of phrases with a cold reverence.

Undeterred by her somewhat haughty demeanour, which Lady Maud only attributed to the novelty of her situation, her ignorance of the world, and her embarrassment under this overpowering condescension, the good-tempered and fussy daughter of Lord de Mowbray proceeded to re-assure Sybil, and to enforce on her that this perhaps unprecedented descent from superiority was not a mere transient courtliness of the moment, and that she really might rely on her patronage and favourable feeling.

'You really must come and see me,' said Lady Maud, 'I shall never be happy till you have made me a visit. Where do you live? I will come and fetch you myself in the carriage. Now let us fix a day at once. Let me see; this is Saturday. What say you to next Monday?'

'I thank you,' said Sybil, very gravely, 'but I never quit my home.'

'What a darling!' exclaimed Lady Maud looking round at her friends. 'Is not she? I know exactly what you feel. But really you shall not be the least embarrassed. It may feel strange at first, to be sure, but then I shall be there; and do you know I look upon you quite as my protégée.'

'Protégée,' said Sybil. 'I live with my father.'

'What a dear!' said Lady Maud, looking round to Lord Milford. 'Is not she naïve?'

'And are you the guardian of these beautiful flowers,' said Mr. Mountchesney.

Sybil signified a negative, and added, 'Mrs. Trafford is very proud of them.'

'You must see the flowers at Mowbray Castle,' said Lady Maud. 'They are unprecedented, are they not, Lord Milford? You know you said the other day that they were equal to Mrs. Lawrence's. I am charmed to find you are fond of flowers,' continued Lady Maud; 'you will be so delighted with Mowbray. Ah! mama is calling us. Now fix; shall it be Monday?'

'Indeed,' said Sybil, 'I never leave my home. I am one of the lower order, and live only among the lower order. I am here to-day merely for a few hours to pay an act of homage to a benefactor.'

'Well I shall come and fetch you,' said Lady Maud, covering her surprise and mortification by a jaunty air that would not confess defeat.

'And so shall I,' said Mr. Mountchesney.

'And so shall I,' whispered Lord Milford, lingering a little behind.

The great and distinguished party had disappeared; their glittering barouche, their prancing horses, their gay grooms, all had vanished; the sound of their wheels was no longer heard. Time flew on; the bell announced that the labour of the week had closed. There was a half holiday always on the last day of the week at Mr. Trafford's settlement; and every man, woman, and child, were paid their wages in the great room before they left the mill. Thus the expensive and evil habits which result from wages being paid in public-houses were prevented. There was also in this system another great advantage for the work-people. They received their wages early enough to repair to the neighbouring markets and make their purchases for the morrow. This added greatly to their comfort, and, rendering it unnecessary for them to run in debt to the shopkeepers, added really to their wealth. Mr. Trafford thought that next to the amount of wages, the most important consideration was the method in which wages are paid; and those of our readers who may have read or can recall the sketches, neither coloured nor exaggerated, which we have given in the early part of this volume of the very different manner in which the working classes may receive the remuneration for their toil, will probably agree with the sensible and virtuous master of Walter Gerard.

He, accompanied by his daughter and Egremont, is now on his way home. A soft summer afternoon; the mild beam still gilding the tranquil scene; a river, green meads full of kine, woods vocal with the joyous song of the thrush and the blackbird; and in the distance, the lofty breast of the purple moor, still blazing in the sun: fair sights and renovating sounds after a day of labour passed in walls and amid the ceaseless and monotonous clang of the spindle and the loom. So Gerard felt it, as he stretched his great limbs in the air and inhaled its perfumed volume.

'Ah! I was made for this Sybil,' he exclaimed; 'but never mind, my child, never mind; tell me more of your fine visitors.'

Egremont found the walk too short; fortunately, from the undulation of the vale, they could not see the cottage until within a hundred yards of it. When they were in sight, a man came forth from the garden to greet them; Sybil gave an exclamation of pleasure; it was MORLEY.

CHAPTER 9

MORLEY greeted Gerard and his daughter with great warmth, and then looked at Egremont. 'Our companion in the ruins of Marney Abbey,' said Gerard; 'you and our friend Franklin here should become acquainted, Stephen, for you both follow the same craft. He is a journalist like yourself, and is our neighbour for a time, and yours.'

'What journal are you on, may I ask?' inquired Morley.

Egremont reddened, was confused, and then replied, 'I have no claim to the distinguished title of a journalist. I am but a reporter; and have some special duties here.'

'Hem!' said Morley; and then taking Gerard by the arm, he walked away with him, leaving Egremont and Sybil to follow them.

'Well I have found him, Walter.'

'What, Hatton?'

'No, no; the brother.'

'And what knows he?'

'Little enough; yet something. Our man lives and prospers; these are facts, but where he is, or what he is: not a clue.'

'And his brother cannot help us?'

'On the contrary, he sought information from me; he is a savage, beneath even our worst ideas of popular degradation. All that is ascertained is that our man exists and is well to do in the world. There comes an annual and anonymous contribution, and not a light one, to his brother. I examined the post-marks of the letters, but they all varied, and were evidently arranged to mislead. I fear you will deem I have not done much; yet it was wearisome enough I can tell you.'

'I doubt it not; and I am sure, Stephen, you have done all that man could. I was fancying that I should hear from you to-day; for what think you has happened? My Lord himself, his family and train, have all been in state to visit the works, and I had to show them. Queer that, wasn't it? He offered me money when it was over. How much I know not, I would not look at it. Though to be sure, they were perhaps my own rents, eh? But I pointed to the sick box, and his own dainty hand deposited the sum there.'

' 'Tis very strange. And you were with him face to face?'

'Face to face. Had you brought me news of the papers, I should have thought that Providence had rather a hand in it; but now, we are still at sea.'

'Still at sea,' said Morley musingly, 'but he lives and prospers. He will turn up yet, Walter.'

'Amen! Since you have taken up this thing, Stephen, it is strange how my mind has hankered after the old business, and yet it ruined my father, and mayhap may do as bad for his son.'

'We will not think that,' said Morley. 'At present we will think of other things. You may guess I am a bit wearied; I think I'll say good night; you have strangers with you.'

'Nay, nay, man; nay. This Franklin is a likely lad enough; I think you will take to him. Prithee come in. Sybil will not take it kindly if you go, after so long an absence; and I am sure I shall not.'

So they entered together.

The evening passed in various conversation, though it led frequently to the staple subject of talk beneath the roof of Gerard – the Condition of the People. What Morley had seen in his recent excursion afforded materials for many comments.

'The domestic feeling is fast vanishing among the working classes of this country,' said Gerard; 'nor is it wonderful; the Home no longer exists.'

'But there are means of reviving it,' said Egremont; 'we have witnessed them to-day. Give men homes, and they will have soft and homely notions. If all men acted like Mr. Trafford, the condition of the people would be changed.'

'But all men will not act like Mr. Trafford,' said Morley. 'It requires a sacrifice of self which cannot be expected, which is unnatural. It is not individual influence that can renovate society; it is some new principle that must reconstruct it. You lament the expiring idea of Home. It would not be expiring if it were worth retaining. The domestic principle has fulfilled its purpose. The irresistible law of progress demands that another should be developed. It will come; you may advance or retard, but you cannot prevent it. It will work out like the development of organic nature. In the present state of civilisation, and with the scientific means of happiness at our command, the notion of home should be obsolete. Home is a barbarous idea; the method of a rude age; home is isolation; therefore anti-social. What we want is Community.'

'It is all very fine,' said Gerard, 'and I dare say you are right, Stephen; but I like stretching my feet on my own hearth.'

CHAPTER 10

TIME passes with a measured and memorable wing during the first period of a sojourn in a new place, among new characters and new manners. Every person, every incident, every feeling, touches and stirs the imagination. The restless mind creates and observes at the same time. Indeed, there is scarcely any popular tenet more erroneous than that which holds that when time is slow, life is dull. It is very often, and very much the reverse. If we look back on those passages of our life which dwell most upon the memory, they are brief periods full of action and novel sensation. Egremont found this so during the first days of his new residence in Mowedale. The first week, an epoch in his life, seemed an age; at the end of the first month, he began to deplore the swiftness of time, and almost to moralise over the brevity of existence. He found that he was leading a life of perfect happiness, but of remarkable simplicity; he wished it might never end, but felt difficulty in comprehending how, in the first days of his experience of it, it had seemed so strange; almost as strange as it was sweet. The day, that commenced early, was passed in reading; books lent him often, too, by Sybil Gerard; sometimes in a ramble with her and Morley, who had time much at his command, to some memorable spot in the neighbourhood, or in the sport which the river and the rod secured Egremont. In the evening, he invariably repaired to the cottage of Gerard, beneath whose humble roof he found every female charm that can fascinate, and conversation that stimulated his intelligence. Gerard was ever the same; hearty, simple, with a depth of feeling and native thought on the subjects on which they touched, and with a certain grandeur of sentiment and conception which contrasted with his social position, but which became his idiosyncrasy. Sybil spoke little, but hung upon the accents of her father; yet ever and anon her rich tones conveyed to the charmed ear of Egremont some deep conviction, the earnestness of her intellect as remarkable as the almost sacred repose of her mien and manner. Of Morley, at first Egremont saw a great deal: he lent our friend books, opened, with unreserve and with great richness of speculative and illustrative power, on the questions which ever engaged him, and which were new and highly interesting to his companion. But, as time advanced, whether it were that the occupations of Morley increased, and the calls on his hours left him fewer occasions for the indulgence of social intercourse, Egremont saw him seldom, except at Gerard's cottage, where generally he might be found in the course of the week, and their rambles together had entirely ceased.

Alone, Egremont mused much over the daughter of Gerard, but, shrinking from the precise and the definite, his dreams were delightful, but vague. All that he asked was, that his present life could go on for ever; he wished for no change, and at length almost persuaded himself that no change could arrive; as men who are basking in a summer sun, surrounded by bright and beautiful objects, cannot comprehend how the seasons can ever alter; that the sparkling foliage should shrivel and fall away, the foaming waters become icebound, and the blue serene a dark and howling space.

In this train of mind, the early days of October having already stolen on him, an incident occurred which startled him in his retirement, and rendered it necessary that he should instantly quit it. Egremont had entrusted the secret of his residence to a faithful servant who communicated with him, when necessary, under his assumed name. Through these means he received a letter from his mother, written from London, where she had unexpectedly arrived, entreating him, in urgent terms, to repair to her without a moment's delay, on a matter of equal interest and importance to herself and him. Such an appeal from such a quarter, from the parent that had ever been kind, and the friend that had been ever faithful, was not for a moment to be neglected. Already a period had elapsed since its transmission, which Egremont regretted. He resolved at once to quit Mowedale, nor could he console himself with the prospect of an immediate return. Parliament was to assemble in the ensuing month, and, independently of the unknown cause which summoned him immediately to town, he was well aware that much disagreeable business awaited him which could no longer be postponed. He had determined not to take his seat unless the expenses of his contest were previously discharged, and, despairing of his brother's aid, and shrinking from trespassing any further on his mother's resources, the future looked gloomy enough: indeed, nothing but the frequent presence and the constant influence of Sybil had driven from his mind the ignoble melancholy which, relieved by no pensive fancy, is the invariable attendant of pecuniary embarrassment.

And now he was to leave her. The event, rather the catastrophe, which, under any circumstances, could not be long
postponed, was to be precipitated. He strolled up to the cottage to bid her farewell, and to leave kind words for her father.
Sybil was not there. The old dame who kept their home informed him that Sybil was at the convent, but would return
in the evening. It was impossible to quit Mowedale without
seeing Sybil; equally impossible to postpone his departure.
But by travelling through the night, the lost hours might be
regained. So Egremont made his arrangements, and awaited
with anxiety and impatience the last evening.

The evening, like his heart, was not serene. The soft air
that had lingered so long with them, a summer visitant in an
autumnal sky, and loth to part, was no more present. A cold
harsh wind, gradually rising, chilled the system, and grated
on the nerves. There was misery in its blast, and depression
in its moan. Egremont felt infinitely dispirited. The landscape
around him, that he had so often looked upon with love and
joy, was dull and hard; the trees dingy, the leaden waters
motionless, the distant hills rough and austere. Where was
that translucent sky, once brilliant as his enamoured fancy;
those bowery groves of aromatic fervour wherein he had loved
to roam and muse; that river of swift and sparkling light that
flowed and flashed like the current of his enchanted hours?
All vanished, as his dreams.

He stood before the cottage of Gerard; he recalled the eve
that he had first gazed upon its moonlit garden. What wild
and delicious thoughts were then his! They were gone like
the illumined hour. Nature and fortune had alike changed.
Prescient of sorrow, almost prophetic of evil, he opened the
cottage door, and the first person his eye encountered was
Morley.

Egremont had not met him for some time, and his cordial
greeting of Egremont to-night contrasted with the coldness,
not to say estrangement, which to the regret and sometimes
the perplexity of Egremont had gradually grown up between
them. Yet on no occasion was his presence less desired by our
friend. Morley was talking, as Egremont entered, with great
animation; in his hand a newspaper, on a paragraph contained
in which he was commenting. The name of Marney caught

the ear of Egremont, who turned rather pale at the sound, and hesitated on the threshold. The unembarrassed welcome of his friends, however, re-assured him, and in a moment he even ventured to inquire the subject of their conversation. Morley, immediately referring to the newspaper, said, 'This is what I have just read:

' "EXTRAORDINARY SPORT AT THE EARL OF MARNEY'S. On Wednesday, in a small cover called the Horns, near Marney Abbey, his grace the Duke of Fitz-Aquitaine, the Earl of Marney, Colonel Rippe, and Captain Grouse, with only four hours' shooting, bagged the extraordinary numbers of seven hundred and thirty head of game, namely, hares three hundred and thirty-nine; pheasants two hundred and twenty-one; partridges thirty-four; rabbits eighty-seven; and the following day upwards of fifty hares, pheasants, &c. (wounded the previous day), were picked up. Out of the four hours' shooting, two of the party were absent an hour and a half, namely, the Earl of Marney and Captain Grouse, attending an agricultural meeting in the neighbourhood; the noble earl, with his usual considerate condescension. having kindly consented personally to distribute the various prizes to the labourers whose good conduct entitled them to the distinction."

'What do you think of that, Franklin?' said Morley. 'That is our worthy friend of Marney Abbey, where we first met. You do not know this part of the country, or you would smile at the considerate condescension of the worst landlord in England; and who was, it seems, thus employed the day or so after his battue, as they call it.' And Morley turning the paper read another paragraph:

'At a Petty Sessions holden at the Green Dragon Inn, Marney, Friday, October —, 1837.

'Magistrates present: The Earl of Marney, the Rev. Felix Flimsey, and Captain Grouse.

'Information against Thomas Hind for a trespass in pursuit of game in Blackrock Wood, the property of Sir Vavasour Firebrace, Bart. The case was distinctly proved; several wires being found in the pocket of the defendant. Defendant was fined in the full penalty of forty shillings and costs twenty-seven; the Bench being of opinion there was no excuse for him, Hind being a regular employ as a farm-labourer and gaining his seven shillings a-week. Defendant, being unable to pay the penalty, was sent for two months to Marham gaol.'

'What a pity,' said Morley, 'that Thomas Hind,* instead of meditating the snaring of a hare, had not been fortunate enough to pick up a maimed one crawling about the fields the day after the battue. It would certainly have been better for himself; and if he has a wife and family, better for the parish.'

'Oh!' said Gerard, 'I doubt not they were all picked up by the poulterer who has the contract: even the Normans did not sell their game.'

'The question is,' said Morley, 'would you rather be barbarous or mean; that is the alternative presented by the real and the pseudo Norman nobility of England. Where I have been lately, there is a Bishopsgate Street merchant who has been made for no conceivable public reason a baron bold. Bigod and Bohun* could not enforce the forest laws* with such severity as this dealer in cotton and indigo.'

'It is a difficult question to deal with, this affair of the game laws,' said Egremont; 'how will you reach the evil? Would you do away with the offence of trespass? And if so, what is your protection for property?'

'It comes to a simple point though,' said Morley, 'the Territorialists must at length understand that they cannot at the same time have the profits of a farm and the pleasures of a chase.'

At this moment entered Sybil. At the sight of her, the remembrance that they were about to part, nearly overwhelmed Egremont. Her supremacy over his spirit was revealed to him, and nothing but the presence of other persons could have prevented him from avowing his entire subjection. His hand trembled as he touched hers, and his eye, searching yet agitated, would have penetrated her serene soul. Gerard and Morley, somewhat withdrawn, pursued their conversation; while Egremont, hanging over Sybil, attempted to summon courage to express to her his sad adieu. It was in vain. Alone, perhaps he might have poured forth a passionate farewell. But constrained he became embarrassed; and his conduct was at the same time tender and perplexing. He asked and repeated questions which had already been answered. His thoughts wandered from their conversation, but not from her with whom he should have conversed. Once their eyes met, and Sybil observed his suffused with tears. Once he looked round and caught the glance of Morley, instantly withdrawn, but not easy to be forgotten.

Shortly after this and earlier than his wont, Morley rose and wished them good night. He shook hands with Egremont and bade him farewell with some abruptness. Harold, who seemed half asleep, suddenly sprang from the side of his mistress and gave an agitated bark. Harold was never very friendly to Morley, who now tried to soothe him, but in vain. The dog looked fiercely at him and barked again, but, the moment Morley had disappeared, Harold resumed his usual air of proud, high-bred gentleness, and thrust his nose into the hand of Egremont, who patted him with fondness.

The departure of Morley was a great relief to Egremont, though the task that was left was still a painful effort. He rose and walked for a moment up and down the room, and commenced an unfinished sentence, approached the hearth, and leant over the mantel; and then at length extending his hand to Gerard, he exclaimed, in a trembling voice, 'Best of friends, I must leave Mowedale.'

'I am very sorry,' said Gerard; 'and when?'

'Now,' said Egremont.

'Now!' said Sybil.

'Yes; this instant. My summons is urgent. I ought to have left this morning. I came here then to bid you farewell,' he said, looking at Sybil, 'to express to you how deeply I was indebted to you for all your goodness; how dearly I shall cherish the memory of these happy days, the happiest I have ever known;' and his voice faltered. 'I came also to leave a kind message for you, my friend, a hope that we might meet again and soon, but your daughter was absent, and I could not leave Mowedale without seeing either of you. So I must contrive to get on through the night.'

'Well, we lose a pleasant neighbour,' said Gerard; 'we shall miss you, I doubt not, eh, Sybil?'

But Sybil had turned away her head; she was leaning over and seemed to be caressing Harold, and was silent.

How much Egremont would have liked to have offered or

invited correspondence; to have proffered his services, when the occasion permitted; to have said or proposed many things that might have cherished their acquaintance or friendship; but, embarrassed by his incognito and all its consequent deception, he could do nothing but tenderly express his regret at parting, and speak vaguely and almost mysteriously of their soon meeting again. He held out again his hand to Gerard, who shook it heartily: then approaching Sybil, Egremont said, 'You have shown me a thousand kindnesses, which I cherish,' he added in a lower tone, 'above all human circumstances. Would you deign to let this volume lie upon your table,' and he offered Sybil an English translation of Thomas à Kempis, illustrated by some masterpieces. In its first page was written 'Sybil, from a faithful friend.'

'I accept it,' said Sybil, with a trembling voice and rather pale, 'in remembrance of a friend.' She held forth her hand to Egremont, who retained it for an instant, and then bending very low, pressed it to his lips. As with an agitated heart he hastily crossed the threshold of the cottage, something seemed to hold him back. He turned round. The bloodhound had seized him by the coat, and looked up at him with an expression of affectionate remonstrance against his departure. Egremont bent down, caressed Harold, and released himself from his grasp.

When Egremont left the cottage, he found the country enveloped in a thick white mist, so that had it not been for some huge black shadows which he recognised as the crests of trees, it would have been very difficult to discriminate the earth from the sky, and the mist thickening as he advanced, even these fallacious landmarks threatened to disappear. He had to walk to Mowbray to catch a night train for London. Every moment was valuable, but the unexpected and increasing obscurity rendered his progress slow and even perilous. The contiguity to the river made every step important. He had, according to his calculations, proceeded nearly as far as his old residence, and notwithstanding the careless courage of youth and the annoyance of relinquishing a project, intolerable at that season of life, was meditating the expediency of renouncing that night the attempt on Mowbray and of gaining his former quarters for shelter. He stopped, as he had stopped several times before, to calculate rather than to observe. The mist was so thick that he could not see his own extended hand. It was not the first time that it had occurred to him that some one or some thing was hovering about his course.

'Who is there?' exclaimed Egremont. But no one answered.

He moved on a little, but very slowly. He felt assured that his ear caught a contiguous step. He repeated his interrogatory in a louder tone, but it obtained no response. Again he stopped. Suddenly he was seized; an iron grasp assailed his throat, a hand of steel gripped his arm. The unexpected onset hurried him on. The sound of waters assured him that he was approaching the precipitous bank of that part of the river which, from a ledge of pointed rocks, here formed rapids. Vigorous and desperate, Egremont plunged like some strong animal on whom a beast of prey had made a fatal spring. His feet clung to the earth as if they were held by some magnetic power. With his disengaged arm he grappled with his mysterious and unseen foe.

At this moment he heard the deep bay of a hound.

'Harold!' he exclaimed. The dog, invisible, sprang forward and seized upon his assailant.* So violent was the impulse that Egremont staggered and fell, but as he fell freed from his dark enemy. Stunned and exhausted, some moments elapsed before he was entirely himself. The wind had suddenly changed; a violent gust had partially dispelled the mist; the outline of the landscape was in many places visible. Beneath him were the rapids of the Mowe, over which a watery moon threw a faint, flickering light. Egremont was lying on its precipitous bank; and Harold panting was leaning over him and looking in his face, and sometimes licking him with that tongue which, though not gifted with speech, had spoken so seasonably in the moment of danger.

END OF THE THIRD BOOK.

BOOK IV

*

CHAPTER I

'ARE you going down to the House, Egerton?' inquired Mr. Berners at Brooks', of a brother M.P., about four o'clock in the early part of the spring of 1839.

'The moment I have sealed this letter; we will walk down together, if you like;' and in a few minutes they left the club.

'Our fellows are in a sort of fright about this Jamaica bill,'* said Mr. Egerton, in an undertone, as if he were afraid a passer-by might hear him. 'Don't say anything about it, but there's a screw loose.'

'The deuce! But how do you mean?'

'They say the Rads are going to throw us over.'

'Talk, talk. They have threatened this half-a-dozen times. Smoke, sir; it will end in smoke.'

'I hope it may; but I know, in great confidence mind you, that Lord John was saying something about it yesterday.'

'That may be; I believe our fellows are heartily sick of the business, and perhaps would be glad of an excuse to break up the government: but we must not have Peel in; nothing could prevent dissolution.'

'Their fellows go about and say that Peel would not dissolve if he came in.'

'Trust him!'

'He has had enough of dissolutions they say.'

'Why, after all, they have not done him much harm. Even '34 was a hit.'

'Whoever dissolves,' said Mr. Egerton, 'I do not think there will be much of a majority either way in our time.'

'We have seen strange things,' said Mr. Berners.

'They never would think of breaking up the government without making their peers,' said Mr. Egerton.

'The queen is not over partial to making more peers; and when parties are in the present state of equality, the Sovereign is no longer a mere pageant.'

'They say her Majesty is more touched about these affairs of the Chartists* than anything else', said Mr. Egerton.

'They are rather queer; but for my part I have no serious fears of a Jacquerie.'*

'Not if it comes to an ourbreak; but a passive resistance Jacquerie is altogether a different thing. When we see a regular Convention assembled in London and holding its daily meetings in Palace Yard, and a general inclination evinced throughout the country to refrain from the consumption of excisable articles, I cannot help thinking that affairs are more serious than you imagine. I know the government are all on the' 'qui vive.''

'Just the fellows we wanted!' exclaimed Lord Fitz-Heron, who was leaning on the arm of Lord Milford, and who met Mr. Egerton and his friend in Pall Mall.

'We want a brace of pairs,' said Lord Milford. 'Will you two fellows pair?'

'I must go down,' said Mr. Egerton; 'but I will pair from half past-seven to eleven.'

'I just paired with Ormsby at White's,' said Berners, 'not half an hour ago. We are both going to dine at Eskdale's and so it was arranged. Have you any news today?'

'Nothing; except thay say that Alfred Mountchesney is going to marry Lady Joan Fitz-Warene,' said Lord Milford.

'She has been given to so many,' said Mr. Egerton.

'It is always so with these great heiresses,'· said his companion. 'They never marry. They cannot bear the thought of sharing their money. I bet Lady Joan will turn out another specimen of the TABITHA CRŒSUS.'

'Well, put down our pair, Egerton,' said Lord Fitz-Heron. 'You do not dine at Sidonia's by any chance?'

'Would that I did! You will have the best dishes and the best guests. I feed at old Matlon's: perhaps a tête-à-tête: Scotch broth and to tell him the news!'

'There is nothing like being a dutiful nephew, particularly when one's uncle is a bachelor and has twenty thousand a-year,' said Lord Milford. 'Au revoir! I suppose there will be no division to-night.'

'No chance.'

Egerton and Berners walked on a little further. As they

came to the Golden Ball, a lady quitting the shop was just
about to get into her carriage; she stopped as she recognised
them. It was Lady Firebrace.

'Ah! Mr. Berners, how d'ye do? You were just the person
I wanted to see! How is Lady Augusta, Mr. Egerton? You
have no idea, Mr. Berners, how I have been fighting your
battles!'

'Really, Lady Firebrace,' said Mr. Berners, rather uneasy,
for he had perhaps, like most of us, a peculiar dislike to being
attacked or cheapened. 'You are too good.'

'Oh! I don't care what a person's politics are!' exclaimed
Lady Firebrace, with an air of affectionate devotion. 'I should
be very glad indeed to see you one of us. You know your
father was! But if any one is my friend, I never will hear him
attacked behind his back without fighting his battles: and I
certainly did fight yours last night.'

'Pray tell me where it was?'

'Lady Crumbleford—'

'Confound Lady Crumbleford!' said Mr. Berners, indignant, but a little relieved.

'No, no; Lady Crumbleford told Lady Alicia Severn.'

'Yes, yes,' said Berners, a little pale, for he was touched.

'But I cannot stop,' said Lady Firebrace. 'I must be with
Lady St. Julians exactly at a quarter past four;' and she sprang
into her carriage.

'I would sooner meet any woman in London than Lady
Firebrace,' said Mr. Berners; 'she makes me uneasy for the
day; she contrives to convince me that the whole world are
employed behind my back in abusing or ridiculing me.

'It is her way,' said Egerton; 'she proves her zeal by showing you that you are odious. It is very successful with people
of weak nerves. Scared at their general unpopularity, they
seek refuge with the very person who at the same time assures
them of their odium and alone believes it unjust. She rules
that poor old goose, Lady Gramshawe, who feels that Lady
Firebrace makes her life miserable, but is convinced that if
she break with the torturer, she loses her only friend.'

'There goes a man who is as much altered as any fellow of
our time.'

'Not in his looks; I was thinking the other night that he was better-looking than ever.'

'Oh! no; not in his looks; but in his life. I was at Christchurch with him, and we entered the world about the same time. I was rather before him. He did everything; and did it well. And now one never sees him, except at the House. He goes nowhere; and they tell me he is a regular reading man.'

'Do you think he looks to office?'

'He does not put himself forward.'

'He attends; and his brother will always be able to get anything for him,' said Egerton.

'Oh! he and Marney never speak; they hate each other.'

'By Jove! however, there is his mother; with this marriage of hers and Deloraine House, she will be their grandest dame.'

'She is the only good woman the tories have: I think their others do them harm, from Lady St. Julians down to your friend Lady Firebrace. I wish Lady Deloraine were with us. She keeps their men together wonderfully; makes her house agreeable; and then her manner, it certainly is perfect; natural, and yet refined.'

'Lady Mina Blake has an idea that, far from looking to office, Egremont's heart is faintly with his party; and that if it were not for the Marchioness—'

'We might gain him, eh?'

'Hem; I hardly know that: he has got crotchets about the people, I am told.'

'What, the ballot and household suffrage?'

'Gad, I believe it is quite a different sort of a thing. I do not know what it is exactly; but I understand he is crotchetty.'

'Well, that will not do for Peel. He does not like crotchetty men. Do you see that, Egerton?'

At this moment, Mr. Egerton and his friend were about to step over from Trafalgar-square to Charing Cross. They observed the carriages of Lady St. Julians and the Marchioness of Deloraine drawn up side by side in the middle of the street, and those two eminent stateswomen in earnest conversation. Egerton and Berners bowed and smiled, but could not hear the brief but not uninteresting words that have nevertheless reached us.

'I give them eleven,' said Lady St. Julians.

'Well, Charles tells me,' said Lady Deloraine, 'that Sir Thomas says so, and he certainly is generally right; but it is not Charles's own opinion.'

'Sir Thomas, I know, gives them eleven,' said Lady St. Julians; 'and that would satisfy me; and we will say eleven. But I have a list here,' and she slightly elevated her brow, and then glanced at Lady Deloraine with a piquant air, 'which proves that they cannot have more than nine; but this is in the greatest confidence: of course between us there can be no secrets. It is Mr. Tadpole's list; nobody has seen it but myself; not even Sir Robert. Lord Grubminster has had a stroke; they are concealing it, but Mr. Tadpole has found it out. They wanted to pair him off with Colonel Fantomme, who they think is dying; but Mr. Tadpole has got a Mesmerist* who has done wonders for him, and who has guaranteed that he shall vote. Well, that makes a difference of one.'

'And then Sir Henry Churton—'

'Oh! you know it,' said Lady St. Julians, looking slightly mortified. 'Yes; he votes with us.'

Lady Deloraine shook her head. 'I think,' she said, 'I know the origin of that report. Quite a mistake. He is in a bad humour, has been so the whole session, and he was at Lady Alice Fermyne's and did say all sorts of things. All that is true. But he told Charles this morning on a committee, that he should vote with the Government.'

'Stupid man!' exclaimed Lady St. Julians; 'I never could bear him. And I have sent his vulgar wife and great staring daughter a card for next Wednesday! Well, I hope affairs will soon be brought to a crisis, for I do not think I can bear much longer this life of perpetual sacrifice,' added Lady St. Julians, a little out of temper, both because she had lost a vote and found her friend and rival better informed than herself.

'There is no chance of a division to-night,' said Lady Deloraine.

'That is settled,' said Lady St. Julians. 'Adieu, my dear friend. We meet, I believe, at dinner?'

'Plotting,' said Mr. Egerton to Mr. Berners, as they passed the great ladies.

'The only consolation one has,' said Berners, 'is, that if they do turn us out, Lady Deloraine and Lady St. Julians must quarrel, for they both want the same thing.'

'Lady Deloraine will have it,' said Egerton.

Here they picked up Mr. Jermyn, a young tory M.P., whom perhaps the reader may remember at Mowbray Castle; and they walked on together. Egerton and Berners trying to pump him as to the expectations of his friends.

'How will Trodgits go?' said Egerton.

'I think Trodgits will stay away,' said Jermyn.

'Whom do you give that new man to, that north-country borough fellow; what's his name?' said Berners.

'Blugsby! oh, Blugsby dined with Peel,' said Jermyn.

'Our fellows say dinners are no good,' said Egerton; 'and they certainly are a cursed bore: but you may depend upon it they do for the burgesses. We don't dine our men half enough. Now Blugsby was just the sort of fellow to be caught by dining with Peel; and I dare say they made Peel remember to take wine with him. We got Melbourne to give a grand feed the other day to some of our men who want attention they say, and he did not take wine with a single guest. He forgot. I wonder what they are doing at the House! Here is Spencer May, he will tell us. Well, what is going on?'

'WISHY is down, and WASHY up.'

'No division, of course?'

'Not a chance; a regular covey ready on both sides.'

CHAPTER 2

ON the morning of the same day that Mr. Egerton and his friend Mr. Berners walked down together to the House of Commons, as appears in our last chapter, Egremont had made a visit to his mother, who had married, since the commencement of this history, the Marquis of Deloraine, a great noble who had always been her admirer. The family had been established by a lawyer, and recently in our history. The present Lord Deloraine, though he was gartered and had been a viceroy, was only the grandson of an attorney, but one who, conscious of his powers, had been called to the bar, and died an ex-chancellor. A certain talent was hereditary in the family. The attorney's son had been a successful courtier, and had planted himself in the cabinet for a quarter of a century. It was a maxim in this family to make great alliances; so the blood progressively refined, and the connections were always distinguished by power and fashion. It was a great hit, in the second generation of an earldom, to convert the coronet into that of a marquis; but the son of the old chancellor lived in stirring times, and cruised for his object with the same devoted patience with which Lord Anson watched for the galleon. It came at last, as everything does if men are firm and calm. The present marquis, through his ancestry and his first wife, was allied with the highest houses of the realm, and looked their peer. He might have been selected as the personification of aristocracy: so noble was his appearance, so distinguished his manner; his bow gained every eye, his smile every heart. He was also very accomplished, and not ill-informed; had read a little, and thought a little, and was in every respect a superior man; alike famed for his favour by the fair, and the constancy of his homage to the charming Lady Marney.

Lord Deloraine was not rich; but he was not embarrassed, and had the appearance of princely wealth; a splendid family mansion with a courtyard; a noble country seat with a magnificent park, including a quite celebrated lake, but with few farms attached to it. He however held a good patent place which had been conferred on his descendants by the old chancellor, and this brought in annually some thousands. His marriage with Lady Marney was quite an affair of the heart; her considerable jointure however did not diminish the lustre of his position.

It was this impending marriage, and the anxiety of Lady Marney to see Egremont's affairs settled before it took place, which about a year and a half ago had induced her to summon him so urgently from Mowedale, which the reader perhaps may not have forgotten. And now Egremont is paying one of his almost daily visits to his mother at Deloraine House.

'A truce to politics, my dear Charles,' said Lady Marney; 'you must be wearied with my inquiries. Besides, I do not take the sanguine view of affairs in which some of our friends indulge. I am one of those who think the pear is not ripe. These men will totter on, and longer perhaps than even themselves imagine. I want to speak of something very different. To-morrow, my dear son, is your birth-day. Now I should grieve were it to pass without your receiving something which showed that its recollection was cherished by your mother. But of all silly things in the world, the silliest is a present that is not wanted. It destroys the sentiment a little, perhaps, but it enhances the gift, if I ask you in the most literal manner to assist me in giving you something that really would please you?'

'But how can I, my dear mother?' said Egremont. 'You have ever been so kind and so generous that I literally want nothing.'

'Oh! you cannot be such a fortunate man as to want nothing, Charles,' said Lady Marney with a smile. 'A dressing-case you have; your rooms are furnished enough: all this is in my way; but there are such things as horses and guns, of which I know nothing, but which men always require. You must want a horse or a gun, Charles. Well, I should like you to get either; the finest, the most valuable that money can purchase. Or a brougham, Charles; what do you think of a new brougham? Would you like that Barker should build you a brougham?'

'You are too good, my dear mother. I have horses and guns enough; and my present carriage is all I can desire.'

'You will not assist me, then? You are resolved that I shall do something very stupid. For to give you something I am determined.'

'Well, my dear mother,' said Egremont smiling, and looking round, 'give me something that is here.'

'Choose then,' said Lady Marney; and she looked round the satin walls of her apartment, covered with cabinet pictures of exquisite art, and then at her tables crowded with precious and fantastic toys.

'It would be plunder my dear mother,' said Egremont.

'No, no; you have said it; you shall choose something. Will you have those vases?' and she pointed to an almost matchless specimen of old Sevres porcelain.

'They are in too becoming a position to be disturbed,' said

Egremont, 'and would ill suit my quiet chambers, where a bronze or a marble is my greatest ornament. If you would permit me, I would rather choose a picture?'

'Then select one at once,' said Lady Marney; 'I make no reservation, except that Watteau, for it was given to me by your father before we were married. Shall it be this Cuyp?'*

'I would rather choose this,' said Egremont; and he pointed to the portrait of a saint by Allori:* the face of a beautiful young girl, radiant and yet solemn, with rich tresses of golden brown hair, and large eyes dark as night, fringed with ebon lashes that hung upon the glowing cheek.

'Ah! you choose that! Well, that was a great favourite of poor Sir Thomas Lawrence.* But for my part I have never seen any one in the least like it, and I think I am sure that you have not.'

'It reminds me,' said Egremont musingly.

'Of what you have dreamed,' said Lady Marney.

'Perhaps so,' said Egremont; 'indeed I think it must have been a dream.'

'Well, the vision shall still hover before you,' said his mother; 'and you shall find this portrait to-morrow over your chimney in the Albany.'

CHAPTER 3

'STRANGERS must withdraw.'

'Division: clear the gallery. Withdraw.'

'Nonsense; no; it's quite ridiculous; quite absurd. Some fellow must get up. Send to the Carlton; send to the Reform; send to Brooks'. Are your men ready? No; are yours? I am sure I can't say. What does it mean? Most absurd! Are there many fellows in the library? The smoking room is quite full. All our men are paired till half-past eleven. It wants five minutes to the half-hour. What do you think of Trenchard's speech?* I don't care for ourselves; I am sorry for him. Well, that is very charitable. Withdraw, withdraw; you must withdraw.'

'Where are you going, Fitzheron?' said a Conservative whipling.

'I must go; I am paired till half-past eleven, and it wants some minutes, and my man is not here.'

'Confound it!'

'How will it go?'

'Gad, I don't know.'

'Fishy, eh?'

'Deuced!' said the under-whip in an under-tone, pale, and speaking behind his teeth.

The division bell was still ringing; peers and diplomatists and strangers were turned out; members came rushing in from the library and smoking-room; some desperate cabs just arrived in time to land their passengers in the waiting-room. The doors were locked.

The mysteries of the Lobby are only for the initiated. Three quarters of an hour after the division was called, the result was known to the exoteric world. Majority for Ministers thirty-seven! Never had the Opposition made such a bad division, and this too on their trial of strength for the session. Everything went wrong. Lord Milford was away without a pair. Mr. Ormsby, who had paired with Mr. Berners, never came, and let his man poll; for which he was infinitely accursed, particularly by the expectant twelve hundred a-yearers, but, not wanting anything himself, and having an income of forty thousand pounds paid quarterly, Mr. Ormsby bore their reported indignation like a lamb.

There were several other similar or analogous mischances; the whigs contrived to poll Lord Grubminster in a wheeled chair; he was unconscious, but had heard as much of the debate as a good many. Colonel Fantomme, on the other hand, could not come to time; the Mesmerist had thrown him into a trance from which it was fated he never should awake: but the crash of the night was a speech made against the Opposition by one of their own men, Mr. Trenchard, who voted with the Government.

'The rest may be accounted for,' said Lady St. Julians to Lady Deloraine the morning after; 'it is simply vexatious; it was a surprise and will be a lesson: but this affair of this Mr. Trenchard, and they tell me that William Latimer was absolutely cheering him the whole time, what does it mean? Do you know the man?'

'I have heard Charles speak of him, and I think much in his favour,' said Lady Deloraine; 'if he were here, he would tell us more about it. I wonder he does not come: he never misses looking in after a great division and giving me all the news.'

'Do you know, my dear friend,' said Lady St. Julians, with an air of some solemnity, 'I am half meditating a great move? This is not a time for trifling. It is all very well for these people to boast of their division of last night, but it was a surprise, and as great to them as to us. I know there is dissension in the camp; ever since that Finality speech of Lord John,* there has been a smouldering sedition. Mr. Tadpole knows all about it; he has liaisons with the frondeurs.* This affair of Trenchard may do us the greatest possible injury. When it comes to a fair fight, the Government have not more than twelve or so. If Mr. Trenchard and three or four others choose to make themselves of importance, you see? The danger is imminent, it must be met with decision.'

'And what do you propose doing?'

'Has he a wife?'

'I really do not know. I wish Charles would come, perhaps he could tell us.'

'I have no doubt he has,' said Lady St. Julians. 'One would have met him, somehow or other, in the course of two years, if he had not been married. Well, married or unmarried, with his wife, or without his wife, I shall send him a card for Wednesday.' And Lady St. Julians paused, overwhelmed as it were by the commensurate vastness of her idea and her sacrifice.

'Do not you think it would be rather sudden?' said Lady Deloraine.

'What does that signify? He will understand it; he will have gained his object; and all will be right.'

'But are you sure it is his object? We do not know the man.'

'What else can be his object?' said Lady St. Julians, 'People get into Parliament to get on; their aims are indefinite. If they have indulged in hallucinations about place before they enter the House, they are soon freed from such distempered fancies; they find they have no more talent than other people, and if they had, they learn that power, patronage, and pay are reserved for us and our friends. Well then, like practical men, they look to some result, and they get it. They are asked out to dinner more than they would be; they move rigmarole resolutions at nonsensical public meetings; and they get invited with their women to assemblies at their leader's, where they see stars and blue ribbons, and above all, us, who, they little think, in appearing on such occasions, make the greatest conceivable sacrifice. Well, then, of course such people are entirely in one's power, if one only had time and inclination to notice them. You can do anything with them. Ask them to a ball, and they will give you their votes; invite them to dinner, and, if necessary, they will rescind them; but cultivate them, remember their wives at assemblies, and call their daughters, if possible, by their right names; and they will not only change their principles or desert their party for you; but subscribe their fortunes, if necessary, and lay down their lives in your service.'

'You paint them to the life, my dear Lady St. Julians,' said Lady Deloraine laughing; 'but, with such knowledge and such powers, why did you not save our boroughs?'

'We had lost our heads, then, I must confess,' said Lady St. Julians. 'What with the dear King and the dear Duke, we really had brought ourselves to believe that we lived in the days of Versailles or nearly; and I must admit I think we had become a little too exclusive. Out of the cottage circle, there was really no world, and after all we were lost, not by insulting the people, but by snubbing the aristocracy.'

The servant announced Lady Firebrace. 'Oh! my dear Lady Deloraine. O! my dear Lady St. Julians!' and she shook her head.

'You have no news, I suppose,' said Lady St. Julians.

'Only about that dreadful Mr. Trenchard; you know the reason why he ratted?'

'No, indeed,' said Lady St. Julians with a sigh.

'An invitation to Lansdowne House, for himself and his wife!'

'Oh! he is married then?'

'Yes; she is at the bottom of it all. Terms regularly settled beforehand. I have a note here; all the facts.' And Lady Firebrace twirled in her hand a bulletin from Mr. Tadpole.

'Lansdowne House is destined to cross me,' said Lady St. Julians with bitterness.

'Well it is provoking,' said Lady Deloraine, 'when you had made up your mind to ask them for Wednesday.'

'Yes, that alone is a sacrifice,' said Lady St. Julians.

'Talking over the division, I suppose,' said Egremont as he entered.

'Ah! Mr. Egremont,' said Lady St. Julians. 'What a *hachis** you made of it!'

Lady Firebrace shook her head, as it were reproachfully.

'Charles,' said Lady Deloraine, 'we were talking of this Mr. Trenchard. Did I not once hear you say you knew something of him?'

'Why, he is one of my intimate acquaintances.'

'Heavens! what a man for a friend!' said Lady St. Julians.

'Heavens!' echoed Lady Firebrace raising her hands.

'And why did you not present him to me, Charles,' said Lady Deloraine.

'I did; at Lady Peel's.'

'And why did you not ask him here?'

'I did several times; but he would not come.'

'He is going to Lansdowne House, though,' said Lady Firebrace.

'I suppose you wrote the leading article in the Standard which I have just read,' said Egremont smiling. 'It announces in large type the secret reasons of Mr. Trenchard's vote.'

'It is a fact,' said Lady Firebrace.

'That Trenchard is going to Lansdowne House to-night; very likely. I have met him at Lansdowne House half-a-dozen times. He is intimate with the family, and lives in the same county.'

'But his wife,' said Lady Firebrace; 'that's the point: he never could get his wife there before.'

'He has none,' said Egremont quietly.

'Then we may regain him,' said Lady St. Julians with energy. 'You shall make a little dinner to Greenwich, Mr. Egremont, and I will sit next to him.'

'Fortunate Trenchard!' said Egremont. 'But do you know I fear he is hardly worthy of his lot. He has a horror of fine ladies; and there is nothing in the world he more avoids than

what you call society. At home, as this morning when I break-
fasted with him, or in a circle of his intimates, he is the best
company in the world; no one so well informed, fuller of rich
humour, and more sincerely amiable. He is popular with all
who know him, except Taper, Lady St. Julians, Tadpole, and
Lady Firebrace.'

'Well, I think I will ask him still for Wednesday,' said Lady
St. Julians; 'and I will write him a little note. If society is not
his object, what is?'

'Ay!' said Egremont, 'there is a great question for you and
Lady Firebrace to ponder over. This is a lesson for you fine
ladies, who think you can govern the world by what you call
your social influences: asking people once or twice a-year to
an inconvenient crowd in your house; now haughtily smirking,
and now impertinently staring, at them; and flattering yourselves all this time, that, to have the occasional privilege of
entering your saloons, and the periodical experience of your
insolent recognition, is to be a reward for great exertions, or,
if necessary, an inducement to infamous tergiversation.'

CHAPTER 4

IT was night; clear and serene, though the moon had not
risen; and a vast concourse of persons were assembling on
Mowbray Moor. The chief gathering collected in the vicinity
of some huge rocks, one of which, pre-eminent above its
fellows, and having a broad flat head, on which some twenty
persons might easily stand at the same time, was called the
Druid's Altar.* The ground about was strewn with stony
fragments, covered to-night with human beings, who found
a convenient resting-place amid these ruins of some ancient
temple, or relics of some ancient world. The shadowy concourse increased, the dim circle of the nocturnal assemblage
each moment spread and widened; there was the hum and
stir of many thousands. Suddenly in the distance the sound of
martial music: and instantly, quick as the lightning, and far
more wild, each person present brandished a flaming torch,
amid a chorus of cheers, that, renewed and resounding,
floated far away over the broad bosom of the dusk wilderness.

The music and the banners denoted the arrival of the leaders of the people. They mounted the craggy ascent that led to the summit of the Druid's Altar, and there, surrounded by his companions, amid the enthusiastic shouts of the multitude, Walter Gerard came forth to address a TORCH-LIGHT MEETING.

His tall form seemed colossal in the uncertain and flickering light, his rich and powerful voice reached almost to the limit of his vast audience, now still with expectation and silent with excitement. Their fixed and eager glance, the mouth compressed with fierce resolution or distended by novel sympathy, as they listened to the exposition of their wrongs, and the vindication of the sacred rights of labour; the shouts and waving of the torches as some bright or bold phrase touched them to the quick; the cause, the hour, the scene, all combined to render the assemblage in a high degree exciting.

'I wonder if Warner will speak to-night,' said Dandy Mick to Devilsdust.

'He can't pitch it in like Gerard,' replied his companion.

'But he is a trump in the tender,' said the Dandy. 'The Hand-looms looks to him as their man, and that's a powerful section.'

'If you come to the depth of a question, there's nothing like Stephen Morley,' said Devilsdust. ' 'Twould take six clergymen any day to settle him. He knows the principles of society by heart. But Gerard gets hold of the passions.'

'And that's the way to do the trick,' said Dandy Mick. 'I wish he would say march, and no mistake.'

'There is a great deal to do before saying that,' said Devilsdust. 'We must have discussion, because when it comes to reasoning, the oligarchs have not got a leg to stand on; and we must stop the consumption of excisable articles, and when they have no tin to pay the bayonets and their b——y police, they are dished.'

'You have a long head, Dusty,' said Mick.

'Why I have been thinking of it ever since I knew two and two made four,' said his friend. 'I was not ten years old when I said to myself, it's a pretty go this, that I should be toiling in a shoddy-hole to pay the taxes for a gentleman what drinks his port wine and stretches his legs on a Turkey carpet. Hear,

hear,' he suddenly exclaimed, as Gerard threw off a stinging sentence, 'Ah! that's the man for the people. You will see, Mick, whatever happens, Gerard is the man who will always lead.'

Gerard had ceased amid enthusiastic plaudits, and Warner, that hand-loom weaver whom the reader may recollect, and who had since become a popular leader and one of the principal followers of Gerard, had also addressed the multitude. They had cheered and shouted, and voted resolutions, and the business of the night was over. Now they were enjoined to disperse in order and depart in peace. The band sounded a triumphant retreat; the leaders had descended from the Druid's Altar; the multitude were melting away, bearing back to the town their high resolves and panting thoughts, and echoing in many quarters the suggestive appeals of those who had addressed them. Dandy Mick and Devilsdust departed together; the business of their night had not yet commenced, and it was an important one.

They took their way to that suburb whither Gerard and Morley repaired the evening of their return from Marney Abbey, but it was not on this occasion to pay a visit to Chaffing Jack and his brilliant saloon. Winding through many obscure lanes, Mick and his friend at length turned into a passage which ended in a square court of a not inconsiderable size, and which was surrounded by high buildings that had the appearance of warehouses. Entering one of these, and taking up a dim lamp that was placed on the stone of an empty hearth, Devilsdust led his friend through several unoccupied and unfurnished rooms, until he came to one in which there were some signs of occupation.

'Now, Mick,' said he, in a very earnest, almost solemn tone, 'are you firm?'

'All right, my hearty,' replied his friend, though not without some affectation of ease.

'There is a good deal to go through,' said Devilsdust. 'It tries a man.'

'You don't mean that?'

'But if you are firm, all's right. Now I must leave you.'

'No, no, Dusty,' said Mick.

'I must go,' said Devilsdust; 'and you must rest here till

you are sent for. Now mind, whatever is bid you, obey; and whatever you see, be quiet. There,' and Devilsdust taking a flask out of his pocket, held it forth to his friend, 'give a good pull, man, I can't leave it you, for though your heart must be warm, your head must be cool,' and so saying he vanished.

Notwithstanding the animating draught, the heart of Mick Radley trembled. There are some moments when the nervous system defies even brandy. Mick was on the eve of a great and solemn incident, round which for years his imagination had gathered and brooded. Often in that imagination he had conceived the scene, and successfully confronted its perils or its trials. Often had the occasion been the drama of many a triumphant reverie, but the stern presence of reality had dispelled all his fancy and all his courage. He recalled the warning of Julia, who had often dissuaded him from the impending step; that warning received with so much scorn and treated with so much levity. He began to think that women were always right; that Devilsdust was after all a dangerous counsellor; he even meditated over the possibility of a retreat. He looked around him; the glimmering lamp scarcely indicated the outline of the obscure chamber. It was lofty, nor in the obscurity was it possible for the eye to reach the ceiling, which several huge beams seemed to cross transversely, looming in the darkness. There was apparently no window, and the door by which they had entered was not easily to be recognised. Mick had just taken up the lamp and was surveying his position, when a slight noise startled him, and looking round he beheld at some little distance two forms which he hoped were human.

Enveloped in dark cloaks and wearing black masks, a conical cap of the same colour adding to their considerable height, each held a torch. They stood in silence, two awful sentries.

Their appearance appalled, their stillness terrified Mick: he remained with his mouth open, and the lamp in his extended hand. At length, unable any longer to sustain the solemn mystery, and plucking up his natural audacity, he exclaimed, 'I say, what do you want?'

All was silent.

'Come, come,' said Mick, much alarmed; 'none of this sort of thing. I say, you must speak though.'

The figures advanced; they stuck their torches in a niche that was by; and then they placed each of them a hand on the shoulder of Mick.

'No, no; none of that,' said Mick, trying to disembarrass himself.

But, notwithstanding this fresh appeal, one of the silent masks pinioned his arms; and in a moment the eyes of the helpless friend of Devilsdust were bandaged.

Conducted by these guides, it seemed to Mick that he was traversing interminable rooms, or rather galleries, for, once stretching out his arm, while one of his supporters had momentarily quitted him to open some gate or door, Mick touched a wall. At length one of the masks spoke, and said, 'In five minutes you will be in the presence of the SEVEN: prepare.'

At this moment rose the sound of distant voices singing in concert, and gradually increasing in volume as Mick and the masks advanced. One of these attendants now notifying to their charge that he must kneel down, Mick found he rested on a cushion, while at the same time, his arms still pinioned, he seemed to be left alone.

The voices became louder and louder; Mick could distinguish the words and burthen of the hymn; he was sensible that many persons were entering the apartment; he could distinguish the measured tread of some solemn procession. Round the chamber, more than once, they moved with slow and awful step. Suddenly that movement ceased; there was a pause of a few minutes; at length a voice spoke. 'I denounce John Briars.'

'Why?' said another.

'He offers to take nothing but piece-work; the man who does piece-work is guilty of less defensible conduct than a drunkard. The worst passions of our nature are enlisted in support of piece-work. Avarice, meanness, cunning, hypocrisy, all excite and feed upon the miserable votary who works by the task and not by the hour. A man who earns by piece-work forty shillings per week, the usual wages for day-work being twenty, robs his fellows of a week's employment; therefore I denounce John Briars.'

'Let it go forth,' said the other voice; 'John Briars is denounced. If he receive another week's wages by the piece, he shall not have the option of working the week after for time. No. 87, see to John Briars.'

'I denounce Claughton and Hicks,' said another voice.

'Why?'

'They have removed Gregory Ray from being a superintendent because he belonged to this lodge.'

'Brethren, is it your pleasure that there shall be a turn out for ten days at Claughton and Hicks?'

'It is our pleasure,' cried several voices.

'No. 34, give orders to-morrow that the works at Claughton and Hicks stop till further orders.'

'Brethren,' said another voice, 'I propose the expulsion from this Union, of any member who shall be known to boast of his superior ability, as to either the quantity or quality of work he can do, either in public or private company. Is it your pleasure?'

'It is our pleasure.'

'Brethren,' said a voice that seemed a presiding one, 'before we proceed to the receipt of the revenue from the different districts of this lodge, there is, I am informed, a stranger present, who prays to be admitted into our fraternity. Are all robed in the mystic robe? Are all masked in the secret mask?'

'All!'

'Then let us pray!' And thereupon, after a movement which intimated that all present were kneeling, the presiding voice offered up an extemporary prayer of power and even eloquence. This was succeeded by the Hymn of Labour, and at its conclusion the arms of the neophyte were unpinioned, and then his eyes were unbandaged.

Mick found himself in a lofty and spacious room lighted with many tapers. Its walls were hung with black cloth; at a table covered with the same material, were seated seven persons in surplices and masked, the president on a loftier seat; above which, on a pedestal, was a skeleton complete. On each side of the skeleton was a man robed and masked, holding a drawn sword; and on each side of Mick was a man in the same garb holding a battle-axe. On the table was the sacred volume open and at a distance, ranged in order on each side of the room, was a row of persons in white robes and white masks, and holding torches.

'Michael Radley,' said the President. 'Do you voluntarily swear in the presence of Almighty God and before these witnesses, that you will execute with zeal and alacrity, so far as in you lies, every task and injunction that the majority of your brethren, testified by the mandate of this grand committee, shall impose upon you, in furtherance of our common welfare, of which they are the sole judges; such as the chastisement of Nobs, the assassination of oppressive and tyrannical masters, or the demolition of all mills, works and shops that shall be deemed by us incorrigible? Do you swear this in the presence of Almighty God, and before these witnesses?'

'I do swear it,' replied a tremulous voice.

'Then rise and kiss that book.'

Mick slowly rose from his kneeling position, advanced with a trembling step, and bending, embraced with reverence the open volume.

Immediately every one unmasked; Devilsdust came forward, and taking Mick by the hand, led him to the President, who received him pronouncing some mystic rhymes. He was covered with a robe and presented with a torch, and then ranged in order with his companions. Thus terminated the initiation of Dandy Mick into a TRADES UNION.

CHAPTER 5

'HIS lordship has not yet rung his bell, gentlemen.'

It was the valet of Lord Milford that spoke, addressing from the door of a house n Belgrave Square, about noon, a deputation from the National Convention, consisting of two of its delegates, who waited on the young viscount, in common with other members of the legislature, in order to call his particular attention to the National Petition which the Convention had prepared, and which, in the course of the session, was to be presented by one of the members for Birmingham.

'I fear we are too early for these fine birds,' said one delegate to the other. 'Who is next on our list?'

'No. 27, — Street, close by; Mr. THOROUGH BASE: he ought to be with the people, for his father was only a fiddler; but I understand he is quite an aristocrat, and has married a widow of quality.'

'Well, knock.'

Mr. Thorough Base was not at home; had received the card of the delegates apprising him of the honour of their intended visit, but had made up his mind on the subject.

No. 18 in the same street received them more courteously. Here resided Mr. KREMLIN, who, after listening with patience if not with interest, to their statement, apprised them that forms of government were of no consequence, and domestic policy of no interest; that there was only one subject which should engage the attention of public men, because everything depended on it; that was, our external system; and that the only specific for a revival of trade and the contentment of the people, was a general settlement of the boundary questions. Finally, Mr. Kremlin urged upon the National Convention to recast their petition with this view, assuring them that on foreign policy they would have the public with them.

The deputation, in reply, might have referred, as an evidence of the general interest excited by questions of foreign policy, to the impossibility even of a leader making a house on one; and to the fact, that there are not three men in the House of Commons who even pretend to have any acquaintance with the external circumstances of the country; they might have added, that, even in such an assembly, Mr. Kremlin himself was distinguished for ignorance, for he had only one idea, and that was wrong.

Their next visit was to WRIGGLE, a member for a metropolitan district, a disciple of Progress, who went with the times but who took particular good care to ascertain their complexion; and whose movements if expedient could partake of a regressive character. As the charter might some day turn up trumps as well as so many other unexpected cards and colours, Wriggle gave his adhesion to it, but, of course, only provisionally; provided, that is to say, he might vote against it at present. But he saw no harm in it, not he, and should be prepared to support it when circumstances, that is to say, the temper of the times, would permit him. More could hardly be expected from a gentleman in the delicate position in which Wriggle found himself at this moment, for he had solicited a baronetcy of the whigs, and had secretly pledged himself to Taper to vote against them on the impending Jamaica division.

BOMBASTES RIP snubbed them, which was hard, for he had been one of themselves, had written confidential letters in 1831 to the secretary of the Treasury, and, 'provided his expenses were paid,' offered to come up from the manufacturing town he now represented, at the head of a hundred thousand men, and burn down Apsley House.* But now Bombastes Rip talked of the great middle class; of public order and public credit. He would have said more to them, but had an appointment in the city, being an active member of the committee for raising a statue to the Duke of Wellington.

FLOATWELL received them in the politest manner, though he did not agree with them. What he did agree with it was difficult to say. Clever, brisk, and bustling, with a university reputation, and without patrimony, Floatwell shrunk from the toils of a profession, and in the hurry-skurry of reform found himself to his astonishment a parliament man. There he had remained, but why, the Fates, alone knew. The fun of such a thing must have evaporated with the novelty. Floatwell had entered public life in complete ignorance of every subject which could possibly engage the attention of a public man. He knew nothing of history, national or constitutional law, had indeed none but puerile acquirements, and had seen nothing of life. Assiduous at committees, he gained those superficial habits of business which are competent to the conduct of ordinary affairs, and picked up in time some of the slang of economical questions. Floatwell began at once with a little success, and he kept his little success; nobody envied him it; he hoarded his sixpences without exciting any evil emulation. He was one of those characters who above all things shrink from isolation, and who imagine they are getting on if they are keeping company with some who stick like themselves. He was always an idolator of some great personage who was on the shelf, and who, he was convinced, because the great personage assured him of it after dinner, would sooner or later turn out *the* man. At present, Floatwell swore by Lord Dunderhead; and the game of this little coterie, who dined together and thought they were a party, was to be courteous to the Convention.

After the endurance of an almost interminable lecture on the currency from Mr. Kite, who would pledge himself to the charter if the charter would pledge itself to one-pound notes, the two delegates had arrived in Piccadilly, and the next member upon the list was Lord Valentine.

'It is two o'clock,' said one of the delegates, 'I think we may venture;' so they knocked at the portal of the court yard, and found they were awaited.

A private staircase led to the suite of rooms of Lord Valentine, who lived in the family mansion. The delegates were ushered through an antechamber into a saloon which opened into a fanciful conservatory, where amid tall tropical plants played a fountain. The saloon was hung with blue satin, and adorned with brilliant mirrors; its coved ceiling was richly painted, and its furniture became the rest of its decorations. On one sofa were a number of portfolios, some open, full of drawings of costumes; a table of pietra dura* was covered with richly-bound volumes that appeared to have been recently referred to; several ancient swords of extreme beauty were lying on a couch; in a corner of the room was a figure in complete armour, black and gold, richly inlaid, and grasping in its gauntlet the ancient standard of England.

The two delegates of the National Convention stared at each other, as if to express their surprise that a dweller in such an abode should ever have permitted them to enter it; but ere either of them could venture to speak, Lord Valentine made his appearance.

He was a young man, above the middle height, slender, broad-shouldered, small-waisted, of a graceful presence; he was very fair, with dark blue eyes, bright and intelligent, and features of classic precision; a small Greek cap crowned his long light-brown hair, and he was enveloped in a morning robe of Indian shawls.

'Well, gentlemen,' said his lordship, as he invited them to be seated, in a clear and cheerful voice, and with an unaffected

tone of frankness which put his guests at their ease; 'I promised to see you; well, what have you got to say?'

The delegates made their accustomed statement; they
wished to pledge no one; all that the people desired was a
respectful discussion of their claims; the national petition,
signed by nearly a million and a half of the flower of the
working-classes, was shortly to be presented to the House of
Commons, praying the House to take into consideration the
five points in which the working-classes deemed their best
interests involved; to wit, universal suffrage, vote by ballot,
annual parliaments salaried members, and the abolition of the
property qualification.

'And supposing these five points conceded,' said Lord
Valentine, 'what do you mean to do?'

The people then being at length really represented,' replied one of the delegates, 'they would decide upon the measures which the interests of the great majority require.'

'I am not so clear about that,' said Lord Valentine; 'that is
the very point at issue. I do not think the great majority are
the best judges of their own interests. At all events, gentlemen, the respective advantages of aristocracy and democracy
are a moot point. Well then, finding the question practically
settled in this country, you will excuse me for not wishing
to agitate it. I give you complete credit for the sincerity of
your convictions; extend the same confidence to me. You are
democrats; I am an aristocrat. My family has been ennobled
for nearly three centuries; they bore a knightly name before
their elevation. They have mainly and materially assisted in
making England what it is. They have shed their blood in
many battles; I have had two ancestors killed in the command
of our fleets. You will not underrate such services, even if
you do not appreciate their conduct as statesmen, though
that has often been laborious, and sometimes distinguished.
The finest trees in England were planted by my family; they
raised several of your most beautiful churches; they have built
bridges, made roads, dug mines, and constructed canals and
drained a marsh of a million of acres which bears our name to
this day. and is now one of the most flourishing portions of
the country. You talk of our taxation and our wars; and of
your inventions and your industry. Our wars converted an

island into an empire, and at any rate developed that industry
and stimulated those inventions of which you boast. You tell
me that you are the delegates of the unrepresented working
classes of Mowbray. Why, what would Mowbray have been
if it had not been for your aristocracy and their wars? Your
town would not have existed; there would have been no
working classes there to send up delegates. In fact, you owe
your very existence to us. I have told you what my ancestors
have done; I am prepared, if the occasion requires it, not to
disgrace them; I have inherited their great position, and I tell
you fairly, gentlemen, I will not relinquish it without a
struggle.'

'Will you combat the people in that suit of armour, my
lord,' said one of the delegates smiling, but in a tone of kindness and respect.

'That suit of armour has combated for the people before
this,' said Lord Valentine, 'for it stood by Simon de Montfort
on the field of Evesham.'*

'My lord,' said the other delegate, 'it is well known that
you come from a great and honoured race; and we have seen
enough to-day to show that in intelligence and spirit you are
not unworthy of your ancestry. But the great question, which
your lordship has introduced, not we, is not to be decided by
a happy instance. Your ancestors may have done great things.
What wonder! They were members of a very limited class,
which had the monopoly of action. And the people, have not
they shed their blood in battle, though they may have commanded fleets less often than your lordship's relatives? And
these mines and canals that you have excavated and constructed, these woods you have planted, these waters you
have drained: had the people no hand in these creations?
What share in these great works had that faculty of Labour
whose sacred claims we now urge, but which for centuries
have been passed over in contemptuous silence? No, my lord,
we call upon you to decide this question by the result. The
Aristocracy of England have had for three centuries the exercise of power; for the last century and a half that exercise has
been uncontrolled; they form at this moment the most prosperous class that the history of the world can furnish; as rich
as the Roman senators, with sources of convenience and en-

joyment which modern science could alone supply. All this is not denied. Your order stands before Europe, the most gorgeous of existing spectacles; though you have of late years dexterously thrown some of the odium of your polity upon that middle class which you despise, and who are despicable only because they imitate you, your tenure of power is not in reality impaired. You govern us still with absolute authority, and you govern the most miserable people on the face of the globe.'

'And is this a fair description of the people of England?' said Lord Valentine. 'A flash of rhetoric, I presume, that would place them lower than the Portuguese or the Poles, the serfs of Russia, or the lazzaroni of Naples.'

'Infinitely lower,' said the delegate, 'for they are not only degraded, but conscious of their degradation. They no longer believe in any innate difference between the governing and the governed classes of this country. They are sufficiently enlightened to feel they are victims. Compared with the privileged classes of their own land, they are in a lower state than any other population compared with its privileged classes. All is relative, my lord, and believe me, the relations of the working classes of England to its privileged orders are relations of enmity, and therefore of peril.'

'The people must have leaders,' said Lord Valentine.

'And they have found them,' said the delegate.

'When it comes to a push they will follow their nobility,' said Lord Valentine.

'Will their nobility lead them?' said the other delegate. 'For my part, I do not pretend to be a philosopher, and if I saw a Simon de Montfort again I should be content to fight under his banner.'

'We have an aristocracy of wealth,' said the delegate who had chiefly spoken. 'In a progressive civilization, wealth is the only means of class distinction; but a new disposition of wealth may remove even this.'

'Ah! you want to get at our estates,' said Lord Valentine, smiling; 'but the effort on your part may resolve society into its original elements, and the old sources of distinction may again develop themselves.'

'Tall barons will not stand against Paixhans' rockets,'*

said the delegate. 'Modern science has vindicated the natural equality of man.'

'And I must say I am very sorry for it,' said the other delegate; 'for human strength always seems to me the natural process of settling affairs.'

'I am not surprised at your opinion,' said Lord Valentine, turning to the delegate and smiling. 'I should not be over-glad to meet you in a fray. You stand some inches above six feet, or I am mistaken.'

'I was six feet two inches when I stopped growing,' said the delegate; 'and age has not stolen any of my height yet.'

'That suit of armour would fit you,' said Lord Valentine, as they all rose.

'And might I ask your lordship,' said the tall delegate, 'why it is here?'

'I am to represent Richard Cœur de Lion at the Queen's ball,'* said Lord Valentine; 'and before my sovereign I will not don a Drury Lane cuirass, so I got this up from my father's castle.'

'Ah! I almost wish the good old times of Cœur de Lion were here again,' said the tall delegate.

'And we should be serfs,' said his companion.

'I am not sure of that,' said the tall delegate. 'At any rate there was the free forest.'

'I like that young fellow,' said the tall delegate to his companion, as they descended the staircase.

'He has awful prejudices,' said his friend.

'Well, well; he has his opinions, and we have ours. But he is a man; with clear, straightforward ideas, a frank, noble presence; and as good-looking a fellow as I ever set eyes on. Where are we now?'

'We have only one more name on our list to-day, and it is at hand. Letter K, No. 1, Albany. Another member of the aristocracy, the Honourable Charles Egremont.'

'Well, I prefer them, so far as I can judge, to Wriggle, and Rip, and Thorough Base,' said the tall delegate laughing. 'I dare say we should have found Lord Milford a very jolly fellow, if he had only been up.'

'Here we are,' said his companion, as he knocked. 'Mr. Egremont, is he at home?'

'The gentleman of the deputation? Yes, my master gave particular orders that he was at home to you. Will you walk in, gentlemen?'

'There, you see,' said the tall delegate. 'This would be a lesson to Thorough Base.'

They sat down in an antechamber; the servant opened a mahogany folding-door which he shut after him, and announced to his master the arrival of the delegates. Egremont was seated in his library, at a round table covered with writing materials, books, and letters. On another table were arranged his parliamentary papers, and piles of blue books. The room was classically furnished. On the mantelpiece were some ancient vases, which he had brought with him from Italy, standing on each side of that picture of Allori of which we have spoken.

The servant returned to the ante-room, and announcing to the delegates that his master was ready to receive them, ushered into the presence of Egremont, WALTER GERARD and STEPHEN MORLEY.

CHAPTER 6

IT is much to be deplored that our sacred buildings are generally closed, except at the stated periods of public resort. It is still more to be regretted that, when with difficulty entered, there is so much in their arrangements to offend the taste and outrage the feelings. In the tumult of life, a few minutes occasionally passed in the solemn shadow of some lofty and ancient aisle, exercise very often a salutary influence: they purify the heart and elevate the mind; dispel many haunting fancies, and prevent many an act which otherwise might be repented. The church would in this light still afford us a sanctuary; not against the power of the law but against the violence of our own will; not against the passions of man but against our own.

The Abbey of Westminster rises amid the strife of factions. Around its consecrated precinct some of the boldest and some of the worst deeds have been achieved or perpetrated; sacrilege, rapine, murder, and treason. Here robbery has been

practised on the greatest scale known in modern ages: here
ten thousand manors belonging to the order of the Templars,
without any proof, scarcely with a pretext, were forfeited in
one day and divided among the monarch and his chief nobles;
here the great estate of the church, which, whatever its articles
of faith, belonged and still belongs to the people, was seized
at various times, under various pretences, by an assembly that
continually changed the religion of their country and their
own by a parliamentary majority, but which never refunded
the booty. Here too was brought forth that monstrous conception which even patrician Rome in its most ruthless period
never equalled, the mortgaging of the industry of the country
to enrich and to protect property; an act which is now bringing its retributive consequences in a degraded and alienated
population. Here too have the innocent been impeached and
hunted to death; and a virtuous and able monarch* martyred,
because, among other benefits projected for his people, he
was of opinion that it was more for their advantage that the
economic service of the state should be supplied by direct
taxation levied by an individual known to all, than by indirect taxation, raised by an irresponsible and fluctuating
assembly. But, thanks to parliamentary patriotism, the people
of England were saved from ship-money, which money the
wealthy paid, and only got in its stead the customs and excise,*
which the poor mainly supply. Rightly was King Charles surnamed the Martyr; for he was the holocaust of direct taxation.
Never yet did man lay down his heroic life for so great a
cause: the cause of the Church and the cause of the Poor.

Even now, in the quiet times in which we live, when public
robbery is out of fashion and takes the milder title of a commission of inquiry, and when there is no treason except voting
against a Minister, who, though he may have changed all the
policy which you have been elected to support, expects your
vote and confidence all the same; even in this age of mean
passions and petty risks, it is something to step aside from
Palace Yard, and instead of listening to a dull debate, where
the facts are only a repetition of the blue books you have already read, and the fancy an ingenious appeal to the recrimi-
nation of Hansard, to enter the old Abbey and listen to an
anthem!

This was a favourite habit of Egremont, and, though the mean discipline and sordid arrangements of the ecclesiastical body to which the guardianship of the beautiful edifice is intrusted have certainly done all that could injure and impair the holy genius of the place, it still was a habit often full of charm and consolation.

There is not perhaps another metropolitan population in the world that would tolerate such conduct as is pursued to 'that great lubber, the public,' by the Dean and Chapter of Westminster, and submit in silence to be shut out from the only building in the two cities which is worthy of the name of a cathedral. But the British public will bear anything; they are so busy in speculating in railway shares.*

When Egremont had entered on his first visit to the Abbey by the south transept, and beheld the boards and the spikes with which he seemed to be environed, as if the Abbey were in a state of siege; iron gates shutting him out from the solemn nave and the shadowy aisles; scarcely a glimpse to be caught of a single window; while on a dirty form, some noisy vergers sat like ticket-porters or babbled like tapsters at their ease, the visions of abbatial perfection, in which he had early and often indulged among the ruins of Marney, rose on his outraged sense, and he was then about hastily to retire from the scene he had so long purposed to visit, when suddenly the organ burst forth, a celestial symphony floated in the lofty roof, and voices of plaintive melody blended with the swelling sounds. He was fixed to the spot.

Perhaps it was some similar feeling that influenced another individual on the day after the visit of the deputation to Egremont. The sun, though in his summer heaven he had still a long course, had passed his meridian by many hours, the service was performing in the choir, and a few persons entering by the door into that part of the Abbey Church which is so well known by the name of Poets' Corner, proceeded through the unseemly stockade which the chapter have erected, and took their seats. One only, a female, declined to pass, notwithstanding the officious admonitions of the vergers that she had better move on, but approaching the iron grating that shut her out from the body of the church, looked wistfully down the long dim perspective of the beautiful southern aisle.

And thus motionless she remained in contemplation, or it might be prayer, while the solemn peals of the organ and the sweet voices of the choir enjoyed that holy liberty for which she sighed, and seemed to wander at their will in every sacred recess and consecrated corner.

The sounds, those mystical and thrilling sounds that at once exalt the soul and touch the heart, ceased; the chanting of the service recommenced; the motionless form moved; and as she moved Egremont came forth from the choir, and his eye was at once caught by the symmetry of her shape and the picturesque position which she gracefully occupied; still gazing through that grate, while the light, pouring through the western window, suffused the body of the church with a soft radiance, just touching the head of the unknown with a kind of halo. Egremont approached the transept door with a lingering pace, so that the stranger who he observed was preparing to leave the church, might overtake him. As he reached the door, anxious to assure himself that he was not mistaken, he turned round and his eye at once caught the face of Sybil. He started, he trembled; she was not two yards distant, she evidently recognized him; he held open the swinging postern of the Abbey that she might pass, which she did, and then stopped on the outside, and said 'Mr. Franklin!'

It was therefore clear that her father had not thought fit, or had not yet had an opportunity, to communicate to Sybil the interview of yesterday. Egremont was still Mr. Franklin. This was perplexing. Egremont would like to have been saved the pain and awkwardness of the avowal, yet it must be made, though not with unnecessary crudeness. And so at present he only expressed his delight, the unexpected delight he experienced at their meeting. And then he walked on by her side.

'Indeed,' said Sybil, 'I can easily imagine you must have been surprised at seeing me in this great city. But many things, strange and unforeseen, have happened to us since you were at Mowedale. You know, of course, you with your pursuits must know, that the People have at length resolved to summon their own Parliament in Westminster. The people of Mowbray had to send up two delegates to the Convention, and they chose my father for one of them. For, so great is their confidence in him, none other would content them.'

'He must have made a great sacrifice in coming?' said Egremont.

'Oh! what are sacrifices in such a cause!' said Sybil. 'Yes; he made great sacrifices,' she continued earnestly; 'great sacrifices, and I am proud of them. Our home, which was a happy home, is gone; he has quitted the Traffords, to whom we were knit by many, many ties,' and her voice faltered, 'and for whom, I know well he would have perilled his life. And now we are parted,' said Sybil, with a sigh, 'perhaps for ever. They offered to receive me under their roof,' she continued, with emotion. 'Had I needed shelter there was another roof which has long awaited me; but I could not leave my father at such a moment. He appealed to me; and I am here. All I desire, all I live for, is to soothe and support him in his great struggle; and I should die content if the People were only free, and a Gerard had freed them.'

Egremont mused: he must disclose all, yet how embarrassing to enter into such explanations in a public thoroughfare! Should he bid her after a while farewell, and then make his confession in writing? Should he at once accompany her home, and there offer his perplexing explanations? Or should he acknowledge his interview of yesterday with Gerard, and then leave the rest to the natural consequences of that acknowledgment when Sybil met her father? Thus pondering, Egremont and Sybil quitting the court of the Abbey, entered Abingdon Street.

'Let me walk home with you,' said Egremont, as Sybil seemed to intimate her intention here to separate.

'My father is not there,' said Sybil; 'but I will not fail to tell him that I have met his old companion.'

'Would he had been as frank!' thought Egremont. And must he quit her in this way? Impossible. 'You must indeed let me attend you!' he said aloud.

'It is not far,' said Sybil. 'We live almost in the Precinct, in an old house, with some kind old people, the brother of one of the nuns of Mowbray. The nearest way to it is straight along this street but that is too bustling for me. I have discovered,' she added with a smile, 'a more tranquil path.' And guided by her, they turned up College Street.

'And how long have you been in London?'

'A fortnight. 'Tis a great prison. How strange it is that, in a vast city like this, one can scarcely walk alone!'

'You want Harold,' said Egremont. 'How is that most faithful of friends?'

'Poor Harold! To part with him too was a pang.'

'I fear your hours must be heavy,' said Egremont.

'Oh! no,' said Sybil, 'there is so much at stake; so much to hear the moment my father returns. I take so much interest too in their discussions; and sometimes I go to hear him speak .None of them can compare with him. It seems to me that it would be impossible to resist our claims if our rulers only heard them from his lips.'

Egremont smiled. 'Your Convention is in its bloom, or rather its bud,' he said; 'all is fresh and pure now; but a little while and it will find the fate of all popular assemblies. You will have factions.'

'But why?' said Sybil. 'They are the real representatives of the people. and all that the people want is justice; that Labour should be as much respected by law and society as Property.'

While they thus conversed, they passed through several clean, still streets, that had rather the appearance of streets in a very quiet country town, than of abodes in the greatest city in the world, and in the vicinity of palaces and parliaments Rarely was a shop to be remarked among the neat little tenements, many of them built of curious old brick, and all of them raised without any regard to symmetry or proportion. Not the sounds of a single wheel was heard; sometimes not a single individual was visible or stirring. Making a circuitous course through this tranquil and orderly district, they at last found themselves in an open place in the centre of which rose a church of vast proportions, and built of hewn stone in that stately, not to say ponderous, style which Vanbrugh introduced. The area round it, which was sufficiently ample, was formed by buildings, generally of a mean character: the long back premises of a carpenter, the straggling yard of a hackneyman; sometimes a small, narrow isolated private residence, like a waterspout in which a rat might reside; sometimes a group of houses of more pretension. In the extreme corner of this area, which was dignified by the name of Smith's Square, instead of taking a more appropriate title from the church of St John which it encircled, was a large old house, that had been masked at the beginning of the century with a modern front of pale-coloured bricks, but which still stood in its courtyard surrounded by its iron railings, withdrawn as it were from the vulgar gaze like an individual who had known higher fortunes, and blending with his humility something of the reserve which is prompted by the memory of vanished greatness.

'This is my home,' said Sybil. 'It is a still place, and suits us well.'

Near the house was a narrow passage which was a thoroughfare into the most populous quarter of the neighbourhood. As Egremont was opening the gate of the courtyard, Gerard ascended the steps of this passage, and approached them.

CHAPTER 7

WHEN Gerard and Morley quitted the Albany after their visit to Egremont, they separated, and Stephen, whom we will accompany, proceeded in the direction of the Temple, in the vicinity of which he himself lodged, and where he was about to visit a brother journalist, who occupied chambers in that famous inn of court. As he passed under Temple Bar his eye caught a portly gentleman stepping out of a public cab, with a bundle of papers in his hand, and immediately disappearing through that well-known archway which Morley was on the point of reaching. The gentleman indeed was still in sight, descending the way, when Morley entered, who observed him drop a letter.* Morley hailed him, but in vain; and fearing the stranger might disappear in one of the many inextricable courts, and so lose his letter, he ran forward, picked up the paper, and then pushed on to the person who dropped it, calling out so frequently that the stranger at length began to suspect that he himself might be the object of the salute, and stopped and looked round. Morley almost mechanically glanced at the outside of the letter, the seal of which was broken, and which was however addressed to a name that immediately fixed his interest. The direction was to 'Baptist Hatton, Esq., Inner Temple.'

'This letter is I believe addressed to you, Sir,' said Morley, looking very intently upon the person to whom he spoke, a portly man and a comely; florid, gentleman-like, but with as little of the expression which Morley in imagination had associated with that Hatton over whom he once pondered, as can easily be imagined.

'Sir, I am extremely obliged to you,' said the strange gentleman; 'the letter belongs to me, though it is not addressed to me. I must have this moment dropped it. My name, Sir, is Firebrace, Sir Vavasour Firebrace, and this letter is addressed to a – a – not exactly my lawyer, but a gentleman, a professional gentleman, whom I am in the habit of frequently seeing; daily, I may say. He is employed in a great question in which I am deeply interested. Sir, I am vastly obliged to you, and I trust that you are satisfied.'

'Oh! perfectly, Sir Vavasour;' and Morley bowed; and going in different directions, they separated.

'Do you happen to know a lawyer by name Hatton in this Inn?' inquired Morley of his friend the journalist, when, having transacted their business, the occasion served.

'No lawyer of that name; but the famous Hatton lives here,' was the reply.

'The famous Hatton! And what is he famous for? You forget I am a provincial.'

'He has made more peers of the realm than our gracious Sovereign,' said the journalist. 'And since the reform of parliament the only chance of a tory becoming a peer is the favour of Baptist Hatton; though who he is no one knows, and what he is no one can describe.'

'You speak in conundrums,' said Morley; 'I wish I could guess them. Try to adapt yourself to my somewhat simple capacity.'

'In a word, then,' said his friend, 'if you must have a definition, Hatton may rank under the genus "antiquary," though his species is more difficult to describe. He is an heraldic antiquary; a discoverer, inventor, framer, arranger of pedigrees; profound in the mysteries of genealogies; an authority I believe unrivalled in everything that concerns the constitution and elements of the House of Lords; consulted by lawyers, though not professing the law; and startling and alarming the noblest families in the country by claiming the ancient baronies which they have often assumed without authority, for obscure pretenders, many of whom he has succeeded in seating in the parliament of his country.'

'And what part of the country did he come from; do you happen to know?' inquired Morley, evidently much interested, though he attempted to conceal his emotion.

'He may be a veritable subject of the kingdom of Cockaigne,* for aught I know,' replied his friend. 'He has been buried in this inn I believe for years; for very many before I settled here; and for a long time I apprehend was sufficiently obscure, though doing they say a great deal in a small way; but the Mallory case made his fortune about ten years ago. That was a barony by writ of summons which had been claimed a century before, and failed. Hatton seated his man, and the precedent enabled three or four more gentlemen under his auspices to follow that example. They were Roman Catholics, which probably brought him the Mallory case, for Hatton is of the old church; better than that, they were all gentlemen of great estate, and there is no doubt their champion was well rewarded for his successful service. They say he is very rich. At present all the business of the country connected with descents flows into his chambers. Not a pedigree in dispute, not a peerage in abeyance, which is not submitted to his consideration. I don't know him personally; but you can now form some idea of his character; and if you want to claim a peerage,' the journalist added laughingly, 'he is your man.'

A strong impression was on the mind of Morley that this was his man; he resolved to inquire of Gerard, whom he should see in the evening, as to the fact of their Hatton being a Catholic, and if so, to call on the antiquary on the morrow.

In the meantime we must not forget one who is already making that visit. Sir Vavasour Firebrace is seated in a spacious library that looks upon the Thames and the gardens

of the Temple. Though piles of parchments and papers cover
the numerous tables, and in many parts intrude upon the
Turkey carpet, an air of order, of comfort, and of taste,
pervades the chamber. The hangings of crimson damask silk
blend with the antique furniture of oak; the upper panes of the
windows are tinted by the brilliant pencil of feudal Germany,
while the choice volumes that line the shelves are clothed in
bindings which become their rare contents. The master of this
apartment was a man of ordinary height, inclined to corpu-
lency, and in the wane of middle life, though his unwrinkled
cheek, his undimmed blue eye, and his brown hair, very
apparent, though he wore a cap of black velvet, did not betray
his age, or the midnight studies by which he had in a great
degree acquired that learning for which he was celebrated.
The general expression of his countenance was pleasing,
though dashed with a trait of the sinister. He was seated in an
easy chair, before a kidney table at which he was writing.
Near at hand was a long tall open desk, on which were several
folio volumes open, and some manuscripts which denoted
that he had recently been engaged with them. At present Mr.
Hatton, with his pen still in his hand and himself in a chamber-
robe of the same material as his cap, leant back in his chair,
while he listened to his client, Sir Vavasour. Several beautiful
black and tan spaniels of the breed of King Charles II were
reposing near him on velvet cushions, with a haughty
luxuriousness which would have become the beauties of the
merry monarch; and a white Persian cat, with blue eyes, a long
tail, and a visage not altogether unlike that of its master, was
resting with great gravity on the writing-table, and assisting at
the conference.

Sir Vavasour had evidently been delivering himself of a
long narrative, to which Mr. Hatton had listened with that
imperturbable patience which characterised him, and which
was unquestionably one of the elements of his success. He
never gave up anything, and he never interrupted anybody.
And now in a silvery voice he replied to his visitor:

'What you tell me, Sir Vavasour, is what I foresaw, but
which, as my influence could not affect it, I dismissed from
my thoughts. You came to me for a specific object. I accomplished it. I undertook to ascertain the rights and revive

the claims of the baronets of England. That was what you required of me; I fulfilled your wish. Those rights are ascertained; these claims are revived. A great majority of the Order have given in their adhesion to the organised movement. The nation is acquainted with your demands, accustomed to them, and the monarch once favourably received them. I can do no more; I do not pretend to make baronets, still less can I confer on those already made the right to wear stars and coronets, the dark green dress of Equites aurati, or white hats with white plumes of feathers. These distinctions, even if their previous usage were established, must flow from the gracious permission of the Crown, and no one could expect, in an age hostile to personal distinctions, that any ministry would recommend the Sovereign to a step which with vulgar minds would be odious, and by malignant ones might be rendered ridiculous.'

'Ridiculous!' said Sir Vavasour.

'All the world,' said Mr. Hatton, 'do not take upon these questions the same enlightened view as ourselves, Sir Vavasour. I never could for a moment believe that the Sovereign would consent to invest such a numerous body of men with such privileges.'

'But you never expressed this opinion,' said Sir Vavasour.

'You never asked for my opinion,' said Mr. Hatton; 'and if I had given it, you and your friends would not have been influenced by it. The point was one on which you might with reason hold yourselves as competent judges as I am. All you asked of me was to make out your case, and I made it out. I will venture to say a better case never left these chambers; I do not believe there is a person in the kingdom who could answer it except myself. They have refused the Order their honours, Sir Vavasour, but it is some consolation that they have never answered their case.'

'I think it only aggravates the oppression,' said Sir Vavasour, shaking his head; 'but cannot you advise any new step, Mr. Hatton? After so many years of suspense, after so much anxiety and such a vast expenditure, it really is too bad that I and Lady Firebrace should be announced at court in the same style as our fishmonger, if he happens to be a sheriff.'

'I can make a peer,' said Mr. Hatton, leaning back in his

chair and playing with his seals, 'but I do not pretend to make baronets. I can place a coronet with four balls on a man's brow; but a coronet with two balls is an exercise of the prerogative with which I do not presume to interfere.'

'I mention it in the utmost confidence,' said Sir Vavasour, in a whisper; 'but Lady Firebrace has a sort of promise that, in the event of a change of government, we shall be in the first batch of peers.'

Mr. Hatton shook his head with a slight smile of contemptuous incredulity.

'Sir Robert,' he said, 'will make no peers; take my word for that. The whigs and I have so deluged the House of Lords, that you may rely upon it as a secret of state, that if the tories come in, there will be no peers made. I know the Queen is sensitively alive to the cheapening of all honours of late years. If the whigs go out to-morrow, mark me, they will disappoint all their friends. Their underlings have promised so many, that treachery is inevitable, and if they deceive some they may as well deceive all. Perhaps they may distribute a coronet or two among themselves; and I shall this year make three; and those are the only additions to the peerage which will occur for many years. You may rely on that. For the tories will make none, and I have some thoughts of retiring from business.'

It is difficult to express the astonishment, the perplexity, the agitation, that pervaded the countenance of Sir Vavasour while his companion thus coolly delivered himself. High hopes extinguished and excited at the same moment; cherished promises vanishing, mysterious expectations rising up; revelations of astounding state secrets; chief ministers voluntarily renouncing their highest means of influence, and an obscure private individual distributing those distinctions which sovereigns were obliged to hoard, and to obtain which the first men in the country were ready to injure their estates and to sacrifice their honour! At length Sir Vavasour said, 'You amaze me, Mr. Hatton. I could mention to you twenty members at Boodle's, at least, who believe they will be made peers the moment the tories come in.'

'Not a man of them,' said Hatton peremptorily. 'Tell me

one of their names, and I will tell you whether they will be made peers.'

'Well, then, there is Mr. Tubbe Sweete, a county member, and his son in Parliament too; I know he has a promise.'

'I repeat to you, Sir Vavasour, the tories will not make a single peer; the candidates must come to me; and I ask you what can I do for a Tubbe Sweete, the son of a Jamaica cooper? Are there any old families among your twenty members of Boodle's?'

'Why I can hardly say,' said Sir Vavasour; 'there is Sir Charles Featherly, an old baronet.'

'The founder a Lord Mayor in James the First's reign. That is not the sort of old family that I mean,' said Mr. Hatton.

'Well, there is Colonel Cockawhoop,' said Sir Vavasour. 'The Cockawhoops are a very good family I have always heard.'

'Contractors of Queen Anne; partners with Marlborough and Solomon Medina; a very good family indeed: but I do not make peers out of good families, Sir Vavasour; old families are the blocks out of which I cut my Mercuries.'

'But what do you call an old family?' said Sir Vavasour.

'Yours,' said Mr. Hatton; and he threw a full glance on the countenance on which the light rested.

'We were in the first batch of baronets,' said Sir Vavasour.

'Forget the baronets for a while,' said Hatton. 'Tell me, what was your family before James I.?'

'They always lived on their lands,' said Sir Vavasour. 'I have a room full of papers that would, perhaps tell us something about them. Would you like to see them?'

'By all means; bring them all here. Not that I want them to inform me of your rights; I am fully acquainted with them. You would like to be a peer, sir. Well, you are really Lord Vavasour, but there is a difficulty in establishing your undoubted right from the single writ of summons difficulty. I will not trouble you with technicalities, Sir Vavasour; sufficient that the difficulty is great, though perhaps not unmanageable. But we have no need of management. Your claim on the barony of Lovel is good: I could recommend your pursuing it, did not another more inviting still present itself. In a word, if you wish to be Lord Bardolf, I will under-take to make you so, before, in all probability, Sir Robert Peel obtains office; and that I should think would gratify Lady Firebrace.'

'Indeed it would,' said Sir Vavasour, 'for if it had not been for this sort of a promise of a peerage made, I speak in great confidence, Mr. Hatton, made by Mr. Taper, my tenants would have voted for the whigs the other day at the ——shire election, and the Conservative candidate would have been beaten. Lord Masque had almost arranged it, but Lady Firebrace would have a written promise from a high quarter, and so it fell to the ground.'

'Well, we are independent of all these petty arrangements now,' said Mr. Hatton.

'It is wonderful,' said Sir Vavasour, rising from his chair and speaking, as it were, to himself. 'And what do you think our expenses will be in this claim?' he inquired.

'Bagatelle!' said Mr. Hatton. 'Why, a dozen years ago I have known men lay out nearly half a million in land and not get two per cent. for their money, in order to obtain a borough influence, which might ultimately obtain them a spick and span coronet; and now you are going to put one on your head, which will give you precedence over every peer on the roll, except three; and I made those; and it will not cost you a paltry twenty or thirty thousand pounds. Why, I know men who would give that for the precedence alone. Here!' and he rose and took up some papers from a table: 'Here is a case; a man you know, I dare say; an earl, and of a decent date as earls go; George I. The first baron was a Dutch valet of William III. Well, I am to terminate an abeyance in his favour through his mother, and give him one of the baronies of the Herberts. He buys off the other claimant, who is already ennobled, with a larger sum than you will expend on your ancient coronet. Nor is that all. The other claimant is of French descent and name; came over at the revocation of the Edict of Nantes.* Well, besides the hush-money, my client is to defray all the expense of attempting to transform the descendant of the silkweaver of Lyons into the heir of a Norman conqueror. So you see, Sir Vavasour, I am not unreasonable. Pah! I would sooner gain five thousand pounds by restoring you to your rights, than fifty thousand in establishing any of these pretenders in their base assumptions. I must work in my craft, Sir Vavasour, but I love the old English blood, and have it in my veins.'

'I am satisfied, Mr. Hatton,' said Sir Vavasour; 'let no time be lost. All I regret is, that you did not mention all this to me before; and then we might have saved a great deal of trouble and expense.'

'You never consulted me,' said Mr. Hatton. 'You gave me your instructions, and I obeyed them. I was sorry to see you in that mind, for to speak frankly, and I am sure now you will not be offended, my lord, for such is your real dignity, there is no title in the world for which I have such a contempt as that of a baronet.'

Sir Vavasour winced, but the future was full of glory and the present of excitement; and he wished Mr. Hatton good morning, with a promise that he would himself bring the papers on the morrow.

Mr. Hatton was buried for a few moments in a reverie, during which he played with the tail of the Persian cat.

CHAPTER 8

WE left Sybil and Egremont just at the moment that Gerard arrived at the very threshold which they had themselves reached.

'Ah! my father,' exclaimed Sybil, and then with a faint blush, of which she was perhaps unconscious, she added, as if apprehensive Gerard would not recall his old companion, 'you remember Mr. Franklin?'

'This gentleman and myself had the pleasure of meeting yesterday,' said Gerard, embarrassed, while Egremont himself changed colour and was infinitely confused. Sybil felt surprised that her father should have met Mr. Franklin and not have mentioned a circumstance naturally interesting to her. Egremont was about to speak when the street-door was opened. And were they to part again, and no explanation? And was Sybil to be left with her father, who was evidently in no haste, perhaps had no great tendency, to give that explanation? Every feeling of an ingenuous spirit urged Egremont personally to terminate this prolonged misconception.

'You will permit me, I hope,' he said, appealing as much to Gerard as to his daughter, 'to enter with you for a few moments.'

It was not possible to resist such a request, yet it was conceded on the part of Gerard with no cordiality. So they entered the large gloomy hall of the house, and towards the end of a long passage Gerard opened a door, and they all went into a spacious melancholy room, situate at the back of the house, and looking upon a small square plot of dank grass, in the midst of which rose a weatherstained Cupid, with one arm broken, and the other raised in the air, and with a long shell to its mouth. It seemed that in old days it might have been a fountain. At the end of the plot, the blind side of a house offered a high wall which had once been painted in fresco. Though much of the coloured plaster had cracked and peeled away, and all that remained was stained and faded, still some traces of the original design might yet be detected: festive wreaths, the colonnades and perspective of a palace.

The walls of the room itself were wainscoted in panels of dark-stained wood; the window-curtains were of coarse green worsted, and encrusted by dust so ancient and irremoveable, that it presented almost a lava-like appearance; the carpet, that had once been bright and showy, was entirely threadbare, and had become grey with age. There were several heavy mahogany arm-chairs in the room, a Pembroke table,* and an immense unwieldy sideboard, garnished with a few wineglasses of a deep blue colour. Over the lofty uncouth mantel was a portrait of the Marquis of Granby, which might have been a sign, and opposite to him, over the sideboard, was a large tawdry-coloured print, by Bunbury,* of Ranelagh* in its most festive hour. The general appearance of the room, however, though dingy, was not squalid; and what with its spaciousness, its extreme repose, and the associations raised by such few images as it did suggest, the impression on the mind of the spectator was far from unpleasing, partaking indeed of that vague melancholy which springs from the contemplation of the past, and which at all times softens the spirit.

Gerard walked to the window and looked at the grassplot; Sybil seating herself, invited their guest to follow her example; Egremont, not without agitation, seemed suddenly to make an effort to collect himself, and then, in a voice not distinguished by its accustomed clearness, he said, 'I explained yesterday to one whom, I hope, I may still call my friend, why I assumed a name to which I have no right.'

Sybil started a little, slightly stared, but did not speak.

'I should be happy if you also would give me credit, in taking that step, at least for motives of which I need not be ashamed; even,' he added in a hesitating voice, 'even if you deemed my conduct indiscreet.'

Their eyes met: astonishment was imprinted on the countenance of Sybil, but she uttered not a word; and her father, whose back was turned to them, did not move.

'I was told,' continued Egremont, 'that an impassable gulf divided the Rich from the Poor; I was told that the Privileged and the People formed Two Nations, governed by different laws, influenced by different manners, with no thoughts or sympathies in common; with an innate inability of mutual comprehension. I believed that if this were indeed the case, the ruin of our common country was at hand; I would have endeavoured, feebly perchance, but not without zeal, to resist such a catastrophe; I possessed a station which entailed on me some portion of its responsibility; to obtain that knowledge which could alone qualify me for beneficial action, I resolved to live without suspicion among my fellow-subjects who were estranged from me; even void of all celebrity as I am, I could not have done that without suspicion, had I been known; they would have recoiled from my class and my name, as you yourself recoiled, Sybil, when they were once accidentally mentioned before you. These are the reasons, these the feelings, which impelled, I will not say justified, me to pass your threshold under a feigned name. I entreat you to judge kindly of my conduct; to pardon me; and not to make me feel the bitterness that I have forfeited the good opinion of one for whom under all circumstances and in all situations, I must ever feel the highest conceivable respect, I would say a reverential regard.'

His tones of passionate emotion ceased. Sybil, with a

countenance beautiful and disturbed, gazed at him for an instant, and seemed about to speak, but her trembling lips refused the office; then with an effort, turning to Gerard, she said, 'My father, I am amazed; tell me, then, who is this gentleman who addresses me?'

'The brother of Lord Marney, Sybil,' said Gerard, turning to her.

'The brother of Lord Marney!' repeated Sybil, with an air almost of stupor.

'Yes,' said Egremont; 'a member of that family of sacrilege, of those oppressors of the people, whom you have denounced to me with such withering scorn.'

The elbow of Sybil rested on the arm of her chair, and her cheek upon her hand; as Egremont said these words she shaded her face, which was thus entirely unseen: for some moments there was silence. Then looking up with an expression grave but serene, and as if she had just emerged from some deep thinking, Sybil said, 'I am sorry for my words; sorry for the pain I unconsciously gave you; sorry indeed for all that has passed; and that my father has lost a pleasant friend.'

'And why should he be lost?' said Egremont mournfully, and yet with tenderness. 'Why should we not still be friends?'

'Oh, sir!' said Sybil, haughtily; 'I am one of those who believe the gulf is impassable. Yes,' she added, slightly, but with singular grace waving her hands, and somewhat turning away her head, 'utterly impassable.'

There are tumults of the mind, when, like the great convulsions of nature, all seems anarchy and returning chaos, yet often, in those moments of vast disturbance, as in the material strife itself, some new principle of order, or some new impulse of conduct, develops itself, and controls, and regulates, and brings to an harmonious consequence, passions and elements which seemed only to threaten despair and subversion. So it was with Egremont. He looked for a moment in despair upon this maiden, walled out from sympathy by prejudices and convictions more impassable than all the mere consequences of class. He looked for a moment, but only for a moment, in despair. He found in his tortured spirit energies that responded to the exigency of the occasion. Even the otherwise em-

barrassing presence of Gerard would not have prevented –
but just at this moment the door opened, and Morley and
another person entered the room.

CHAPTER 9

MORLEY paused as he recognised Egremont; then advancing
to Gerard, followed by his companion, he said, 'This is Mr.
Hatton of whom we were speaking last night, and who
claims to be an ancient acquaintance of yours.'

'Perhaps I should rather say of your poor dear father,' said
Hatton, scanning Gerard with his clear blue eye; and then he
added, 'He was of great service to me in my youth, and one is
not apt to forget such things.'

'One ought not,' said Gerard; 'but it is a sort of memory,
as I have understood, that is rather rare. For my part I remember you very well, Baptist Hatton,' said Gerard, examining his guest with almost as complete a scrutiny as he had
himself experienced. 'The world has gone well with you, I am
glad to hear and see.'

'Qui laborat, orat,' said Hatton in a silvery voice, 'is the
gracious maxim of our Holy Church; and I venture to believe
my prayers and vigils have been accepted, for I have laboured
in my time;' and as he was speaking these words, he turned
and addressed them to Sybil.

She beheld him with no little interest; this mysterious name
that had sounded so often in her young ears, and was associated with so many strange and high hopes, and some
dark blending of doubt and apprehension, and discordant
thoughts. Hatton in his appearance realised little of the
fancies in which Sybil had sometimes indulged with regard to
him. That appearance was prepossessing: a frank and even
benevolent expression played upon his intelligent and handsome countenance; his once rich brown hair, still long, though
thin, was so arranged as naturally to conceal his baldness; he
was dressed with great simplicity, but with remarkable taste
and care; nor did the repose and suavity of his manner and the
hushed tone of his voice detract from the favourable effect that
he always at once produced.

'Qui laborat, orat,' said Sybil with a smile, 'is the privilege of the people.'

'Of whom I am one,' said Hatton, bowing, well recollecting that he was addressing the daughter of a chartist delegate.

'But is your labour, their labour?' said Sybil. 'Is yours that life of uncomplaining toil wherein there is so much of beauty and of goodness, that, by the fine maxim of our Church, it is held to include the force and efficacy of prayer?'

'I am sure that I should complain of no toil that would benefit you,' said Hatton; and then addressing himself again to Gerard, he led him to a distant part of the room where they were soon engaged in earnest converse. Morley at the same moment approached Sybil, and spoke to her in a subdued tone. Egremont, feeling embarrassed, advanced and bade her farewell. She rose and returned his salute with some ceremony; then hesitating while a soft expression came over her countenance, she held forth her hand, which he retained for a moment, and withdrew.

'I was with him more than an hour,' continued Morley. 'At first he recollected nothing; even the name of Gerard, though he received it as familiar to him, seemed to produce little impression; he recollected nothing of any papers; was clear that they must have been quite insignificant; whatever they were, he doubtless had them now, as he never destroyed papers; would order a search to be made for them, and so on. I was about to withdraw, when he asked me carelessly a question about your father; what he was doing, and whether he were married, and had children. This led to a long conversation, in which he suddenly seemed to take great interest. At first he talked of writing to see your father, and I offered that Gerard should call upon him. He took down your direction, in order that he might write to your father, and give him an appointment; when, observing that it was Westminster, he said that his carriage was ordered to go to the House of Lords in a quarter of an hour, and that, if not inconvenient to me, he would propose that I should at once accompany him. I thought, whatever might be the result, it must be a satisfaction to Gerard at last to see this man, of whom he has talked and thought so much; and so we are here.'

'You did well, good Stephen, as you always do,' said Sybil with a musing and abstracted air; 'no one has so much forethought, and so much energy as you.'

He threw a glance at her; and immediately withdrew it. Their eyes had met: hers were kind and calm.

'And this Egremont,' said Morley rather hurriedly and abruptly, and looking on the ground, 'how came he here? When we discovered him yesterday, your father and myself agreed that we should not mention to you the – the mystification of which we had been dupes.'

'And you did wrong,' said Sybil. 'There is no wisdom like frankness. Had you told me, he would not have been here to-day. He met and addressed me, and I only recognised an acquaintance who had once contributed so much to the pleasantness of our life. Had he not accompanied me to this door and met my father, which precipitated an explanation on his part which he found had not been given by others, I might have remained in an ignorance which hereafter might have produced inconvenience.'

'You are right,' said Morley looking at her rather keenly. 'We have all of us opened ourselves too unreservedly before this aristocrat.'

'I should hope that none of us have said to him a word that we wish to be forgotten,' said Sybil. 'He chose to wear a disguise, and can hardly quarrel with the frankness with which we spoke of his order or his family. And for the rest, he has not been injured from learning something of the feelings of the people by living among them.'

'And yet if anything were to happen to-morrow,' said Morley, 'rest assured this man has his eye on us. He can walk into the government offices like themselves and tell his tale, for, though one of the pseudo-opposition, the moment the people move, the factions become united.'

Sybil turned and looked at him, and then said, 'And what could happen to-morrow, that we should care for the government being acquainted with it or us? Do not they know everything? Do not you meet in their very sight? You pursue an avowed and legal aim by legal means, do you not? What then is there to fear? And why should anything happen that should make us apprehensive?'

'All is very well at this moment,' said Morley, 'and all may continue well; but popular assemblies breed turbulent spirits, Sybil. Your father takes a leading part; he is a great orator, and is in his element in this clamorous and fiery life. It does not much suit me; I am a man of the closet. This convention, as you well know, was never much to my taste. Their Charter is a coarse specific for our social evils. The spirit that would cure our ills must be of a deeper and finer mood.'

'Then why are you here?' said Sybil.

Morley shrugged his shoulders, and then said, 'An easy question. Questions are always easy. The fact is, in active life one cannot afford to refine. I could have wished the movement to have taken a different shape, and to have worked for a different end; but it has not done this. But it is still a movement and a great one, and I must work it for my end and try to shape it to my form. If I had refused to be a leader, I should not have prevented the movement; I should only have secured my own insignificance.'

'But my father has not these fears; he is full of hope and exultation,' said Sybil. 'And surely it is a great thing that the people have their Parliament lawfully meeting in open day, and their delegates from the whole realm declaring their grievances in language which would not disgrace the conquering race which has in vain endeavoured to degrade them. When I heard my father speak the other night, my heart glowed with emotion; my eyes were suffused with tears; I was proud to be his daughter; and I gloried in a race of forefathers who belonged to the oppressed and not to the oppressors.'

Morley watched the deep splendour of her eye and the mantling of her radiant cheek, as she spoke these latter words with not merely animation but fervour. Her bright hair, that hung on either side her face in long tresses of luxuriant richness, was drawn off a forehead that was the very throne of thought and majesty, while her rich lip still quivered with the sensibility which expressed its impassioned truth.

'But your father, Sybil, stands alone,' at length Morley replied; 'surrounded by votaries who have nothing but enthusiasm to recommend them; and by emulous and intriguing rivals, who watch every word and action, in order that they may discredit his conduct, and ultimately secure his downfall.'

'My father's downfall!' said Sybil. 'Is he not one of themselves? And is it possible, that among the delegates of the People there can be other than one and the same object?'

'A thousand,' said Morley; 'we have already as many parties as in St. Stephen's itself.'

'You terrify me,' said Sybil. 'I knew we had fearful odds to combat against. My visit to this city alone has taught me how strong are our enemies. But I believed that we had on our side God and Truth.'

'They know neither of them in the National Convention,' said Morley. 'Our career will be a vulgar caricature of the bad passions and the low intrigues, the factions and the failures, of our oppressors.'

At this moment Gerard and Hatton, who were sitting in the remote part of the room, rose together and came forward; and this movement interrupted the conversation of Sybil and Morley. Before, however, her father and his new friend could reach them, Hatton, as if some point on which he had not been sufficiently explicit had occurred to him, stopped, and placing his hand on Gerard's arm, withdrew him again, saying in a voice which could be heard only by the individual whom he addressed, 'You understand; I have not the slightest doubt myself of your moral right: I believe that on every principle of justice, Mowbray Castle is as much yours as the house that is built by the tenant on the lord's land: but can we prove it? We never had the legal evidence. You are in error in supposing that these papers were of any vital consequence: mere memoranda; very useful no doubt; I hope I shall find them; but of no validity. If money were the only difficulty, trust me, it should not be wanting; I owe much to the memory of your father, my good Gerard; I would fain serve you: and your daughter. I'll not tell you what I would do for you, my good Gerard. You would think me foolish; but I am alone in the world, and seeing you again and talking of old times: I really am scarcely fit for business. Go, however, I must; I have an appointment at the House of Lords. Good bye. I must say farewell to the Lady Sybil.'

CHAPTER 10

'YOU can't have that table, sir, it is engaged,' said a waiter at
the Athenæum* to a member of the club who seemed un-
mindful of the type of appropriation which, in the shape of
an inverted plate, ought to have warned him off the coveted
premises.

'It is always engaged,' grumbled the member. 'Who has
taken it?'

'Mr. Hatton, sir.'

And indeed at this very moment, it being about eight
o'clock of the same day on which the meeting detailed in the
last chapter had occurred, a handsome dark brougham with
a beautiful horse was stopping in Waterloo Place before the
portico of the Athenæum Club-house, from which equipage
immediately emerged the prosperous person of Baptist
Hatton.

This club was Hatton's only relaxation. He had never
entered society; and now his habits were so formed, that the
effort would have been a painful one; though, with a first-
rate reputation in his calling, and supposed to be rich, the
openings were numerous to a familiar intercourse with those
middle-aged nameless gentlemen of easy circumstances who
haunt clubs, and dine a great deal at each other's houses and
chambers; men who travel regularly a little, and gossip regularly a great deal; who lead a sort of facile, slipshod existence, doing nothing, yet mightily interested in what others
do; great critics of little things; profuse in minor luxuries, and
inclined to the respectable practice of a decorous profligacy;
peering through the window of a club-house as if they were
discovering a planet; and usually much excited about things
with which they have no concern, and personages who never
heard of them.

All this was not in Hatton's way, who was free from all
pretension, and who had acquired, from his severe habits of
historical research, a respect only for what was authentic.
These nonentities flitted about him, and he shrunk from an
existence that seemed to him at once dull and trifling. He had
a few literary acquaintances that he had made at the Anti-

quarian Society, of which he was a distinguished member; a vice-president of that body had introduced him to the Athenæum. It was the first and only club that Hatton had ever belonged to, and he delighted in it. He liked splendour and the light and bustle of a great establishment. They saved him from that melancholy which after a day of action is the doom of energetic celibacy. A luxurious dinner, without trouble, suited him after his exhaustion; sipping his claret, he revolved his plans. Above all, he revelled in the magnificent library, and perhaps was never happier, than when, after a stimulating repast, he adjourned up stairs, and buried himself in an easy chair with Dugdale,* or Selden,* or an erudite treatise on forfeiture or abeyance.

To-day, however, Hatton was not in this mood. He came in exhausted and excited: ate rapidly and rather ravenously; despatched a pint of champagne; and then called for a bottle of Lafitte. His table cleared, a devilled biscuit placed before him, a cool bottle and a fresh glass, he indulged in that reverie which the tumult of his feelings and the physical requirements of existence had hitherto combined to prevent.

'A strange day,' he thought as, with an abstracted air, he filled his glass, and sipping the wine, leant back in his chair. 'The son of Walter Gerard! A chartist delegate! The best blood in England! What would I not be, were it mine!

'Those infernal papers! They made my fortune; and yet, I know not how it is, the deed has cost me many a pang. Yet it seemed innoxious; the old man dead, insolvent; myself starving; his son ignorant of all, to whom too they could be of no use, for it required thousands to work them, and even with thousands they could only be worked by myself. Had I not done it, I should ere this probably have been swept from the surface of the earth, worn out with penury, disease, and heart-ache. And now I am Baptist Hatton, with a fortune almost large enough to buy Mowbray itself, and with knowledge that can make the proudest tremble.

'And for what object all this wealth and power? What memory shall I leave? What family shall I found? Not a relative in the world, except a solitary barbarian, from whom, when years ago I visited him as a stranger, I recoiled with unutterable loathing.

'Ah! had I a child: a child like the beautiful daughter of Gerard!'

And here mechanically Hatton filled his glass, and quaffed at once a bumper.

'And I have deprived her of a principality! That seraphic being, whose lustre even now haunts my vision; the ring of whose silver tone even now lingers in my ear. He must be a fiend who could injure her. I am that fiend. Let me see; let me see!'

And now he seemed wrapt in the very paradise of some creative vision; still he filled the glass, but this time he only sipped it, as if he were afraid to disturb the clustering images around him.

'Let me see; let me see. I could make her a baroness. Gerard is as much Baron Valence as Shrewsbury is Talbot. Her name is Sybil. Curious how, even when peasants, the good blood keeps the good old family names! The Valences were ever Sybils.

'I could make her a baroness. Yes! and I could give her wherewith to endow her state. I could compensate for the broad lands which should be hers, and which perhaps through me she has forfeited.

'Could I do more? Could I restore her to the rank she would honour, assuage these sharp pangs of conscience, and achieve the secret ambition of my life? What if my son were to be Lord Valence?

'Is it too bold? A chartist delegate; a peasant's daughter! With all that shining beauty that I witnessed, with all the marvellous gifts that their friend Morley so descanted on, would she shrink from me? I'm not a crook-backed Richard.

'I could proffer much: I feel I could urge it plausibly. She must be very wretched. With such a form, such high imaginings, such thoughts of power and pomp as I could breathe in her, I think she'd melt. And to one of her own faith, too! To build up a great Catholic house again; of the old blood, and the old names, and the old faith: by holy Mary it is a glorious vision!'

CHAPTER II

ON the evening of the day that Egremont had met Sybil in the Abbey of Westminster, and subsequently parted from her under circumstances so distressing, the Countess of Marney held a great assembly at the family mansion in St. James' Square, which Lord Marney intended to have let to a new club, and himself and his family to have taken refuge for a short season at an hotel; but he drove so hard a bargain that, before the lease was signed, the new club, which mainly consisted of an ingenious individual who had created himself secretary, had vanished. Then it was agreed that the family mansion should be inhabited for the season by the family; and to-night Arabella was receiving all that great world of which she herself was a distinguished ornament.

'We come to you as early as possible, my dear Arabella,' said Lady Deloraine to her daughter-in-law.

'You are always so good! Have you seen Charles? I was in hopes he would have come,' Lady Marney added, in a somewhat mournful tone.

'He is at the House; otherwise I am sure he would have been here,' said Lady Deloraine, glad that she had so good a reason for an absence which under any circumstances she well knew would have occurred.

'I fear you will be sadly in want of beaus this evening, my love. We dined at the Duke of Fitz-Aquitaine's, and all our cavaliers vanished. They talk of an early division.'

'I really wish all these divisions were over,' said Lady Marney. 'They are very anti-social. Ah! here is Lady de Mowbray.'

Alfred Mountchesney hovered round Lady Joan Fitz-Warene, who was gratified by the devotion of the Cupid of May Fair. He uttered inconceivable nothings, and she replied to him in incomprehensible somethings. Her learned profundity and his vapid lightness effectively contrasted. Occasionally he caught her eye, and conveyed to her the anguish of his soul in a glance of self-complacent softness.

Lady St. Julians, leaning on the arm of the Duke of Fitz-Aquitaine, stopped to speak to Lady Joan. Lady St. Julians was determined that the heiress of Mowbray should marry one of her sons. She watched, therefore, with a restless eye all those who attempted to monopolise Lady Joan's attention, and contrived perpetually to interfere with their manœuvres. In the midst of a delightful conversation that seemed to approach a crisis, Lady St. Julians was sure to advance, and interfere with some affectionate appeal to Lady Joan, whom she called 'her dear child' and 'sweetest love,' while she did not deign even to notice the unhappy cavalier whom she had thus as it were unhorsed.

'My sweet child!' said Lady St. Julians to Lady Joan, 'you have no idea how unhappy Frederick is this evening, but he cannot leave the House, and I fear it will be a late affair.'

Lady Joan looked as if the absence or presence of Frederick was to her a matter of great indifference, and then she added, 'I do not think the division so important as is generally imagined. A defeat upon a question of colonial government does not appear to me of sufficient weight to dissolve a cabinet.'

'Any defeat will do that now,' said Lady St. Julians, 'but to tell you the truth I am not very sanguine. Lady Deloraine says they will be beat: she says the radicals will desert them; but I am not so sure. Why should the radicals desert them? And what have we done for the radicals? Had we indeed foreseen this Jamaica business, and asked some of them to dinner, or given a ball or two to their wives and daughters! I am sure if I had had the least idea that we had so good a chance of coming in, I should not have cared myself to have done something; even to have invited their women.'

'But you are such a capital partisan, Lady St. Julians,' said the Duke of Fitz-Aquitaine, who, with the viceroyalty of Ireland dexterously dangled before his eyes for the last two years, had become a thorough conservative, and had almost as much confidence in Sir Robert as in Lord Stanley.

'I have made great sacrifices,' said Lady St. Julians. 'I went once and stayed a week at Lady Jenny Spinner's to gain her looby of a son and his eighty thousand a year, and Lord St. Julians proposed him at White's; and then, after all, the whigs made him a peer! They certainly make more of their social influences than we do. That affair of that Mr. Trenchard was a blow. Losing a vote at such a critical time, when, if I had had only a remote idea of what was passing through his mind, I would have even asked him to Barrowley for a couple of days.'

A foreign diplomatist of distinction had pinned Lord Marney, and was dexterously pumping him as to the probable future.

'But is the pear ripe?' said the diplomatist.

'The pear is ripe, if we have courage to pluck it,' said Lord Marney; 'but our fellows have no pluck.'

'But do you think that the Duke of Wellington – ' and here the diplomatist stopped and looked up in Lord Marney's face, as if he would convey something that he would not venture to express.

'Here he is,' said Lord Marney, 'he will answer the question himself.'

Lord Deloraine and Mr. Ormsby passed by; the diplomatist addressed them; 'You have not been to the Chamber?'

'No,' said Lord Deloraine; 'but I hear there is hot work. It will be late.'

'Do you think – ,' said the diplomatist, and he looked up in the face of Lord Deloraine.

'I think that in the long run everything will have an end,' said Lord Deloraine.

'Ah! said the diplomatist.

'Bah!' said Lord Deloraine as he walked away with Mr. Ormsby. 'I remember that fellow: a sort of equivocal attaché at Paris, when we were with Monmouth at the peace: and now he is a quasi ambassador, and ribboned and starred to the chin.'

'The only stars I have got,' said Mr. Ormsby, demurely, 'are four stars in India stock.'*

Lady Firebrace and Lady Maud Fitz-Warene were announced; they had just come from the Commons: a dame and damsel full of political enthusiasm. Lady Firebrace gave critical reports and disseminated many contradictory estimates of the result; Lady Maud talked only of a speech made by Lord Milford, which from the elaborate noise she made about it, you would have supposed to have been the oration of the evening; on the contrary, it had lasted only a few minutes, and in a thin house had been nearly inaudible; but then, as Lady Maud added, 'it was in such good taste!'

Alfred Mountchesney and Lady Joan Fitz-Warene passed Lady Marney, who was speaking to Lord Deloraine. 'Do you think,' said Lady Marney, 'that Mr. Mountchesney will bear away the prize?'

Lord Deloraine shook his head. 'These great heiresses can never make up their minds. The bitter drop rises in all their reveries.'

'And yet,' said Lady Marney, 'I would just as soon be married for my money as my face.'

Soon after this, there was a stir in the saloons; a murmur, the ingress of many gentlemen; among others Lord Valentine, Lord Milford, Mr. Egerton, Mr. Berners, Lord Fitz-Heron, Mr. Jermyn. The House was up; the great Jamaica division was announced; the radicals had thrown over the government, who, left in a majority of only five, had already intimated their sense of the unequivocal feeling of the House with respect to them. It was known that on the morrow the government would resign.

Lady Deloraine, prepared for the great result, was calm: Lady St. Julians, who had not anticipated it, was in a wild flutter of distracted triumph. A vague yet dreadful sensation came over her, in the midst of her joy, that Lady Deloraine had been beforehand with her; had made her combinations with the new Minister; perhaps even sounded the Court. At the same time that in this agitating vision, the great offices of the palace which she had apportioned to herself and her husband seemed to elude her grasp, the claims and hopes and interests of her various children haunted her perplexed consciousness. What if Charles Egremont were to get the place which she had projected for Frederick or Augustus? What if Lord Marney became master of the horse? Or Lord Deloraine went again to Ireland? In her nervous excitement she credited all these catastrophes: seized upon 'the Duke' in order that Lady Deloraine might not gain his ear, and resolved to get home as soon as possible, in order that she might write without a moment's loss of time to Sir Robert.

'They will hardly go out without making some peers,' said Sir Vavasour Firebrace to Mr. Jermyn.

'Why, they have made enough.'

'Hem! I know Tubbe Sweete has a promise, and so has Cockawhoop. I don't think Cockawhoop could show again at Boodle's without a coronet.'

'I do not see why these fellows should go out,' said Mr. Ormsby. 'What does it signify whether ministers have a majority of five, or ten or twenty? In my time, a proper majority was a third of the House. That was Lord Liverpool's majority. Lord Monmouth used to say, that there were ten families in this country, who, if they could only agree, could always share the government. Ah! those were the good old times! We never had adjourned debates then; but sat it out like gentlemen who had been used all their lives to be up all night, and then supped at Watier's* afterwards.'

'Ah! my dear Ormsby,' said Mr. Berners, 'do not mention Watier's; you make my mouth water.'

'Shall you stand for Birmingham, Ormsby, if there be a dissolution?' said Lord Fitz-Heron.

'I have been asked,' said Mr. Ormsby: 'but the House of Commons is not the House of Commons of my time, and I have no wish to re-enter it. If I had a taste for business, I might be a member of the Marylebone vestry.'

'All I repeat,' said Lord Marney to his mother, as he rose from the sofa where he had been some time in conversation with her, 'is that if there be any idea that I wish Lady Marney should be a lady in waiting, it is an error, Lady Deloraine. I wish that to be understood. I am a domestic man, and I wish Lady Marney to be always with me; and what I want, I want for myself. I hope in arranging the household the domestic character of every member of it will be considered. After all that has occurred the country expects that.'

'But my dear George, I think it is really premature—'

'I dare say it is; but I recommend you, my dear mother, to be alive. I heard Lady St. Julians just now in the supper room asking the Duke to promise her that her Augustus should be a Lord of the Admiralty. She said the Treasury would not do, as there was no house, and that with such a fortune as his wife brought him he could not hire a house under a thousand a year.'

'He will not have the Admiralty,' said Deloraine.

'She looks herself to the Robes.'

'Poor woman!' said Lady Deloraine.

'Is it quite true?' said a great whig dame, to Mr. Egerton, one of her own party.

'Quite,' he said.

'I can endure anything except Lady St. Julians' glance of triumph,' said the whig dame. 'I really think if it were only to ease her Majesty from such an infliction, they ought to have held on.'

'And must the household be changed?' said Mr. Egerton.

'Do not look so serious,' said the whig dame, smiling with fascination; 'we are surrounded by the enemy.'

'Will you be at home to-morrow early?' said Mr. Egerton.

'As early as you please.'

'Very well, we will talk then. Lady Charlotte has heard something: nous verrons.'

'Courage; we have the Court with us, and the Country cares for nothing.'

CHAPTER 12

'IT is all right,' said Mr. Tadpole. 'They are out. Lord Melbourne has been with the Queen, and recommended her Majesty to send for the Duke, and the Duke has recommended her Majesty to send for Sir Robert.'

'Are you sure?' said Mr. Taper.

'I tell you Sir Robert is on his road to the palace at this moment; I saw him pass, full dressed.'

'It is too much,' said Mr. Taper.

'Now what are we to do?' said Mr. Tadpole.

'We must not dissolve,' said Mr. Taper. 'We have no cry.'

'As much cry as the other fellows,' said Mr. Tadpole; 'but no one of course would think of dissolution before the next registration. No, no; this is a very manageable Parliament, depend upon it. The malcontent radicals who have turned them out are not going to bring them in. That makes us equal. Then we have an important section to work upon: the Sneaks, the men who are afraid of a dissolution. I will be bound we make a good working conservative majority of five-and-twenty out of the Sneaks.'

'With the Treasury patronage,' said Mr. Taper; 'fear and

favour combined. An impending dissolution, and all the places we refuse our own men, we may count on the Sneaks.'

'Then there are several religious men who have wanted an excuse for a long time to rat,' said Mr. Tadpole. 'We must get Sir Robert to make some kind of a religious move, and that will secure Sir Litany Lax, and young Mr. Salem.'

'It will never do to throw over the Church Commission,'* said Mr. Taper. 'Commissions and committees ought always to be supported.'

'Besides, it will frighten the saints,' said Mr. Tadpole. 'If we could get him to speak at Exeter Hall,* were it only a slavery meeting, that would do.'

'It is difficult,' said Taper; 'he must be pledged to nothing; not even to the right of search. Yet if we could get up something with a good deal of sentiment and no principle involved; referring only to the past, but with his practised powers touching the present. What do you think of a monument to Wilberforce,* or a commemoration of Clarkson?'*

'There is a good deal in that,' said Mr. Tadpole. 'At present go about and keep our fellows in good humour. Whisper nothings that sound like something. But be discreet; do not let there be more than half a hundred fellows who believe they are going to be Under Secretaries of State. And be cautious about titles. If they push you, give a wink, and press your finger to your lip. I must call here,' continued Mr. Tadpole, as he stopped before the house of the Duke of Fitz-Aquitaine. 'This gentleman is my particular charge. I have been cooking him these three years. I had two notes from him yesterday, and can delay a visit no longer. The worst of it is, he expects that I shall bear him the non-official announcement of his being sent to Ireland, of which he has about as much chance as I have of being Governor-General of India. It must be confessed, ours is critical work sometimes, friend Taper; but never mind, what we have to do to individuals, Peel has to do with a nation, and therefore we ought not to complain.'

The Duke of Fitz-Aquitaine wanted Ireland, and Lord de Mowbray wanted the Garter. Lord Marney, who wanted the Buck-hounds, was convinced that neither of his friends had the slightest chance of obtaining their respective objects, but believed that he had a very good one of securing his own if he used them for his purpose, and persuaded them to combine together for the common good. So at his suggestion they had all met together at the duke's, and were in full conference on the present state of affairs, while Tadpole and Taper were engaged in that interesting and instructive conversation of which we have snatched a passage.

'You may depend upon it,' said Lore Marney, 'that nothing is to be done by delicacy. It is not delicacy that rules the House of Lords. What has kept us silent for years? Threats; and threats used in the most downright manner. We were told that if we did not conform absolutely, and without appeal, to the will and pleasure of one individual, the cards would be thrown up. We gave in; the game has been played, and won. I am not at all clear that it has been won by those tactics, but gained it is; and now what shall we do? In my opinion it is high time to get rid of the dictatorship. The new ruse now for the palace is to persuade her Majesty that Peel is the only man who can manage the House of Lords. Well, then, it is exactly the time to make certain persons understand that the House of Lords are not going to be tools any longer merely for other people. Rely upon it a bold united front at this moment would be a spoke in the wheel. We three form the nucleus; there are plenty to gather round. I have written to Marisforde; he is quite ripe. Lord Hounslow will be here to-morrow. The thing is to be done; and if we are not firm the grand conservative triumph will only end in securing the best posts both at home and abroad for one too powerful family.'

'Who had never been heard of in the time of my father,' said the duke.

'Nor in the time of mine,' said Lord de Mowbray.

'Royal and Norman blood like ours,' said Lord Marney, 'is not to be thrown over in that way.'

It was just at this moment that a servant entered with a card, which the duke looking at, said, 'It is Tadpole; shall we have him in? I dare say he will tell us something.' And, notwithstanding the important character of their conference, political curiosity, and perhaps some private feeling which not one of them cared to acknowledge, made them unanimously agree that Mr. Tadpole should be admitted.

'Lord Marney and Lord de Mowbray with the Duke of

Fitz-Aquitaine,' thought Mr. Tadpole, as he was ushered into the library; and his eye, practised in machinations and prophetic in manœuvres, surveyed the three nobles. 'This looks like business and perhaps means mischief. Very lucky I called!' With an honest smile he saluted them all.

'What news from the palace, Tadpole?' inquired the duke.

'Sir Robert is there,' replied Tadpole.

'That is good news,' exclaimed his grace, echoed by Lord de Mowbray, and backed up with a faint bravo from Lord Marney.

Then arose a conversation in which all affected much interest respecting the Jamaica debate; whether the whigs had originally intended to resign; whether it were Lord Melbourne or Lord John who had insisted on the step; whether, if postponed, they could have tided over the session; and so on. Tadpole, who was somewhat earnest in his talk, seemed to have pinned the duke of Fitz-Aquitaine; Lord Marney, who wanted to say a word alone to Lord de Mowbray, had dexterously drawn that personage aside on the pretence of looking at a picture. Tadpole, who, with a most frank and unsophisticated mien, had an eye for every corner of a room, seized the opportunity for which he had been long cruising. 'I don't pretend to be behind the scenes, duke; but it was said to me to-day, "Tadpole, if you do chance to see the Duke of Fitz-Aquitaine, you may say that positively Lord Killcroppy will not go to Ireland."'

A smile of satisfaction played over the handsome face of the duke: instantly suppressed lest it might excite suspicion; and then, with a friendly and significant nod, that intimated to Tadpole not to dwell on the subject at the present moment, the duke with a rather uninterested air recurred to the Jamaica debate, and soon after appealed on some domestic point to his son-in-law. This broke up the conversation between Lord de Mowbray and Lord Marney. Lord de Mowbray advancing was met accidentally on purpose by Mr. Tadpole, who seemed anxious to push forward to Lord Marney.

'You have heard of Lord Ribbonville?' said Tadpole in a suppressed tone.

'No; what?'

'Can't live the day out. How fortunate Sir Robert is! Two garters to begin with!'

Tadpole had now succeeded in tackling Lord Marney alone; the other peers were far out of ear-shot. 'I don't pretend to be behind the scenes, my Lord,' said the honest gentleman in a peculiarly confidential tone, and with a glance that spoke volumes of state secrecy; 'but it was said to me to-day, "Tadpole, if you do chance to meet Lord Marney, you may say that positively Lord Rambrooke will not have the Buckhounds."'

'All I want,' said Lord Marney, 'is to see men of character about her Majesty. This is a domestic country, and the country expects that no nobleman should take household office, whose private character is not inexpugnable. Now that fellow Rambrooke keeps a Frenchwoman. It is not much known, but it is a fact.'

'Dreadful!' exclaimed Mr. Tadpole. 'I have no doubt of it. But he has no chance of the Buck-hounds, you may rely on that. Private character is to be the basis of the new government. Since the Reform Act, that is a qualification much more esteemed by the constituency than public services. We must go with the times, my lord. A virtuous middle class shrinks with horror from French actresses; and the Wesleyans, the Wesleyans must be considered, Lord Marney.'

'I always subscribe to them,' said his lordship.

'Ah!' said Mr. Tadpole, mysteriously, 'I am glad to hear that. Nothing I have heard to-day has given me so much pleasure as those few words. One may hardly jest on such a subject,' he added, with a sanctimonious air; 'but I think I may say,' and here he broke into a horse smile, 'I think I may say that those subscriptions will not be without their fruit.' And with a bow honest Tadpole disappeared, saying to himself as he left the house, 'If you were ready to be conspirators when I entered the room, my lords you were at least prepared to be traitors when I quitted it.'

In the meantime Lord Marney, in the best possible humour, said to Lord de Mowbray, 'You are going to White's, are you? If so, take me.'

'I am sorry, my dear lord, but I have an appointment in the city. I have to go to the Temple, and I am already behind my time.'

CHAPTER 13

AND why was Lord de Mowbray going to the Temple? He had received the day before, when he came home to dress, a disagreeable letter from some lawyers, apprising him that they were instructed by their client, Mr. Walter Gerard, to commence proceedings against his lordship on a writ of right, with respect to his manors of Mowbray, Valence, Mowedale, Mowbray Valence, and several others carefully enumerated in their precise epistle, and the catalogue of which read like an extract from Domesday Book.

More than twenty years had elapsed since the question had been mooted; and though the discussion had left upon Lord de Mowbray an impression from which at times he had never entirely recovered, still circumstances had occurred since the last proceedings which gave him a moral, if not a legal, conviction that he should be disturbed no more. And these were the circumstances: Lord de Mowbray, after the death of the father of Walter Gerard, had found himself in communication with the agent who had developed and pursued the claim for the yeoman, and had purchased for a good round sum the documents on which that claim was founded, and by which alone apparently that claim could be sustained.

The vendor of these muniments was Baptist Hatton, and the sum which he obtained for them, by allowing him to settle in the metropolis, pursue his studies, purchase his library and collections, and otherwise give himself that fair field which brains without capital can seldom command, was in fact the foundation of his fortune. Many years afterwards, Lord de Mowbray had recognised Hatton in the prosperous parliamentary agent who often appeared at the bar of the House of Lords, and before committees of privilege, and who gradually obtained an unrivalled reputation and employment in peerage cases. Lord de Mowbray renewed his acquaintance with a man who was successful; bowed to Hatton whenever they met; and finally consulted him respecting the barony of Valence, which had been in the old Fitz-Warene and Mowbray families, and to which it was thought the present earl might prefer some hocus-pocus claim through his deceased mother;

so that, however recent was his date as an English earl, he might figure on the roll as a Plantagenet baron, which in the course of another century would complete the grand mystification of high nobility. The death of his son, dexterously christened Valence, had a little damped his ardour in this respect; but still there was a sufficiently intimate connection kept up between him and Hatton; so that, before he placed the letter he had received in the hands of his lawyers, he thought it desirable to consult his ancient ally.

This was the reason that Lord de Mowbray was at the present moment seated in the same chair, in the same library, as was a few days back that worthy baronet, Sir Vavasour Firebrace. Mr. Hatton was at the same table similarly employed; his Persian cat on his right hand, and his choice spaniels reposing on their cushions at his feet.

Mr. Hatton held forward his hand to receive the lettter of which Lord de Mowbray had been speaking to him, and which he read with great attention, weighing as it were each word. Singular! as the letter had been written by himself, and the firm who signed it were only his instruments, obeying the spring of the master hand.

'Very remarkable!' said Mr. Hatton.

'Is it not?' said Lord de Mowbray.

'And your lordship received this yestereday?'

'Yesterday. I lost no time in communicating with you.'

'Jubb and Jinks,' continued Mr. Hatton, musingly, surveying the signature of the letter. 'A respectable firm.'

'That makes it more strange,' said his lordship.

'It does,' said Mr. Hatton.

'A respectable firm would hardly embark in such a proceeding without some show of pretext,' said Lord de Mowbray.

'Hardly,' said Mr. Hatton.

'But what can they have?' urged his lordship.

'What indeed!' said Mr. Hatton. 'Mr. Walter Gerard, without his pedigree, is a mere flash in the pan; and I defy him to prove anything without the deed of '77.'

'Well, he has not got that,' said Lord de Mowbray.

'Safe, of course?' said Mr. Hatton.

'Certain. I almost wish I had burnt it as well as the whole boxful.'

'Destroy that deed and the other muniments, and the Earl de Mowbray will never be Baron Valence,' said Mr. Hatton.

'But what use are these deeds now?' said his lordship. 'If we produce them, we may give a colour to this fellow's claim.'

'Time will settle his claim,' said Mr. Hatton; 'it will mature yours. You can wait.'

'Alas! since the death of my poor boy—'

'It has become doubly important. Substantiate the barony, it will descend to your eldest daughter, who, even if married, will retain your name. Your family will live, and ennobled. The Fitz-Warenes Lords Valence will yield to none in antiquity; and, as to rank, so long as Mowbray Castle belongs to them, the revival of the earldom is safe at the first coronation, or the first ministry that exists with a balanced state of parties.'

'That is the right view of the case,' said Lord de Mowbray; 'and what do you advise?'

'Be calm, and you have nothing to fear. This is the mere revival of an old claim, too vast to be allowed to lapse from desuetude. Your documents, you say, are all secure?'

'Be sure of that. They are at this moment in the muniment room of the great tower of Mowbray Castle; in the same iron box and in the same cabinet they were deposited—'

'When, by placing them in your hands,' said Mr. Hatton, finishing a sentence which might have been awkward, 'I had the satisfaction of confirming the rights and calming the anxieties of one of our ancient houses. I would recommend your lordship to instruct your lawyers to appear to this writ as a matter of course. But enter into no details, no unnecessary confidence with them. They are needless. Treat the matter lightly, especially to them. You will hear no more of it.'

'You feel confidence?'

'Perfect. Walter Gerard has no documents of any kind. Whatever his claim might be, good or bad, the only evidence that can prove his pedigree is in your possession, and the only use to which it ever will be put, will be in due time to seat your grandson in the House of Lords.'

'I am glad I called upon you,' said Lord de Mowbray.

'To be sure. Your lordship can speak to me without reserve, and I am used to these start-ups. It is part of the trade; but an old soldier is not to be deceived by such feints.'

'Clearly a feint, you think?'

'A feint! a feint.'

'Good morning. I am glad I called. How goes on my friend Sir Vavasour?'

'Oh! I shall land him at last.'

'Well, he is an excellent neighbourly man. I have a great respect for Sir Vavasour. Would you dine with me, Mr. Hatton, on Thursday? It would give me and Lady de Mowbray great pleasure.'

'Your lordship is extremely kind,' said Mr. Hatton bowing with a slight sarcastic smile, 'but I am a hermit.'

'But your friends should see you sometimes,' said Lord de Mowbray.

'Your lordship is too good, but I am a mere man of business, and know my position. I feel I am not at home in ladies' society.'

'Well then, come to-morrow: I am alone, and I will ask some persons to meet you whom you know and like: Sir Vavasour and Lord Shaftesbury, and a most learned Frenchman who is over here, a Vicomte de Narbonne, who is very anxious to make your acquaintance. Your name is current, I can tell you, at Paris.'

'Your lordship is too good; another day: I have a great pressure of affairs at present.'

'Well, well; so be it. Good morning, Mr. Hatton.'

Hatton bowed lowly. The moment the door was shut, rubbing his hands, he said, 'In the same box and in the same cabinet: the muniment room in the great tower of Mowbray Castle! They exist and I know their whereabouts. I'll have 'em.'

CHAPTER 14

Two and even three days had rolled over since Mr. Tadpole had reported Sir Robert on his way to the palace, and marvellously little had transpired. It was of course known that a cabinet was in formation, and the daily papers reported to the public the diurnal visits of certain noble lords and right honourable gentlemen to the new first minister. But the world of high politics had suddenly become so cautious that nothing leaked out. Even gossip was at fault. Lord Marney had not received the Buck-hounds, though he never quitted his house for ride or lounge without leaving precise instructions with Captain Grouse as to the identical time he should return home, so that his acceptance should not be delayed. Ireland was not yet governed by the Duke of Fitz-Aquitaine, and the Earl de Mowbray was still ungartered. These three distinguished noblemen were all of them anxious – a little fidgetty; but at the same time it was not even whispered that Lord Rambrooke or any other lord had received the post which Lord Marney had appropriated to himself; nor had Lord Killcroppy had a suspicious interview with the prime minister, which kept the Duke of Fitz-Aquitaine quiet though not easy; while not a shadow of coming events had glanced over the vacant stall of Lord Ribbonville in St. George's Chapel, and this made Lord de Mowbray tranquil, though scarcely content. In the meantime, daily and hourly they all pumped Mr. Tadpole, who did not find it difficult to keep up his reputation for discretion; for knowing nothing, and beginning himself to be perplexed at the protracted silence, he took refuge in oracular mystery, and delivered himself of certain Delphic sentences, which adroitly satisfied those who consulted him while they never committed himself.

At length one morning there was an odd whisper in the circle of first initiation. The blood mantled on the cheek of Lady St. Julians; Lady Deloraine turned pale. Lady Firebrace wrote confidential notes with the same pen to Mr. Tadpole and Lord Masque. Lord Marney called early in the morning on the Duke of Fitz-Aquitaine, and already found Lord de Mowbray there. The clubs were crowded even at noon. Everywhere a mysterious bustle and an awful stir.

What could be the matter? What has happened?

'It is true,' said Mr. Egerton to Mr. Berners at Brooks'.

'Is it true?' asked Mr. Jermyn of Lord Valentine at the Carlton.

'I heard it last night at Crockford's,' said Mr. Ormsby; 'one always hears things there four-and-twenty hours before other places.'

The word was employed the whole of the morning in asking and anwering this important question 'Is it true?' Towards dinner-time, it was settled universally in the affirmative, and then the world went out to dine and to ascertain why it was true and how it was true.

And now what had really happened? What had happened was what is commonly called a 'hitch.' There was undoubtedly a hitch somewhere and somehow; a hitch in the construction of the new cabinet. Who could have thought it? The whig ministers it seems had resigned, but somehow or other had not entirely and completely gone out. What a constitutional dilemma! The Houses must evidently meet, address the throne, and impeach its obstinate counsellors. Clearly the right course, and party feeling ran so high, that it was not impossible that something might be done. At any rate, it was a capital opportunity for the House of Lords to pluck up a little courage and take what is called, in high political jargon, the initiative. Lord Marney, at the suggestion of Mr. Tadpole, was quite ready to do this; and so was the Duke of Fitz-Aquitaine, and almost the Earl de Mowbray.

But then, when all seemed ripe and ready, and there appeared a probability of the 'Independence of the House of Lords' being again the favourite toast of conservative dinners, the oddest rumour in the world got about, which threw such ridicule on these great constitutional movements in petto,* that, even with the Buck-hounds in the distance and Tadpole at his elbow, Lord Marney hesitated. It seemed, though of course no one could for a moment credit it, that these wrong-headed, rebellious ministers who would not go out, wore – petticoats!*

And the great Jamaica debate that had been cooked so long, and anxiously-expected yet almost despaired-of defection of the independent radical section, and the full-dressed visit to the palace that had gladdened the heart of Tadpole, were they all to end in this? Was Conservatism, that mighty mystery of the nineteenth century, was it after all to be brained by a fan?

Since the farce of the 'Invincibles'* nothing had ever been so ludicrously successful.

Lady Deloraine consoled herself for the 'Bedchamber Plot,' by declaring that Lady St. Julians was indirectly the cause of it, and that, had it not been for the anticipation of her official entrance into the royal apartments, the conspiracy would not have been more real than the Meal-tub plot,* or any other of the many imaginary machinations that still haunt the page of history, and occasionally flit about the prejudiced memory of nations. Lady St. Julians, on the contrary, wrung her hands over the unhappy fate of her enthralled sovereign, deprived of her faithful presence, and obliged to put up with the society of personages of whom she knew nothing, and who called themselves the friends of her youth. The ministers who had missed, especially those who had received, their appointments looked as all men do when they are jilted: embarrassed, and affecting an awkward ease; as if they knew something which, if they told, would free them from the supreme ridicule of their situation, but which, as men of delicacy and honour, they refrained from revealing. All those who had been in fluttering hopes, however faint, of receiving preferment, took courage now that the occasion had passed, and loudly complained of their cruel and undeniable deprivation. The constitution was wounded in their persons. Some fifty gentlemen, who had not been appointed under-secretaries of state, moaned over the martyrdom of young ambition.

'Peel ought to have taken office,' said Lord Marney. 'What are the women to us?'

'Peel ought to have taken office,' said the Duke of Fitz-Aquitaine. 'He should have remembered how much he owed to Ireland.'

'Peel ought to have taken office,' said Lord de Mowbray. 'The garter will become now a mere party badge.'

Perhaps it may be allowed to the impartial pen that traces these memoirs of our times to agree, though for a different reason, with these distinguished followers of Sir Robert Peel. One may be permitted to think that, under all circumstances, he should have taken office in 1839. His withdrawal seems to

have been a mistake. In the great heat of parliamentary faction
which had prevailed since 1831, the royal prerogative, which,
unfortunately for the rights and liberties and social welfare of
the people, had since 1688 been more or less oppressed, had
waned fainter and fainter. A youthful princess on the throne,
whose appearance touched the imagination, and to whom her
people were generally inclined to ascribe something of that
decision of character which becomes those born to command,
offered a favourable opportunity to restore the exercise of that
regal authority, the usurpation of whose functions has entailed on the people of England so much suffering, and so
much degradation. It was unfortunate that one who, if any,
should have occupied the proud and national position of the
leader of the tory party, the chief of the people and the champion of the throne, should have commenced his career as
minister under Victoria by an unseemly contrariety to the
personal wishes of the Queen. The reaction of public opinion,
disgusted with years of parliamentary tumult and the inco-
herence of party legislation, the balanced state in the kingdom
of political parties themselves, the personal character of the
sovereign; these were all causes which intimated that a movement in favour of prerogative was at hand. The leader of the
tory party should have vindicated his natural position, and
availed himself of the gracious occasion; he missed it; and, as
the occasion was inevitable, the whigs enjoyed its occur-
rence. And thus England witnessed for the first time the
portentous anomaly of the oligarchical or Venetian party,
which had in the old days destroyed the free monarchy of
England, retaining power merely by the favour of the Court.

But we forget, Sir Robert Peel is not the leader of the tory
party; the party that resisted the ruinous mystification that
metamorphosed direct taxation by the Crown into indirect
taxation by the Commons; that denounced the system which
mortgaged industry to protect property; the party that rules
Ireland by a scheme which reconciled both churches, and by a
series of parliaments which counted among them lords and
commons of both religions; that has maintained at all times
the territorial constitution of England as the only basis and
security for local government, and which nevertheless once
laid on the table of the House of Commons a commercial

tariff negotiated at Utrecht, which is the most rational that was ever devised by statesmen; a party that has prevented the Church from being the salaried agent of the state, and has supported through many struggles the parochial polity of the country which secures to every labourer a home.

In a parliamentary sense, that great party has ceased to exist; but I will believe that it still lives in the thought and sentiment and consecrated memory of the English nation. It has its origin in great principles and in noble instincts; it sympathises with the lowly, it looks up to the Most High; it can count its heroes and its martyrs; they have met in its behalf plunder, proscription, and death. Nor, when it finally yielded to the iron progress of oligarchical supremacy, was its catastrophe inglorious. Its genius was vindicated in golden sentences and with fervent arguments of impassioned logic by St. John; and breathed in the intrepid eloquence and patriot soul of William Wyndham.* Even now it is not dead, but sleepeth; and, in an age of political materialism, of confused purposes and perplexed intelligence, that aspires only to wealth because it has faith in no other accomplishment, as men rifle cargoes on the verge of shipwreck, toryism will yet rise from the tomb over which Bolingbroke shed his last tear, to bring back strength to the Crown, liberty to the Subject, and to announce that power has only one duty: to secure the social welfare of the PEOPLE.

CHAPTER 15

DURING the week of political agitation which terminated with the inglorious catastrophe of the Bedchamber plot, Sybil remained tranquil, and would have been scarcely conscious of what was disturbing so many right honourable hearts, had it not been for the incidental notice of their transactions by her father and his friends. To the Chartists, indeed, the factious embroilment at first was of no great moment, except as the breaking up and formation of cabinets might delay the presentation of the National Petition. They had long ceased to distinguish between the two parties who then and now contend for power. And they were right. Between the noble lord

who goes out, and the right honourable gentleman who
comes in, where is the distinctive principle? A shadowy
difference may be simulated in opposition, to serve a cry and
stimulate the hustings; but the mask is not worn, even in
Downing Street; and the conscientious conservative seeks, in
the pigeon-holes of a whig bureau, for the measures against
which for ten years he has been sanctioning, by the speaking
silence of an approving nod, a general wail of frenzied alarm.

Once it was otherwise; once the people recognised a party
in the state whose principles identified them with the rights
and privileges of the multitude: but when they found the
parochial constitution of the country sacrificed without a
struggle, and a rude assault made on all local influences in
order to establish a severely organised centralisation, a blow
was given to the influence of the priest and of the gentleman,
the ancient champions of the people against arbitrary courts
and rapacious parliaments, from which they will find that it
requires no ordinary courage and wisdom to recover.

The unexpected termination of the events of May, 1839, in
the re-establishment in power of a party confessedly too weak
to carry on the parliamentary government of the country, was
viewed however by the Chartists in a very different spirit from
that with which they had witnessed the outbreak of these
transactions. It had unquestionably a tendency to animate their
efforts, and imparted a bolder tone to their future plans and
movements. They were encouraged to try a fall with a feeble
administration. Gerard from this moment became engrossed
in affairs; his correspondence greatly increased; and he was so
much occupied that Sybil saw daily less and less of her father.

It was on the morning after the day that Hatton had made
his first and unlooked-for visit in Smith Square, that some of
the delegates, who had caught the rumour of the resignation
of the whigs, had called early on Gerard, and he had soon after
left the house in their company; and Sybil was alone. The
strange incidents of the preceding day were revolving in her
mind, as her eye wandered vaguely over her book. The
presence of that Hatton who had so often, and in such different scenes, occupied their conversation; the re-appearance of
that stranger, whose unexpected entrance into their little
world had eighteen months ago so often lent interest and

pleasure to their life: these were materials for pensive sentiment. Mr. Franklin had left some gracious memories with Sybil; the natural legacy of one so refined, intelligent, and gentle, whose temper seemed never ruffled, and who evidently so sincerely relished their society. Mowedale rose before her in all the golden beauty of its autumnal hour; their wild rambles and hearty greetings, and earnest converse when her father returned from his daily duties, and his eye kindled with pleasure as the accustomed knock announced the arrival of his almost daily companion. In spite of the excitement of the passing moment, its high hopes and glorious aspirations, and visions perchance of greatness and of power, the eye of Sybil was dimmed with emotion as she recalled that innocent and tranquil dream.

Her father had heard from Franklin after his departure more than once; but his letters, though abounding in frank expressions of deep interest in the welfare of Gerard and his daughter, were in some degree constrained; a kind of reserve seemed to envelop him; they never learnt anything of his life and duties; he seemed sometimes as it were meditating a departure from his country. There was undoubtedly about him something mysterious and unsatisfactory. Morley was of opinion that he was a spy; Gerard, less suspicious, ultimately concluded that he was harassed by his creditors, and when at Mowedale was probably hiding from them.

And now the mystery was at length dissolved. And what an explanation! A Norman, a noble, an oppressor of the people, a plunderer of the church: all the characters and capacities that Sybil had been bred up to look upon with fear and aversion and to recognise as the authors of the degradation of her race.

Sybil sighed; the door opened, and Egremont stood before her. The blood rose to her cheek, her heart trembled; for the first time in his presence she felt embarrassed and constrained. His countenance on the contrary was collected, serious, and pale.

'I am an intruder,' he said advancing, 'but I wish much to speak to you,' and he seated himself near her. There was a momentary pause. 'You seemed to treat with scorn yesterday,' resumed Egremont, in accents less sustained, 'the belief that sympathy was independent of the mere accidents of position.

Pardon me, Sybil, but even you may be prejudiced.' He paused.

'I should be sorry to treat anything you said with scorn,' replied Sybil, in a subdued tone. 'Many things happened yesterday,' she added, 'which might be offered as some excuse for an unguarded word.'

'Would that it had been unguarded!' said Egremont, in a voice of melancholy. 'I could have endured it with less repining. No, Sybil, I have known you, I have had the happiness and the sorrow of knowing you too well to doubt the convictions of your mind, or to believe that they can be lightly removed, and yet I would strive to remove them. You look upon me as an enemy, as a natural foe, because I am born among the privileged. I am a man, Sybil, as well as a noble.' Again he paused; she looked down, but did not speak.

'And can I not feel for men, my fellows, whatever be their lot? I know you will deny it; but you are in error, Sybil; you have formed your opinions upon tradition, not upon experience. The world that exists is not the world of which you have read; the class that calls itself your superior is not the same class as ruled in the time of your fathers. There is a change in them as in all other things, and I participate in that change. I shared it before I knew you, Sybil; and if it touched me then, at least believe it does not influence me less now.'

'If there be a change,' said Sybil, 'it is because in some degree the People have learnt their strength.'

'Ah! dismiss from your mind those fallacious fancies,' said Egremont. 'The People are not strong; the People never can be strong. Their attempts at self-vindication will end only in their suffering and confusion. It is civilisation that has effected, that is effecting, this change. It is that increased knowledge of themselves that teaches the educated their social duties. There is a dayspring in the history of this nation, which perhaps those only who are on the mountain tops can as yet recognise. You deem you are in darkness, and I see a dawn. The new generation of the aristocracy of England are not tyrants, not oppressors, Sybil, as you persist in believing. Their intelligence, better than that, their hearts, are open to the responsibility of their position. But the work that is before them is no holiday-work. It is not the fever of superficial impulse that can remove the deep-fixed barriers of centuries of ignorance and crime. Enough that their sympathies are awakened; time and thought will bring the rest. They are the natural leaders of the People, Sybil; believe me they are the only ones.'

'The leaders of the People are those whom the People trust,' said Sybil, rather haughtily.

'And who may betray them,' said Egremont.

'Betray them!' exclaimed Sybil. 'And can you believe that my father –'

'No, no; you can feel, Sybil, though I cannot express, how much I honour your father. But he stands alone in the single-ness and purity of his heart. Who surround him?'

'Those whom the People have also chosen; and from a like confidence in their virtues and abilities. They are a senate supported by the sympathy of millions, with only one object in view, the emancipation of their race. It is a sublime spectacle, these delegates of labour advocating the sacred cause in a manner which might shame your haughty factions. What can resist a demonstration so truly national! What can withstand the supremacy of its moral power!'

Her eye met the glance of Egremont. That brow, full of thought and majesty, was fixed on his. He encountered that face radiant as a seraph's; those dark eyes flashing with the inspiration of the martyr.

Egremont rose, moved slowly to the window, gazed in abstraction for a few moments on the little garden, with its dank turf that no foot ever trod, its mutilated statue, and its mouldering frescoes. What a silence; how profound! What a prospect; how drear! Suddenly he turned, and advancing with a more rapid pace, he approached Sybil. Her head was averted, and leaning on her left arm, she seemed lost in reverie. Egre-mont fell upon his knee, and gently taking her hand, he press-ed it to his lips. She started, she looked round, agitated, alarmed, while he breathed forth in tremulous accents, 'Let me express to you my adoration!

'Ah! not now for the first time, but for ever; from the moment I first beheld you in the starlit arch of Marney, has your spirit ruled my being, and softened every spring of my affections. I followed you to your home, and lived for a time content in the silent worship of your nature. When I came the last morning to the cottage, it was to tell, and to ask, all. Since then for a moment your image has never been absent from my consciousness; your picture consecrates my hearth, and your approval has been the spur of my career. Do not reject my love; it is deep as your nature, and fervent as my own. Banish those prejudices that have embittered your existence, and, if persisted in, may wither mine. Deign to retain this hand! If I be a noble, I have none of the accidents of nobility: I cannot offer you wealth, splendour, or power; but I can offer you the devotion of an entranced being, aspirations that you shall guide, an ambition that you shall govern.'

'These words are mystical and wild,' said Sybil with an amazed air; 'they came upon me with convulsive suddenness.' And she paused for an instant, collecting as it were her mind with an expression almost of pain upon her countenance.' These changes of life are so strange and rapid that it seems to me I can scarcely meet them. You are Lord Marney's brother; it was by yesterday, only yesterday, I learnt it. I thought then I had lost your friendship, and now you speak of – love! love of me! Retain your hand and share your life and fortunes! You forget what I am. But though I learnt only yesterday what you are, I will not be so remiss. Once you wrote upon a page you were my faithful friend; and I have pondered over that line with kindness often. I will be your faithful friend; I will recall you to yourself. I will at least not bring you shame and degradation.'

'Oh, Sybil, beloved, beautiful Sybil, not such bitter words; no, no!'

'No bitterness to you! that would indeed be harsh,' and she covered with her hand her streaming eyes.

'Why, what is this?' after a pause and with an effort she exclaimed. 'A union between the child and brother of nobles and a daughter of the people! Estrangement from your family, and with cause, their hopes destroyed, their pride outraged; alienation from your order, and justly, all their prejudices insulted. You will forfeit every source of worldly content and cast off every spring of social success. Society for you will become a great confederation to deprive you of self-complacency. And rightly. Will you not be a traitor to the cause? No, no, kind friend, for such I'll call you. Your opinion of me, too good and great as I feel it, touches me deeply. I am not used to such passages in life; I have read of such. Pardon me, feel for me, if I receive them with some disorder. They sound to me for the first time, and for the last. Perhaps they ought never to have reached my ear. No matter now; I have a life of penitence before me, and I trust I shall be pardoned.' And she wept.

'You have indeed punished me for the fatal accident of birth, if it deprives me of you.'

'Not so,' she added, weeping; 'I shall never be the bride of earth; and but for one, whose claims though earthly are to me irresistible, I should have ere this forgotten my hereditary sorrows in the cloister.'

All this time Egremont had retained her hand, which she had not attempted to withdraw. He had bent his head over it as she spoke; it was touched with his tears. For some moments there was silence; then, looking up and in a smothered voice, Egremont made one more effort to induce Sybil to consider his suit. He combated her views as to the importance to him of the sympathies of his family and of society; he detailed to her his hopes and plans for their future welfare; he dwelt with passionate eloquence on his abounding love. But, with a solemn sweetness, and as it were a tender inflexibility, the tears trickling down her soft cheek, and pressing his hand in both of hers, she subdued and put aside all his efforts.

'Believe me,' she said, 'the gulf is impassable.'

END OF THE FOURTH BOOK

BOOK V

*

'TERRIBLE news from Birmingham,' ssid Mr. Egerton at Brooks'. 'They have massacred the police, beat off the military, and sacked the town. News just arrived.'

'I have known it these two hours,' said a grey-headed gentleman, speaking without taking his eyes off the newspaper. 'There is a cabinet sitting now.'

'Well, I always said so,' said Mr. Egerton; 'our fellows ought to have put down that Convention.'

'It is deuced lucky,' said Mr. Berners, 'that the Bedchamber business is over, and we are all right. This affair, in the midst of the Jamaica hitch, would have been fatal to us.'

'These Chartists evidently act upon a system,' said Mr. Egerton. 'You see they were perfectly quiet till the National Petition was presented and debated; and now, almost simultaneously with our refusing to consider their petition, we have news of this outbreak.'

'I hope they will not spread,' said the grey-headed gentleman. 'There are not troops enough in the country if there be anything like a general movement. I hear they have sent the Guards down by a special train, and a hundred more of the police. London is not over-garrisoned.'

'They are always ready for a riot at Birmingham,' said a Warwickshire peer. 'Trade is very bad there and they suffer a good deal. But I should think it would not go farther.'

'I am told,' said the grey-headed gentleman, 'that business is getting slack in all the districts.'

'It might be better,' said Mr. Egerton, 'but they have got work.'

Here several gentlemen entered, inquiring whether the evening papers were in, and what was the news from Birmingham.

'I am told,' said one of them, 'that the police were regularly smashed.'

'Is it true that the military were really beat off?'

'Quite untrue: the fact is, there were no proper preparations; the town was taken by surprise, the magistrates lost their heads; the people were masters of the place; and when the police did act, they were met by a triumphant populace, who two hours before would have fled before them. They say they have burnt down forty houses.'

'It is a bad thing, this beating the police,' said the grey-headed gentleman.

'But what is the present state of affairs?' inquired Mr. Berners. 'Are the rioters put down?'

'Not in the least,' said Mr. Egerton, 'as I hear. They are encamped in the Bull Ring amid smoking ruins, and breathe nothing but havoc.'

'Well, I voted for taking the National Petition into consideration,' said Mr. Berners. 'It could do us no harm, and would have kept things quiet.'

'So did every fellow on our side,' said Mr. Egerton, 'who was not in office or about to be. Well, Heaven knows what may come next. The Charter may some day be as popular in this club as the Reform Act.'

'The oddest thing in that debate,' said Mr. Berners, 'was Egremont's move.'

'I saw Marney last night at Lady St. Julians',' said Mr Egerton, 'and congratulated him on his brother's speech. He looked daggers, and grinned like a ghoul.'

'It was a very remarkable speech, that of Egremont,' said the grey-headed gentlemen. 'I wonder what he wants.'

'I think he must be going to turn radical,' said the Warwickshire peer.

'Why, the whole speech was against radicalism,' said Mr. Egerton.

'Ah, then he is going to turn whig, I suppose.'

'He is ultra anti-whig,' said Egerton.

'Then what the deuce is he?' said Mr. Berners.

'Not a conservative certainly, for Lady St. Julians does nothing but abuse him.'

'I suppose he is crotchety,' suggested the Warwickshire noble.

'That speech of Egremont was the most really democratic speech that I ever read,' said the grey-headed gentleman. 'How was it listened to?'

'Oh! capitally,' said Mr. Egerton. 'He has seldom spoken before, and always slightly though well. He was listened to with mute attention; never was a better house. I should say made a great impression, though no one knew exactly what he was after.'

'What does he mean by obtaining the results of the Charter without the intervention of its machinery?'* inquired Lord Loraine, a mild, middle-aged, lounging, languid man, who passed his life in crossing from Brooks' to Boodle's, and from Boodle's to Brooks', and testing the comparative intelligence of these two celebrated bodies; himself gifted with no ordinary abilities cultivated with no ordinary care, but the victim of sauntering, his sultana queen, as it was, according to Sheffield, Duke of Buckingham,* of the second Charles Stuart.

'He spoke throughout in an exoteric vein,' said the grey-headed gentleman, 'and I apprehend was not very sure of his audience; but I took him to mean, indeed it was the gist of the speech, that if you wished for a time to retain your political power, you could only effect your purpose by securing for the people greater social felicity.'

'Well, that is sheer radicalism,' said the Warwickshire peer; 'pretending that the people can be better off than they are, is radicalism and nothing else.'

'I fear, if that be radicalism,' said Lord Loraine, 'we must all take a leaf out of the same book. Sloane was saying at Boodle's just now that he looked forward to the winter in his country with horror.'

'And they have no manufactures there,' said Mr. Egerton.

'Sloane was always a croaker,' said the Warwickshire peer. 'He always said the New Poor Law would not act, and there is no part of the country where it works so well as in his own.'

'They say at Boodle's there is to be an increase to the army,' said Lord Loraine; 'ten thousand men immediately; decided on by the cabinet this afternoon.'

'It could hardly have leaked out by this time,' said the grey-headed gentleman. 'The cabinet were sitting less than an hour ago.'

'They have been up a good hour,' said Lord Loraine, 'quite long enough for their decisions to be known in St.

James' Street. In the good old times, George Farnley used always to walk from Downing Street to this place the moment the council was up and tell us everything.'

'Ah! those were the good old gentleman-like times,' said Mr. Berners, 'when members of Parliament had nobody to please and ministers of State nothing to do.'

The riots of Birmingham occurred two months after the events that closed our last book. That period, so far as the obvious movements of the Chartists were concerned, had been passed in preparations for the presentation and discussion of the National Petition, which the parliamentary embroilments of the spring of that year had hitherto procrastinated and prevented. The petition was ultimately carried down to Westminster on a triumphal car, accompanied by all the delegates of the Convention in solemn procession. It was necessary to construct a machine in order to introduce the huge bulk of parchment, signed by a million and a half of persons, into the House of Commons; and thus supported, its vast form remained on the floor of the House during the discussion. The House, after a debate which was not deemed by the people commensurate with the importance of the occasion, decided on rejecting the prayer of the Petition, and from that moment the party in the Convention who advocated a recourse to physical force in order to obtain their purpose, was in the ascendant. The National Petition, and the belief that, although its objects would not at present be obtained, yet a solemn and prolonged debate on its prayer would at least hold out to the working classes the hope, that their rights might from that date rank among the acknowledged subjects of parliamentary discussion, and ultimately, by the force of discussion, be recognised, as other rights of other portions of the people once equally disputed, had been the means by which the party in the Convention who upheld on all occasions the supremacy of moral power had been able to curb the energetic and reckless minority, who derided from the first all other methods but terror and violence as effective of their end. The hopes of all, the vanity of many, were frustrated and shocked by finding that the exertions and expenditure of long months were not only fruitless, but had not even attracted as numerous an assembly, or excited as much interest, as an ordinary party struggle on some petty point of factitious interest, forgotten as soon as fought. The attention of the working classes was especially called by their leaders to the contrast between the interest occasioned by the endangered constitution of Jamaica, a petty and exhausted colony, and the claims for the same constitutional rights by the working millions of England. In the first instance, not a member was absent from his place; men were brought indeed from distant capitals to participate in the struggle and to decide it; the debate lasted for days, almost for weeks; not a public man of light and leading in the country withheld the expression of his opinion; the fate of governments was involved in it; cabinets were overthrown and reconstructed in the throes and tumult of the strife, and, for the first time for a long period, the Sovereign personally interposed in public transactions with a significance of character, which made the working classes almost believe that the privileged had at last found a master, and the unfranchised regained their natural chief. The mean position which the Saxon multitude occupied, as distinguished from the Jamaica planters, sunk deep into their hearts. From that moment all hope of relief from the demonstration of a high moral conduct in the millions, and the exhibition of that well-regulated order of public life which would intimate their fitness for the possession and fulfilment of public rights, vanished. The party of violence, a small minority, as is usually the case, but consisting of men of determined character, triumphed; and the outbreak at Birmingham was the first consequence of those reckless counsels that were destined in the course of the ensuing years to inflict on the working classes of this country so much suffering and disaster.

It was about this time, a balmy morning of July, that Sybil, tempted by the soft sunshine, and a longing for the sight of flowers and turf and the spread of winding waters, went forth from her gloomy domicile to those beautiful gardens that bloom in that once melancholy region of marsh, celebrated in old days only for its Dutch canal and its Chinese bridge, and now not unworthy of the royal park that encloses them. Except here and there a pretty nursery-maid with her interesting charge; some beautiful child with nodding plume, immense bow, and gorgeous sash; the gardens were vacant. Indeed it was only at this early hour, that Sybil found from experience that it was agreeable in London for a woman unaccompanied to venture abroad. There is no European city where our fair sisters are so little independent as in our metropolis; to our shame.

Something of the renovating influence of a beautiful nature was needed by the daughter of Gerard. She was at this moment anxious and dispirited. The outbreak at Birmingham, the conviction that such proceedings must ultimately prove fatal to the cause to which she was devoted, the dark apprehension that her father was in some manner implicated in this movement, which had commenced with so much public disaster, and which menaced consequences still more awful; all these events, and fears, and sad forebodings, acted with immense influence on a temperament which, though gifted with even a sublime courage, was singularly sensitive. The quick and teeming imagination of Sybil conjured up a thousand fears which were in some degree unfounded, in a great degree exaggerated; but this is the inevitable lot of the creative mind practising on the inexperienced.

The shock too had been sudden. The two months that had elapsed since she had parted, as she supposed for ever, from Egremont, while they had not less abounded than the preceding time in that pleasing public excitement which her father's career, in her estimation alike, useful, honourable, and distinguished, occasioned her, and been fruitful in some sources of satisfaction of a softer and more domestic character. The acquaintance of Hatton, of whom they saw a great deal, had very much contributed to the increased amenity of her life. He was a most agreeable, instructive, and obliging companion who seemed peculiarly to possess the art of making life pleasant by the adroit management of unobtrusive resources. He lent Sybil books; and all that he recommended to her notice were of a kind that harmonised with her sentiment and taste. He furnished her from his library with splendid works of art, illustrative of those periods of our history, and those choice and costly edifices which were associated with her fondest thought and fancy. He placed in her room the best periodical literature of the day, which for her was a new world; he furnished her with newspapers whose columns of discussion

taught her, that the opinions she had embraced were not un-
questioned: as she had never seen a journal in her life before,
except a stray number of the 'Mowbray Phalanx,' or the
metropolitan publication which was devoted to the cause of
the National Convention, and reported her father's speeches,
the effect of this reading on her intelligence was, to say the
least, suggestive.

Many a morning too when Gerard was disengaged, Hatton
would propose that they should show Sybil something of the
splendour or the rarities of the metropolis; its public buildings, museums, and galleries of art. Sybil, though uninstructed
in painting, had that native taste which requires only observation to arrive at true results. She was much interested with
all she saw and all that occurred, and her gratification was
heightened by the society of an individual, who not only sym-
pathised with all she felt, but who, if she made an inquiry, was
ever ready with an instructive reply. Hatton poured forth the
taste and treasures of a well-stored and refined intelligence.
And then too always easy, bland, and considerate; and though
with luxuries and conveniences at his command, to participate
in which, under any other circumstances, might have been
embarrassing to his companions, with so much tact, that
either by an allusion to early days, happy days when he owed
so much to Gerard's father, or some other mode equally feli-
citous, he contrived completely to maintain among them the
spirit of social equality. In the evening, Hatton generally
looked in when Gerard was at home, and on Sundays they
were always together. Their common faith was a bond of
union which led them to the same altar, and on that day
Hatton had obtained their promise always to dine with him.
He was careful to ascertain each holy day at what chapel the
music was most exquisite, that the most passionate taste of
Sybil might be gratified. Indeed, during this residence in London, the opportunity it afforded of making her acquainted
with some of the great masters of the human voice was perhaps to Sybil a source of pleasure not the least important. For,
though it was not deemed consistent with the future discipline
which she contemplated to enter a theatre, there were yet
occasions which permitted her, under every advantage, to
enlist to the performance of the master-pieces of sacred

melody. Alone, with Hatton and her father, she often poured forth those tones of celestial sweetness and ethereal power that had melted the soul of Egremont amid the ruins of Marney Abbey.

More intimately acquainted with Sybil Gerard, Hatton had shrunk from the project that he had at first so crudely formed. There was something about her that awed, while it fascinated him. He did not relinquish his purpose, for it was a rule of his life never to do that; but he postponed the plans of its fulfilment. Hatton was not, what is commonly understood by the phrase, in love with Sybil; certainly not passionately in love with her. With all his daring and talents, and fine taste, there was in Hatton such a vein of thorough good sense, that it was impossible for him to act or even to think anything that was ridiculous. He wished still to marry Sybil for the great object that we have stated; he had a mind quite equal to appreciate her admirable qualities, but sense enough to wish that she were a less dazzling creature, because then he would have a better chance of accomplishing his end. He perceived, when he had had a due opportunity to study her character, that the cloister was the natural catastrophe impending over a woman who, with an exalted mind, great abilities, a fine and profound education, and almost supernatural charms, found herself born and rooted in the ranks of a degraded population. All this Hatton understood; it was a conclusion he had gradually arrived at by a gradual process of induction, and by vigilant observation that in its study of character had rarely been deceived; and when, one evening, with an art that could not be suspected, he sounded Gerard on the future of his daughter, he found that the clear intellect and straightforward sagacity of the father had arrived at the same result. 'She wishes,' said Gerard, 'to take the veil and, I only oppose it for a time, that she may have some knowledge of life and a clear conception of what she is about to do. I wish not that she should hereafter reproach her father. But, to my mind, Sybil is right. She cannot look at marriage: no man that she could marry would be worthy of her.'

During these two months, and especially during the last, Morley was rarely in London, though ever much with Gerard, and often with his daughter, during his visits. The necessary impulse had been given to the affairs of the Convention, the delegates had visited the members, the preparations for the presentation of the National Petition had been completed; the overthrow of the whig government, the abortive effort of Sir Robert Peel, the return of the whig administration, and the consequent measures had occasioned a delay of two months in the presentation of the great document; it was well for Gerard to remain, who was a leader in debate, and whose absence for a week would have endangered his position as the head of a party, but these considerations did not influence Morley, who had already found great inconvenience in managing his journal at a distance; so, about the middle of May, he had returned to Mowbray, coming up occasionally by the train if anything important were stirring, or his vote could be of service to his friend and colleague. The affair of Birmingham, however, had alarmed Morley, and he had written up to Gerard that he should instantly repair to town. Indeed he was expected the very morning that Sybil, her father having gone to the Convention, where there were at this very moment fiery debates, went forth to take the morning air of summer in the gardens of St. James' Park.

It was a real summer day; large, round, glossy, fleecy clouds, as white and shining as glaciers, studded with their immense and immovable forms the deep blue sky. There was not even a summer breeze, though the air was mellow, balmy, and exhilarating. These was a bloom upon the trees, the waters glittered, the prismatic wild-fowl dived, breathed again, and again disappeared. Beautiful children, fresh and sweet as the new-born rose, glanced about with the gestures and sometimes the voices of Paradise. And in the distance rose the sacred towers of the great Western Minster.

How fair is a garden amid the toils and passions of existence! A curse upon those who vulgarise and desecrate these holy haunts; breaking the hearts of nursery-maids, and smoking tobacco in the palace of the rose!

The mental clouds dispelled as Sybil felt the freshness and fragrance of nature. The colour came to her cheek; the deep brightness returned to her eye: her step, that at first had been languid, and if not melancholy, at least contemplative, became active and animated. She forgot the cares of life, and was touched by all the sense of all its enjoyment. To move, to breathe, to feel the sunbeam, were sensible and surpassing pleasures. Cheerful by nature, not withstanding her stately thoughts and solemn life, a brilliant smile played on her seraphic face, as she marked the wild passage of the daring birds, or watched the thoughtless grace of infancy.

She rested herself on a bench beneath a branching elm, and her eye, which for some time had followed the various objects that had attracted it, was now fixed in abstraction on the sunny waters. The visions of past life rose before her. It was one of those reveries when the incidents of our existence are mapped before us, when each is considered with relation to the rest, and assumes in our knowledge its distinct and absolute position; when, as it were, we take stock of our experience, and ascertain how rich sorrow and pleasure, feeling and thought, intercourse with our fellow-creatures and the fortuitous mysteries of life, have made us in wisdom.

The quick intelligence and the ardent imagination of Sybil had made her comprehend with fervour the two ideas that had been impressed on her young mind; the oppression of her Church and the degradation of her people. Educated in solitude and exchanging thoughts only with individuals of the same sympathies, these impressions had resolved themselves into one profound and gloomy conviction that the world was divided only between the oppressors and the oppressed. With her, to be one of the people was to be miserable and innocent; one of the privileged, a luxurious tyrant. In the cloister, in her garden, amid the scenes of suffering which she often visited and always solaced, she had raised up two phantoms which with her represented human nature.

But the experience of the last few months had operated a great change in these impressions. She had seen enough to suspect that the world was a more complicated system than she had preconceived. There was not that strong and rude simplicity in its organisation which she had supposed. The characters were more various, the motives more mixed, the classes more blended, the elements of each more subtle and diversified, than she had imagined. The people, she found, was not that pure embodiment of unity of feeling, of interest, and of purpose, which she had pictured in her abstractions.

The people had enemies among the people; their own passions; which made them often sympathise, often combine, with the privileged. Her father, with all his virtues, all his abilities, singleness of purpose, and simplicity of aim, encountered rivals in their own Convention, and was beset by open, or, still worse, secret foes.

Sybil, whose mind had been nurtured with great thoughts, and with whom success or failure alike partook of the heroic, who had hoped for triumph, but who was prepared for sacrifice, found to her surprise that great thoughts have very little to do with the business of the world; that human affairs, even in an age of revolution, are the subject of compromise; and that the essence of compromise is littleness. She thought that the People, calm and collected, conscious at last of their strength and confident in their holy cause, had but to express their pure and noble convictions by the delegates of their choice, and that an antique and decrepit authority must bow before the irresistible influence of their moral power. These delegates of their choice turned out to be a plebeian senate of wild ambitions and sinister and selfish ends, while the decrepit authority that she had been taught existed only by the sufferance of the millions, was compact and organised, with every element of physical power at its command. and supported by the interests, the sympathies, the honest convictions, and the strong prejudices of classes influential not merely from their wealth but even by their numbers.

Nor could she resist the belief that the feeling of the rich towards the poor was not that sentiment of unmingled hate and scorn which she associated with Norman conquerors and feudal laws. She would ascribe rather the want of sympathy that unquestionably exists between Wealth and Work in England, to mutual ignorance between the classes which possess these two great elements of national prosperity; and though the source of that ignorance was to be sought in antecedent circumstances of violence and oppression, the consequences perhaps had outlived the causes, as customs survive opinions.

Sybil looked towards Westminster, to those proud and passionate halls where assembles the Parliament of England; that rapacious, violent, and haughty body, which had brought kings and prelates to the block; spoiled churches and then seized the sacred manors for their personal prey; invested their own possessions with infinite privileges and, then mortgaged for their state and empire the labour of countless generations. Could the voice of solace sound from such a quarter?

Sybil unfolded a journal which she had brought; not now to be read for the first time; but now for the first time to be read alone, undisturbed, in a scene of softness and serenity. It contained a report of the debate in the House of Commons on the presentation of the National Petition; that important document which had been the means of drawing forth Sybil from her solitude, and of teaching her something of that world of which she had often pondered, and yet which she had so inaccurately preconceived.

Yes! there was one voice that had sounded in that proud Parliament, that, free from the slang of faction, had dared to express immortal truths: the voice of a noble, who without being a demagogue, had upheld the popular cause; had pronounced his conviction that the rights of labour were as sacred as those of property; that if a difference were to be established, the interests of the living wealth ought to be preferred; who had declared that the social happiness of the millions should be the first object of a statesman, and that, if this were not achieved, thrones and dominions, the pomp and power of courts and empires, were alike worthless.

With a heart not without emotion, with a kindling cheek, and eyes suffused with tears, Sybil read the speech of Egremont. She ceased; still holding the paper with one hand, she laid on it the other with tenderness, and looked up to breathe as it were for relief. Before her stood the orator himself.

CHAPTER 2

EGREMONT had recognised Sybil as she entered the garden. He was himself crossing the park to attend a committee of the House of Commons which had sat for the first time that morning. The meeting had been formal and brief, the committee soon adjourned, and Egremont repaired to the spot where he was in the hope of still finding Sybil.

He approached her not without some restraint, with reserve, and yet with tenderness. 'This is a great, an unexpected pleasure indeed,' he said in a faltering tone. She had looked up; the expression of an agitation, not distressful, on her beautiful countenance could not be concealed. She smiled through a gushing vision; and, with a flushed cheek, impelled perhaps by her native frankness, perhaps by some softer and irresistible feeling of gratitude, respect, regard, she said in a low voice, 'I was reading your beautiful speech.'

'Indeed,' said Egremont much moved, 'that is an honour, a pleasure, a reward, I never could have even hoped to attain.'

'By all,' continued Sybil with more self-possession, 'it must be read with pleasure, with advantage, but by me, oh! with what deep interest.'

'If anything that I said finds an echo in your breast,' and here he hesitated: 'it will give me confidence for the future,' he hurriedly added.

'Ah! why do not others feel like you!' said Sybil, 'all would not then be hopeless.'

'But you are not hopeless?' said Egremont, and he seated himself on the bench, but at some distance from her.

Sybil shook her head.

'But when we spoke last,' said Egremont, 'you were full of confidence; in your cause, and in your means.'

'It is not very long ago,' said Sybil, 'since we thus spoke, and yet time in the interval has taught me some bitter truths.'

'Truth is precious,' said Egremont, 'to us all; and yet I fear I could not sufficiently appreciate the cause that deprived you of your sanguine faith.'

'Alas!' said Sybil mournfully, 'I was but a dreamer of dreams: I wake from my hallucination, as others have done, I suppose, before me. Like them, too, I feel the glory of life has gone; but my content at least,' and she bent her head meekly, 'has never rested, I hope, too much on this world.'

'You are depressed, dear Sybil?'

'I am unhappy. I am anxious about my father. I fear that he is surrounded by men unworthy of his confidence. These scenes of violence alarm me. Under any circumstances I should shrink from them, but I am impressed with the conviction that they can bring us nothing but disaster and disgrace.'

'I honour your father,' said Egremont; 'I know no man whose character I esteem so truly noble; such a just compound of intelligence and courage, and gentle and generous impulse. I should deeply grieve were he to compromise himself. But you have influence over him, the greatest, as you have over all. Counsel him to return to Mowbray.'

'Can I give counsel?' said Sybil, 'I who have been wrong in all my judgments? I came up to this city with him, to be his guide, his guardian. What arrogance! What short-sighted pride! I thought the People all felt as I feel; that I had nothing to do but to sustain and animate him; to encourage him when he flagged, to uphold him when he wavered. I thought that moral power must govern the world, and that moral power was embodied in an assembly whose annals will be a series of petty intrigues, or, what is worse, of violent machinations.'

'Exert every energy,' said Egremont, 'that your father should leave London immediately; to-morrow, to-night if possible. After this business at Birmingham, the government must act. I hear that they will immediately increase the army and the police; and that there is a circular from the Secretary of State to the Lord Lieutenants of counties. But the government will strike at the Convention. The members who remain will be the victims. If your father return to Mowbray, and be quiet, he has a chance of not being disturbed.'

'An ignoble end of many lofty hopes,' said Sybil.

'Let us retain our hopes,' said Egremont, 'and cherish them.'

'I have none,' she replied.

'And I am sanguine,' said Egremont.

'Ah! because you have made a beautiful speech. But they will listen to you, they will cheer you, but they will never follow you. The dove and the eagle will not mate; the lion and the lamb will not lie down together; and the conquerors will never rescue the conquered.'

Egremont shook his head. 'You still will cherish these phantoms, dear Sybil! and why? They are not visions of delight. Believe me, they are as vain as they are distressing. The mind of England is the mind ever of the rising race. Trust me, it is with the People. And not the less so, because this feeling is one of which even in a great degree it is unconscious.

Those opinions which you have been educated to dread and mistrust, are opinions that are dying away. Predominant opinions are generally the opinions of the generation that is vanishing. Let an accident, which speculation could not foresee, the balanced state at this moment of parliamentary parties, cease, and in a few years, more or less, cease it must, and you will witness a development of the new mind of England, which will make up by its rapid progress for its retarded action. I live among these men; I know their inmost souls; I watch their instincts and their impulses; I know the principles which they have imbibed, and I know, however hindered by circumstances for the moment, those principles must bear their fruit. It will be a produce hostile to the oligarchical system. The future principle of English politics will not be a levelling principle; not a principle adverse to privileges, but favourable to their extension. It will seek to ensure equality, not by levelling the Few, but by elevating the Many.'

Indulging for some little time in the mutual reflections which the tone of the conversation suggested, Sybil at length rose, and, saying that she hoped by this time her father might have returned, bade farewell to Egremont, but he, also rising, would for a time accompany her. At the gate of the gardens, however, she paused, and said with a soft sad smile. 'Here we must part,' and extended to him her hand.

'Heaven will guard over you!' said Egremont, 'for you are a celestial charge.'

CHAPTER 3

As Sybil approached her home, she recognised her father in the court before their house, accompanied by several men, with whom he seemed on the point of going forth. She was so anxious to speak to Gerard, that she did not hesitate at once to advance. There was a stir as she entered the gate; the men ceased talking, some stood aloof, all welcomed her with silent respect. With one or two Sybil was not entirely unacquainted; at least by name or person. To them, as she passed, she bent her head; and then, going up to her father, who was about to welcome her, she said, in a tone of calmness, and

with a semblance of composure, 'If you are going out, dear
father, I should like to see you for one moment first.'

'A moment, friends,' said Gerard, 'with your leave;' and
he accompanied his daughter into the house. He would have
stopped in the hall, but she walked on to their room, and
Gerard, though pressed for time, was compelled to follow
her. When they had entered their chamber, Sybil closed the
door with care, and then, Gerard sitting, or rather leaning
carelessly, on the edge of the table, she said, 'We are once
more together, dear father; we will never again be separated.'

Gerard sprang quickly on his legs, his eye kindled, his
cheek flushed. 'Something has happened to you, Sybil!'

'No,' she said, shaking her head, mournfully, 'not that; but
something may happen to you.'

'How so, my child?' said her father, relapsing into his
customary good-tempered placidity, and speaking in an easy,
measured, almost drawling tone that was habitual to him.

'You are in danger,' said Sybil, 'great and immediate. No
matter at this moment how I am persuaded of this: I wish
no mysteries, but there is no time for details. The government will strike at the Convention; they are resolved. This
outbreak at Birmingham has brought affairs to a crisis. They
have already arrested the leaders there; they will seize those
who remain here in avowed correspondence with them.'

'If they arrest all who are in correspondence with the Convention,' said Gerard, 'they will have enough to do.'

'Yes: but you take a leading part,' said Sybil; 'you are the
individual they would select.'

'Would you have me hide myself,' said Gerard, 'just because something is going on besides talk?'

'Besides talk!' exclaimed Sybil. 'O! my father, what
thoughts are these! It may be that words are vain to save us;
but feeble deeds are vainer far than words.'

'I do not see that the deeds, though I have nothing to do
with them, are so feeble,' said Gerard; 'their boasted police
are beaten, and by the isolated movement of an unorganised
mass. What if the outbreak had not been a solitary one? What
if the people had been disciplined?'

'What if everything were changed, if everything were contrary to what it is?' said Sybil. 'The people are not disciplined;

their action will not be, cannot be, coherent and uniform; these are riots in which you are involved, not revolutions; and you will be a victim, and not a sacrifice.'

Gerard looked thoughtful, but not anxious: after a momentary pause, he said, 'We must not be scared at a few arrests, Sybil. These are haphazard pranks of a government that wants to terrify, but is itself frightened. I have not counselled, none of us have counselled, this stir at Birmingham. It is a casualty. We were none of us prepared for it. But great things spring from casualties. I say the police were beaten, and the troops alarmed; and I say this was done without organisation, and in a single spot. I am as much against feeble deeds as you can be, Sybil; and to prove this to you, our conversation at the moment you arrived was to take care for the future that there shall be none. Neither vain words, nor feeble deeds, for the future,' added Gerard, and he moved to depart.

Sybil approached him with gentleness; she took his hand as if to bid him farewell; she retained it for a moment, and looked him steadfastly in the face, with a glance at the same time serious and soft. Then, throwing her arms round his neck and leaning her cheek upon his breast, she murmured, 'O! my father, your child is most unhappy.'

'Sybil,' exclaimed Gerard, in a tone of tender reproach, 'this is womanish weakness; I love but must not share it.'

'It may be womanish,' said Sybil, 'but it is wise: for what should make us unhappy if not the sense of impending, yet unknown, danger?'

'And why danger?' said Gerard.

'Why mystery?' said Sybil. 'Why are you ever pre-occupied and involved in dark thoughts, my father? It is not the pressure of business, as you will perhaps tell me, that occasions this change in a disposition so frank and even careless. The pressure of affairs is not nearly so great, cannot be nearly so great, as in the early period of your assembling, when the eyes of the whole country were on you, and you were in communication with all parts of it. How often have you told me that there was no degree of business which you found irksome? Now you are all dispersed and scattered: no discussions no committees, little correspondence; and you yourself are ever brooding, and ever in conclave too, with persons who,

I know, for Stephen has told me so, are the preachers of violence; violence perhaps that some of them may preach, yet will not practise: both bad; traitors it may be, or, at the best, hare-brained men.'

'Stephen is prejudiced,' said Gerard. 'He is a visionary, indulging in impossible dreams, and if possible, little desirable. He knows nothing of the feeling of the country or the character of his countrymen. Englishmen want none of his joint-stock felicity; they want their rights, rights consistent with the rights of other classes, but without which the rights of other classes cannot and ought not to be secure.'

'Stephen is at least your friend, my father; and once you honoured him.'

'And do so now, and love him very dearly. I honour him for his great abilities and knowledge. Stephen is a scholar; I have no pretensions that way; but I can feel the pulse of a people, and can comprehend the signs of the times, Sybil. Stephen was all very well talking in our cottage and garden at Mowbray, when we had nothing to do; but now we must act, or others will act for us. Stephen is not a practical man; he is crotchety, Sybil, and that's just it.'

'But violence and action,' said Sybil, 'are they identical, my father?'

'I did not speak of violence.'

'No; but you looked it. I know the language of your countenance, even to the quiver of your lip. Action, as you and Stephen once taught me, and I think wisely, was to prove to our rulers by an agitation, orderly and intellectual, that we were sensible of our degradation; and that it was neither Christianlike nor prudent, neither good nor wise, to let us remain so. That you did, and you did it well; the respect of the world, even of those who differed from you in interest or opinion, was not withheld from you, and can be withheld from none who exercise the moral power that springs from great talents and a good cause. You have let this great moral power, this pearl of price,' said Sybil, with emotion; 'we cannot conceal it from ourselves, my father; you have let it escape from your hands.'

Gerard looked at her as she spoke, with an earnestness unusual with him. As she ceased, he cast his eyes down, and seemed for a moment in thought; then, looking up, he said, 'The season for words is past. I must begone, dear Sybil.' And he moved towards the door.

'You shall not leave me,' said Sybil, springing forward, and seizing his arm.

'What would you, what would you?' said Gerard, distressed.

'That we should quit this city to-night.'

'What, quit my post?'

'Why yours? Have not your colleagues dispersed? Is not your assembly formally adjourned to another town? Is it not known that the great majority of the delegates have returned to their homes? And why not you to yours?'

'I have no home,' said Gerard, almost in a voice of harshness. 'I came here to do the business that was wanting, and, by the blessing of God, I will do it. I am no changeling, nor can I refine and split straws, like your philosophers and Morleys; but if the people will struggle, I will struggle with them; and die, if need be, in the front. Nor will I be deterred from my purpose by the tears of a girl,' and he released himself from the hand of his daughter with abruptness.

Sybil looked up to heaven with streaming eyes, and clasped her hands in unutterable woe. Gerard moved again towards the door, but before he reached it his step faltered, and he turned again and looked at his daughter with tenderness and anxiety. She remained in the same position, save that her arms that had fallen were crossed before her, and her downward glance seemed fixed in deep abstraction. Her father approached her unnoticed; he took her hand; she started, and looking round with a cold and distressed expression, said, in a smothered tone, 'I thought you had gone.'

'Not in anger, my sweet child,' and Gerard pressed her to his heart.

'But you go,' murmured Sybil.

'These men await me,' said Gerard. 'Our council is of importance. We must take some immediate steps for the aid of our brethren in distress at Birmingham, and to discountenance similar scenes of outbreak to this affair: but, the moment this is over, I will come back to you; and, for the rest, it shall be as you desire; to-morrow we will return to Mowbray.'

Sybil returned her father's embrace with a warmth which expressed her sense of his kindness and her own soothed feelings, but she said nothing; and, bidding her now to be of good cheer, Gerard quitted the apartment.

CHAPTER 4

THE clock of St. John's church struck three, and the clock of St. John's church struck four; and the fifth hour sounded from St. John's church; and the clock of St. John's was sounding six. And Gerard had not yet returned.

The time for awhile after his departure had been comparatively light-hearted and agreeable. Easier in her mind and for a time busied with the preparations for their journey, Sybil sat by the open window more serene and cheerful than for a long period had been her wont. Sometimes she turned for a moment from her volume and fell into a reverie of the morrow and of Mowbray. Viewed through the magic haze of time and distance, the scene of her youth assumed a character of tenderness and even of peaceful bliss. She sighed for the days of their cottage and their garden, when the discontent of her father was only theoretical, and their political conclaves were limited to a discussion between him and Morley on the rights of the people or the principles of society. The bright waters of the Mowe and its wooded hills; her matin walks to the convent to visit Ursula Trafford, a pilgrimage of piety and charity and love; the faithful Harold, so devoted and so intelligent; even the crowded haunts of labour suffering among which she glided like an angel, blessing and blessed; they rose before her, those touching images of the past, and her eyes were suffused with tears, of tenderness, not of gloom.

And blended with them the thought of one who had been for a season the kind and gentle companion of her girlhood, that Mr. Franklin whom she had never quite forgotten, and who, alas! was not Mr. Franklin after all. Ah! that was a wonderful history; a somewhat thrilling chapter in the memory of one so innocent and so young! His voice even now lingered in her ear. She recalled without an effort those tones of the morning, tones of tenderness, and yet of wisdom and considerate thought, that had sounded only for her welfare. Never had Egremont appeared to her in a light so subduing. He was what man should be to woman ever: gentle, and yet a guide. A thousand images dazzling and wild rose in her mind; a thousand thoughts, beautiful and quivering as the twilight, clustered round her heart; for a moment she indulged in impossible dreams, and seemed to have entered a newly discovered world. The horizon of her experience expanded like the glittering heaven of a fairy tale. Her eye was fixed in lustrous contemplation, the flush on her cheek was a messenger from her heart, the movement of her mouth would have in an instant become a smile, when the clock of St. John's struck four, and Sybil started from her reverie.

The clock of St. John's struck four, and Sybil became anxious; the clock of St. John's struck five, and Sybil became disquieted; restless and perturbed, she was walking up and down the chamber, her long books since thrown aside, when the clock of St. John's struck six.

She clasped her hands and looked up to heaven. There was a knock at the street door; she herself sprang out to open it. It was not Gerard. It was Morley.

'Ah! Stephen,' said Sybil, with a countenance of undisguised disappointment, 'I thought it was my father.'

'I should have been glad to have found him here,' said Morley. 'However, with your permission I will enter.'

'And he will soon arrive,' said Sybil; 'I am sure he will soon arrive. I have been expecting him every minute—'

'For hours,' added Morley, finishing her sentence, as they entered the room. 'The business that he is on,' he continued, throwing himself into a chair with a recklessness very unlike his usual composure and even precision, 'the business that he is on is engrossing.'

'Thank Heaven,' said Sybil, 'we leave this place to-morrow.'

'Hah!' said Morley, starting, 'who told you so?'

'My father has so settled it; has indeed promised me that we shall depart.'

'And you were anxious to do so.'

'Most anxious; my mind is prophetic only of mischief to him if we remain.'

'Mine too. Otherwise I should not have come up to-day.'

'You have seen him, I hope?' said Sybil.

'I have; I have been hours with him.'

'I am glad. At this conference which he talked of?'

'Yes; at this headstrong council; and I have seen him since; alone. Whatever hap to him, my conscience is assoiled.'

'You terrify me, Stephen,' said Sybil, rising from her seat. 'What can happen to him? What would he do, what would you resist? Tell me, tell me, dear friend.'

'Oh! yes,' said Morley, pale, and with a slight bitter smile, 'Oh! yes; dear friend!'

'I said dear friend, for so I deemed you,' said Sybil; 'and so we have ever found you. Why do you stare at me so strangely, Stephen?'

'So you deem me, and so you have ever found me,' said Morley, in a slow and measured tone, repeating her words. 'Well; what more would you have? What more should any of us want?' he asked abruptly.

'I want no more,' said Sybil, innocently.

'I warrant me, you do not. Well, well; nothing matters. And so,' he added in his ordinary tone, 'you are waiting for your father?'

'Whom you have not long since seen,' said Sybil, 'and whom you expected to find here?'

'No!' said Morley, shaking his head with the same bitter smile; 'no, no, I didn't. I came to find you.'

'You have something to tell me,' said Sybil, earnestly. 'Something has happened to my father. Do not break it to me; tell me at once,' and she advanced and laid her hand upon his arm.

Morley trembled; and then in a hurried and agitated voice, said, 'No, no, no! nothing has happened. Much may happen, but nothing has happened. And we may prevent it,'

'Tell me what may happen; tell me what to do.'

'Your father,' said Morley, slowly rising from his seat and pacing the room, and speaking in a low calm voice, 'your father, and my friend, is in this position, Sybil; he is conspiring against the State.'

'Yes, yes,' said Sybil, very pale, speaking almost in a whisper, and with her gaze fixed intently on her companion. 'Tell me all.'

'I will. He is conspiring, I say, against the State. To-night they meet in secret, to give the last finish to their plans; and to-night they will be arrested.'

'O God!' said Sybil, clasping her hands. 'He told me truth.'

'Who told you truth?' said Morley, springing to her side, in a hoarse voice, and with an eye of fire.

'A friend,' said Sybil, dropping her arms and bending her head in woe; 'a kind, good friend. I met him but this morn, and he warned me of all this.'

'Hah, hah!' said Morley, with a sort of stifled laugh; 'Hah, hah! he told you, did he? the kind good friend whom you met this morning? Did I not warn you, Sybil, of the traitor? Did I not tell you to beware of taking this false aristocrat to your hearth; to worm out all the secrets of that home that he once polluted by his espionage and, now would desolate by his treason?'

'Of whom and what do you speak?' said Sybil, throwing herself into a chair.

'I speak of that base spy, Egremont.'

'You slander an honourable man,' said Sybil, with dignity. 'Mr. Egremont has never entered this house since you met him here for the first time; save once.'

'He needed no entrance to this house to worm out its secrets,' said Morley, maliciously. 'That could be more adroitly done by one who had assignations at command with the most charming of its inmates.'

'Unmannerly churl!' exclaimed Sybil, starting in her chair, her eye flashing lightning, her distended nostril quivering with scorn.

'Oh! yes, I am a churl,' said Morley; 'I know I am a churl. Were I a noble, the daughter of the people would perhaps condescend to treat me with less contempt.'

'The daughter of the people loves truth and manly bearing, Stephen Morley; and will treat with contempt all those who slander women, whether they be nobles or serfs.'

'And where is the slanderer?'

'Ask him who told you I held assignations with Mr. Egremont, or with any one.'

'Mine eyes, mine own eyes, were my informant,' said Morley. 'This morn, the very morn I arrived in London, I learnt how your matins were now spent. Yes!' he added, in a tone of mournful anguish, 'I passed the gate of the gardens; I witnessed your adieus.'

'We met by hazard,' said Sybil in a calm tone, and with an expression that denoted she was thinking of other things, 'and in all probability we shall never meet again. Talk not of these trifles, Stephen; my father, how can we save him?'

'Are they trifles?' said Morley, slowly and earnestly, walking to her side, and looking her intently in the face. 'Are they indeed trifles, Sybil? Oh! make me credit that, and then—' he paused.

Sybil returned his gaze: the deep lustre of her dark orb rested on his peering vision; his eye fled from the unequal contest; his heart throbbed, his limbs trembled; he fell upon his knee.

'Pardon me, pardon me,' he said, and he took her hand. 'Pardon the most miserable and the most devoted of men!'

'What need of pardon, dear Stephen?' said Sybil in a soothing tone. 'In the agitated hour wild words escape. If I have used them, I regret; if you, I have forgotten.'

The clock of St. John's told that the sixth hour was more than half-past.

'Ah!' said Sybil, withdrawing her hand, 'you told me how precious was time. What can we do?'

Morley rose from his kneeling position, and again paced the chamber, lost for some moments in deep meditation. Suddenly he seized her arm, and said, 'I can endure no longer the anguish of my life: I love you, and if you will not be mine, I care for no one's fate.'

'I am not born for love,' said Sybil, frightened, yet endeavouring to conceal her alarm.

'We are all born for love,' said Morley. 'It is the principle of existence and its only end. And love of you, Sybil,' he continued, in a tone of impassioned pathos, 'has been to me for years the hoarded treasure of my life. For this I have haunted your hearth and hovered round your home; for this I have served your father like a slave, and embarked in a cause with which I have little sympathy, and which can meet with no success. It is your image that has stimulated my ambition, developed my powers, sustained me in the hour of humiliation, and secured me that material prosperity which I can now command. Oh! deign to share it; share it with the impassioned heart and the devoted life that now bow before you; and do not shrink from them because they are the feelings and the fortunes of the People.'

'You astound, you overwhelm me,' said Sybil, agitated. 'You came for another purpose, we were speaking of other feelings; it is the hour of exigency you choose for these strange, these startling words.'

'I also have my hour of exigency,' said Morley, 'and its minutes are now numbering. Upon it all depends.'

'Another time,' said Sybil, in a low and deprecatory voice; 'speak of these things another time!'

'The caverns of my mind are open,' said Morley, 'and they will not close.'

'Stephen,' said Sybil, 'dear Stephen, I am grateful for your kind feelings; but indeed this is not the time for such passages: cease, my friend!'

'I came to know my fate,' said Morley, doggedly.

'It is a sacrilege of sentiment,' said Sybil, unable any longer to restrain her emotion, 'to obtrude its expression on a daughter at such a moment.'

'You would not deem it so if you loved, or if you could love, me, Sybil,' said Morley, mournfully. 'Why, it is a moment of deep feeling, and suited for the expression of deep feeling. You would not have answered thus, if he who had been kneeling here had been named Egremont.'

'He would not have adopted a course,' said Sybil, unable any longer to restrain her displeasure, 'so selfish, so indecent.'

'Ah! she loves him!' exclaimed Morley, springing on his legs, and with a demoniac laugh.

There was a pause. Under ordinary circumstances Sybil would have left the room and terminated a distressing interview, but in the present instance that was impossible; for on the continuance of that interview any hope of assisting her father depended. Morley had thrown himself into a chair opposite to her, leaning back in silence with his face covered; Sybil was disinclined to revive the conversation about her father, because she had already perceived that Morley was only too much aware of the command which the subject gave him over her feelings and even conduct. Yet time, time now full of terror, time was stealing on. It was evident that Morley would not break the silence. At length, unable any longer to repress her tortured heart, Sybil said, 'Stephen, be generous; speak to me of your friend.'

'I have no friend,' said Morley, without taking his hands from his face.

'The Saints in heaven have mercy on me,' said Sybil, 'for I am very wretched.'

'No, no, no!' said Morley, rising rapidly from his seat, and again kneeling at her side, 'not wretched; not that tone of anguish! What can I do? what say? Sybil, dearest Sybil. I love you so much, so fervently, so devotedly; more can love you as I do; say not you are wretched!'

'Alas! alas!' said Sybil.

'What shall I do? what say?' said Morley.

'You know what I would have you say,' said Sybil. 'Speak of one who is my father, if no longer your friend: you know what I would have you do: save him; save him from death and me from despair.'

'I am ready,' said Morley; 'I came for that. Listen. There is a meeting to-night at half-past eight o'clock; they meet to arrange a general rising in the country: their intention is known to the government; they will be arrested. Now it is in my power, which it was not when I saw your father this morning, to convince him of the truth of this, and were I to see him before eight o'clock, which I could easily do, I could prevent his attendance, certainly prevent his attendance, and he would be saved; for the government depend much upon the papers, some proclamations, and things of that kind, which will be signed this evening, for their proofs. Well, I am ready to save Gerard, my friend, for so I'll call him, as you wish it; one I have served before and long; one whom I came up from Mowbray this day to serve and save; I am ready to do that which you require; you yourself admit it is no light deed; and coming from one you have known so long, and, as you confess, so much regarded, should be doubly cherished; I am ready to do this great service; to save the father from death and the daughter from despair, if she would but only say to me, "I have but one reward, and it is yours." '

'I have read of something of this sort,' said Sybil, speaking in a murmuring tone, and looking round her with a wild expression, 'this bargaining of blood, and shall I call it love? But that was ever between the oppressors and the oppressed. This is the first time that a child of the people has been so assailed by one of her own class, and who exercises his power from the confidence which the sympathy of the sorrows alone caused. It is bitter; bitter for me and mine: but for you, pollution.'

'Am I answered?' said Morley.

'Yes,' said Sybil, 'in the name of the holy Virgin.'

'Good night, then,' said Morley, and he approached the door. His hand was on it. The voice of Sybil made him turn his head.

'Where do they meet to-night?' she enquired in a smothered tone.

'I am bound to secrecy,' said Morley.

'There is no softness in your spirit,' said Sybil.

'I am met with none.'

'We have ever been your friends.'

'A blossom that has brought no fruit.'

'This hour will be remembered at the judgment-seat,' said Sybil.

'The holy Virgin will perhaps interpose for me,' said Morley with a sneer.

'We have merited this,' said Sybil, 'who have taken an infidel to our hearts.'

'If he had been a heretic, like Egremont!' said Morley.

Sybil burst into tears. Morley sprang to her. 'Swear by the holy Virgin, swear by all the saints, swear by your hope of heaven and by your own sweet name; without equivocation, without reserve, with fulness and with truth, that you will never give your heart or hand to Egremont; and I will save your father.'

As in a low voice, but with a terrible earnestness, Morley dictated this oath, Sybil, already pale, became white as the marble saint of some sacred niche. Her large dark eyes seemed fixed; a fleet expression of agony flitted over her beautiful brow like a cloud; and she said, 'I swear that I will never give my hand to ——'

'And your heart, your heart,' said Morley eagerly. 'Omit not that. Swear by the holy oaths again you do not love him. She falters! Ah! she blushes!' For a burning brightness now suffused the cheek of Sybil. 'She loves him,' exclaimed Morley, wildly, and he rushed frantically from the room.

CHAPTER 5

AGITATED and overcome by these unexpected and passionate appeals, and these outrageous ebullitions acting on her at a time when she herself was labouring under no ordinary excitement, and was distracted with disturbing thoughts, the mind of Sybil seemed for a moment to desert her; neither by sound nor gesture did she signify her sense of Morley's last words and departure: and it was not until the loud closing of the street door, echoing through the long passage, recalled her to herself, that she was aware how much was at stake in that incident. She darted out of the room to recall him; to make one more effort for her father; but in vain. By the side of their house was an intricate passage leading into a labyrinth of small streets. Through this Morley had disappeared; and his name, more than once sounded in a voice of anguish in that silent and most obsolete Smith Square, received no echo.

Darkness and terror came over the spirit of Sybil; a sense of confounding and confusing woe, with which it was in vain to cope. The conviction of her helplessness prostrated her. She sat her down upon the steps before the door of that dreary house, within the railings of that gloomy court, and buried her face in her hands; a wild vision of the past and the future, without thought or feeling, coherence or consequence; sunset gleams of vanished bliss, and stormy gusts of impending doom.

The clock of St. John's struck seven.

It was the only thing that spoke in that still and dreary square; it was the only voice that ever seemed to sound there; but it was a voice from heaven, it was the voice of St. John.

Sybil looked up; she looked up at the holy building. Sybil listened; she listened to the holy sounds. St. John told her that the danger of her father was so much more advanced.

Oh! why are these saints in heaven if they cannot aid the saintly! The oath that Morley would have enforced came whispering in the ear of Sybil, 'Swear by the holy Virgin, and by all the saints.'

And shall she not pray to the holy Virgin, and all the saints? Sybil prayed; she prayed to the holy Virgin, and all the saints; and especially to the beloved St. John, most favoured among Hebrew men, who reposed on the breast of the divine Friend.

Brightness and courage returned to the spirit of Sybil; a sense of animating and exalting faith that could move mountains, and combat without fear a thousand perils. The conviction of celestial aid inspired her. She rose from her sad resting-place, and re-entered the house; only, however, to provide herself with her walking attire, and then, alone and without a guide, the shades of evening already descending, this child of innocence and divine thoughts, born in a cottage and bred in a cloister, went forth, on a great enterprise of duty and devotion, into the busiest and the wildest haunts of the greatest of modern cities.

Sybil knew well her way to Palace Yard. This point was soon reached; she desired the cabman to drive her to a street in the Strand, in which was a coffee-house, where during the last weeks of their stay in London, the scanty remnants of the National Convention had held their sittings. It was by a mere accident that Sybil had learnt this circumstance, for, when she had attended the meetings of the Convention in order to hear her father's speeches, it was in the prime of their gathering, and when their numbers were great, and when they met in audacious rivalry opposite to that St. Stephen's which they wished to supersede. This accidental recollection, however, was her only clue in the urgent adventure on which she had embarked.

She cast an anxious glance at the clock of St. Martin's, as she passed that church; the hand was approaching the half hour of seven. She urged on the driver; they were in the Strand: there was an agitating stoppage; she was about to descend when the obstacle was removed; and in a few minutes they turned down the street which she sought.

'What number, Ma'am?' asked the cabman.

' 'Tis a coffee-house; I know not the number, nor the name of him who keeps it. 'Tis a coffee-house. Can you see one? Look, look, I pray you! I am much pressed.'

'Here's a coffee-house, Ma'am,' said the man in a hoarse voice.

'How good you are! Yes; I will get out. You will wait for me, I am sure.'

'All right,' said the cabman, as Sybil entered the illumined door. 'Poor young thing! she's very anxious about summut.'

Sybil at once stepped into a rather capacious room, fitted up in the old-fashioned style of coffee-rooms, with mahogany boxes, in several of which were men drinking coffee, and reading newspapers by a painful glare of gas. There was a waiter in the middle of the room, who was throwing some fresh sand upon the floor, but who stared immensely when, looking up, he beheld Sybil.

'Now, Ma'am, if you please,' said the waiter enquiringly.

'Is Mr. Gerard here?' said Sybil.

'No, Ma'am; Mr. Gerard has not been here to-day, nor yesterday neither;' and he went on throwing the sand.

'I should like to see the master of the house,' said Sybil very humbly.

'Should you, Ma'am?' said the waiter, but he gave no indication of assisting her in the fulfilment of her wish.

Sybil repeated that wish, and this time the waiter said nothing.

This vulgar and insolent neglect, to which she was so little accustomed, depressed her spirit. She could have encountered tyranny and oppression, and she would have tried to struggle with them; but this insolence of the insignificant made her feel her insignificance; and the absorption all this time of the guests in their newspapers, aggravated her nervous sense of her utter helplessness. All her feminine reserve and modesty came over her; alone in this room among men, she felt overpowered, and she was about to make a precipitate retreat when the clock of the coffee-room sounded the half hour. In a paroxysm of nervous excitement, she exclaimed, 'Is there not one among you who will assist me?'

All the newspaper readers put down their journals, and stared.

'Hoity, toity!' said the waiter, and he left off throwing the sand.

'Well, what's the matter now?' said one of the guests.

'I wish to see the master of the house on business of urgency,' said Sybil, 'to himself, and to one of his friends, and his servant here will not even reply to my enquiries.'

'I say, Saul, why don't you answer the young lady?' said another guest.

'So I did,' said Saul. 'Did you call for coffee, Ma'am?'

'Here's Mr. Tanner, if you want him, my dear,' said the first guest, as a lean black-looking individual, with grizzled hair and a red nose, entered the coffee-room from the interior. 'Tanner, here's a lady wants you.'

'And a very pretty girl too,' whispered one to another.

'What's your pleasure?' said Mr. Tanner abruptly.

'I wish to speak to you alone,' said Sybil; and advancing towards him, she said in a low voice, ' 'Tis about Walter Gerard I would speak to you.'

'Well, you can step in here if you like,' said Tanner, discourteously; 'there's only my wife;' and he led the way to the inner room, a small close parlour, adorned with portraits of Tom Paine,* Cobbett,* Thistlewood,* and General Jackson;* with a fire, though it was a hot July, and a very fat woman affording still more heat, and who was drinking shrub* and water, and reading the police reports. She stared rudely at Sybil as she entered, following Tanner, who himself, when the door was closed, said, 'Well, now what have you got to say?'

'I wish to see Walter Gerard.'

'Do you indeed!'

'And,' continued Sybil, notwithstanding his sneering remark, 'I come here that you may tell me where I may find him.'

'I believe he lives somewhere in Westminster,' said Tanner, 'that's all I know about him; and if this be all you had to say, it might have been said in the coffee-room.'

'It is not all that I have to say,' said Sybil; 'and I beseech you, sir, listen to me. I know where Gerard lives; I am his daughter, and the same roof covers our heads. But I wish to know where they meet to-night: you understand me;' and she looked at his wife, who had resumed her police reports; ' 'tis urgent.'

'I don't know nothing about Gerard,' said Tanner, 'except that he comes here and goes away again.'

'The matter on which I would see him,' said Sybil, 'is as urgent as the imagination can conceive, and it concerns you as well as himself; but, if you know not where I can find him,' and she moved, as if about to retire, ' 'tis of no use.'

'Stop,' said Tanner, 'you can tell it to me.'

'Why so? You know not where he is; you cannot tell it to him.'

'I don't know that,' said Tanner. 'Come, let's have it out; and if it will do him any good, I'll see if we can't manage to find him.'

'I can impart my news to him, and no one else,' said Sybil. 'I am solemnly bound.'

'You can't have a better counseller than Tanner,' urged his wife, getting curious; 'you had better tell us.'

'I want no counsel; I want that which you can give me if you choose, information. My father instructed me that if, certain circumstances occurring, it was a matter of the last urgency that I should see him this evening, and, before nine o'clock, I was to call here, and obtain from you the direction where to find him; the direction,' she added in a lowered tone, and looking Tanner full in the face, 'where they hold their secret council to-night.'

'Hem,' said Tanner; 'I see you're on the free-list. And pray how am I to know you *are* Gerard's daughter?'

'You do not doubt I am his daughter!' said Sybil, proudly.

'Hem!' said Tanner; 'I do not know that I do very much,' and he whispered to his wife. Sybil removed from them as far as she was able.

'And this news is very urgent,' resumed Tanner; 'and concerns me, you say?'

'Concerns you all,' said Sybil; 'and every minute is of the last importance.'

'I should like to have gone with you myself, and then there could have been no mistake,' said Tanner; 'but that can't be; we have a meeting here at half-past eight in our great room. I don't much like breaking rules, especially in such a business;

and yet, concerning all of us, as you say, and so very urgent, I don't see how it could do harm; and I might, I wish I was quite sure you were the party.'

'How can I satisfy you?' said Sybil, distressed.

'Perhaps the young person have got her mark on her linen,' suggested the wife. 'Have you got a handkerchief, Ma'am?' and she took Sybil's handkerchief, and looked at it, and examined it at every corner. It had no mark. And this unforeseen circumstance of great suspicion might have destroyed everything, had not the production of the handkerchief by Sybil also brought forth a letter addressed to her from Hatton.

'It seems to be the party,' said the wife.

'Well,' said Tanner, 'you know St. Martin's Lane, I suppose? Well, you go up St. Martin's Lane to a certain point, and then you will get into Seven Dials;* and then you'll go on. However, it is impossible to direct you; you must find your way. Hunt Street, going out of Silver Street, No. 22. 'Tis what you call a blind street, with no thoroughfare, and then you go down an alley. Can you recollect that?'

'Fear not.'

'No. 22, Hunt Street, going out of Silver Street. Remember the alley. It's an ugly neighbourhood; but you go of your own accord.'

'Yes, yes. Good night.'

CHAPTER 6

URGED by Sybil's entreaties the cab-driver hurried on. With all the skilled experience of a thorough cockney charioteer, he tried to conquer time and space by his rare knowledge of short cuts and fine acquaintance with unknown thoroughfares. He seemed to avoid every street which was the customary passage of mankind. The houses, the population, the costume, the manners, the language, through which they whirled their way, were of a different state and nation from those with which the dwellers of the dainty quarters of this city are acquainted. Now dark streets of frippery and old stores, now market-places of entrails and carrion, with gutters running gore, sometimes the way was enveloped in the yeasty fumes of a colossal brewery, and sometimes they plunged into a labyrinth of lanes teeming with life, and where the dog-stealer and the pick-pocket, the burglar and the assassin, found a sympathetic multitude of all ages; comrades for every enterprise, and a market for every booty.

The long summer twilight was just expiring; the pale shadows of the moon were just stealing on; the gas was beginning to glare in shops of tripe and bacon, and the paper lanterns to adorn the stall and the stand. They crossed a broad street which seemed the metropolis of the district; it flamed with gin palaces; a multitude were sauntering in the mild though tainted air; bargaining, blaspheming, drinking, wrangling; and varying their business and their potations, their fierce strife and their impious irreverence, with flashes of rich humour, gleams of native wit, and racy phrases of idiomatic slang.

Absorbed in her great mission, Sybil was almost insensible to the scenes through which she passed, and her innocence was thus spared many a sight and sound that might have startled her vision or alarmed her ear. They could not now be very distant from the spot; they were crossing this broad way, and then were about to enter another series of small obscure dingy streets, when the cabdriver giving a flank to his steed to stimulate it to a last effort, the horse sprang forward, and the wheel of the cab came off.

Sybil extricated herself from the vehicle unhurt; a group immediately formed round the cab, a knot of young thieves, almost young enough for infant schools, a dustman, a woman nearly naked and very drunk, and two unshorn ruffians with brutality stamped on every feature, with pipes in their mouths, and their hands in their pockets.

'I can take you no further,' said the cabman: 'my fare is three shillings.'

'What am I to do?' said Sybil, taking out her purse.

'The best thing the young lady can do,' said the dustman, in a hoarse voice, 'is to stand something to us all.'

'That's your time o'day,' squeaked a young thief.

'I'll drink to your health with very great pleasure, my dear,' hiccupped the woman.

'How much have you got there?' said the young thief making a dash at her purse, but he was not quite tall enough, and failed.

'No wiolence,' said one of the ruffians taking his pipe out of his mouth and sending a volume of smoke into Sybil's face, 'we'll take the young lady to Mother Poppy's, and then we'll make a night of it.'

But at this moment appeared a policeman, one of the permanent garrison of the quarter, who seeing one of her Majesty's carriages in trouble thought he must interfere. 'Hilloa,' he said, 'what's all this?' And the cabman, who was a good fellow though in too much trouble to aid Sybil, explained in the terse and picturesque language of Cockaigne, doing full justice to his late fare, the whole circumstances.

'Oh! that's it,' said the policeman, 'the lady's respectable, is she? Then I'd advise you and Hell Fire Dick to stir your chalks, Splinterlegs. Keep moving's the time of day, Madam; you get on. Come;' and taking the woman by her shoulder he gave her a spin that sent her many a good yard. 'And what do you want?' he asked gruffly of the lads.

'We wants a ticket for the Mendicity Society,'* said the captain of the infant band, putting his thumb to his nose and running away, followed by his troop.

'And so you want to go to Silver Street?' said her official preserver to Sybil, for she had not thought it wise to confess her ultimate purpose, and indicate under the apprehended circumstances the place of rendezvous to a member of the police.

'Well; that's not very difficult now. Go a-head; take the second turning to your right, and the third to your left, and you're landed.'

Aided by these instructions, Sybil hastened on, avoiding notice as much as was in her power, and assisted in some degree by the advancing gloom of night. She reached Silver Street; a long, narrow, hilly street; and now she was at fault. There were not many persons about, and there were few shops here; yet one was at last at hand, and she entered to enquire her way. The person at the counter was engaged, and many customers awaited him: time was very precious: Sybil had made the enquiry and received only a supercilious stare from the shopman, who was weighing with precision some articles that he was serving. A young man, shabby, but of a superior appearance to the people of this quarter, good-looking, though with a dissolute air, and who seemed waiting for a customer in attendance, addressed Sybil. 'I am going to Hunt Street,' he said, 'shall I show you the way?'

She accepted this offer thankfully. 'It is close at hand, I believe?'

'Here it is,' he said; and he turned down a street. 'What is your house?'

'No. 22: a printing-office,' said Sybil; for the street she had entered was so dark she despaired of finding her way, and ventured to trust so far a guide who was not a policeman.

'The very house I am going to,' said the stranger: 'I am a printer.' And they walked on some way, until they at length stopped before a glass illuminated door, covered with a red curtain. Before it was a group of several men and women brawling, but who did not notice Sybil and her companion.

'Here we are,' said the man; and he pushed the door open, inviting Sybil to enter. She hesitated; it did not agree with the description that had been given her by the coffee-house keeper, but she had seen so much since, and felt so much, and gone through so much, that she had not at the moment that clear command of her memory for which she was otherwise remarkable; but while she faltered, an inner door was violently thrown open, and Sybil moving aside, two girls, still beautiful in spite of gin and paint, stepped into the street.

'This cannot be the house,' exclaimed Sybil, starting back, overwhelmed with shame and terror. 'Holy Virgin, aid me!'

'And that's a blessed word to hear in this heathen land,' exclaimed an Irishman, who was one of the group on the outside.

'If you be of our holy church,' said Sybil, appealing to the man who had thus spoken and whom she gently drew aside, 'I beseech you by everything we hold sacred, to aid me.'

'And will I not?' said the man; 'and I should like to see the arm that would hurt you;' and he looked round, but the young man had disappeared. 'You are not a countrywoman, I am thinking,' he added.

'No, but a sister in Christ,' said Sybil; 'listen to me, good

friend. I hasten to my father, he is in great danger, in Hunt
Street; I know not my way, every moment is precious; guide
me, I beseech you, honestly and truly guide me!'

'Will I not? Don't you be afraid, my dear. And her poor
father is ill! I wish I had such a daughter! We have not far to
go. You should have taken the next turning. We must walk up
this again, for 'tis a small street with no thoroughfare. Come
on without fear.'

Nor did Sybil fear; for the description of the street which
the honest man had incidentally given, tallied with her instructions. Encouraging her with many kind words, and full
of rough courtesies, the good Irishman led her to the spot she
had so long sought. There was the court she was told to enter.
It was well lit, and, descending the steps, she stopped at the
first door on her left, and knocked.

CHAPTER 7

ON the same night that Sybil was encountering so many
dangers, the saloons of Deloraine House blazed with a thousand lights to welcome the world of power and fashion to a
festival of almost unprecedented magnificence. Fronting a
royal park, its long lines of illumined windows and the bursts
of gay and fantastic music that floated from its walls attracted
the admiration and curiosity of another party that was assembled in the same fashionable quarter, beneath a canopy not
less bright and reclining on a couch scarcely less luxurious, for
they were lit by the stars and reposed upon the grass.

'I say, Jim,' said a young genius of fourteen, stretching
himself upon the turf, 'I pity them ere jarvies* a sitting on
their boxes all the night and waiting for the nobs what is
dancing. They as no repose.'

'But they as porter,' replied his friend, a sedater spirit, with
the advantage of an additional year or two of experience;
'they takes their pot of half-and-half by turns, and if their
name is called, the link* what they subscribe for to pay,
sings out, "Here;" and that's the way their guvners is done.'

'I think I should like to be a link, Jim,' said the young one.

'I wish you may get it,' was the response: 'it's the next best thing to a crossing; it's what everyone looks to when he enters public life, but he soon finds 'tain't to be done without a deal of interest. They keeps it to themselves, and never lets anyone in unless he makes himself very troublesome and gets up a party agin 'em.'

'I wonder what the nobs has for supper,' said the young one pensively. 'Lots of kidneys, I dare say.'

'Oh! no; sweets is the time of day in these here blowouts; syllabubs like blazes, and snapdragon as makes the flunkies quite pale.'

'I would thank you, sir, not to tread upon this child,' said a widow. She had three others with her slumbering around, and this was the youngest wrapt in her only shawl.

'Madam,' replied the person whom she addressed, in tolerable English, but with a marked accent, 'I have bivouacked in many lands, but never with so young a comrade: I beg you a thousand pardons.'

'Sir, you are very polite. These warm nights are a great blessing, but I am sure I know not what we shall do in the fall of the leaf.'

'Take no thought of the morrow,' said the foreigner, who was a Pole, had served as a boy beneath the suns of the Peninsula under Soult,* and fought against Diebitsch* on the banks of the icy Vistula. 'It brings many changes.' And, arranging the cloak which he had taken that day out of pawn around him, he delivered himself up to sleep with that facility which is not uncommon among soldiers.

Here broke out a brawl; two girls began fighting and blaspheming; a man immediately came up, chastised, and separated them. 'I am the Lord Mayor of the night,' he said, 'and I will have no row here. 'Tis the like of you that makes the beaks threaten to expel us from our lodgings.' His authority seemed generally recognised, the girls were quiet; but they had disturbed a sleeping man, who roused himself, looked around him, and said with a scared look, 'Where am I? What's all this?'

'Oh! it's nothin',' said the elder of the two lads we first

noticed, 'only a couple of unfortinate gals who've prigged* a watch from a cove what was lushy, and fell asleep under the trees, between this and Kinsington.'

'I wish they had not waked me,' said the man, 'I walked as far as from Stokenchurch, and that's a matter of forty mile, this morning, to see if I could get some work, and went to bed here without any supper. I'm blessed if I worn't dreaming of a roast leg of pork.'

'It has not been a lucky day for me,' rejoined the lad; 'I could not find a single gentleman's horse to hold, so help me, except one what was at the House of Commons, and he kept me there two mortal hours, and said, when he came out, that he would remember me next time. I ain't tasted no wittals to-day, except some cat's-meat, and a cold potato, what was given me by a cabman; but I have got a quid* here, and if you are very low, I'll give you half.'

In the meantime Lord Valentine, and the Princess Stephanie of Eurasberg, with some companions worthy of such a pair, were dancing a new Mazurka before the admiring assembly at Deloraine House. The ball was in the statue gallery, illumined on this night in the Russian fashion, which, while it diffused a brilliant light throughout the beautiful chamber, was peculiarly adapted to develop the contour of the marble forms of grace and loveliness that were ranged around.

'Where is Arabella?' inquired Lord Marney of his mother; 'I want to present young Huntingford to her. He can be of great use to me, but he bores me so, I cannot talk to him. I want to present him to Arabella.'

'Arabella is in the blue drawing-room. I saw her just now with Mr. Jermyn and Charles. Count Soudriaffsky is teaching them some Russian tricks.'

'What are Russian tricks to me? she must talk to young Huntingford; everything depends on his working with me against the Cut-and-Come-again branch-line; they have refused me my compensation, and I am not going to have my estate cut up into ribbons without compensation.'

'My dear Lady Deloraine,' said Lady de Mowbray, 'how beautiful your gallery looks to-night! Certainly there is nothing in London that lights up so well.'

'Its greatest ornaments are its guests. I am charmed to see Lady Joan looking so well.'

'You think so?'

'Indeed.'

'I wish—' and here Lady de Mowbray gave a smiling sigh. 'What do you think of Mr. Mountchesney?'

'He is universally admired.'

'So everyone says, and yet—'

'Well, what do you think of the Dashville, Fitz?' said Mr. Berners to Lord Fitzheron, 'I saw you dancing with her.'

'I can't bear her: she sets up to be natural, and is only rude; mistakes insolence for innocence; says everything which comes first to her lips, and thinks she is gay when she is only giddy.'

'"Tis brilliant,' said Lady Joan to Mr. Mountchesney.

'When you are here,' he murmured.

'And yet a ball in a gallery of art is not, in my opinion, in good taste. The associations which are suggested by sculpture are not festive. Repose is the characteristic of sculpture. Do not you think so?'

'Decidedly,' said Mr. Mountchesney. 'We danced in the gallery at Matfield this Christmas, and I thought all the time that a gallery is not the place for a ball; it is too long and too narrow.'

Lady Joan looked at him, and her lip rather curled.

'I wonder if Valentine has sold that bay cob of his,' said Lord Milford to Lord Eugene de Vere.

'I wonder,' said Lord Eugene.

'I wish you would ask him, Eugene,' said Lord Milford; 'you understand, I don't want him to know I want it.'

' 'Tis such a bore to ask questions,' said Lord Eugene.

'Shall we carry Chichester?' asked Lady Firebrace of Lady St. Julians.

'Oh! do not speak to me ever again of the House of Commons,' she replied in a tone of affected despair. 'What use is winning our way by units? It may take years. Lord Protocol says, that "one is enough." That Jamaica affair has really ended by greatly strengthening them.'

'I do not despair,' said Lady Firebrace. 'The unequivocal

adhesion of the Duke of Fitz-Aquitane is a great thing. It gives us the northern division at a dissolution.'

'That is to say in five years, my dear Lady Firebrace. The country will be ruined before that.'

'We shall see. Is it a settled thing between Lady Joan and Mr. Mountchesney?'

'Not the slightest foundation. Lady Joan is a most sensible girl, as well as a most charming person, and my dear friend. She is not in a hurry to marry, and quite right. If indeed Frederick were a little more steady; but nothing shall ever induce me to consent to his marrying her, unless I thought he was worthy of her.'

'You are such a good mother,' exclaimed Lady Firebrace, 'and such a good friend! I am glad to hear it is not true about Mr. Mountchesney.'

'If you could only help me, my dear Lady Firebrace, to put an end to that affair between Frederick and Lady Wallington. It is so silly, and getting talked about; and in his heart too he really loves Lady Joan; only he is scarcely aware of it himself.'

'We must manage it,' said Lady Firebrace, with a look of encouraging mystery.

'Do, my dear creature; speak to him; he is very much guided by your opinion. Tell him everybody is laughing at him, and any other little thing that occurs to you.'

'I will come directly,' said Lady Marney to her husband, 'only let me see this.'

'Well, I will bring Huntingford here. Mind you speak to him a great deal; take his arm, and go down to supper with him, if you can. He is a very nice sensible young fellow, and you will like him very much, I am sure; a little shy at first, but he only wants bringing out.'

A dexterous description of one of the most unlicked and unlickable cubs that ever entered society with forty thousand a year; courted by all, and with just that degree of cunning that made him suspicious of every attention.

'This dreadful Lord Huntingford!' said Lady Marney.

'Jermyn and I will interfere,' said Egremont, 'and help you.'

'No, no,' said Lady Marney, shaking her head, 'I must do it.'

At this moment, a groom of the chambers advanced, and drew Egremont aside, saying in a low tone, 'Your servant, Mr. Egremont, is here, and wishes to see you instantly.'

'My servant! Instantly! What the deuce can be the matter? I hope the Albany is not on fire,' and he quitted the room.

In the outer hall, amid a crowd of footmen, Egremont recognised his valet, who immediately came forward.

'A porter has brought this letter, sir, and I thought it best to come on with it at once.'

The letter directed to Egremont, bore also on its super-scription these words: 'This letter must be instantly carried by the bearer to Mr. Egremont, wherever he may be.'

Egremont, with some change of countenance, drew aside, and opening the letter, read it by a lamp at hand. It must have been very brief; but the face of him to whom it was addressed, became, as he perused its lines, greatly agitated. When he had finished reading it, he seemed for a moment lost in profound thought; then looking up, he dismissed his servant without instructions, and hastening back to the assembly, he enquired of the groom of the chambers whether Lord John Russell, whom he had observed in the course of the evening, was still present; and he was answered in the affirmative.

About a quarter of an hour after this incident, Lady Firebrace said to Lady St. Julians in a tone of mysterious alarm, 'Do you see that?'

'No! what?'

'Do not look as if you observed them: Lord John and Mr. Egremont, in the furthest window; they have been there these ten minutes, in the most earnest conversation. I am afraid we have lost him.'

'I have always been expecting it,' said Lady St. Julians. 'He breakfasts with that Mr. Trenchard, and does all those sort of things. Men who breakfast out are generally liberals. Have not you observed that? I wonder why?'

'It shows a restless revolutionary mind,' said Lady Fire-brace, 'that can settle to nothing; but must be running after gossip the moment they are awake.'

'Yes,' said Lady St. Julians. 'I think those men who break-fast out, or who give breakfasts, are generally dangerous characters; at least, I would not trust them. The Whigs are very fond of that sort of thing. If Mr. Egremont joins them, I really do not see what shadow of a claim Lady Deloraine can urge to have anything.'

'She only wants one thing,' said Lady Firebrace, 'and we know she cannot have that.'

'Why?'

'Because Lady St. Julians will have it.'

'You are too kind,' with many smiles.

'No, I assure you Lord Masque told me that her Majesty—' and here Lady Firebrace whispered.

'Well,' said Lady St. Julians, evidently much gratified, 'I do not think I am one who am likely to forget my friends.'

'That I am sure you are not!' said Lady Firebrace.

CHAPTER 8

BEHIND the printing-office in the alley at the door of which we left Sybil, was a yard that led to some premises that had once been used as a workshop, but were now generally unoccupied. In a rather spacious chamber, over which was a loft, five men, one of whom was Gerard, were busily engaged. There was no furniture in the room except a few chairs and a deal table, on which were a solitary light and a variety of papers.

'Depend upon it,' said Gerard, 'we must stick to the National Holiday:* we can do nothing effectively, unless the movement is simultaneous. They have not troops to cope with a simultaneous movement, and the Holiday is the only machinery to secure unity of action. No work for six weeks, and the rights of Labour will be acknowledged!'

'We shall never be able to make the people unanimous in a cessation of labour,' said a pale young man, very thin, but with a countenance of remarkable energy. 'The selfish instincts will come into play and will balk our political object, while a great increase of physical suffering must be inevitable.'

'It might be done,' said a middle-aged thickset man, in a thoughtful tone. 'If the Unions were really to put their shoulder to the wheel, it might be done.'

'And if it is not done,' said Gerard, 'what do you propose? The people ask you to guide them. Shrink at such a conjuncture, and our influence over them is forfeited, and justly forfeited.'

'I am for partial but extensive insurrections,' said the young man. 'Sufficient in extent and number to demand all the troops and yet to distract the military movements. We can count on Birmingham again, if we act at once before their new Police Act is in force;* Manchester is ripe, and several of the cotton towns; but above all I have letters that assure me that at this moment we can do anything in Wales.'

'Glamorganshire is right to a man,' said Wilkins, a Baptist teacher. 'And trade is so bad that the Holiday at all events must take place there, for the masters themselves are extinguishing their furnaces.'

'All the north is seething,' said Gerard.

'We must contrive to agitate the metropolis,' said Maclast, a shrewd carroty-haired paper-stainer. 'We must have weekly meetings at Kennington and demonstrations at White Conduit House:* we cannot do more here, I fear, than talk, but a few thousand men on Kennington Common* every Saturday and some spicy resolutions will keep the Guards in London.'

'Aye, ay,' said Gerard; 'I wish the woollen and cotton trades were as bad to do as the iron, and we should need no holiday as you say, Wilkins. However it will come. In the mean time the Poor-law pinches and terrifies, and will make even the most spiritless turn.'

'The accounts to-day from the north are very encouraging though,' said the young man. 'Stevens is producing a great effect, and this plan of our people going in procession and taking possession of the churches very much affects the imagination of the multitude.'

'Ah!' said Gerard, 'if we could only have the Church on our side, as in the good old days, we would soon put an end to the demon tyranny of Capital.'

'And now,' said the pale young man, taking up a manuscript paper, 'to our immediate business. Here is the draft of the projected proclamation of the Convention on the Birmingham outbreak. It enjoins peace and order, and counsels the people to arm themselves in order to secure both. You understand: that they may resist if the troops and the police endeavour to produce disturbance.'

'Ay, ay,' said Gerard. 'Let it be stout. We will settle this at once, and so get it out to-morrow. Then for action.'

'But we must circulate this pamphlet of the Polish Count on the manner of encountering cavalry with pikes,' said Maclast.

' 'Tis printed,' said the stout thickset man; 'we have set it up on a broadside.* We have sent ten thousand to the north and five thousand to John Frost.* We shall have another delivery to-morrow. It takes very generally.'

The pale young man then read the draft of the proclamation; it was canvassed and criticised, sentence by sentence; altered, approved; finally put to the vote, and unanimously carried. On the morrow it was to be posted in every thoroughfare of the metropolis, and circulated in every great city of the provinces and every populous district of labour.

'And now,' said Gerard, 'I shall to-morrow to the north, where I am wanted. But before I go, I propose, as suggested yesterday, that we five, together with Langley, whom I counted on seeing here to-night, now form ourselves into a committee for arming the people. Three of us are permanent in London; Wilkins and myself will aid you in the provinces. Nothing can be decided on this head till we see Langley, who will make a communication from Birmingham that cannot be trusted to writing. The seven o'clock train must have long since arrived. He is now a good hour behind his time.'

'I hear footsteps,' said Maclast.

'He comes,' said Gerard.

The door of the chamber opened and a woman entered. Pale, agitated, exhausted, she advanced to them in the glimmering light.

'What is this?' said several of the council.

'Sybil!' exclaimed the astonished Gerard, and he rose from his seat.

She caught the arm of her father, and leant on him for a moment in silence. Then looking up, with an expression which seemed to indicate that she was rallying her last energies, she said, in a voice low, yet so distinct that it reached the ear of all present, 'There is not an instant to lose; fly!'

The men rose hastily from their seats; they approached the

messenger of danger; Gerard waved them off, for he perceived his daughter was sinking. Gently he placed her in his chair; she was sensible, for she grasped his arm, and she murmured, still she murmured, 'fly!'

' 'Tis very strange,' said Maclast.

'I feel queer,' said the thickset man.

'Methinks she looks like a heavenly messenger,' said Wilkins.

'I had no idea that earth had anything so fair,' said the youthful scribe of proclamations.

'Hush, friends,' said Gerard; and then he bent over Sybil, and said in a low soothing voice, 'Tell me, my child, what is it?'

She looked up to her father, a glance as it were of devotion and despair; her lips moved, but they refused their office, and expressed no words. There was a deep silence in the room.

'She is gone,' said her father.

'Water,' said the young man, and he hurried away to obtain some.

'I feel queer,' said his thickset colleague to Maclast.

'I will answer for Langley as for myself,' said Maclast; 'and there is not another human being aware of our purpose.'

'Except Morley.'

'Yes; except Morley. But I should as soon doubt Gerard as Stephen Morley.'

'Certainly.'

'I cannot conceive how she traced me,' said Gerard. 'I have never even breathed to her of our meeting. Would we had some water! Ah! here it comes.'

'I arrest you in the Queen's name,' said a serjeant of police. 'Resistance is vain.' Maclast blew out the light, and then ran up into the loft, followed by the thickset man, who fell down the stairs. Wilkins got up the chimney. The serjeant took a lantern from his pocket, and threw a powerful light on the chamber, while his followers entered, seized and secured all the papers, and commenced their search.

The light fell upon a group that did not move; the father holding the hand of his insensible child, while he extended his other arm as if to preserve her from the profanation of the touch of the invaders.

'You are Walter Gerard, I presume?' said the serjeant; six foot two, without shoes.

'Whoever I may be,' he replied, 'I presume you will produce your warrant, friend, before you touch me.'

' 'Tis here. We want five of you, named herein, and all others that may happen to be found in your company.'

'I shall obey the warrant,' said Gerard, after he had examined it; 'but this maiden, my daughter, knows nothing of this meeting or its purpose. She has but just arrived, and how she traced me I know not. You will let me recover her, and then permit her to depart.'

'Can't let no one out of my sight found in this room.'

'But she is innocent, even if we were guilty; she could be nothing else but innocent, for she knows nothing of this meeting and its business, both of which I am prepared at the right time and place to vindicate. She entered this room a moment only before yourself, entered and swooned.'

'Can't help that; must take her; she can tell the magistrate anything she likes, and he must decide.'

'Why, you are not afraid of a young girl?'

'I am afraid of nothing, but I must do my duty. Come, we have no time for talk. I must take you both.'

'By G—d, you shall not take her;' and letting go her hand, Gerard advanced before her and assumed a position of defence. 'You know, I find, my height; my strength does not shame my stature! Look to yourself. Advance and touch this maiden, and I will fell you and your minions like oxen at their pasture.'

The inspector took a pistol from his pocket, and pointed it at Gerard. 'You see,' he said, 'resistance is quite vain.'

'For slaves and cravens, but not for us. I say, you shall not touch her till I am dead at her feet. Now, do your worst.'

At this moment, two policemen who had been searching the loft, descended with Maclast, who had vainly attempted to effect his escape over a neighbouring roof; the thickset man was already secured; and Wilkins had been pulled down the chimney, and made his appearance in as grimy a state as such a shelter would naturally have occasioned. The young man too, their first prisoner, who had been captured before they had entered the room, was also brought in; there was now abundance of light; the four prisoners were ranged and well guarded at the end of the apartment; Gerard standing before Sybil still maintained his position of defence, and the serjeant was, a few yards away, in his front with his pistol in his hand.

'Well, you are a queer chap,' said the serjeant; 'but I must do my duty. I shall give orders to my men to seize you, and if you resist them, I shall shoot you through the head.'

'Stop!' called out one of the prisoners, the young man who drew proclamations, 'she moves. Do with us as you think fit, but you cannot be so harsh as to seize one that is senseless, and a woman!'

'I must do my duty,' said the serjeant, rather perplexed at the situation. 'Well, if you like, take steps to restore her, and when she has come to herself, she shall be moved in a hackney coach alone with her father.'

The means at hand to recover Sybil were rude, but they assisted a reviving nature. She breathed, she sighed, slowly opened her beautiful dark eyes, and looked around. Her father held her death-cold hand; she returned his pressure; her lips moved, and still she murmured 'fly!'

Gerard looked at the serjeant. 'I am ready,' he said, 'and I will carry her.' The officer nodded assent. Guarded by two policemen, the tall delegate of Mowbray bore his precious burthen out of the chamber through the yard, the printing-offices, up the alley, till a hackney-coach received them in Hunt Street, round which a mob had already collected, though kept at a discreet distance by the police. One officer entered the coach with them; another mounted the box. Two other coaches carried the rest of the prisoners and their guards, and within half an hour from the arrival of Sybil at the scene of the secret meeting, she was on her way to Bow Street to be examined as a prisoner of state.

Sybil rallied quickly during their progress to the police-office. Satisfied to find herself with her father, she would have enquired as to all that had happened, but Gerard at first discouraged her; at length he thought it wisest gradually to convey to her that they were prisoners, but he treated the matter lightly, did not doubt that she would immediately be discharged, and added that though he might be detained for a day or so, his offence was at all events bailable, and he had friends on whom he could rely. When Sybil clearly compre-

hended that she was a prisoner, and that her public examination was impending, she became silent, and, leaning back in
the coach, covered her face with her hands.

The prisoners arrived at Bow Street; they were hurried into
a back office, where they remained some time unnoticed,
several policemen remaining in the room. At length, about
twenty minutes having elapsed, a man dressed in black and of
a severe aspect, entered the room, accompanied by an inspector of police. He first inquired whether these were the
prisoners, what were their names and descriptions, which each
had to give and which were written down, where they were
arrested, why they were arrested; then scrutinising them
sharply, he said the magistrate was at the Home Office, and he
doubted whether they could be examined until the morrow.
Upon this Gerard commenced stating the circumstances under
which Sybil had unfortunately been arrested, but the gentleman in black, with a severe aspect, immediately told him to
hold his tongue, and, when Gerard persisted, declared that, if
he did not immediately cease, he should be separated from the
other prisoners, and be ordered into solitary confinement.

Another half-hour of painful suspense. The prisoners were
not permitted to hold any conversation. Sybil sat half reclining on a form with her back against the wall, and her face
covered, silent and motionless. At the end of half an hour, the
inspector of police, who had visited them with the gentleman
in black entered, and announced that the prisoners could not
be brought up for examination that evening, and they must
make themselves as comfortable as they could for the night.
Gerard made a last appeal to the inspector that Sybil might be
allowed a separate chamber, and in this he was unexpectedly
successful.

The inspector was a kind-hearted man: he lived at the office
and his wife was the housekeeper. He had already given her an
account, an interesting account, of his female prisoner. The
good woman's imagination was touched as well as her heart;
she had herself suggested that they ought to soften the rigour
of the fair prisoner's lot; and her husband therefore almost
anticipated the request of Gerard. He begged Sybil to accompany him to his better half, and at once promised all the
comforts and convenience which they could command. As,

attended by him, she took her way to the apartments of his family, they passed through a room in which there were writing materials; and Sybil, speaking for the first time, and in a faint voice, enquired of the inspector whether it were permitted to apprise a friend of her situation. She was answered in the affirmative, on condition that the note was previously perused by him.

'I will write it at once,' she said, and taking up a pen inscribed these words: –

'I followed your counsel; I entreated him to quit London this night. He pledged himself to do so on the morrow.

'I learnt he was attending a secret meeting; that there was urgent peril. I tracked him through scenes of terror. Alas! I arrived only in time to be myself seized as a conspirator, and I have been arrested and carried a prisoner to Bow Street, where I write this.

'I ask you not to interfere for him; that would be vain; but if I were free, I might at least secure him justice. But I am not free; I am to be brought up for public examination tomorrow, if I survive this night.

'You are powerful; you know all; you know what I say is truth. None else will credit it. Save me!'

'And now,' said Sybil to the inspector in a tone of mournful desolation and of mild sweetness, 'all depends on your faith to me,' and she extended him the letter, which he read.

'Whoever he may be, and wherever he may be,' said the man with emotion, for the spirit of Sybil had already controlled his nature, 'provided the person to whom this letter is addressed is within possible distance, fear not it shall reach him.'

'I will seal and address it then,' said Sybil, and she addressed the letter to

'THE HON. CHARLES EGREMONT, M.P.,

adding that superscription the sight of which had so agitated Egremont at Deloraine House.

CHAPTER 9

NIGHT waned: and Sybil was at length slumbering. The cold
that precedes the dawn had stolen over her senses, and calmed
the excitement of her nerves. She was lying on the ground,
covered with a cloak of which her kind hostess had prevailed
on her to avail herself, and was partly resting on a chair, at
which she had been praying when exhausted nature gave way
and she slept. Her bonnet had fallen off, and her rich hair,
which had broken loose, covered her shoulder like a mantle.
Her slumber was brief and disturbed, but it had in a great
degree soothed the irritated brain. She woke, however, in
terror from a dream in which she had been dragged through a
mob, and carried before a tribunal. The coarse jeers, the
brutal threats, still echoed in her ear; and when she looked
around, she could not for some moments recall or recognise
the scene. In one corner of the room, which was sufficiently
spacious, was a bed occupied by the still sleeping wife of the
inspector; there was a great deal of heavy furniture of dark
mahogany; a bureau, several chests of drawers; over the
mantel was a piece of faded embroidery framed, that had been
executed by the wife of the inspector, when she was at school,
and opposite to it, on the other side, were portraits of Dick
Curtis and Dutch Sam,* who had been the tutors of her husband, and now lived as heroes in his memory.

Slowly came over Sybil the consciousness of the dreadful
eve that was past. She remained for some time on her knees in
silent prayer: then, stepping lightly, she approached the
window. It was barred. The room which she inhabited was a
high storey of the house; it looked down upon one of those
half-tawdry, half-squalid streets that one finds in the vicinity of
our theatres; some wretched courts, haunts of misery and
crime, blended with gin palaces and slang taverns,* burnished
and brazen; not a being was stirring. It was just that single
hour of the twenty-four when crime ceases, debauchery is
exhausted, and even desolation finds a shelter.

It was dawn, but still grey. For the first time since she had
been a prisoner, Sybil was alone. A prisoner, and in a few
hours to be examined before a public tribunal! Her heart sank.

How far her father had committed himself was entirely a mystery to her; but the language of Morley, and all that she had witnessed, impressed her with the conviction that he was deeply implicated. He had indeed spoken in their progress to the police-office with confidence as to the future, but then he had every motive to encourage her in her despair, and to support her under the overwhelming circumstances in which she was so suddenly involved. What a catastrophe to all his high aspirations! It tore her heart to think of him! As for herself, she would still hope that ultimately she might obtain justice, but she could scarcely flatter herself that at the first any distinction would be made between her case and that of the other prisoners. She would probably be committed for trial; and though her innocence on that occasion might be proved, she would have been a prisoner in the interval, instead of devoting all her energies in freedom to the support and assistance of her father. She shrank, too, with all the delicacy of a woman, from the impending examination in open court before the magistrate. Supported by her convictions, vindicating a sacred principle, there was no trial, perhaps, to which Sybil could not have been superior, and no test of her energy and faith which she would not have triumphantly encountered; but to be hurried like a criminal to the bar of a police-office, suspected of the lowest arts of sedition, ignorant even of what she was accused, without a conviction to support her, or the ennobling consciousness of having failed at least in a great cause: all these were circumstances which infinitely disheartened and depressed her. She felt sometimes that she should be unable to meet the occasion; had it not been for Gerard, she could almost have wished that death might release her from its base perplexities.

Was there any hope? In the agony of her soul she had confided last night in one; with scarcely a bewildering hope that he could save her. He might not have the power, the opportunity, the wish. He might shrink from mixing himself up with such characters and such transactions; he might not have received her hurried appeal in time to act upon it, even if the desire of her soul were practicable. A thousand difficulties, a thousand obstacles now occurred to her; and she felt her hopelessness.

Yet, notwithstanding her extreme anxiety, and the absence
of all surrounding objects to soothe and to console her, the
expanding dawn revived and even encouraged Sybil. In spite
of the confined situation, she could still partially behold a sky
dappled with rosy hues; a sense of freshness touched her; she
could not resist endeavouring to open the window and feel the
air, notwithstanding all the bars. The wife of the inspector
stirred, and half slumbering, murmured, 'Are you up? It
cannot be more than five o'clock. If you open the window we
shall catch cold; but I will rise and help you to dress.'

This woman, like her husband, was naturally kind, and at
once influenced by Sybil. They both treated her as a superior
being; and if, instead of the daughter of a lowly prisoner and
herself a prisoner, she had been the noble child of a captive
minister of state, they could not have extended to her a more
humble and even delicate solicitude.

It had not yet struck seven, and the wife of the inspector
suddenly stopping and listening, said, 'They are stirring early:'
and then, after a moment's pause, she opened the door, at
which she stood for some time, endeavouring to catch the
meaning of the mysterious sounds. She looked back at Sybil,
and saying, 'Hush, I shall be back directly,' she withdrew,
shutting the door.

In little more than two hours, as Sybil had been informed,
she would be summoned to her examination. It was a
sickening thought. Hope vanished as the catastrophe advanced.
She almost accused herself for having without authority
sought out her father; it had been, as regarded him, a fruitless
mission, and, by its results on her, had aggravated his present
sorrows and perplexities. Her mind again recurred to him
whose counsel had indirectly prompted her rash step, and to
whose aid in her infinite hopelessness she had appealed. The
woman who had all this time been only standing on the
landing-place without the door, now re-entered with a puzzled and curious air, saying, 'I cannot make it out; some one
has arrived.'

'Some one has arrived.' Simple yet agitating words. 'Is it
unusual,' enquired Sybil in a trembling tone, 'for persons to
arrive at this hour?'

'Yes,' said the wife of the inspector. 'They never bring

them from the stations until the office opens. I cannot make it out. Hush!' and at this moment some one tapped at the door.

The woman returned to the door and reopened it, and some words were spoken which did not reach Sybil, whose heart beat violently as a wild thought rushed over her mind. The suspense was so intolerable, her agitation so great, that she was on the point of advancing and asking if – when the door was shut and she was again left alone. She threw herself on the bed. It seemed to her that she had lost all control over her intelligence. All thought and feeling merged in that deep suspense, when the order of our being seems to stop and quiver as it were upon its axis.

The woman returned; her countenance was glad. Perceiving the agitation of Sybil, she said, 'You may dry your eyes, my dear. There is nothing like a friend at court; there's a warrant from the Secretary of State for your release.'

'No, no,' said Sybil springing from her chair. 'Is he here?'

'What, the Secretary of State!' said the woman.

'No, no; I mean is anyone here?'

'There is a coach waiting for you at the door with the messenger from the office, and you are to depart forthwith. My husband is here; it was he who knocked at the door. The warrant came before the office was opened.'

'My father! I must see him.'

The inspector at this moment tapped again at the door and then entered. He caught the last request of Sybil, and replied to it in the negative. 'You must not stay,' he said; 'you must be off immediately. I will tell all to your father. And take a hint; this affair may be bailable or it may not be. I can't give an opinion, but it depends on the evidence. If you have any good man you know, I mean a householder long established and well to do in the world, I advise you to lose no time in looking him up. That will do your father much more good than saying good bye and all that sort of thing.'

Bidding farewell to his kind wife, and leaving many weeping messages for her father, Sybil descended the stairs with the inspector. The office was not opened; a couple of policemen only were in the passage, and, as she appeared, one of them went forth to clear the way for Sybil to the coach that was waiting for her. A milkwoman or two, a stray chimney-sweep, a pieman with his smoking apparatus, and several of those nameless nothings that always congregate and make the nucleus of a mob, probably our young friends who had been passing the night in Hyde Park, had already gathered round the office door. They were dispersed and returned again and took up their position at a more respectful distance, abusing with many racy execrations that ancient body which from a traditionary habit they still called the New Police.*

A man in a loose white great coat, his countenance concealed by a shawl which was wound round his neck and by his slouched hat, assisted Sybil into the coach, and pressed her hand at the same time with great tenderness. Then he mounted the box by the driver, and ordered him to make the best of his way to Smith Square.

With a beating heart, Sybil leant back in the coach and clasped her hands. Her brain was too wild to think; the incidents of her life during the last four-and-twenty hours had been so strange and rapid that she seemed almost to resign any quality of intelligent control over her fortunes, and to deliver herself up to the shifting visions of the startling dream. His voice had sounded in her ear as his hand had touched hers. And on those tones her memory lingered, and that pressure had reached her heart. What tender devotion! What earnest fidelity! What brave and romantic faith! Had she breathed on some talisman, and called up some obedient genie to her aid, the spirit could not have been more loyal, nor the completion of her behest more ample and precise.

She passed the towers of the church of St. John; of the saint who had seemed to guard over her in the exigency of her existence. She was approaching her threshold; the blood left her cheek, her heart palpitated. The coach stopped. Trembling and timid, she leant upon his arm and yet dared not look upon his face. They entered the house; they were in the room where two months before he had knelt to her in vain, which yesterday had been the scene of so many heart-rending passions.

As in some delicious dream, when the enchanted fancy has traced for a time with coherent bliss the stream of bright adventures and sweet and touching phrase, there comes at last some wild gap in the flow of fascination, and by means which we cannot trace, and by an agency which we cannot pursue, we find ourselves in some enrapturing situation that is, as it were, the ecstasy of our life; so it happened now, that, while in clear and precise order there seemed to flit over the soul of Sybil all that had passed, all that he had done, all that she felt, by some mystical process which memory could not recall, Sybil found herself pressed to the throbbing heart of Egremont, nor shrinking from the embrace, which expressed the tenderness of his devoted love!

CHAPTER 10

MOWBRAY was in a state of great excitement. It was Saturday evening; the mills were closed; the news had arrived of the arrest of the Delegate.

'Here's a go!' said Dandy Mick to Devilsdust. 'What do you think of this?'

'It's the beginning of the end,' said Devilsdust.

'The deuce!' said the Dandy, who did not clearly comprehend the bent of the observation of his much pondering and philosophic friend, but was touched by its oracular terseness.

'We must see Warner,' said Devilsdust, 'and call a meeting of the people on the Moor for to-morrow evening. I will draw up some resolutions. We must speak out; we must terrify the Capitalists.'

'I am all for a strike,' said Mick.

' 'Tisn't ripe,' said Devilsdust.

'But that's what you always say, Dusty,' said Mick.

'I watch events,' said Devilsdust. 'If you want to be a leader of the people you must learn to watch events.'

'But what do you mean by watching events?'

'Do you see Mother Carey's stall?' said Dusty, pointing in the direction of the counter of the good-natured widow.

'I should think I did; and what's more, Julia owes her a tick for herrings.'*

'Right,' said Devilsdust, 'and nothing but herrings are to be seen on her board. Two years ago it was meat.'

'I twig,' said Mick.

'Wait till it's wegetables; when the people can't buy even

fish. Then we will talk about strikes. That's what I call watching events.'

Julia, Caroline, and Harriet came up to them.

'Mick,' said Julia, 'we want to go to the Temple.'

'I wish you may get it,' said Mick shaking his head. 'When you have learnt to watch events, Julia, you will understand that under present circumstances the Temple is no go.'

'And why so, Dandy?' said Julia.

'Do you see Mother Carey's stall?' said Mick, pointing in that direction. 'When there's a tick at Madam Carey's there is no tin for Chaffing Jack. That's what I call watching events.'

'Oh! as for the tin,' said Caroline, 'in these half-time days that's quite out of fashion. But they do say it's the last night at the Temple, for Chaffing Jack means to shut up, it does not pay any longer; and we want a lark. I'll stand treat; I'll put my ear-rings up the spout; they must go at last, and I would sooner at any time go to my uncle's* for frolic than woe.'

'I am sure I should like very much to go to the Temple if anyone would pay for me,' said Harriet, 'but I won't pawn nothing.'

'If we only pay and hear them sing,' said Julia in a coaxing tone.

'Very like,' said Mick; 'there's nothing that makes one so thirsty as listening to a song, particularly if it touches the feelings. Don't you remember, Dusty, when we used to encore that German fellow in "Scots wha ha"? We always had it five times. Hang me if I wasn't blind drunk at the end of it.'

'I tell you what, young ladies,' said Devilsdust, looking very solemn, 'you're dancing on a volcano.'

'Oh! my,' said Caroline, 'I am sure I wish we were; though what you mean exactly I don't quite know.'

'I mean that we shall all soon be slaves,' said Devilsdust.

'Not if we get the Ten-Hour Bill,' said Harriet.

'And no cleaning of machinery in meal time,' said Julia; 'that is a shame.'

'You don't know what you are talking about,' said Devilsdust. 'I tell you, if the Capitalists put down Gerard we're done for another ten years, and by that time we shall be all used up.'

'Lor! Dusty, you quite terrify one,' said Caroline.

'It's a true bill though. Instead of going to the Temple we must meet on the Moor, and in as great numbers as possible. Go you and get all your sweethearts. I must see your father, Harriet; he must preside. We will have the hymn of Labour sung by a hundred thousand voices in chorus. It will strike terror into the hearts of the Capitalists. This is what we must all be thinking of, if we wish Labour to have a chance, not of going to Chaffing Jack's, and listening to silly songs. D'ye understand?'

'Don't we!' said Caroline; 'and for my part, for a summer eve, I prefer Mowbray Moor to all the Temples in the world, particularly if it's a sociable party, and we have some good singing.'

This evening it was settled among the principal champions of the cause of Labour, among whom Devilsdust was now included, that on the morrow there should be a monster meeting on the Moor, to take into consideration the arrest of the delegate of Mowbray. Such was the complete organisation of this district, that by communicating with the various lodges of the Trades Unions, fifty thousand persons, or even double that number, could within four-and-twenty hours, on a great occasion and on a favourable day, be brought into the field. The morrow being a day of rest, was favourable and the seizure of their cherished delegate was a stimulating cause. The excitement was great, the enthusiasm earnest and deep. There was enough distress to make people discontented, without depressing them. And Devilsdust, after attending a council of the Union, retired to rest, and dreamed of strong speeches and spicy resolutions, bands and banners, the cheers of assembled thousands, and the eventual triumph of the sacred rights.

The post of the next morning brought great and stirring news to Mowbray. Gerard had undergone his examination at Bow Street. It was a long and laborious one; he was committed for trial, for a seditious conspiracy, but he was held to bail. The bail demanded was heavy; but it was prepared, and instantly proffered. His sureties were Morley and a Mr. Hatton. By this post Morley wrote to his friends, apprising them that both Gerard and himself intended to leave London instantly, and that they might be expected to arrive at Mowbray by the evening train.

The monster meeting of the Moor, it was instantly resolved, should be converted into a triumphant procession, or rather be preceded by one. Messengers on horseback were sent to all the neighbouring towns to announce the great event. Every artisan felt as a Moslem summoned by the sacred standard. All went forth with their wives and their children to hail the return of the patriot and the martyr. The Trades of Mowbray mustered early in the morning, and in various processions took possession of all the churches. Their great pride was entirely to fill the church of Mr. St. Lys, who, not daunted by their demonstration, and seizing the offered opportunity, suppressed the sermon with which he had supplied himself, and preached to them an extemporary discourse on 'Fear God and honour the King.' In the dissenting chapels, thanksgivings were publicly offered that bail had been accepted for Walter Gerard. After the evening service, which the Unions again attended, they formed in the High Street, and lined it with their ranks and banners. Every half-hour a procession arrived from some neighbouring town, with its music and streaming flags. Each was received by Warner, or some other member of the managing committee, who assigned to them their appointed position, which they took up without confusion, nor was the general order for a moment disturbed. Sometimes a large party arrived without music or banners, but singing psalms, and headed by their minister; sometimes the children walked together, the women following, then the men, each with a ribbon of the same colour in his hat; all hurried, yet spontaneous and certain, indications how mankind, under the influence of high and earnest feelings, recur instantly to ceremony and form; how, when the imagination is excited, it appeals to the imagination, and requires for its expression something beyond the routine of daily life.

It was arranged that, the moment the train arrived and the presence of Gerard was ascertained, the Trade in position nearest to the station should commence the hymn of Labour, which was instantly to be taken up by its neighbour, and so on in succession, so that by an almost electrical agency the whole population should almost simultaneously be assured of his arrival.

At half-past six o'clock the bell announced that the train

was in sight; a few minutes afterwards Dandy Mick hurried up to the leader of the nearest Trade, spoke a few words, and instantly the signal was given and the hymn commenced. It was taken up as the steeples of a great city in the silence of the night take up the new hour that has just arrived; one by one, the mighty voices rose till they all blended in one vast waving sea of sound. Warner and some others welcomed Gerard and Morley, and ushered them, totally unprepared for such a reception, to an open carriage drawn by four white horses that was awaiting them. Orders were given that there was to be no cheering, no irregular clamour. The hymn alone was heard. As the carriage passed each Trade, they followed and formed in procession behind it; thus all had the opportunity of beholding their chosen chief, and he the proud consolation of looking on the multitude who thus enthusiastically recognised the sovereignty of his services.

The interminable population, the mighty melody, the incredible order, the simple yet awful solemnity, this representation of the great cause to which she was devoted under an aspect that at once satisfied the reason, captivated the imagination, and elevated the heart; her admiration of her father, thus ratified as it were by the sympathy of a nation, added to all the recent passages of her life teeming with such strange and trying interest, overcame Sybil. The tears fell down her cheek as the carriage bore away her father, while she remained under the care of one unknown to the people of Mowbray, but who had accompanied her from London; this was Hatton.

The last light of the sun was shed over the Moor when Gerard reached it, and the Druid's altar, and its surrounding crags, were burnished with its beam.

CHAPTER 11

It was the night following the day after the return of Gerard to Mowbray. Morley, who had lent to him and Sybil his cottage in the dale, was at the office of his newspaper, the Mowbray Phalanx, where he now resided. He was alone in his room writing, occasionally rising from his seat, and pacing the chamber, when some one knocked at his door. Receiving a permission to come in, there entered Hatton.

'I fear I am disturbing an article?' said the guest.

'By no means; the day of labour is not at hand. I am very pleased to see you.'

'My quarters are not inviting,' continued Hatton. 'It is remarkable what bad accommodation you find in these great trading towns. I should have thought that the mercantile traveller had been a comfortable animal, not to say a luxurious; but I find everything mean and third-rate. The wine execrable. So I thought I would come and bestow my tediousness on you. 'Tis hardly fair.'

'You could not have pleased me better. I was, rather from distraction than from exigency, throwing some thoughts on paper. But the voice of yesterday still lingers in my ear.'

'What a spectacle!'

'Yes; you see what a multitude presents who have recognised the predominance of Moral Power,' said Morley. 'The spectacle was august; but the results to which such a public mind must lead are sublime.'

'It must have been deeply gratifying to our friend,' said Hatton.

'It will support him in his career,' said Morley.

'And console him in his prison,' added Hatton.

'You think that it will come to that?' said Morley enquiringly.

'It has that aspect; but appearances change.'

'What should change them?'

'Time and accident, which change, everything.'

'Time will bring the York Assizes,' said Morley musingly; 'and as for accident, I confess the future seems to me dreary. What can happen for Gerard?'

'He might win his writ of right,' said Hatton demurely, stretching out his legs, and leaning back in his chair. 'That also may be tried at the York Assizes.'

'His writ of right! I thought that was a feint, a mere affair of tactics to keep the chance of the field.'

'I believe the field may be won,' said Hatton very composedly.

'Won!'

'Ay! the castle and manor of Mowbray, and half the lord-ships round, to say nothing of this good town. The people are prepared to be his subjects; he must give up equality, and be content with being a popular sovereign.'

'You jest, my friend.'

'Then I speak truth in jest; sometimes, you know, the case.'

'What mean you?' said Morley rising and approaching Hatton; 'for, though I have often observed you like a biting phrase, you never speak idly. Tell me what you mean.'

'I mean,' said Hatton, looking Morley earnestly in the face, and speaking with great gravity, 'that the documents are in existence which prove the title of Walter Gerard to the proprietorship of this great district; that I know where the documents are to be found; and that it requires nothing but a resolution equal to the occasion to secure them.'

'Should that be wanting?' said Morley.

'I should think not,' said Hatton. 'It would belie our nature to believe so.'

'And where are these documents?'

'In the muniment room of Mowbray Castle.'

'Hah!' exclaimed Morley in a prolonged tone.

'Kept closely by one who knows their value, for they are the title-deeds not of his right but of his confusion.'

'And how can we obtain them?'

'By means more honest than those they were acquired by.'

'They are not obvious.'

'Two hundred thousand human beings yesterday ac-knowledged the supremacy of Gerard,' said Hatton. 'Suppose they had known that within the walls of Mowbray Castle were contained the proofs that Walter Gerard was the lawful possessor of the lands on which they live; I say suppose that had been the case. Do you think they would have contented themselves with singing psalms? What would have become of moral power then? They would have taken Mowbray Castle by storm; they would have sacked and gutted it; they would have appointed a chosen band to rifle the round tower; they would have taken care that every document in it, especially an iron chest, painted blue, and blazoned with the shield of Valence, should have been delivered to you, to me, to anyone that Gerard appointed for the office. And what could be the remedy of the Earl de Mowbray? He could scarcely bring an action against the hundred for the destruction of the castle, which we would prove was not his own. And the most he could do would be to transport some poor wretches who had got drunk in his plundered cellars, and then set fire to his golden saloons.'

'You amaze me,' said Morley, looking with an astonished expression on the person who had just delivered himself of these suggestive details with the same coolness and arid accuracy that he would have entered into the details of a pedigree.

' 'Tis a practical view of the case,' remarked Mr. Hatton.

Morley paced the chamber disturbed; Hatton remained silent and watched him with a scrutinising eye.

'Are you certain of your facts?' at length said Morley, abruptly stopping.

'Quite so; Lord de Mowbray informed me of the circumstances himself before I left London, and I came down here in consequence.'

'You know him?'

'No one better.'

'And these documents, some of them, I suppose,' said Morley with a cynical look, 'were once in your own possession then?'

'Possibly. Would they were now! But it is a great thing to know where they may be found.'

'Then they once were the property of Gerard?'

'Hardly that. They were gained by my own pains, and often paid for with my own purse. Claimed by no one, I parted with them to a person to whom they were valuable. It is not merely to serve Gerard that I want them now, though I would willingly serve him. I have need of some of these papers with respect to an ancient title, a claim to which by a person in whom I am interested they would substantiate. Now listen, good friend Morley; moral force is a fine thing, especially in speculation, and so is a community of goods, especially when a man has no property, but when you have lived as long as I have, and have tasted of the world's delights, you'll comprehend the rapture of acquisition, and learn that it is generally secured by very coarse means. Come, I have a mind that you

should prosper. The public spirit is inflamed here; you are a
leader of the people. Let us have another meeting on the
Moor, a preconcerted outbreak; you can put your fingers in a
trice on the men who will do our work. Mowbray Castle is in
their possession; we secure our object. You shall have ten
thousand pounds on the nail, and I will take you back to
London with me besides, and teach you what is fortune.'

'I understand you,' said Morley. 'You have a clear brain and
a bold spirit; you have no scruples, which indeed are generally
the creatures of perplexity rather than of principle. You ought
to succeed.'

'We ought to succeed, you mean,' said Hatton, 'for I have
long perceived that you only wanted opportunity to mount.'

'Yesterday was a great burst of feeling occasioned by a very
peculiar cause,' said Morley musingly; 'but it must not mislead us. The discontent here is not deep. The people are still
employed, though not fully. Wages have fallen, but they must
drop more. THE PEOPLE are not ripe for the movement you
intimate. There are thousands who would rush to the rescue of
the castle. Besides there is a priest here, one St. Lys, who
exercises a most pernicious influence over the people. It will
require immense efforts and great distress to root him out.
No: it would fail.'

'Then we must wait awhile,' said Hatton, 'or devise some
other means.'

' 'Tis a very impracticable case,' said Morley.

'There is a combination for every case,' said Hatton.
'Ponder and it comes. This seemed simple; but you think, you
really think it would not answer?'

'At this moment, not; that is my conviction.'

'Well, suppose instead of an insurrection we have a burglary.
Can you assist me to the right hands here?'

'Not I indeed!'

'What is the use then of this influence over the people of
which you and Gerard are always talking? After yesterday, I
thought you could do anything here.'

'We have not hitherto had the advantage of your worldly
knowledge; in future we shall be wiser.'

'Well then,' said Hatton, 'we must now think of Gerard's
defence. He shall have the best counsel. I shall retain Kelly

specially. I shall return to town to-morrow morning. You will keep me alive to the state of feeling here, and if things get more mature, drop me a line and I will come down.'

'This conversation had better not be mentioned to Gerard.'

'That is obvious; it would only disturb him. I did not preface it by a stipulation of confidence, because that is idle. Of course you will keep the secret; it is your interest; it is a great possession. I know very well you will be most jealous of sharing it. I know it is as safe with you as with myself.'

And with these words Hatton wished him a hearty farewell and withdrew.

'He is right,' thought Morley; 'he knows human nature well. The secret is safe. I will not breathe it to Gerard. I will treasure it up. It is knowledge; it is power: great knowledge, great power. And what shall I do with it? Time will teach me.'

END OF THE FIFTH BOOK

BOOK VI

*

'ANOTHER week,' exclaimed a gentleman in Downing Street on the 5th August, 1842, 'and we shall be prorogued. You can surely keep the country quiet for another week.'

'I cannot answer for the public peace for another four-and-twenty hours,' replied his companion.

'This business at Manchester must be stopped at once; you have a good force there?'

'Manchester is nothing; these are movements merely to distract. The serious work is not now to be apprehended in the cotton towns. The state of Staffordshire and Warwickshire is infinitely more menacing. Cheshire and Yorkshire alarm me. The accounts from Scotland are as bad as can be. And though I think the sufferings of '39 will keep Birmingham and the Welsh collieries in check, we cannot venture to move any of our force from those districts.'

'You must summon a council for four o'clock. I have some deputations to receive, which I will throw over; but to Windsor I must go. Nothing has yet occurred to render any notice of the state of the country necessary in the speech from the Throne.'

'Not yet,' said his companion; 'but what will to-morrow bring forth?'

'After all it is only a turn-out. I cannot recast her Majesty's speech and bring in rebellion and closed mills, instead of loyalty and a good harvest.'

'It would be a bore. Well, we will see to-morrow;' and the colleague left the room.

'And now for these deputations,' said the gentleman in Downing Street; 'of all things in the world I dislike a deputation. I do not care how much I labour in the Closet or the House; that's real work; the machine is advanced. But receiving a deputation is like sham marching: an immense dust and no progress. To listen to their views! As if I did not know what their views were before they stated them! And to put on a countenance of respectful candour while they are developing their exploded or their impracticable systems! Were it not that, at a practised crisis, I permit them to see conviction slowly stealing over my conscience, I believe the fellows would never stop. I cannot really receive these deputations. I must leave them to Hoaxem,' and the gentleman in Downing Street rang his bell.

'Well, Mr. Hoaxem,' resumed the gentleman in Downing Street, as that faithful functionary entered, 'there are some deputations I understand, to-day. You must receive them, as I am going to Windsor. What are they?'

'There are only two, sir, of moment. The rest I could easily manage.'

'And these two?'

'In the first place, there is our friend Colonel Bosky, the members for the county of Calfshire, and a deputation of tenant farmers.'

'Pah!'

'These must be attended to. The members have made a strong representation to me, that they really cannot any longer vote with government unless the Treasury assists them in satisfying their constituents.'

'And what do they want?'

'Statement of grievances; high taxes and low prices; mild expostulations and gentle hints that they have been thrown over by their friends; Polish corn, Holstein cattle, and British income-tax.'*

'Well, you know what to say,' said the gentleman in Downing Street. 'Tell them generally, that they are quite mistaken; prove to them particularly that my only object has been to render protection more protective, by making it practical, and divesting it of the surplusage of odium; that no foreign corn can come in at fifty-five shillings; that there are not enough cattle in all Holstein to supply the parish of Pancras daily with beef-steaks; and that as for the income-tax, they will be amply compensated for it, by their diminished cost of living through the agency of that very tariff of which they are so superficially complaining.'

'Their diminished cost of living!' said Mr. Hoaxem, a little confused. 'Would not that assurance, I humbly suggest, clash a little with my previous demonstration that we had arranged that no reduction of prices should take place ?'

'Not at all; your previous demonstration is of course true, but at the same time you must impress upon them the necessity of general views to form an opinion of particular instances. As for example, a gentleman of five thousand pounds per annum pays to the income-tax, which by the bye always call property-tax, one hundred and fifty pounds a-year. Well, I have materially reduced the duties on eight hundred articles. The consumption of each of those articles by an establishment of five thousand pounds per annum cannot be less than one pound per article. The reduction of price cannot be less than a moiety; therefore a saving of four hundred per annum; which, placed against the deduction of the property-tax, leaves a clear increase of income of two hundred and fifty pounds per annum; by which you see that a property-tax, in fact, increases income.'

'I see,' said Mr. Hoaxem, with an admiring glance. 'And what am I to say to the deputation of the manufacturers of Mowbray, complaining of the great depression of trade, and the total want of remunerating profits ?'

'You must say exactly the reverse,' said the gentleman in Downing Street. 'Show them how much I have done to promote the revival of trade. First of all, in making provisions cheaper; cutting off at one blow half the protection on corn, as, for example, at this moment under the old law the duty on foreign wheat would have been twenty-seven shillings a quarter; under the new law it is thirteen. To be sure, no wheat could come in at either price, but that does not alter the principle. Then, as to live cattle, show how I have entirely opened the trade with the Continent in live cattle. Enlarge upon this, the subject is speculative and admits of expansive estimates. If there be any dissenters on the deputation, who, having freed the negroes, have no subject left for their foreign sympathies, hint at the tortures of the bull-fight and the immense consideration to humanity, that, instead of being speared at Seville, the Andalusian Toro will probably in future be cut up at Smithfield. This cheapness of provisions will permit them to compete with the foreigner in all neutral markets, in time beat them in their own. It is a complete compensation too for the property-tax, which, impress upon them, is a great experiment and entirely for their interests. Ring the changes on great measures and great experiments till it is time to go down and make a House. Your official duties, of course, must not be interfered with. They will take the hint. I have no doubt you will get through the business very well, Mr. Hoaxem, particularly if you be "frank and explicit;" that is the right line to take when you wish to conceal your own mind and to confuse the minds of others. Good morning!'

CHAPTER 2

Two days after this conversation in Downing Street, a special messenger arrived at Marney Abbey from the Lord Lieutenant of the county, the Duke of Fitz-Aquitaine. Immediately after reading the despatch of which he was the bearer, there was a great bustle in the house; Lady Marney was sent for to her husband's library, and there enjoined immediately to write various letters, which were to prevent certain expected visitors from arriving; Captain Grouse was in and out of the same library every five minutes, receiving orders and counter-orders, and finally mounting his horse was flying about the neighbourhood with messages and commands. All this stir signified that the Marney regiment of Yeomanry were to be called out directly.

Lord Marney, who had succeeded in obtaining a place in the Household, and was consequently devoted to the insti-tutions, of the country, was full of determination to uphold them; but at the same time, with characteristic prudence, was equally resolved that the property principally protected should be his own, and that the order of his own district should chiefly engage his solicitude.

'I do not know what the Duke means by marching into the disturbed districts,' said Lord Marney to Captain Grouse. 'These are disturbed districts. There have been three fires in one week, and I want to know what disturbance can be worse than that? In my opinion this is a mere anti-corn-law riot to frighten the government; and suppose they do stop the mills, what then? I wish they were all stopped, and then one might live like a gentleman again.'

Egremont, between whom and his brother a sort a bad-tempered good understanding had of late years to a certain degree flourished, in spite of Lord Marney remaining child-less, which made him hate Egremont with double-distilled virulence, and chiefly by the affectionate manœuvres of their mother, but whose annual visits to Marney had generally been limited to the yeomanry week, arrived from London the same day as the letter of the Lord Lieutenant, as he had learnt that his brother's regiment, in which he commanded a troop, as well as the other yeomanry corps in the North of England, must immediately take the field.

Five years had elapsed since the commencement of our history, and they had brought apparently much change to the character of the brother of Lord Marney. He had become, especially during the last two or three years, silent and re-served; he rarely entered society; even the company of those who were once his intimates had ceased to attract him; he was really a melancholy man. The change in his demeanour was observed by all; his mother and his sister-in-law were the only persons who endeavoured to penetrate its cause, and sighed over the failure of their sagacity. Quit the world and the world forgets you; and Egremont would have soon been a name no longer mentioned in those brilliant saloons which he once adorned, had not occasionally a sensation, produced by an effective speech in the House of Commons, recalled his name to his old associates, who then remembered the pleasant hours passed in his society, and wondered why he never went any-where now.

'I suppose he finds society a bore,' said Lord Eugene de Vere; 'I am sure I do: but then, what is a fellow to do? I am not in Parliament, like Egremont. I believe, after all, that's the thing; for I have tried everything else, and everything else is a bore.'

'I think one should marry, like Alfred Mountchesney,' said Lord Milford.

'But what is the use of marrying if you do not marry a rich woman? and the heiresses of the present age will not marry. What can be more unnatural! It alone ought to produce a revolution. Why, Alfred is the only fellow who has made a coup; and then he has not got it down.'

'She behaved in a most unprincipled manner to me, that Fitzwarene,' said Lord Milford, 'always took my bouquets and once made me write some verses.'

'By Jove!' said Lord Eugene, 'I should like to see them. What a bore it must have been to write verses!'

'I only copied them out of Mina Blake's album: but I sent them in my own handwriting.'

Baffled sympathy was the cause of Egremont's gloom. It is the secret spring of most melancholy. He loved and loved in vain. The conviction that his passion, though hopeless, was not looked upon with disfavour, only made him the more wretched, for the disappointment is more acute in proportion as the chance is better. He had never seen Sybil since the morning he quitted her in Smith Square, immediately before her departure for the North. The trial of Gerard had taken place at the assizes of that year: he had been found guilty, and sentenced to eighteen months' imprisonment in York Castle; the interference of Egremont, both in the House of Commons and with the government, saved him from the felon confinement with which he was at first threatened, and from which assuredly state prisoners should be exempt. During this effort some correspondence had taken place between Egremont and Sybil, which he would willingly have encouraged and maintained; but it ceased nevertheless with its subject. Sybil, through the influential interference of Ursula Trafford, lived at the convent at York during the imprisonment of her father, and visited him daily.

The anxiety to take the veil which had once characterised Sybil had certainly waned. Perhaps her experience of life had impressed her with the importance of fulfilling vital duties. Her father, though he had never opposed her wish, had never encouraged it; and he had now increased and interesting claims on her devotion. He had endured great trials, and had fallen on adverse fortunes. Sybil would look at him, and though his noble frame was still erect and his countenance still displayed that mixture of frankness and decision which had distinguished it of yore, she could not conceal from herself that there were ravages which time could not have produced.

A year and a half of imprisonment had shaken to its centre a frame born for action, and shrinking at all times from the resources of sedentary life. The disappointment of high hopes had jarred and tangled even the sweetness of his noble disposition. He needed solicitude and solace: and Sybil resolved that if vigilance and sympathy could soothe an existence that would otherwise be embittered, these guardian angels should at least hover over the life of her father.

When the term of his imprisonment had ceased, Gerard had returned with his daughter to Mowbray. Had he deigned to accept the offers of his friends, he need not have been anxious as to his future. A public subscription for his service had been collected: Morley, who was well to do in the world, for the circulation of the Mowbray Phalanx daily increased with the increasing sufferings of the people, offered his friend to share his house and purse: Hatton was munificent; there was no limit either to his offers or his proffered services. But all were declined; Gerard would live by labour. The post he had occupied at Mr. Trafford's was not vacant, even if that gentleman had thought fit again to receive him; but his reputation as a first-rate artizan soon obtained him good employment, though on this occasion in the town of Mowbray, which for the sake of his daughter he regretted. He had no pleasant home now for Sybil, but he had the prospect of one, and until he obtained possession of it, Sybil sought a refuge, which had been offered to her from the first, with her kindest and dearest friend; so that, at this period of our history, she was again an inmate of the convent at Mowbray, whither her father and Morley had attended her the eve of the day she had first visited the ruins of Marney Abbey.

CHAPTER 3

'I have seen a many things in my time, Mrs. Trotman,' said Chaffing Jack, as he took the pipe from his mouth in the silent bar-room of the Cat and Fiddle; 'but I never see any like this. I think I ought to know Mowbray if anyone does, for, man and boy, I have breathed this air for a matter of half a century. I sucked it in when it tasted of primroses, and this tavern was a cottage covered with honeysuckle in the middle of green fields, where the lads came and drank milk from the cow with their lasses; and I have inhaled what they call the noxious atmosphere, when a hundred chimneys have been smoking like one; and always found myself pretty well. Nothing like business to give one an appetite. But when shall I feel peckish again, Mrs. Trotman?'

'The longest lane has a turning, they say, Mr. Trotman.'

'Never knew anything like this before,' replied her husband, 'and I have seen bad times: but I always used to say, "Mark my words, friends, Mowbray will rally." My words carried weight, Mrs. Trotman, in this quarter, as they naturally should, coming from a man of my experience, especially when I gave tick. Every man I chalked up was of the same opinion as the landlord of the Cat and Fiddle, and always thought that Mowbray would rally. That's the killing feature of these times, Mrs. Trotman, there's no rallying in the place.'

'I begin to think it's the machines,' said Mrs. Trotman.

'Nonsense,' said Mr. Trotman; 'it's the corn laws. The town of Mowbray ought to clothe the world with our resources. Why, Shuffle and Screw can turn out forty mile of calico per day; but where's the returns? That's the point. As the American gentleman said, who left his bill unpaid, "Take my bread-stuffs and I'll give you a cheque at sight on the Pennsylvanian Bank."'

'It's very true,' said Mrs. Trotman. 'Who's there?'

'Nothing in my way?' said a woman with a basket of black cherries, with a pair of tin scales thrown upon their top.

'Ah! Mrs. Carey,' said Chaffing Jack, 'is that you?'

'My mortal self, Mr. Trotman, tho' I be sure I feel more like a ghost than flesh and blood.'

'You may well say that, Mrs. Carey; you and I have known Mowbray as long, I should think, as any in this quarter—'

'And never see such times as these, Mr. Trotman, nor the like of such. But I always thought it would come to this, every-thing turned topsy-turvy as it were, the children getting all the wages, and decent folk turned adrift to pick up a living as they could. It's something of a judgment in my mind, Mr. Trotman.'

'It's the trade leaving the country, widow, and no mistake.'

'And how shall we bring it back again?' said the widow; 'the police ought to interfere.'

'We must have cheap bread,' said Mr. Trotman.

'So they tell me,' said the widow; 'but whether bread be cheap or dear don't much signify, if we have nothing to buy it with. You don't want anything in my way, neighbour? It's not very tempting, I fear,' said the good widow in a rather mournful tone; 'but a little fresh fruit cools the mouth in this sultry time, and at any rate it takes me into the world. It seems like business, tho' very hard to turn a penny by; but one's neighbours are very kind, and a little chat about the dreadful times always puts me in spirits.'

'Well, we will take a pound for the sake of trade, widow,' said Mrs. Trotman.

'And here's a glass of gin-and-water, widow,' said Mr. Trotman, 'and when Mowbray rallies you shall come and pay for it.'

'Thank you both very kindly,' said the widow, 'a good neighbour, as our minister says, is the pool of Bethesda; and as you say, Mowbray will rally.'

'I never said so,' exclaimed Chaffing Jack, interrupting her. 'Don't go about for to say that I said Mowbray would rally. My words have some weight in this quarter, widow; Mowbray rally! Why should it rally? Where's the elements?'

'Where indeed?' said Devilsdust as he entered the Cat and Fiddle with Dandy Mick, 'there is not the spirit of a louse in Mowbray.'

'That's a true bill,' said Mick.

'Is there another white-livered town in the whole realm where the operatives are all working half-time, and thanking the Capitalists for keeping the mills going, and only starving them by inches?' said Devilsdust, in a tone of scorn.

'That's your time of day,' said Mick.

'Very glad to see you, gentlemen,' said Mr. Trotman, 'pray be seated. There's a little backy left yet in Mowbray, and a glass of twist at your service.'

'Nothing exciseable for me,' said Devilsdust.

'Well, it ayn't exactly the right ticket, Mrs. Trotman, I believe,' said Mick, bowing gallantly to the lady; 'but 'pon my soul I am so thirsty, that I'll take Chaffing Jack at his word;' and so saying, Mick and Devilsdust ensconced themselves in the bar, while goodhearted Mrs. Carey sipped her glass of gin-and-water, which she frequently protested was a pool of Bethesda.*

'Well, Jack,' said Devilsdust, 'I suppose you have heard the news?'

'If it be anything that has happened at Mowbray, especially in this quarter, I should think I had. Times must be very bad indeed that some one does not drop in to tell me anything that has happened, and to ask my advice.'

'It's nothing to do with Mowbray.'

'Thank you kindly, Mrs. Trotman,' said Mick, 'and here's your very good health.'

'Then I am in the dark,' said Chaffing Jack, replying to the previous observation of Devilsdust, 'for I never see a newspaper now except a week old, and that lent by a friend, I who used to take my Sun* regular, to say nothing of the Dispatch,* and Bell's Life.* Times is changed, Mr. Radley.'

'You speak like a book, Mr. Trotman,' said Mick, 'and here's your very good health. But as for newspapers, I'm all in the dark myself, for the Literary and Scientific is shut up, and no subscribers left, except the honorary ones, and not a journal to be had except the Moral World, and that's gratis.'

'As bad as the Temple,' said Chaffing Jack, 'it's all up with the institutions of the country. And what then is the news?'

'Labour is triumphant in Lancashire,' said Devilsdust, with bitter solemnity.

'The deuce it is,' said Chaffing Jack. 'What, have they raised wages?'

'No,' said Devilsdust, 'but they have stopped the mills.'

'That won't mend matters much,' said Jack with a puff.

'Won't it?'

'The working classes will have less to spend than ever.'

'And what will the Capitalists have to spend?' said Devilsdust.

'Worse and worse,' said Mr. Trotman, 'you will never get institutions like the Temple re-opened on this system.'

'Don't you be afraid, Jack,' said Mick, tossing off his tumbler; 'if we only get our rights, won't we have a blow out!'

'We must have a struggle,' said Devilsdust, 'and teach the Capitalists on whom they depend, so that in future they are not to have the lion's share, and then all will be right.'

'A fair day's wage for a fair day's work,' said Mick; 'that's your time of day.'

'It began at Staleybridge,' said Devilsdust, 'and they have stopped them all; and now they have marched into Manchester ten thousand strong. They pelted the police—'

'And cheered the red-coats like fun,' said Mick.

'The soldiers will fraternise,' said Devilsdust.

'Do what?' said Mrs. Trotman.

'Stick their bayonets into the Capitalists, who have hired them to cut the throats of the working classes,' said Devilsdust.

'The Queen is with us,' said Mick. 'It's well known she sets her face against gals working in mills like blazes.'

'Well, this is news,' said Mrs. Carey. 'I always thought some good would come of having a woman on the throne;' and repeating her thanks and pinning on her shawl, the widow retired, eager to circulate the intelligence.

'And now that we are alone,' said Devilsdust, 'the question is, what are we to do here; and we came to consult you, Jack, as you know Mowbray better than any living man. This thing will spread. It won't stop short. I have a bird too singing something in my ear these two days past. If they do not stop it in Lancashire, and I defy them, there will be a general rising.'

'I have seen a many things in my time,' said Mr. Trotman; 'some risings and some strikes, and as stiff turn-outs as may be. But to my fancy there is nothing like a strike in prosperous times; there's more money spent under those circumstances than you can well suppose, young gentlemen. It's as good as Mowbray Staty* any day.'

'But now to the point,' said Devilsdust. 'The people are regularly sold; they want a leader.'

'Why, there's Gerard,' said Chaffing Jack; 'never been a better man in my time. And Warner, the greatest man the Handlooms ever turned out.'

'Ay, ay,' said Devilsdust; 'but they have each of them had a year and a half, and that cools blood.'

'Besides,' said Mick, 'they are too old; and Stephen Morley

has got round them, preaching moral force, and all that sort of gammon.'

'I never heard that moral force won the battle of Waterloo,' said Devilsdust. 'I wish the Capitalists would try moral force a little, and see whether it would keep the thing going. If the Capitalists will give up their redcoats, I would be a moral force man to-morrow.'

'And the new police,' said Mick. 'A pretty go, when a fellow in a blue coat fetches you the Devil's own con on your head, and you get moral force for a plaster.'

'Why, that's all very well,' said Chaffing Jack; 'but I am against violence; at least, much. I don't object to a moderate riot, provided it is not in my quarter of the town.'

'Well, that's not the ticket now,' said Mick. 'We don't want no violence; all we want is to stop all the mills and hands in the kingdom, and have a regular national holiday for six weeks at least.'

'I have seen a many things in my time,' said Chaffing Jack solemnly, 'but I have always observed, that if the people had worked generally for half-time for a week, they would stand anything.'

'That's a true bill,' said Mick.

'Their spirit is broken,' said Chaffing Jack, 'or else they never would have let the Temple have been shut up.'

'And think of our Institute, without a single subscriber!' said Mick. 'The gals is the only thing what has any spirit left, Julia told me just now she would go to the cannon's mouth for the Five Points any summer day.'

'You think the spirit can't be raised, Chaffing Jack,' said Devilsdust seriously. 'You ought to be a judge.'

'If I don't know Mowbray, who does? Trust my word, the house won't draw.'

'Then it is U-P,' said Mick.

'Hush!' said Devilsdust. 'But suppose it spreads?'

'It won't spread,' said Chaffing Jack. 'I've seen a deal of these things. I fancy from what you say it's a cotton squall. It will pass, Sir. Let me see the miners out, and then I will talk to you.'

'Stranger things than that have happened,' said Devilsdust.

'Then things get serious,' said Chaffing Jack. 'Them miners

is very stubborn, and when they gets excited ayn't it a bear at play, that's all?'

'Well,' said Devilsdust, 'what you say is well worth attention; but all the same I feel we are on the eve of a regular crisis.'

'No, by jingo!' said Mick, and, tossing his cap into the air, he snapped his fingers with delight at the anticipated amusement.

CHAPTER 4

'I don't think I can stand this much longer,' said Mr. Mountchesney, the son-in-law of Lord de Mowbray, to his wife, as he stood before the empty fire-place with his back to the mantelpiece and his hands thrust into the pockets of his coat. 'This living in the country in August bores me to extinction. I think we will go to Baden, Joan.'

'But papa is so anxious, dearest Alfred, that we should remain here at present and see the neighbours a little.'

'I might be induced to remain here to please your father, but as for your neighbours I have seen quite enough of them. They are not a sort of people that I ever met before, or that I wish to meet again. I do not know what to say to them, nor can I annex an idea to what they say to me. Heigho! certainly the country in August is a thing of which no one who has not tried it has the most remote conception.'

'But you always used to say you doted on the country, Alfred,' said Lady Joan in a tone of tender reproach.

'So I do; I never was happier than when I was at Melton, and even enjoyed the country in August when I was on the Moors.'

'But I cannot well go to Melton,' said Lady Joan.

'I don't see why you can't. Mrs. Shelldrake goes with her husband to Melton, and so does Lady Di with Barham; and a very pleasant life it is.'

'Well, at any rate we cannot go to Melton now,' said Lady Joan mortified; 'and it is impossible for me to go to the Moors.'

'No, but I could go,' said Mr. Mountchesney, 'and leave you here. I might have gone with Eugene de Vere and Milford and Fitz-heron. They wanted me very much. What a capital party it would have been, and what capital sport we should have had! And I need not have been away for more than a month, or perhaps six weeks, and I could have written to you every day, and all that sort of thing.'

Lady Joan sighed and affected to recur to the opened volume which, during this conversation, she had held in her hand.

'I wonder where Maud is,' said Mr. Mountchesney; 'I shall want her to ride with me to-day. She is a capital horse-woman, and always amuses me. As you cannot ride now, Joan, I wish you would let Maud have Sunbeam.'

'As you please.'

'Well, I am going to the stables and will tell them. Who is this?' Mr. Mountchesney exclaimed, and then walked to the window that, looking over the park, showed at a distance the advance of a showy equipage.

Lady Joan looked up.

'Come here, Joan, and tell me who this is;' and Lady Joan was at his side in a moment.

'It is the livery of the Bardolfs,' said Lady Joan.

'I always call them Firebrace: I cannot get out of it,' said Mr. Mountchesney. 'Well, I am glad it is they; I thought it might be an irruption of barbarians. Lady Bardolf will bring us some news.'

Lord and Lady Bardolf were not alone; they were accompanied by a gentleman who had been staying on a visit at Firebrace, and who, being acquainted with Lord de Mowbray, had paid his respects to the castle on his way to London. This gentleman was the individual who had elevated them to the peerage, Mr. Hatton. A considerable intimacy had sprung up between him and his successful clients. Firebrace was an old place rebuilt in the times of the Tudors, but with something of its more ancient portions remaining, and with a storehouse of muniments that had escaped the civil wars. Hatton revelled in them, and in pursuing his researches had already made discoveries which might perhaps place the coronet of the earldom of Lovel on the brow of the former champion of the baronet-age, who now however never mentioned the order. Lord de Mowbray was well content to see Mr. Hatton, a gentleman in whom he did not repose the less confidence, because his advice given him three years ago, respecting the writ of right and the claim upon his estate, had proved so discreet and correct. Acting on that advice, Lord de Mowbray had instructed his lawyers to appear to the action without entering into any unnecessary explanation of the merits of his case. He counted on the accuracy of Mr. Hatton's judgment, that the claim would not be pursued; and he was right: after some fencing and preliminary manœuvring, the claim had not been pursued. Lord de Mowbray therefore, always gracious, was disposed to accord a very distinguished reception to his confidential counsellor. He pressed very much his guests to remain with him some days, and, though that was not practicable, Mr. Hatton promised that he would not leave the neighbourhood without paying another visit to the castle.

'And you continue quiet here?' said Mr. Hatton to Lord de Mowbray.

'And I am told we shall keep so,' said Lord de Mowbray. 'The mills are mostly at work, and the men take the reduced wages in a good spirit. The fact is, our agitators in this neighbourhood suffered pretty smartly in '39, and the Chartists have lost their influence.'

'I am sorry for poor Lady St. Julians,' said Lady Bardolf to Lady de Mowbray. 'It must be such a disappointment, and she has had so many; but I understand there is nobody to blame but herself. If she had only left the Prince alone; but she would not be quiet.'

'And where are the Deloraines?'

'They are at Munich; with which they are delighted. And Lady Deloraine writes me that Mr. Egremont has promised to join them there. If he do, they mean to winter at Rome.'

'Somebody said he was going to be married,' said Lady de Mowbray.

'His mother wishes him to marry,' said Lady Bardolf; 'but I have heard nothing.'

Mr. Mountchesney came in and greeted the Bardolfs with some warmth. 'How delightful in the country in August to meet somebody that you have seen in London in June!' he exclaimed. 'Now, dear Lady Bardolf, do tell me something, for you can conceive nothing so triste as we are here. We never get a letter. Joan only corresponds with philosophers, and Maud with clergymen; and none of my friends ever write to me.'

'Perhaps you never write to them?'

'Well, I never have been a letter-writer, because really I never wanted to write or be written to. I always knew what was going on because I was on the spot. I was doing the things that people were writing letters about; but now, not being in the world any longer, doing nothing, living in the country, and the country in August, I should like to receive letters every day, but I do not know whom to fix upon as a correspondent. Eugène de Vere will not write, Milford cannot; and as for Fitz-heron, he is so very selfish, he always wants his letters answered.'

'That is unreasonable,' said Lady Bardolf.

'Besides, what can they tell me at this moment? They have gone to the Moors and are enjoying themselves. They asked me to go with them, but I could not go, because you see I could not leave Joan; though why I could not leave her, I really cannot understand, because Egerton has got some moors this year, and he leaves Lady Augusta with her father.'

Lady Maud entered the room in her bonnet, returning from an airing. She was all animation, charmed to see everybody; she had been to Mowbray to hear some singing at the Roman Catholic chapel in that town; a service had been performed and a collection made for the suffering workpeople of the place. She had been apprised of it for some days, was told that she would hear the most beautiful voice that she had ever listened to, but it had far exceeded her expectations. A female voice it seemed; no tones could be conceived more tender and yet more thrilling: in short, seraphic.

Mr. Mountchesney blamed her for not taking him. He liked music, singing, especially female singing; when there was so little to amuse him, he was surprised that Lady Maud had not been careful that he should have been present. His sister-in-law reminded him that she had particularly requested him to drive her over to Mowbray, and he had declined the honour as a bore.

'Yes,' said Mr. Mountchesney, 'but I thought Joan was going with you, and that you would be shopping.'

'It was a good thing our House was adjourned before these disturbances in Lancashire,' said Lord Bardolf to Lord de Mowbray.

'The best thing we can all do is to be on our estates, I believe,' said Lord de Mowbray.

'My neighbour Marney is in a state of great excitement,' said Lord Bardolf; 'all his yeomanry out.'

'But he is quiet at Marney?'

'In a way; but these fires puzzle us. Marney will not believe that the condition of the labourer has anything to do with them; and he certainly is a very acute man. But still I don't know what to say to it. The poor-law is very unpopular in my parish. Marney will have it that the incendiaries are all strangers, hired by the Anti-Corn-law League.'*

'Ah! here is Lady Joan,' exclaimed Lady Bardolf, as the wife of Mr. Mountchesney entered the room. 'My dearest Lady Joan!'

'Why, Joan,' said Mr. Mountchesney, 'Maud has been to Mowbray, and heard the most delicious singing. Why did we not go?'

'I did mention it to you, Alfred.'

'I remember you said something about going to Mowbray, and that you wanted to go to several places. But there is nothing I hate so much as shopping. It bores me more than anything. And you are so peculiarly long when you are shopping. But singing, and beautiful singing in a Catholic chapel by a woman, perhaps a beautiful woman, that is quite a different thing; and I should have been amused, which nobody seems ever to think of here. I do not know how you find it, Lady Bardolf, but the country to me in August is a something—' and not finishing his sentence, Mr. Mountchesney gave a look of inexpressible despair.

'And you did not see this singer?' said Mr. Hatton, sidling up to Lady Maud, and speaking in a subdued tone.

'I did not, but they tell me she is most beautiful; something extraordinary; I tried to see her, but it was impossible.'

'Is she a professional singer?'

'I should imagine not; a daughter of one of the Mowbray people, I believe.'

'Let us have her over to the Castle, Lady de Mowbray,' said Mr. Mountchesney.

'If you like,' replied Lady de Mowbray, with a languid smile.

'Well, at last I have got something to do,' said Mr. Mountchesney. 'I will ride over to Mowbray, find out the beautiful singer, and bring her to the Castle.'

CHAPTER 5

THE beam of the declining sun, softened by the stained panes of a small gothic window, suffused the chamber of the Lady Superior of the convent of Mowbray. The vaulted room, of moderate dimensions, was furnished with great simplicity, and opened into a small oratory. On a table were several volumes, an ebon cross was fixed in a niche, and leaning in a high-backed chair, sat Ursula Trafford. Her pale and refined complexion, that in her youth had been distinguished for its lustre, became her spiritual office; and indeed her whole countenance, the delicate brow, the serene glance, the small aquiline nose, and the well-shaped mouth, firm and yet benignant, betokened the celestial soul that inhabited that gracious frame.

The Lady Superior was not alone; on a low seat by her side, holding her hand, and looking up into her face with a glance of reverential sympathy, was a maiden, over whose head five summers have revolved since first her girlhood broke upon our sight amid the ruins of Marney Abbey; five summers that have realised the matchless promise of her charms, and, while they have added something to her stature, have robbed it of nothing of its grace, and have rather steadied the blaze of her beauty than diminished its radiance.

'Yes, I mourn over them,' said Sybil, 'the deep convictions that made me look forward to the cloister as my home. Is it that the world has assoiled my soul? Yet I have not tasted of worldly joys: all that I have known of it has been suffering and tears. They will return, these visions of my sacred youth: dear friend, tell me that they will return!'

'I too have had visions in my youth, Sybil, and not of the cloister, yet am I here.'

'And what should I infer?' said Sybil inquiringly.

'That my visions were of the world, and brought me to the cloister, and that yours were of the cloister, and have brought you to the world.'

'My heart is sad,' said Sybil; 'and the sad should seek the shade.'

'It is troubled, my child, rather than sorrowful.'

Sybil shook her head.

'Yes, my child,' said Ursula, 'the world has taught you that there are affections which the cloister can neither satisfy nor supply. Ah! Sybil, I too have loved.'

The blood rose to the cheek of Sybil, and then returned as quickly to the heart; her trembling hand pressed that of Ursula as she sighed, and murmured, 'No, no, no.'

'Yes, it is the spirit that hovers over your life, Sybil; and in vain you would forget what haunts your heart. One not less gifted than he, as good, as gentle, as gracious, once too breathed in my ear the accents of joy. He was, like myself, the child of an old house, and Nature had invested him with every quality that can dazzle and can charm. But his heart was as pure, and his soul as lofty, as his intellect and frame were bright,—' and Ursula paused.

Sybil pressed the hand of Ursula to her lips, and whispered, 'Speak on.'

'The dreams of by-gone days,' continued Ursula, in a voice of emotion; 'the wild sorrows that I can recall, and yet feel that I was wisely chastened: he was stricken in his virtuous pride, the day before he was to have led me to that altar where alone I found the consolation that never fails. And thus closed some years of human love, my Sybil,' said Ursula, bending forward and embracing her. 'The world for a season crossed their fair current, and a power greater than the world forbade their banns; but they are hallowed; memory is my sympathy; it is soft and free, and when he came here to inquire after you, his presence and agitated heart recalled the past.'

'It is too wild a thought,' said Sybil, 'ruin to him, ruin to all.

No; we are severed by a fate as uncontrollable as severed you, dear friend; ours is a living death.'

'The morrow is unforeseen,' said Ursula. 'Happy, indeed, would it be for me, my Sybil, that your innocence should be enshrined within these holy walls, and that the pupil of my best years, and the friend of my serene life, should be my successor in this house. But I feel a deep persuasion that the hour has not arrived for you to take the step that never can be recalled.'

So saying, Ursula embraced and dismissed Sybil; for the conversation, the last passages of which we have given, had occurred when Sybil, according to her wont on Saturday afternoon, had come to request the permission of the Lady Superior to visit her father.

It was in a tolerably spacious and not discomfortable chamber, the first floor over the printing-office of the Mowbray Phalanx, that Gerard had found a temporary home. He had not long returned from his factory, and, pacing the chamber with a disturbed step, he awaited the expected arrival of his daughter.

She came; the faithful step, the well-known knock; the father and the daughter embraced; he pressed to his heart the child who had clung to him through so many trials, and who had softened so many sorrows, who had been the visiting angel in his cell, and whose devotion had led captivity captive.

Their meetings, though regular, were now comparatively rare. The sacred day united them, and sometimes for a short period the previous afternoon, but otherwise the cheerful hearth and welcome home were no longer for Gerard. And would the future bring them to him? And what was to be the future of his child? His mind vacillated between the convent of which she now seldom spoke, and which with him was never a cherished idea, and those dreams of restored and splendid fortunes, which his sanguine temperament still whispered him, in spite of hope so long deferred and expectations so often balked, might yet be realised. And sometimes between these opposing visions there rose a third, and more practical, though less picturesque, result; the idea of her marriage. And with whom? It was impossible that one so rarely gifted, and educated with so much daintiness, could ever make a wife of the people. Hatton offered wealth, but Sybil had never seemed to comprehend his hopes and Gerard felt that their ill-assorted ages was a great barrier. There was of all the men of his own order but one, who from his years, his great qualities, his sympathy, and the nature of his toil and means, seemed not unfitted to be the husband of his daughter; and often had Gerard mused over the possibility of these intimate ties with Morley. Sybil had been, as it were, bred up under his eye; an affection had always subsisted between them, and he knew well that in former days Sybil had appreciated and admired the great talents and acquirements of their friend. At one period he almost suspected that Morley was attached to her. And yet, from causes which he had never attempted to penetrate, probably from a combination of unintentional circumstances, Sybil and Morley had for the last two or three years been thrown little together, and their intimacy had entirely died away. To Gerard it seemed that Morley had ever proved his faithful friend: Morley had originally dissuaded him with energy against that course which had led to his discomfiture and punishment; when arrested, his former colleague was his bail, was his companion and adviser during his trial; had endeavoured to alleviate his imprisonment; and on his release had offered to share his means with Gerard, and when these were refused, he at least supplied Gerard with a roof. And yet, with all this, that abandonment of heart and brain, that deep sympathy with every domestic thought which characterised old days, were somehow or other wanting. There was on the part of Morley still devotion, but there was reserve.

'You are troubled, my father,' said Sybil, as Gerard continued to pace the chamber.

'Only a little restless. I am thinking what a mistake it was to have moved in '39.'

Sybil sighed.

'Ah! you were right, Sybil,' continued Gerard; 'affairs were not ripe. We should have waited three years.'

'Three years!' exclaimed Sybil, starting; 'are affairs riper now?'

'The whole of Lancashire is in revolt,' said Gerard. 'There is not a sufficient force to keep them in check. If the miners and colliers rise, and I have cause to believe that it is more than probable they will move before many days are past, the game is up.'

'You terrify me,' said Sybil.

'On the contrary,' said Gerard, smiling, 'the news is good enough; I'll not say too good to be true, for I had it from one of the old delegates who is over here to see what can be done in our north countree.'

'Yes,' said Sybil, inquiringly, and leading on her father.

'He came to the works; we had some talk. There are to be no leaders this time, at least no visible ones. The people will do it themselves. All the children of Labour are to rise on the same day, and to toil no more, till they have their rights. No violence, no bloodshed; but toil halts, and then our oppressors will learn the great economical truth as well as moral lesson, that when Toil plays, Wealth ceases.'

'When Toil ceases the People suffer,' said Sybil. 'That is the only truth that we have learnt, and it is a bitter one.'

'Can we be free without suffering?' said Gerard. 'Is the greatest of human blessings to be obtained as a matter of course; to be plucked like fruit, or seized like a running stream? No, no; we must suffer, but we are wiser than of yore; we will not conspire. Conspiracies are for aristocrats, not for nations.'

'Alas, alas! I see nothing but woe,' said Sybil. 'I cannot believe that, after all that has passed, the people here will move; I cannot believe that, after all that has passed, all that you, that we, have endured, that you, my father, will counsel them to move.'

'I counsel nothing,' said Gerard. 'It must be a great, national instinct that does it; but if all England, if Wales, if Scotland, won't work, is Mowbray to have a monopoly?'

'Ah! that's a bitter jest,' said Sybil. 'England, Wales, Scotland, will be forced to work as they were forced before. How can they subsist without labour? And if they could, there is an organised power that will subdue them.'

'The Benefit Societies, the Sick and Burial Clubs,* have money in the banks that would maintain the whole working classes, with aid in kind that will come, for six weeks, and that will do the business. And as for force, why there are not five soldiers to each town in the kingdom. It's a glittering bugbear, this fear of the military; simultaneous strikes would baffle all the armies in Europe.'

'I'll go back and pray that all this is wild talk,' said Sybil, earnestly. 'After all that has passed, were it only for your child, you should not speak, much less think this, my father. What havoc to our hearts and homes has been all this madness! It has separated us; it has destroyed our happy home; it has done more than this—' and here she wept.

'Nay, nay, my child,' said Gerard coming up and soothing her; 'one cannot weigh one's words before those we love. I can't hear of the people moving with coldness; that's out of nature; but I promise you I'll not stimulate the lads here. I am told they are little inclined to stir. You found me in a moment of what I must call, I suppose, elation; but I hear they beat the red-coats and police at Staleybridge, and that pricked my blood a bit. I have been ridden down before this when I was a lad, Sybil by Yeomanry hoofs. You must allow a little for my feelings.'

She extended her lips to the proffered embrace of her father. He blessed her and pressed her to his heart, and soothed her apprehensions with many words of softness. There was a knock at the door.

'Come in,' said Gerard. And there came in Mr. Hatton.

They had not met since Gerard's release from York Castle. There Hatton had visited him, had exercised his influence to remedy his grievances, and had more than once offered him the means of maintenance on receiving his freedom. There were moments of despondency when Gerard had almost wished that the esteem and regard with which Sybil looked upon Hatton might have matured into sentiments of a deeper nature; but on this subject the father had never breathed a word. Nor had Hatton, except to Gerard, ever intimated his wishes, for we could scarcely call them hopes. He was a silent suitor of Sybil, watching opportunities and ready to avail himself of circumstances which he worshipped. His sanguine disposition, fed by a suggestive and inventive mind, and stimulated by success and a prosperous life, sustained him always to the last. Hatton always believed that everything desirable must happen if a man had energy and watched circumstances. He had confidence too in the influence of his really insinuating manner, his fine taste, his tender tone, his ready sympathy, all which masked his daring courage and absolute recklessness of means.

There were general greetings of the greatest warmth. The eyes of Hatton were suffused with tears as he congratulated Gerard on his restored health, and pressed Sybil's hand with the affection of an old friend between both his own.

'I was down in this part of the world on business,' said Hatton, 'and thought I would come over here for a day to find you all out.' And then, after some general conversation, he said, 'And where do you think I accidentally paid a visit a day or two back? At Mowbray Castle. I see you are surprised. I saw all your friends. I did not ask his lordship how the writ of right went on. I dare say he thinks 'tis all hushed. But he is mistaken. I have learnt something which may help us over the stile yet.'

'Well-a-day!' said Gerard, 'I once thought if I could get back the lands the people would at least have a friend; but that's past. I have been a dreamer of dreams often when I was overlooking them at work. And so we all have, I suppose. I would willingly give up my claim if I could be sure the Lancashire lads will not come to harm this bout.'

' 'Tis a more serious business,' said Hatton, 'than anything of the kind that has yet happened. The government are much alarmed. They talk of sending the Guards down into the north, and bringing over troops from Ireland.'

'Poor Ireland!' said Gerard. 'Well, I think the friezecoats* might give us a helping hand now, and employ the troops at least.'

'No, my dear father, say not such things.'

'Sybil will not let me think of these matters, friend Hatton,' said Gerard, smiling. 'Well, I suppose it's not in my way, at least I certainly did not make the best hand of it in '39; but it was London that got me into that scrape. I cannot help fancying that were I on our Moors here a bit with some good lads, it might be different, and I must say so, I must indeed, Sybil.

'But you are quiet here, I hope,' said Hatton.

'Oh! yes,' said Gerard; 'I believe our spirit is sufficiently broken at Mowbray. Wages weekly dropping, and just work enough to hinder sheer idleness; that sort of thing keeps the people in very humble trim. But wait a bit, and when they have reached starvation point, I fancy we shall hear a murmur.'

'I remember our friend Morley in '39, when we returned from London, gave me a very good character of the disposition of the people here,' said Hatton; 'I hope it continues the same. He feared no outbreak then, and the distress in '39 was severe.'

'Well,' said Gerard, 'the wages have been dropping ever since. The people exist, but you can scarcely say they live. But they are cowed, I fancy. An empty belly is sometimes as apt to dull the heart as inflame the courage. And then they have lost their leaders, for I was away, you see, and have been quiet enough since I came out; and Warner is broken; he has suffered more from his time than I did; which is strange, for he had his pursuits, whereas I was restless enough, and that's the truth, and, had it not been for Sybil's daily visit, I think, though I may never be allowed to live in a castle, I should certainly have died in one.'

'And how is Morley?'

'Right well; the same as you left him; I saw not a straw's change when I came out. His paper spreads. He still preaches moral force, and believes that we shall all end in living in communities. But as the only community of which I have personal experience is a gaol, I am not much more inclined to his theory than heretofore.'

CHAPTER 6

THE reader may not have altogether forgotten Mr. Nixon and his co-mates, the miners and colliers of that district not very remote from Mowbray, which Morley had visited at the commencement of this history, in order to make fruitless researches after a gentleman whom he subsequently so unexpectedly stumbled upon. Affairs were as little flourishing in that region as at Mowbray itself, and the distress fell upon a population less accustomed to suffering, and whose spirit was not daunted by the recent discomfiture and punishment of their leaders.

'It can't last,' said Master Nixon, as he took his pipe from his mouth at the Rising Sun.

He was responded to by a general groan. 'It comes to this,' he continued, 'Natur has her laws, and this is one: a fair day's wage for a fair day's work.'

'I wish you may get it,' said Juggins, 'with a harder stint every week, and a shilling a day knocked off.'

'And what's to come to-morrow?' said Waghorn. 'The butty has given notice to quit in Parker's field this day se'-n-night.* Simmons won't drop wages, but works half time.'

'The boys will be at play afore long,' said a collier.

'Hush!' said Master Nixon, with a reproving glance, 'play is a very serious word. The boys are not to go to play as they used to do without by your leave or with your leave: We must appoint a committee to consider the question, and we must communicate with the other trades.'

'You're the man, Master Nixon, to choose for church-warden,' replied the reproved miner, with a glance of admiration.

'What is Diggs doing?' said Master Nixon, in a solemn tone.

'A-dropping wages, and a-raising tommy like fun,' said Master Waghorn.

'There is a great stir in Hell-house yard,' said a miner who entered the tap-room at this moment, much excited. 'They say that all the workshops will be shut to-morrow; not an order for a month past. They have got a top-sawyer from London there, who addresses them every evening, and says that we have a right to four shillings a-day wages, eight hours' work, and two pots of ale.'

'A fair day's wage for a fair day's work,' said Master Nixon; 'I would not stickle about hours, but the money and the drink are very just.'

'If Hell-house yard is astir,' said Waghorn, 'there will be a good deal to be seen yet.'

'It's grave,' said Master Nixon. 'What think you of a deputation there? It might come to good.'

'I should like to hear the top-sawyer from London,' said Juggins. 'We had a Chartist here the other day, but he did not understand our case at all.'

'I heard him,' said Master Nixon; 'but what's his Five Points to us? Why, he ayn't got tommy among them.'

'Nor long stints,' said Waghorn.

'Nor butties,' said Juggins.

'He's a pretty fellow to come and talk to us,' said a collier. 'He had never been down a pit in all his life.'

The evening passed away in the tap-room of the Rising Sun in reflections on the present critical state of affairs, and in consultations as to the most expedient course for the future. The rate of wages, which for several years in this district had undergone a continuous depression, had just received another downward impulse, and was threatened with still further reduction, for the price of iron became every day lower in the market, and the article itself so little in demand that few but the great capitalists who could afford to accumulate their produce were able to maintain their furnaces in action. The little men who still continued their speculations could only do so partially, by diminishing the days of service and increasing their stints or toil, and by decreasing the rate of wages as well as paying them entirely in goods, of which they had a great stock, and of which they thus relieved themselves at a high profit. Add to all these causes of suffering and discontent among the workmen the apprehension of still greater evils, and the tyranny of the butties or middlemen, and it will with little difficulty be felt that the public mind of this district was well prepared for the excitement of the political agitator, especially if he were discreet enough rather to descant on their physical sufferings and personal injuries, than to attempt the propagation of abstract political principles, with which it was impossible for them to sympathise with the impulse and facility of the inhabitants of manufacturing towns, members of literary and scientific institutes, habitual readers of political journals, and accustomed to habits of discussion of all public questions. It generally happens, however, that where a mere physical impulse urges the people to insurrection, though it is often an influence of slow growth and movement, the effects are more violent, and sometimes more obstinate, than when they move under the blended authority of moral and physical necessity, and mix up together the rights and the wants of Man.

However this may be, on the morning after the conversation at the Rising Sun which we have just noticed, the population having as usual gone to their work, having penetrated the pit, and descended the shaft, the furnaces all blazing, the chimneys all smoking, suddenly there rose a rumour even in the bowels of the earth, that the hour and the man had at length arrived: the hour that was to bring them relief, and the man that was to bear them redress.

'My missus told it me at the pit-head, when she brought me my breakfast,' said a pikeman to his comrade, and he struck a vigorous blow at the broad seam on which he was working.

'It is not ten mile,' said his companion. 'They'll be here by noon.'

'There is a good deal to do in their way,' said the first pikeman. 'All men at work after notice to be ducked, they say, and every engine to be stopped forthwith.'

'Will the police meet them before they reach this?'

'There is none: my missus says that not a man John of them is to be seen. The Hell-cats, as they call themselves, halt at every town and offer fifty pounds for a live policeman.'

'I'll tell you what,' said the second pikeman, 'I'll stop my stint and go up the shaft. My heart's all of a flutter: I can't work no more. We'll have a fair day's wage for a fair day's work yet.'

'Come along, I'm your man; if the doggy stop us, we'll knock him down. The people must have their rights; we're driven to this; but if one shilling a day is dropped, why not two?'

'Very true; the people must have their rights, and eight hours' work is quite enough.'

In the light of day, the two miners soon learnt in more detail the news which the wife of one of them earlier in the morning had given as a rumour. There seemed now no doubt that the people of Wodgate, commonly called the Hell-cats, headed by their Bishop, had invaded in great force the surrounding district, stopped all the engines, turned all the potters out of the manufactories, met with no resistance from the authorities, and issued a decree that labour was to cease until the Charter was the law of the land.

This last edict was not the least surprising part of the whole affair; for no one could have imagined that the Bishop or any of his subjects had ever even heard of the Charter, much less that they could by any circumstances comprehend its nature, or by any means be induced to believe that its operation would further their interests or redress their grievances. But all this had been brought about, as most of the great events of history, by the unexpected and unobserved influence of individual character.

A Chartist leader had been residing for some time at Wodgate, ever since the distress had become severe, and had obtained great influence and popularity by assuring a suffering and half-starving population that they were entitled to four shillings a-day and two pots of ale, and only eight hours' work. He was a man of abilities and of popular eloquence, and his representations produced an effect; their reception invested him with influence, and as he addressed a population who required excitement, being slightly employed and with few resources for their vacant hours, the Chartist, who was careful never to speak of the Charter, became an important personage at Wodgate, and was much patronised by Bishop Hatton and his Lady, whose good offices he was sedulous to conciliate. At the right moment, everything being ripe and well prepared, the Bishop being very drunk and harassed by the complaints of his subjects, the Chartist revealed to him the mysteries of the Charter, and persuaded him not only that the Five Points* would cure everything, but that he was the only man who could carry the Five Points. The Bishop had nothing to do; he was making a lock merely for amusement: he required action; he embraced the Charter, without having a definite idea what it meant, but he embraced it fervently, and he determined to march into the country at the head of the population of Wodgate, and establish the faith.

Since the conversion of Constantine, a more important adoption had never occurred. The whole of the north of England and a great part of the midland counties were in a state of disaffection; the entire country was suffering; hope had deserted the labouring classes; they had no confidence in any future of the existing system. Their organisation, independent of the political system of the Chartists, was complete. Every

trade had its union, and every union its lodge in every town
and its central committee in every district. All that was required was the first move, and the Chartist emissary had long
fixed upon Wodgate as the spring of the explosion, when the
news of the strike in Lancashire determined him to precipitate
the event.

The march of Bishop Hatton at the head of the Hell-cats
into the mining districts was perhaps the most striking popular movement since the Pilgrimage of Grace.* Mounted on a
white mule, wall-eyed and of hideous form, the Bishop brandished a huge hammer with which he had announced that he
would destroy the enemies of the people: all butties, doggies,
dealers in truck and tommy, middle masters and main masters.
Some thousand Hell-cats followed him, brandishing bludgeons, or armed with bars of iron, pick-handles, and hammers.
On each side of the Bishop, on a donkey, was one of his little
sons, as demure and earnest as if he were handling his file. A
flowing standard of silk, inscribed with the Charter, and which
had been presented to him by the delegate, was borne before
him like the oriflamme. Never was such a gaunt, grim crew.
As they advanced, their numbers continually increased, for
they arrested all labour in their progress. Every engine was
stopped, the plug was driven out of every boiler, every fire
was extinguished, every man was turned out. The decree
went forth that labour was to cease until the Charter was the
law of the land: the mine and the mill, the foundry and the
loomshop, were, until that consummation, to be idle: nor
was the mighty pause to be confined to these great enterprises.
Every trade of every kind and description was to be stopped:
tailor and cobbler, brushmaker and sweep, tinker and carter,
mason and builder, all, all; for all an enormous Sabbath, that
was to compensate for any incidental suffering which it induced by the increased means and the elevated condition that
it ultimately would insure; that paradise of artisans, that
Utopia of Toil, embalmed in those ringing words, sounds
cheerful to the Saxon race: 'A fair day's wage for a fair day's
work.'

CHAPTER 7

DURING the strike in Lancashire the people had never plundered, except a few provision shops chiefly rifled by boys, and their acts of violence had been confined to those with whom they were engaged in what, on the whole, might be described as a fair contest. They solicited sustenance often in great numbers, but even then their language was mild and respectful, and they were easily satisfied and always grateful. A body of two thousand persons, for example (the writer speaks of circumstances within his own experience), quitted one morning a manufacturing town in Lancashire, when the strike had continued for some time and began to be severely felt, and made a visit to a neighbouring squire of high degree. They entered his park in order, men, women, and children, and then, seating themselves in the immediate vicinity of the mansion, they sent a deputation to announce that they were starving and to entreat relief. In the instance in question, the lord of the domain was absent in the fulfilment of those public duties which the disturbed state of the country devolved on him. His wife, who had a spirit equal to the occasion, notwithstanding the presence of her young children, who might well have aggravated feminine fears, received the deputation herself; told them that of course she was unprepared to feed so many, but that, if they promised to maintain order and conduct themselves with decorum, she would take measures to satisfy their need. They gave their pledge and remained tranquilly encamped while preparations were making to satisfy them. Carts were sent to a neighbouring town for provisions; the keepers killed what they could, and in a few hours the multitude were fed without the slightest disturbance, or the least breach of their self-organised discipline. When all was over, the deputation waited again on the lady to express to her their gratitude; and, the gardens of this house being of celebrity in the neighbourhood, they requested permission that the people might be allowed to walk through them, pledging themselves that no flower should be plucked and no fruit touched. The permission was granted: the multitude, in order, each file under a chief and each commander of the files obedient to a superior officer, then made a progress through the beautiful gardens of their beautiful hostess. They even passed through the forcing houses and vineries. Not a border was trampled on, not a grape plucked; and, when they quitted the domain, they gave three cheers for the fair castellan.

The Hell-cats and their followers were of a different temper from these gentle Lancashire insurgents. They destroyed and ravaged; sacked and gutted houses; plundered cellars; proscribed bakers as enemies of the people; sequestrated the universal stores of all truck and tommy shops; burst open doors, broke windows; destroyed the gas-works, that the towns at night might be in darkness; took union workhouses by storm, burned rate-books in the market-place, and ordered public distribution of loaves of bread and flitches of bacon to a mob; cheering and laughing amid flames and rapine. In short, they robbed and rioted; the police could make no head against them; there was no military force; the whole district was in their possession; and, hearing that a battalion of the Coldstreams were coming down by a train, the Bishop ordered all railroads to be destroyed, and, if the Hell-cats had not been too drunk to do his bidding and he too tipsy to repeat it, it is probable that a great destruction of these public ways might have taken place.

Does the reader remember Diggs' tommy shop? And Master Joseph? Well, a terrible scene took place there. The Wodgate girl, with a back like a grasshopper, of the Baptist school religion, who had married Tummas, once a pupil of the Bishop, and still his fervent follower, although he had cut open his pupil's head, was the daughter of a man who had worked many years in Diggs' field, had suffered much under his intolerable yoke, and at the present moment was deep in his awful ledger. She had heard from her first years of the oppression of Diggs, and had impressed it on her husband, who was intolerant of any tyranny except at Wodgate. Tummas and his wife, and a few chosen friends, therefore, went out one morning to settle the tommy-book of her father with Mr. Diggs. A whisper of their intention had got about among those interested in the subject. It was a fine summer morning, some three hours from noon; the shop was shut, indeed it had not been opened since the riots, and all the lower windows of the dwelling were closed, barred, and bolted.

A crowd of women had collected. There was Mistress Page and Mistress Prance, old Dame Toddles and Mrs. Mullins, Liza Gray and the comely dame, who was so fond of society that she liked even a riot.

'Master Joseph, they say, has gone to the North,' said the comely dame.

'I wonder if old Diggs is at home?' said Mrs. Mullins.

'He won't show, I'll be sworn,' said old Dame Toddles.

'Here are the Hell-cats,' said the comely dame. 'Well, I do declare, they march like reglars; two, four, six, twelve; a good score at the least.'

The Hell-cats briskly marched up to the elm-trees that shaded the canal before the house, and then formed in line opposite to it. They were armed with bludgeons, crowbars, and hammers. Tummas was at the head, and by his side his Wodgate wife. Stepping forth alone, amid the cheering of the crowd of women, the pupil of the Bishop advanced to the door of Diggs' house, gave a loud knock, and a louder ring. He waited patiently for several minutes: there was no reply from the interior, and then Tummas knocked and rang again.

'It's very awful,' said the comely dame.

'It's what I always dreamt would come to pass,' said Liza Gray, 'ever since Master Joseph cut my poor baby over the eye with his three-foot rule.'

'I think there can be nobody within,' said Mrs. Prance.

'Old Diggs would never leave the tommy without a guard,' said Mrs. Page.

'Now, lads,' said Tummas, looking round him and making a sign; and immediately some half dozen advanced with their crowbars and were about to strike at the door, when a window in the upper story of the house opened, and the muzzle of a blunderbuss was presented at the assailants.

The women all screamed and ran away.

' 'Twas Master Joseph,' said the comely dame, halting to regain her breath.

' 'Twas Master Joseph,' sighed Mrs. Page.

' 'Twas Master Joseph,' moaned Mrs. Prance.

'Sure enough,' said Mrs. Mullins, 'I saw his ugly face.'

'More frightful than the great gun,' said old Dame Toddles.

'I hope the children will get out of the way,' said Liza Gray, 'for he is sure to fire on them.'

In the meantime, while Master Joseph himself was content with his position and said not a word, a benignant countenance exhibited itself at the window, and requested in a mild voice to know, 'What his good friends wanted there?'

'We have come to settle Sam Barlow's tommy-book,' said their leader.

'Our shop is not open to-day, my good friends: the account can stand over; far be it from me to press the poor.'

'Master Diggs,' said a Hell-cat, 'canst thou tell us the price of bacon to-day?'

'Well, good bacon,' said the elder Diggs, willing to humour them, 'may be eightpence a pound.'

'Thou art wrong, Master Diggs,' said the Hell-cat, ' 'tis fourpence and long credit. Let us see half a dozen good flitches at fourpence, Master Diggs; and be quick.'

There was evidently some controversy in the interior as to the course at this moment to be pursued. Master Joseph remonstrated against the policy of concession, called conciliation, which his father would fain follow, and was for instant coercion; but age and experience carried the day, and in a few minutes some flitches were thrown out of the window to the Hell-cats, who received the booty with a cheer.

The women returned.

' 'Tis the tenpence a pound flitch,' said the comely dame, examining the prize with a sparkling glance.

'I have paid as much for very green stuff,' said Mrs. Mullins.

'And now, Master Diggs,' said Tummas, 'what is the price of the best tea a-pound? We be good customers, and mean to treat our wives and sweethearts here. I think we must order half a chest.'

This time there was a greater delay in complying with the gentle hint; but, the Hell-cats getting obstreperous, the tea was at length furnished and divided among the women. This gracious office devolved on the wife of Tummas, who soon found herself assisted by a spontaneous committee, of which the comely dame was the most prominent and active member.

Nothing could be more considerate, good-natured, and offici-ous, than the mode and spirit with which she divided the stores. The flitches were cut up and apportioned in like man-ner. The scene was as gay and bustling as a fair.

'It is as good as grand tommy-day,' said the comely dame, with a self-complacent smile, as she strutted about, smiling and dispensing patronage.

The orders for bacon and tea were followed by a popular demand for cheese. The female committee received all the plunder and were active in its distribution. At length, a rumour got about that Master Joseph was entering the names of all present in the tommy-books, so that eventually the score might be satisfied. The mob had now much increased. There was a panic among the women, and indignation among the men: a Hell-cat advanced and announced that, unless the tommy-books were all given up to be burnt, they would pull down the house. There was no reply; some of the Hell-cats advanced; the women cheered; a crowbar fell upon the door; Master Joseph fired, wounded a woman and killed a child.

There rose one of those universal shrieks of wild passion which announce that men have discarded all the trammels of civilisation, and found in their licentious rage new and un-foreseen sources of power and vengeance. Where it came from, how it was obtained, who prompted the thought, who first accomplished it, were alike impossible to trace; but, as it were in a moment, a number of trusses of straw were piled up before the house and set on fire, the gates of the timber-yard were forced, and a quantity of scantlings and battens soon fed the flame. Everything indeed that could stimulate the fire was employed; and every one was occupied in the service. They ran to the water side and plundered the barges, and threw the huge blocks of coal upon the enormous bonfire. Men, women, and children were alike at work with the eager-ness and energy of fiends. The roof of the house caught fire: the dwelling burned rapidly; you could see the flames like the tongues of wild beasts, licking the bare and vanishing walls; a single being was observed amid the fiery havoc, shrieking and desperate; he clung convulsively to a huge account-book. It was Master Joseph. His father had made his escape from the back of the premises and had counselled his

son instantly to follow him, but Master Joseph wished to
rescue the ledger as well as their lives, and the delay ruined him.

'He has got the tommy-book,' cried Liza Gray.

The glare of the clear flame fell for a moment upon his
countenance of agony; the mob gave an infernal cheer; then,
some part of the building falling in, there rose a vast cloud of
smoke and rubbish, and he was seen no more.

CHAPTER 8

'LIFE's a tumble-about thing of ups and downs,' said Widow
Carey, stirring her tea, 'but I have been down this time longer
than I can ever remember.'

'Nor ever will get up, widow,' said Julia, at whose lodgings herself and several of Julia's friends had met, 'unless we
have the Five Points.'

'I will never marry any man who is not for the Five Points,'
said Caroline.

'I should be ashamed to marry any one who had not the
suffrage,' said Harriet.

'He is no better than a slave,' said Julia.

The widow shook her head. 'I don't like these politics,'
said the good woman, 'they bayn't in a manner of business
for our sex.'

'And I should like to know why?' said Julia. 'Ayn't we as
much concerned in the cause of good government as the
men? And don't we understand as much about it? I am sure
the Dandy never does anything without consulting me.'

'It's fine news for a summer day,' said Caroline, 'to say we
can't understand politics, with a Queen on the throne.'

'She has got her ministers to tell her what to do,' said
Mrs. Carey, taking a pinch of snuff. 'Poor innocent young
creature, it often makes my heart ache to think how she is
beset.'

'Over the left,' said Julia. 'If the ministers try to come into
her bed-chamber, she knows how to turn them to the right
about.'

'And as for that,' said Harriet, 'why are we not to interfere
with politics as much as the swell ladies in London?'

'Don't you remember, too, at the last election here,' said

Caroline, 'how the fine ladies from the Castle came and canvassed for Colonel Rosemary?'

'Ah!' said Julia, 'I must say I wish the Colonel had beat that horrid Muddlefist. If we can't have our own man, I am all for the Nobs against the Middle Class.'

'We'll have our own man soon, I expect,' said Harriet. 'If the people don't work, how are the aristocracy to pay the police?'

'Only think!' said Widow Carey, shaking her head. 'Why, at your time of life, my dears, we never even heard of these things, much less talked of them.'

'I should think you didn't, widow, and because why?' said Julia; 'because there was no march of mind* then. But we know the time of day now as well as any of them.'

'Lord, my dear,' said Mrs. Carey; 'what's the use of all that? What we want is, good wages and plenty to do; and as for the rest, I don't grudge the Queen her throne, nor the noblemen and gentlemen their good things. Live and let live say I.'

'Why you are a regular oligarch, widow,' said Harriet.

'Well, Miss Harriet,' replied Mrs. Carey, a little nettled, ' 'tisn't calling your neighbours names that settles any question. I'm quite sure that Julia will agree to that, and Caroline too. And perhaps I might call you something if I chose, Miss Harriet; I've heard things said before this that I should blush to say, and blush to hear too. But I won't demean myself, no I won't. Holly-hock, indeed! Why holly-hock?'

At this moment entered the Dandy and Devilsdust.

'Well, young ladies,' said the Dandy. 'A-swelling the receipt of customs by the consumption of Congo!* That won't do, Julia; it won't, indeed. Ask Dusty. If you want to beat the enemy, you must knock up the revenue. How d'ye do, widow?'

'The same to you, Dandy Mick. We is deploring the evils of the times here in a neighbourly way.'

'Oh, the times will soon mend,' said the Dandy, gaily.

'Well, so I think.' said the widow; 'for when things are at the worst, they always say ——'

'But you always say they cannot mend, Mick,' said Julia, interrupting her.

'Why in a sense, Julia, in a certain sense, you are right; but there are two senses to everything, my girl,' and Mick began singing, and then executed a hornpipe, to the gratification of Julia and her guests.

' 'Tis genteel,' said Mick, receiving their approbation. 'You remember it at the Circus?'

'I wonder when we shall have the Circus again?' said Caroline.

'Not with the present rate of wages,' said Devilsdust.

'It's very hard,' said Caroline, 'that the Middle Class are always dropping our wages. One really has no amusements now. How I do miss the Temple!'

'We'll have the Temple open again before long,' said the Dandy.

'That will be sweet!' exclaimed Caroline. 'I often dream of that foreign nobleman who used to sing "Oh, no, we never!" '

'Well, I cannot make out what puts you in such spirits, Mick,' said Julia. 'You told me only this morning that the thing was up, and that we should soon be slaves for life; working sixteen hours a-day for no wages, and living on oatmeal porridge and potatoes, served out by the millocrats like a regular Bastile.'

'But, as Madam Carey says, when things are at the worst ——'

'Oh! I did say it,' said the widow, 'surely, because you see, at my years, I have seen so many ups and downs, though I always say ——'

'Come, Dusty,' said Julia, 'you are more silent than ever. You won't take a dish, I know; but tell us the news, for I am sure you have something to say.'

'I should think we had,' said Dusty.

Here all the girls began talking at the same time, and, without waiting for the intelligence, favouring one another with their guesses of its import.

'I am sure its Shuffle and Screw going to work half time,' said Harriet; 'I always said so.'

'It's something to put down the people,' said Julia. 'I suppose the Nobs have met, and are going to drop wages again.'

'I think Dusty is going to be married,' said Caroline.

'Not at this rate of wages, I should hope,' said Mrs. Carey, getting in a word.

'I should think not,' said Devilsdust. 'You are a sensible woman, Mrs. Carey. And I don't know exactly what you mean, Miss Caroline,' he added, a little confused. For Devilsdust was a silent admirer of Caroline, and had been known to say to Mick, who told Julia, who told her friend, that if he ever found time to think of such things, that was the sort of girl he should like to make the partner of his life.

'But, Dusty,' said Julia, 'now what is it?'

'Why, I thought you all knew,' said Mick.

'Now, now,' said Julia, 'I hate suspense. I like news to go round like a fly-wheel.'

'Well,' said Devilsdust, drily, 'this is Saturday, young women, and Mrs. Carey, too, you will not deny that.'

'I should think not,' said Mrs. Carey, 'by the token I kept a stall for thirty year in our market and, never gave it up till this summer, which makes me always think that, though I have seen many up and downs, this ———'

'Well, what has Saturday to do with us?' said Caroline; 'for neither Dandy Mick nor you can take us to the Temple, or any other genteel place, since they are all shut, from the Corn Laws, or some other cause or other.'

'I believe it's the machines more than the Corn Laws that have shut up the Temple,' said Harriet. 'Machines, indeed! Fancy preferring a piece of iron or wood to your own flesh and blood! And they call that Christianlike!'

'It is Saturday,' said Julia, 'sure enough; and if I don't lie in bed to-morrow till sunset, may I get a bate ticket for every day for a week to come.'

'Well, go it, my hearty!' said Mick to Devilsdust. 'It is Saturday, that they have all agreed.'

'And to-morrow is Sunday,' said Devilsdust, solemnly.

'And next day is the blackest day in all the week,' said Julia. 'When I hear the factory bell on Monday morning, I feel just the same as I did when I crossed with my uncle from Liverpool to Seaton to eat shrimps. Wasn't I sick coming home, that's all!'

'You won't hear that bell sound next Monday,' said Devilsdust, solemnly.

'You don't mean that?' said Julia.

'Why, what's the matter?' said Caroline. 'Is the Queen dead?'

'No bell on Monday morning?' said Mrs. Carey, incredulously.

'Not a single ring, if all the Capitalists in Mowbray were to pull together at the same rope,' said Devilsdust.

'What can't it be?' said Julia. 'Come, Mick; Dusty is always so long telling us anything.'

'Why, we are going to have the devil's own strike,' said Mick, unable any longer to contain himself, and dancing with glee.

'A strike!' said Julia.

'I hope they will destroy the machines,' said Harriet.

'And open the Temple,' said Caroline, 'or else it will be very dull.'

'I have seen a many strikes,' said the widow; 'but as Chaffing Jack was saying to me the other day ——'

'Chaffing Jack be hanged!' said Mick. 'Such a slow coach won't do in these high-pressure times. We are going to do the trick, and no mistake. There shan't be a capitalist in England who can get a day's work out of us, even if he makes the operatives his junior partners.'

'I never heard of such things,' said Mrs. Carey, in amazement.

'It's all booked, though,' said Devilsdust. 'We'll clean out the Savings Banks;* the Benefits and Burials will shell out. I am treasurer of the Ancient Shepherds,* and we passed a resolution yesterday unanimously, that we would devote all our funds to the sustenance of Labour in this its last and triumphant struggle against Capital.'

'Lor!' said Caroline; 'I think it will be very jolly.'

'As long as you can give us money, I don't care, for my part, how long we stick out,' said Julia.

'Well,' said Mrs Carey. 'I didn't think there was so much spirit in the place. As Chaffing Jack was saying the other day ——'

'There is no spirit in the place,' said Devilsdust, 'but we mean to infuse some. Some of our friends are going to pay you a visit to-morrow.'

'And who may they be?' said Caroline.

'To-morrow is Sunday,' said Devilsdust, 'and the miners mean to say their prayers in Mowbray Church.'

'Well, that will be a shindy!' said Caroline.

'It's a true bill, though,' said Mick. 'This time to-morrow you will have ten thousand of them in this town, and if every mill and work in it and ten mile round is not stopped, my name is not MICK RADLEY.'

CHAPTER 9

IT was Monday morning. Hatton, enveloped in his chamber robe and wearing his velvet cap, was lounging in the best room of the principal commercial inn of Mowbray, over a breakfast-table covered with all the delicacies of which a northern matin meal may justly boast. There were pies of spiced meat and trout fresh from the stream, hams that Westphalia never equalled, pyramids of bread of every form and flavour adapted to the surrounding fruits, some conserved with curious art, and some just gathered from the bed or from the tree.

'It is very odd,' said Hatton to his companion Morley, 'you can't get coffee anywhere.'

Morley, who had supposed that coffee was about the commonest article of consumption in Mowbray, looked a little surprised; but at this moment Hatton's servant entered with a mysterious yet somewhat triumphant air, ushering in a travelling biggin* of their own, fuming like one of the springs of Geyser.

'Now try that,' said Hatton to Morley, as the servant poured him out a cup; 'you won't find that so bad.'

'Does the town continue pretty quiet?' inquired Morley of the servant, as he was leaving the room.

'Quite quiet, I believe, sir, but a great many people in the streets. All the mills are stopped.'

'Well, this is a strange business,' said Hatton, when they were once more alone. 'You had no idea of it when I met you on Saturday?'

'None; on the contrary, I felt convinced that there were no elements of general disturbance in this district. I thought from the first that the movement would be confined to Lancashire and would easily be arrested; but the feebleness of the government, the want of decision, perhaps the want of means, have permitted a flame to spread, the extinction of which will not soon be witnessed.'

'Do you meant that?'

'Whenever the mining population is disturbed, the disorder is obstinate. On the whole, they endure less physical suffering than most of the working classes, their wages being considerable; and they are so brutalised that they are more difficult to operate on than our reading and thinking population of the factories. But, when they do stir, there is always violence and a determined course. When I heard of their insurrection on Saturday, I was prepared for great disturbances in their district; but that they should suddenly resolve to invade another country, as it were, the seat of another class of labour, and where the hardships, however severe, are not of their own kind, is to me amazing, and convinces me that there is some political head behind the scenes, and that this move, however unintentional on the part of the miners themselves, is part of some comprehensive scheme which, by widening the scene of action and combining several counties and classes of labour in the broil, must inevitably embarrass and perhaps paralyse the government.'

'There is a good deal in what you say,' said Hatton, taking a strawberry with rather an absent air; and then he added, 'You remember a conversation we once had, the eve of my departure from Mowbray in '39?'

'I do,' said Morley, reddening.

'The miners were not so ready then,' said Hatton.

'They were not,' said Morley, speaking with some confusion.

'Well they are here now,' said Hatton.

'They are,' said Morley, thoughtfully, but more collected.

'You saw them enter yesterday?' said Hatton. 'I was sorry I missed it, but I was taking a walk with the Gerards up Dale, to see the cottage where they once lived, and which they used to talk so much about! Was it a strong body?'

'I should say about two thousand men, and, as far as bludgeons and iron staves go, armed.'

'A formidable force with no military to encounter them.'

'Irresistible, especially with a favourable population.'

'You think the people were not grieved to see them?'

'Certainly. Left alone, they might have remained quiet; but they only wanted the spark. We have a number of young men here who have for a long time been murmuring against our inaction and what they call want of spirit. The Lancashire strike set them all agog; and, had any popular leader, Gerard for example, or Warner, resolved to move, they were ready.'

'The times are critical,' said Hatton, wheeling his armchair from the table and resting his feet on the empty fireplace. 'Lord de Mowbray had no idea of all this. I was with him on my way here, and found him quite tranquil. I suppose the invasion of yesterday has opened his eyes a little.'

'What can he do?' said Morley. 'It is useless to apply to the government. They have no force to spare. Look at Lancashire: a few dragoons and rifles, hurried about from place to place and harassed by night service; always arriving too late, and generally attacking the wrong point; some diversion from the main scheme. Now, we had a week ago some of the 17th Lancers here. They have been marched into Lancashire. Had they remained, the invasion would never have occurred.'

'You haven't a soldier at hand?'

'Not a man; they have actually sent for a party of the 73rd from Ireland to guard us. Mowbray may be burnt before they land.'

'And the castle too,' said Hatton, quietly. 'These are indeed critical times, Mr. Morley. I was thinking, when walking with our friend Gerard yesterday, and hearing him and his charming daughter dilate upon the beauties of the residence which they had forfeited, I was thinking what a strange thing life is, and that the fact of a box of papers belonging to him being in the possession of another person who only lives close by, for we were walking through Mowbray woods ——'

At this moment a waiter entered, and said there was one without who wished to speak with Mr. Morley.

'Let him come up,' said Hatton; 'he will give us some news, perhaps.'

And there was accordingly shown up a young man who
had been a member of the Convention in '39 with Morley,
afterwards of the Secret Council with Gerard, the same young
man who had been the first arrested on the night that Sybil
was made a prisoner, having left the scene of their deliberations
for a moment in order to fetch her some water. He too
had been tried, convicted, and imprisoned, though for a
shorter time than Gerard; and he was the Chartist Apostle
who had gone, and resided at Wodgate, preached the faith to
the barbarians, converted them, and was thus the primary
cause of the present invasion of Mowbray.

'Ah! Field,' said Morley, 'is it you?'

'You are surprised to see me;' and then the young man
looked at Hatton.

'A friend,' said Morley; 'speak as you like.'

'Our great man, the leader and liberator of the people,'
said Field, with a smile, 'who has carried all before him, and
who, I verily believe, will carry all before him, for Providence
has given him those superhuman energies which can alone
emancipate a race, wishes to confer with you on the state of
this town and neighbourhood. It has been represented to him
that no one is more knowing and experienced than yourself
in this respect; besides, as the head of our most influential
organ in the Press, it is in every way expedient that you should
see him. He is at this moment below, giving instructions and
receiving reports of the stoppage of all the country works;
but, if you like, I will bring him up here, we shall be less disturbed.'

'By all means,' said Hatton, who seemed to apprehend that
Morley would make some difficulties. 'By all means.'

'Stop,' said Morley; 'have you seen Gerard?'

'No,' said Field. 'I wrote to him some time back, but his
reply was not encouraging. I thought his spirit was perhaps
broken.'

'You know that he is here?'

'I concluded so, but we have not seen him; though, to be
sure, we have seen so many and done so much since our
arrival yesterday, it is not wonderful. By-the-bye, who is this
black-coat you have here, this St. Lys? We took possession
of the church yesterday on our arrival, for it is a sort of thing

that pleases the miners and colliers wonderfully, and I always humour them. This St. Lys preached us such a sermon that I was almost 'afraid at one time the game would be spoiled. Our great man was alarmingly taken by it, was saying his prayers all day, and had nearly marched back again: had it not been for the excellence of the rum-and-water at our quarters, the champion of the Charter would have proved a pious recreant.'

'St. Lys will trouble you,' said Morley. 'Alas, for poor human nature, when violence can only be arrested by superstition!'

'Come, don't you preach,' said the Chartist. 'The Charter is a thing the people can understand, especially when they are masters of the country; but as for moral force, I should like to know how I could have marched from Wodgate to Mowbray with that on my banner.'

'Wodgate,' said Morley, 'that's a queer place.'

'Wodgate,' said Hatton; 'what Wodgate is that?'

At this moment a great noise sounded without the room, the door was banged, there seemed a scuffling, some harsh high tones, the deprecatory voices of many waiters. The door was banged again, and this time flew open; while exclaiming in an insolent coarse voice, 'Don't tell me of your private rooms; who is master here, I should like to know?' there entered a very thick-set man, rather under the middle size, with a brutal and grimy countenance, wearing the unbuttoned coat of a police serjeant conquered in fight, a cocked hat, with a white plume, which was also a trophy of war, a pair of leather breeches and topped boots, which from their antiquity had the appearance of being his authentic property. This was the leader and liberator of the people of England. He carried in his hand a large hammer, which he had never parted with during the whole of the insurrection; and, stopping when he had entered the room and surveying its inmates with an air at once stupid and arrogant, recognising Field the Chartist, he hallooed out, 'I tell you I want him. He's my Lord Chancellor and Prime Minister, my head and principal Doggy; I can't go on without him. Well, what do you think?' he said, advancing to Field; 'here's a pretty go! They won't stop the works at the big country mill you were talking of. They won't, won't they? Is my word the law of the land, or is it not? Have I given my commands that all labour shall cease till the Queen sends me a message that the Charter is established, and is a man who has a mill to shut his gates upon my forces, and pump upon my people with engines? There shall be fire for this water;' and, so saying, the Liberator sent his hammer with such force upon the table, that the plate and porcelain and accumulated luxuries of Mr. Hatton's breakfast perilously vibrated.

'We will inquire into this, sir,' said Field, 'and we will take the necessary steps.'

'We will inquire into this, and we will take the necessary steps,' said the Liberator, looking round with an air of pompous stupidity; and then, taking up some peaches, he began devouring them with considerable zest.

'Would the Liberator like to take some breakfast?' said Mr. Hatton.

The Liberator looked at his host with a glance of senseless intimidation, and then, as if not condescending to communicate directly with ordinary men, he uttered in a more subdued tone to the Chartist these words, 'Glass of ale.'

Ale was instantly ordered for the Liberator, who after a copious draught assumed a less menacing air, and smacking his lips, pushed aside the dishes, and sat down on the table, swinging his legs.

'This is my friend of whom I spoke, and whom you wished to see, sir,' said the Chartist; 'the most distinguished advocate of popular rights we possess, the editor of the Mowbray Phalanx, Mr. Morley.'

Morley slightly advanced; he caught the Liberator's eye, who scrutinised him with extreme earnestness, and then, jumping from the table, shouted: 'Why, this is the muff that called on me in Hell-house Yard three years ago.'

'I had that honour,' said Morley, quietly.

'Honour be hanged!' said the Bishop; 'you know something about somebody; I couldn't squeeze you then, but by G—— I will have it out of you now. Now, cut it short; have you seen him, and where does he live?'

'I came then to gain information, not to give it,' said

Morley. 'I had a friend who wished much to see this gentleman ——'

'He ayn't no gentleman,' said the Bishop; 'he's my brother:
but I tell you what, I'll do something for him now. I'm cock
of the walk, you see; and that's a sort of thing that don't
come twice in a man's life. One should feel for one's flesh
and blood; and if I find him out, I'll make his fortune, or my
name is not Simon Hatton.'

The creator and counsellor of peers started in his chair, and
looked aghast. A glance was interchanged between him and
Morley, which revealed their mutual thoughts; and the great
antiquary, looking at the Liberator with a glance of blended
terror and disgust, walked away to the window.

'Suppose you put an advertisement in your paper,' continued the Bishop. 'I know a traveller who lost his keys at the
Yard, and got them back again by those same means. Go on
advertising till you find him, and my Prime Minister and
principal Doggy here shall give you an order on the town-
council for your expenses.'

Morley bowed his thanks in silence.

The Bishop continued: 'What's the name of the man who
has got the big mill here, about three mile off, who won't
stop his works, and ducked my men this morning with his
engines? I'll have fire, I say, for that water; do you hear that,
Master Newspaper? I'll have fire for that water before I am
many hours older.'

'The Liberator means Trafford,' said the Chartist.

'I'll Trafford him,' said the Liberator, brandishing his
hammer. 'He ducks my messenger, does he? I tell you I'll
have fire for that water;' and he looked around him as if he
courted some remonstrance, in order that he might crush it.

'Trafford is a humane man,' said Morley, in a quiet tone,
'and behaves well to his people.'

'A man with a big mill humane!' exclaimed the Bishop;
'with two or three thousand slaves working under the same
roof, and he doing nothing but eating their vitals. I'll have
no big mills where I'm main master. Let him look to it. Here
goes;' and he jumped off the table. 'Before an hour I'll pay
this same Trafford a visit, and I'll see whether he'll duck me.

Come on, my prime Doggy;' and nodding to the Chartist to
follow him, the Liberator left the room.

Hatton turned his head from the window, and advanced
quickly to Morley. 'To business, friend Morley. This savage
cannot be quiet for a moment; he exists only in destruction
and rapine. If it were not Trafford's mill, it would be something else. I am sorry for the Traffords; they have old blood
in their veins. Before sunset their settlement will be razed to
the ground. Can we prevent it? Why not attack the castle,
instead of the mill?'

CHAPTER 10

ABOUT noon of this day there was a great stir in Mowbray.
It was generally whispered about that the Liberator, at the
head of the Hell-cats, and all others who chose to accompany
them, was going to pay a visit to Mr. Trafford's settlement,
in order to avenge an insult which his envoys had experienced
early in the morning, when, accompanied by a rabble of two
or three hundred persons, they had repaired to the Mowedale
works, in order to signify the commands of the Liberator that
labour should stop, and, if necessary, to enforce those commands. The injunctions were disregarded; and when the mob,
in pursuance of their further instructions, began to force the
great gates of the premises, in order that they might enter the
building, drive the plugs out of the steam-boilers, and free the
slaves enclosed, a masqued battery of powerful engines was
suddenly opened upon them, and the whole band of patriots
were deluged. It was impossible to resist a power which
seemed inexhaustible, and, wet to their skins, and amid the
laughter of their adversaries, they fled. This ridiculous catastrophe had terribly excited the ire of the Liberator. He vowed
vengeance, and as, like all great revolutionary characters and
military leaders, the only foundation of his power was constant employment for his troops and constant excitement for
the populace, he determined to place himself at the head of
the chastising force, and make a great example, which should
establish his awful reputation, and spread the terror of his
name throughout the district.

Field, the Chartist, had soon discovered who were the rising spirits of Mowbray, and Devilsdust and Dandy Mick were both sworn on Monday morning of the council of the Liberator, and took their seats at the board accordingly. Devilsdust, used to public business, and to the fulfilment of responsible duties, was calm and grave, but equally ready and determined. Mick's head, on the contrary, was quite turned by the importance of his novel position. He was greatly excited, could devise nothing, and would do anything, always followed Devilsdust in council; but when he executed their joint decrees, and showed himself about the town, he strutted like a peacock, swore at the men, and winked at the girls, and was the idol and admiration of every gaping or huzzaing younker.*

There was a large crowd assembled in the Market Place, in which were the Liberator's lodgings, many of them armed in their rude fashion, and all anxious to march. Devilsdust was with the great man and Field; Mick below was marshalling the men, and swearing like a trooper at all who disobeyed, or who misunderstood him.

'Come, stupid,' said he, addressing Tummas, 'what are you staring about? Get your men in order, or I'll be among you.'

'Stoopid!' said Tummas, staring at Mick with immense astonishment. 'And who are you who says "Stoopid?" A white-livered handloom as I dare say, or a son-of-a-gun of a factory slave. Stoopid, indeed! What next, when a Hell-cat is to be called stoopid by such a thing as you?'

'I'll give you a piece of advice, young man,' said Master Nixon, taking his pipe out of his mouth, and blowing an immense puff: 'just you go down the shaft for a couple of months, and then you'll learn a little of life, which is wery useful.'

The lively temperament of the Dandy would here probably have involved him in an inconvenient embroilment, had not some one at this moment touched him on the shoulder, and, looking round, he recognised Mr. Morley. Notwithstanding the difference of their political schools, Mick had a profound respect for Morley, though why he could not perhaps precisely express. But he had heard Devilsdust for years declare that Stephen Morley was the deepest head in Mowbray; and though he regretted the unfortunate weakness in favour of that imaginary abstraction, called Moral Force, for which the editor of the Phalanx was distinguished, still Devilsdust used to say, that if ever the great revolution were to occur, by which the rights of labour were to be recognised, though bolder spirits and brawnier arms might consummate the change, there was only one head among them that would be capable, when they had gained their power, to guide it for the public weal, and, as Devilsdust used to add, 'carry out the thing,' and that was Morley.

It was a fine summer day, and Mowdale was as resplendent as when Egremont, amid its beauties, first began to muse over the beautiful. There was the same bloom over the sky, the same shadowy lustre on the trees, the same sparkling brilliancy on the waters. A herdsman, following some kine, was crossing the stone bridge; and, except their lowing as they stopped and sniffed the current of fresh air in its centre, there was not a sound.

Suddenly the tramp and hum of a multitude broke upon the sunshiny silence. A vast crowd, with some assumption of an ill-disciplined order, approached from the direction of Mowbray. At their head rode a man on a white mule. Many of his followers were armed with bludgeons and other rude weapons, and moved in files. Behind them spread a more miscellaneous throng, in which women were not wanting, and even children. They moved rapidly; they swept by the former cottage of Gerard; they were in sight of the settlement of Trafford.

'All the waters of the river shall not dout* the blaze that I will light up to-day,' said the Liberator.

'He is a most inveterate Capitalist,' said Field, 'and would divert the minds of the people from the Five Points by allotting them gardens and giving them baths.'

'We will have no more gardens in England; everything shall be open,' said the Liberator, 'and baths shall only be used to drown the enemies of the People. I always was against washing; it takes the marrow out of a man.'

'Here we are,' said Field, as the roofs and bowers of the village, the spire and the spreading factory, broke upon them. 'Every door and every window closed! The settlement is deserted. Some one has been before us, and apprised them of our arrival.'

'Will they pour water on me?' said the Bishop. 'It must be a stream indeed that shall put out the blaze that I am going to light. What shall we do first? Halt, there, you men,' said the Liberator, looking back with that scowl which his apprentices never could forget. 'Will you halt, or won't you? or must I be among you?'

There was a tremulous shuffling, and then a comparative silence.

The women and children of the village had been gathered into the factory yard, the great gates of which were closed.

'What shall we burn first?' asked the Bishop.

'We may as well parley with them a little,' said Field; 'perhaps we may contrive to gain admission, and then we can sack the whole affair and let the people burn the machinery. It will be a great moral lesson.'

'As long as there is burning,' said the Bishop, 'I don't care what lessons you teach them. I leave them to you, but I will have fire to put out that water.'

'I will advance,' said Field; and so saying, he went forward and rang at the gate; the Bishop, on his mule, with a dozen Hell-cats accompanying him; the great body of the people about twenty yards withdrawn.

'Who rings?' asked a loud voice.

'One who, by the order of the Liberator, wishes to enter and see whether his commands for a complete cessation of labour have been complied with in this establishment.'

'Very good,' said the Bishop.

'There is no hand at work here,' said the voice; 'and you may take my word for it.'

'Your word be hanged,' said the Bishop. 'I want to know ——'

'Hush, hush!' said Field; and then in a louder voice he said, 'It may be so; but as our messengers this morning were not permitted to enter, and were treated with great indignity ——'

'That's it,' said the Bishop.

'With great indignity,' continued Field, 'we must have ocular experience of the state of affairs, and I beg and recommend you therefore at once to let the Liberator enter.'

'None shall enter here,' replied the unseen guardian of the gate.

'That's enough,' cried the Bishop.

'Beware!' said Field.

'Whether you let us in or not, 'tis all the same,' said the Bishop; 'I will have fire for your water, and I have come for that. Now, lads!'

'Stop,' said the voice of the unseen. 'I will speak to you.'

'He is going to let us in,' whispered Field to the Bishop.

And suddenly there appeared on the flat roof of the lodge that was on one side of the gates, Gerard. His air, his figure, his position were alike commanding, and at the sight of him a loud and spontaneous cheer burst from the assembled thousands. It was the sight of one who was, after all, the most popular leader of the people that had ever figured in these parts, whose eloquence charmed and commanded, whose disinterestedness was acknowledged, whose sufferings had created sympathy, whose courage, manly bearing, and famous feats of strength were a source to them of pride. There was not a Mowbray man whose heart did not throb with emotion, and whose memory did not recall the orations from the Druid's altar and the famous meetings on the moor. 'Gerard for ever!' was the universal shout.

The Bishop, who liked no one to be cheered except himself, like many great men, was much disgusted, a little perplexed. 'What does all this mean?' he whispered to Field. 'I came here to burn down the place.'

'Wait awhile,' said Field, 'we must humour the Mowbray men a bit. This is their favourite leader, at least was in old days. I know him well; he is a bold and honest man.'

'Is this the man who ducked my people?' asked the Bishop, fiercely.

'Hush!' said Field; 'he is going to speak.'

'My friends,' said Gerard, 'for if we are not friends, who should be? (loud cheers, and cries of "Very true,") if you come here to learn whether the Mowedale works are stopped, I give you my word there is not a machine or man that stirs here at this moment (great cheering). I believe you'll take my word (cheers and cries of "We will"). I believe I'm known at Mowbray ("Gerard for ever!"), and on Mowbray Moor too (tumultuous cheering). We have met together before this ("That we have"), and shall meet again yet (great cheering). The people haven't so many friends that they should quarrel with well-wishers. The master here has done his best to soften your lots. He is not one of those who deny that Labour has rights (loud cheers). I say that Mr. Trafford has always acknowledged the rights of Labour (prolonged cheers, and cries of "So he has"). Well, is he the man that we should injure? ("No, no.") What if he did give a cold reception to some visitors this morning (groans); perhaps they wore faces he was not used to (loud cheers and laughter from the Mowbray people). I dare say they mean as well as we do; no doubt of that; but still a neighbour's a neighbour (immense cheering). Now, my lads, three cheers for the National Holiday;' and Gerard gave the time, and his voice was echoed by the thousands present. 'The master here has no wish to interfere with the National Holiday; all he wants to secure is that all mills and works should alike stop (cries of "Very just"). And I say so, too,' continued Gerard. 'It is just; just and manly, and like a true-born Englishman, as he is, who loves the people, and whose fathers before him loved the people (great cheering). Three cheers for Mr. Trafford, I say;' and they were given; 'and three cheers for Mrs. Trafford too, the friend of the poor!' Here the mob became not only enthusiastic, but maudlin; all vowing to each other that Trafford was a true-born Englishman and his wife a very good angel upon earth. This popular feeling is so contagious that even the Hell-cats shared it, cheering, shaking hands with each other, and almost shedding tears, though, it must be confessed, they had some vague idea that it was all to end in something to drink.

Their great leader, however, remained unmoved, and nothing but his brutal stupidity could have prevented him from endeavouring to arrest the tide of public feeling; but he was quite bewildered by the diversion, and for the first time failed in finding a prompter in Field. The Chartist was cowed by Gerard; his old companion in scenes that the memory lingered over, and whose superior genius had often controlled and often led him. Gerard, too, had recognised him, and had made some personal allusion and appeal to him, which alike touched his conscience and flattered his vanity. The ranks were broken, the spirit of the expedition had dissolved; the great body were talking of returning, some of the stragglers, indeed, were on their way back; the Bishop, silent and confused, kept knocking the mane of his mule with his hammer.

'Now,' said Morley, who during this scene had stood apart, accompanied by Devilsdust and Dandy Mick, 'now,' said Morley to the latter, 'now is your time.'

'Gentlemen!' sang out Mick.

'A speech, a speech!' cried out several.

'Listen to Mick Radley,' whispered Devilsdust, moving swiftly among the mob, and addressing every one he met of influence. 'Listen to Mick Radley; he has something important.'

'Radley for ever! Listen to Mick Radley! Go it, Dandy! Pitch it into them! Silence for Dandy Mick! Jump up on that ere bank;' and on the bank Mick mounted accordingly.

'Gentlemen,' said Mick.

'Well, you have said that before.'

'I like to hear him say "Gentlemen;" it's respectful.'

'Gentlemen,' said the Dandy, 'the National Holiday has begun ——'

'Three cheers for it!'

'Silence! hear the Dandy!'

'The National Holiday has begun,' continued Mick,' and it seems to me the best thing for the people to do is to take a walk in Lord de Mowbray's park.'

This proposition was received with one of those wild shouts of approbation which indicate that the orator has exactly hit his audience between wind and water. The fact is, the public mind at this instant wanted to be led, and in Dandy Mick a leader appeared. A leader, to be successful, should embody in his system the necessities of his followers, express what every one feels, but no one has had the ability or the courage to pronounce.

The courage, the adroitness, the influence of Gerard had reconciled the people to the relinquishment of the great end for which they had congregated; but neither man nor multitude like to make preparations without obtaining a result. Every one wanted to achieve some object by the movement; and at this critical juncture an object was proposed, and one which promised novelty, amusement, excitement. The Bishop, whose consent must be obtained, but who relinquished an idea with the same difficulty with which he had imbibed it, alone murmured, and kept saying to Field, 'I thought we came to burn down this mill! A bloody-minded Capitalist, a man that makes gardens, and forces the people to wash themselves! What is all this?'

Field said what he could, while Devilsdust, leaning over the mule's shoulder, cajoled the other ear of the Bishop, who at last gave his consent with almost as much reluctance as George the Fourth did to the emancipation of the Roman Catholics;* but he made his terms, and said, in a sulky voice, he must have a glass of ale.

'Drink a glass of ale with Lord de Mowbray,' said Devilsdust.

CHAPTER 11

WHEN the news had arrived in the morning at Mowbray, that the messengers of the Bishop had met with a somewhat queer reception at the Mowedale works, Gerard, prescient that some trouble might in consequence occur there, determined to repair at once to the residence of his late employer. It so happened that Monday was the day on which the cottages up the Dale and on the other side of the river were visited by an envoy of Ursula Trafford, and it was the office of Sybil this morning to fulfil the duties of that mission of charity. She had mentioned this to her father on the previous day, and as, in consequence of the strike, he was no longer occupied, he had proposed to accompany his daughter on the morrow. Together therefore they had walked until they arrived, it being then about two hours to noon, at the bridge, a little above their former residence. Here they were to separate. Gerard embraced his daughter with even more than usual tenderness; and, as Sybil crossed the bridge, she looked round at her father, and her glance caught his, turned for the same fond purpose.

Sybil was not alone; Harold, who had ceased to gambol, but who had gained in stature, majesty, and weight what he had lost of lithe and frolic grace, was by her side. He no

longer danced before his mistress, coursed away and then
returned, or vented his exuberant life in a thousand feats of
playful vigour; but, sedate and observant, he was always at
hand, ever sagacious, and seemed to watch her every glance.

The day was beautiful, the scene was fair, the spot indeed
was one which rendered the performance of gracious offices
to Sybil doubly sweet. She ever begged of the Lady Superior
that she might be her minister to the cottages up Dale. They
were full of familiar faces. It was a region endeared to Sybil
by many memories of content and tenderness. And as she
moved along to-day, her heart was light, and the natural joy-
ousness of her disposition, which so many adverse circumstances had tended to repress, was visible in her sunny face.
She was happy about her father. The invasion of the miners,
instead of prompting him, as she had feared, to some rash
conduct, appeared to have filled him only with disgust. Even
now he was occupied in a pursuit of order and peace, coun-
selling prudence and protecting the benevolent.

She passed through a copse which skirted those woods of
Mowbray wherein she had once so often rambled with one
whose image now hovered over her spirit. Ah! what scenes
and changes, dazzling and dark, had occurred since the careless though thoughtful days of her early girlhood! Sybil
mused: she recalled the moonlit hour, when Mr. Franklin
first paid a visit to their cottage, their walks and wandering,
the expeditions which she planned, and the explanations which
she so artlessly gave him. Her memory wandered to their
meeting in Westminster, and all the scenes of sorrow and of
softness of which it was the herald. Her imagination raised
before her in colours of light and life the morning, the terrible
morning, when he came to her desperate rescue; his voice
sounded in her ear; her cheek glowed as she recalled their
tender farewell.

It was past noon; Sybil had reached the term of her expedition, had visited her last charge; she was emerging from
the hills into the open country, and about to regain the river
road that would in time have conducted her to the bridge.
On one side of her was the moor, on the other a wood that
was the boundary of Mowbray Park. And now a number of
women met her, some of whom she recognised, and had in-

deed visited earlier in the morning. Their movements were disordered; distress and panic were expressed on their countenances. Sybil stopped, she spoke to some, the rest gathered round her. The Hell-cats were coming, they said; they were on the other side of the river, burning mills, destroying all they could put their hands on, man, woman, and child.

Sybil, alarmed for her father, put to them some questions, to which they gave incoherent answers. It was however clear that they had seen no one, and knew nothing of their own experience. The rumour had reached them that the mob was advancing up Dale, those who had apprised them had, according to their statement, absolutely witnessed the approach of the multitude, and so they had locked up their cottages, crossed the bridge, and run away to the woods and moor. Under these circumstances, deeming that there might be much exaggeration, Sybil at length resolved to advance, and in a few minutes those whom she had encountered were out of sight. She patted Harold, who looked up in her face and gave a bark, significant of his approbation of her proceeding, and also of his consciousness that something strange was going on. She had not proceeded very far before two men on horseback, at full gallop, met her. They pulled up as soon as they observed her, and said, 'You had better go back as fast as you can: the mob is out, and coming up Dale in great force.'

Sybil inquired, with much agitation, whether they had themselves seen the people, and they replied that they had not, but that advices had been received from Mowbray of their approach, and, as for themselves, they were hurrying at their utmost speed to a town ten miles off, where they understood some yeomanry were stationed, and to whom the Mayor of Mowbray had last night sent a despatch. Sybil would have inquired whether there were time for her to reach the bridge and join her father at the factory of Trafford, but the horsemen were impatient and rode off. Still she determined to proceed. All that she now aimed at was to reach Gerard and share his fate.

A boat put across the river, with two men and a crowd of women. The mob had been seen; at least there was positively one person present who had distinguished them in the extreme distance, or rather the cloud of dust which they had

created; there were dreadful stories of their violence and devastation. It was understood that a body meant to attack Trafford's works, but, as the narrator added, it was very probable
that the greater part would cross the bridge and so on to the
Moor, where they would hold a meeting.

Sybil would fain have crossed in the boat, but there was
no one to assist her. They had escaped, and meant to lose no
time in finding a place of refuge for the moment. They were
sure if they recrossed now, they must meet the mob. They
were about to leave Sybil in infinite distress, when a lady,
driving herself in a pony carriage, with a couple of grooms
behind her mounted also on ponies of the same form and
colour, came up from the direction of the Moor, and, observing
the group and Sybil much agitated, pulled up and inquired the
cause. One of the men, frequently interrupted by all the
women, immediately entered into a narrative of the state of
affairs, for which the lady was evidently quite unprepared, for
her alarm was considerable.

'And this young person will persist in crossing over,' continued the man. 'It's nothing less than madness. I tell her she
will meet instant death or worse.'

'It seems to me very rash,' said the lady in a kind tone, and
who seemed to recognise her.

'Alas! what am I to do!' exclaimed Sybil. 'I left my father
at Mr. Trafford's!'

'Well, we have no time to lose,' said the man, whose companion had now fastened the boat to the bank, and so, wishing
them good morning, and followed by the whole of his cargo,
they went on their way.

But just at this moment a gentleman, mounted on a knowing little cob, came galloping up, exclaiming, as he reached
the pony carriage, 'My dear Joan, I am looking after you. I
have been in the greatest alarm for you. There are riots on
the other side of the river, and I was afraid you might have
crossed the bridge.'

Upon this Lady Joan related to Mr. Mountchesney how
she had just become acquainted with the intelligence, and
then they conversed together for a moment or so in a whisper:
when, turning round to Sybil, she said, 'I think you had really
better come home with us till affairs are a little more quiet.'

'You are most kind,' said Sybil, 'but if I could get back to the town through Mowbray Park, I think I might do something for my father!'

'We are going to the castle through the park at this moment,' said the gentleman. 'You had better come with us. There you will at least be safe, and perhaps we shall be able to do something for the good people in trouble over the water;' and, so saying, nodding to a groom, who, advancing, held his cob, the gentleman dismounted, and approaching Sybil with great courtesy, said, 'I think we ought all of us to know each other. Lady Joan and myself had once the pleasure of meeting you, I think, at Mr. Trafford's. It was a long time ago, but,' he added in a subdued tone, 'you are not a person to forget.'

Sybil was insensible to Mr. Mountchesney's gallantry, but, alarmed and perplexed, she yielded to the representations of himself and Lady Joan, and got into the phaeton. Turning from the river, they pursued a road which, after a short progress, entered the park, Mr. Mountchesney cantering on before them, Harold following. They took their way for about a mile through a richly-wooded demesne, Lady Joan addressing many observations with great kindness to Sybil, and frequently endeavouring, though in vain, to divert her agitated thoughts, till they at length emerged from the more covered parts into extensive lawns, while on a rising ground, which they rapidly approached, rose Mowbray Castle, a modern castellated building, raised in a style not remarkable for its taste or correctness, but vast, grand, and imposing.

'And now,' said Mr. Mountchesney, riding up to them and addressing Sybil, 'I will send off a scout immediately for news of your father. In the meantime let us believe the best!' Sybil thanked him with cordiality, and then she entered Mowbray Castle.

CHAPTER 12

IN less than an hour after the arrival of Sybil at Mowbray Castle, the scout that Mr. Mountchesney had sent off to gather news returned, and with intelligence of the triumph of

Gerard's eloquence, that all had ended happily, and that the people were dispersing, and returning to the town.

Kind as was the reception accorded to Sybil by Lady de Mowbray and her daughter, on her arrival, the remembrance of the perilous position of her father had totally disqualified her from responding to their advances. Acquainted with the cause of her anxiety and depression, and sympathising with womanly softness with her distress, nothing could be more considerate than their behaviour. It touched Sybil much, and she regretted the harsh thoughts that irresistible circumstances had forced her to cherish respecting persons who, now that she saw them in their domestic and unaffected hour, had apparently many qualities to conciliate and to charm. When the good news arrived of her father's safety, and safety achieved in a manner so flattering to a daughter's pride, it came upon a heart predisposed to warmth and kindness, and all her feelings opened. The tears stood in her beautiful eyes, and they were tears not only of tenderness but gratitude. Fortunately Lord de Mowbray was at the moment absent, and, as the question of the controverted inheritance was a secret to every member of the family except himself, the name of Gerard excited no invidious sensation in the circle. Sybil was willing to please, and to be pleased; every one was captivated by her beauty, her grace, her picturesque expression, and sweet simplicity. Lady de Mowbray serenely smiled, and frequently, when unobserved, viewed her through her eye-glass. Lady Joan, much softened by marriage, would show her the castle; Lady Maud was in ecstasies with all that Sybil said or did; while Mr. Mountchesney, who had thought of little else but Sybil ever since Lady Maud's report of her seraphic singing, and who had not let four-and-twenty hours go by without discovering, with all the practised art of St. James's, the name and residence of the unknown fair, flattered himself he was making great play, when Sybil, moved by his kindness, distinguished him by frequent notice. They had viewed the castle, they were in the music-room. Sybil had been prevailed upon, though with reluctance, to sing. Some Spanish church music which she found there called forth all her powers; all was happiness, delight, rapture, Lady Maud in a frenzy of friendship, Mr. Mountchesney convinced that the country in

August might be delightful, and Lady Joan almost gay because Alfred was pleased. Lady de Mowbray had been left in her boudoir with the 'Morning Post.' Sybil had just finished a ravishing air, there was a murmur of luncheon, when suddenly Harold, who had persisted in following his mistress, and whom Mr. Mountchesney had gallantly introduced into the music-room, rose, and coming forward from the corner in which he reposed, barked violently.

'How now!' said Mr. Mountchesney.

'Harold!' said Sybil in a tone of remonstrance and surprise.

But the dog not only continued to bark, but even howled. At this moment the groom of the chambers entered the room abruptly, and with a face of mystery said that he wished to speak with Mr. Mountchesney. That gentleman immediately withdrew. He was absent some little time, the dog very restless, Lady Joan becoming disquieted, when he returned. His changed air struck the vigilant eye of his wife.

'What has happened, Alfred?' she said.

'Oh! don't be alarmed,' he replied with an obvious affectation of ease. 'There are some troublesome people in the park; stragglers, I suppose, from the rioters. The gatekeeper ought not to have let them pass. I have given directions to Bentley what to do, if they come to the castle.'

'Let us go to mamma,' said Lady Joan.

And they were all about leaving the music-room, when a servant came running in and called out, 'Mr. Bentley told me to say, sir, they are in sight.'

'Very well,' said Mr. Mountchesney in a calm tone, but changing colour. 'You had better go to your mamma, Joan, and take Maud and our friend with you. I will stay below for a while,' and, notwithstanding the remonstrances of his wife, Mr. Mountchesney went to the hall.

'I don't know what to do, sir,' said the house-steward. 'They are a very strong party.'

'Close all the windows, lock and bar all the doors,' said Mr. Mountchesney. 'I am frightened,' he continued, 'about your lord. I fear he may fall in with these people.'

'My lord is at Mowbray,' said Mr. Bentley. 'He must have heard of this mob there.'

And now, emerging from the plantations, and entering on

the lawns, the force and description of the invading party were easier to distinguish. They were numerous, though consisting of only a section of the original expedition, for Gerard had collected a great portion of the Mowbray men, and they preferred being under his command to following a stranger, whom they did not much like, on a somewhat licentious adventure of which their natural leader disapproved. The invading section, therefore, were principally composed of Hellcats, though, singular enough, Morley, of all men in the world, accompanied them, attended by Devilsdust, Dandy Mick, and others of that youthful class of which these last were the idols and heroes. There were perhaps eighteen hundred or two thousand persons armed with bars and bludgeons, in general a grimy crew, whose dress and appearance revealed the kind of labour to which they were accustomed. The difference between them and the minority of Mowbray operatives was instantly recognisable.

When they perceived the castle, this dreadful band gave a ferocious shout. Lady de Mowbray showed blood; she was composed and courageous. She observed the mob from the window, and reassuring her daughters and Sybil, she said she would go down and speak to them. She was on the point of leaving the room with this object, when Mr. Mountchesney entered, and, hearing her purpose, dissuaded her from attempting it. 'Leave all to me,' he said; 'and make yourselves quite easy; they will go away; I am certain they will go away;' and he again quitted them.

In the meantime, Lady de Mowbray and her friends observed the proceedings below. When the main body had advanced within a few hundred yards of the castle, they halted, and seated themselves on the turf. This step reassured the garrison: it was generally held to indicate that the intentions of the invaders were not of a very settled or hostile character; that they had visited the place probably in a spirit of frolic, and if met with tact and civility might ultimately be induced to retire from it without much annoyance. This was evidently the opinion of Mr. Mountchesney from the first, and when an uncouth being, on a white mule, attended by twenty or thirty miners, advanced to the castle, and asked for Lord de Mowbray, Mr. Mountchesney met them with kindness, saying that he regretted his father-in-law was absent, expressed his readiness to represent him, and inquired their pleasure. His courteous bearing evidently had an influence on the Bishop, who, dropping his usual brutal tone, mumbled something about his wish to drink Lord de Mowbray's health.

'You shall all drink his health,' said Mr. Mountchesney humouring him, and he gave directions that a couple of barrels of ale should be broached in the park before the castle. The Bishop was pleased, the people were in good humour, some men began dancing; it seemed that the cloud had blown over, and Mr. Mountchesney sent up a bulletin to Lady de Mowbray that all danger was past, and that he hoped in ten minutes they would all have disappeared.

The ten minutes had expired: the Bishop was still drinking ale, and Mr. Mountchesney still making civil speeches, and keeping his immediate attendants in humour.

'I wish they would go,' said Lady de Mowbray.

'How wonderfully Alfred has managed them,' said Lady Joan.

'After all,' said Lady Maud, 'it must be confessed that the people ——' Her sentence was interrupted; Harold who had been shut out, but had lain down without quietly, though moaning at intervals, now sprang at the door with so much force that it trembled on its hinges, while the dog again barked with renewed violence. Sybil went to him: he seized her dress with his teeth, and would have pulled her away. Suddenly uncouth and mysterious sounds were heard, there was a loud shriek, the gong in the hall thundered, the great alarum-bell of the tower sounded without, and the housekeeper, followed by the female domestics, rushed into the room.

'Oh! my lady, my lady,' they all exclaimed at the same time, 'the Hell-cats are breaking into the castle.'

Before any one of the terrified company could reply, the voice of Mr. Mountchesney was heard. He was approaching them; he was no longer calm. He hurried into the room; he was pale, evidently greatly alarmed. 'I have come to you,' he said; 'these fellows have got in below. While there is time, and we can manage them, you must leave the place.'

'I am ready for anything,' said Lady de Mowbray.

Lady Joan and Lady Maud wrung their hands in frantic terror. Sybil, very pale, said, 'Let me go down; I may know some of these men.'

'No, no,' said Mr. Mountchesney. 'They are not Mowbray people. It would not be safe.'

Dreadful sounds were now heard; a blending of shouts and oaths, and hideous merriment. Their hearts trembled.

'The mob are in the house, sir,' called out Mr. Bentley, rushing up to them. 'They say they will see everything.'

'Let them see everything,' said Lady de Mowbray, 'but make a condition that they first let us go. Try, Alfred, try to manage them before they are utterly ungovernable.'

Mr. Mountchesney again left them on this desperate mission. Lady de Mowbray and all the women remained in the chamber. Not a word was spoken; the silence was complete. Even the maidservants had ceased to sigh and sob. A feeling something like desperation was stealing over them.

The dreadful sounds continued, increased. They seemed to approach nearer. It was impossible to distinguish a word, and yet their import was frightful and ferocious.

'Lord have mercy on us all!' exclaimed the housekeeper, unable to refrain herself. The maids began to cry.

After an absence of about five minutes, Mr. Mountchesney again hurried in, and, leading away Lady de Mowbray, he said, 'You haven't a moment to lose. Follow us!'

There was a general rush, and, following Mr. Mountchesney, they passed rapidly through several apartments, the fearful noises every moment increasing, until they reached the library, which opened on the terrace. The windows were broken, the terrace crowded with people, several of the mob were in the room, even Lady de Mowbray cried out and fell back.

'Come on,' said Mr. Mountchesney. 'The mob have possession of the castle. It is our only chance.'

'But the mob are here,' said Lady de Mowbray, much terrified.

'I see some Mowbray faces,' said Sybil, springing forward, with a flashing eye and a glowing cheek. 'Bamford and Samuel Carr: Bamford, if you be my father's friend, aid us now; and Samuel Carr, I was with your mother this morning:

did she think I should meet her son thus? No, you shall not enter,' said Sybil, advancing. They recognised her, they paused. 'I know you, Couchman; you told us once at the Convent that we might summon you in our need. I summon you now. Oh, men, men!' she exclaimed, clasping her hands, 'what is this? Are you led away by strangers to such deeds? Why, I know you all! You came here to aid, I am sure, and not to harm. Guard these ladies, save them from these foreigners! There's Butler, he'll go with us, and Godfrey Wells. Shall it be said you let your neighbours be plundered and assailed by strangers and never try to shield them? Now, my good friends, I entreat, I adjure you, Butler, Wells, Couchman, what would Walter Gerard say, your friend that you have so often followed, if he saw this?'

'Gerard for ever!' shouted Couchman.

'Gerard for ever!' exclaimed a hundred voices.

' 'Tis his blessed daughter,' said others; ' 'tis Sybil, our angel Sybil!'

'Stand by Sybil Gerard.'

Sybil had made her way upon the terrace, and had collected around her a knot of stout followers, who, whatever may have been their original motive, were now resolved to do her bidding. The object of Mr. Mountchesney was to descend the side-step of the terrace and gain the flower-garden, whence there were means of escape. But the throng was still too fierce to permit Lady de Mowbray and her companions to attempt the passage, and all that Sybil and her followers could at present do, was to keep the mob off from entering the library, and to exert themselves to obtain fresh recruits.

At this moment an unexpected aid arrived.

'Keep back there! I call upon you in the name of God to keep back!' exclaimed a voice of one struggling and communing with the rioters, a voice which all immediately recognised. It was that of Mr. St. Lys. 'Charles Gardner, I have been your friend. The aid I gave you was often supplied to me by this house. Why are you here?'

'For no evil purpose, Mr. St. Lys. I came, as others did, to see what was going on.'

'Then you see a deed of darkness. Struggle against it. Aid me and Philip Warner in this work; it will support you at the

judgment. Tressel, Tressel, stand by me and Warner. That's
good, that's right. And you too, Daventry, and you and you.
I knew you would wash your hands of this fell deed. It is not
Mowbray men would do this. That's right, that's right! Form
a band. Good again. There's not a man that joins us now who
does not make a friend for life.'

Mr. St. Lys had been in the neighbourhood when the news
of the visit of the mob to the castle reached him. He anticipated the perilous consequences. He hastened immediately to
the scene of action. He had met Warner, the handloom weaver,
in his way, and enlisted his powerful influence with the people
on his side.

The respective bands of Sybil and Mr. St. Lys in time contrived to join. Their numbers were no longer contemptible;
they were animated by the words and presence of their leaders:
St. Lys struggling in their midst; Sybil maintaining her position on the terrace, and inciting all around her to courage and
energy.

The multitude were kept back, the passage to the side-steps
of the terrace was clear.

'Now,' said Sybil, and she encouraged Lady de Mowbray,
her daughters, and followers to advance. It was a fearful
struggle to maintain the communication, but it was a successful one. They proceeded breathless and trembling, until they
reached what was commonly called the Grotto, but which
was, in fact, a subterranean way excavated through a hill and
leading to the bank of the river where there were boats. The
entrance of this tunnel was guarded by an iron gate, and Mr.
Mountchesney had secured the key. The gate was opened,
Warner and his friends made almost superhuman efforts at
this moment to keep back the multitude. Lady de Mowbray
and her daughters had passed through, when there came one
of those violent undulations usual in mobs, and which was
occasioned by a sudden influx of persons attracted by what
was occurring, and Sybil and those who immediately surrounded her and were guarding the retreat were carried far
away. The gate was closed, the rest of the party had passed,
but Sybil was left, and found herself entirely among strangers.

In the meantime the castle was in the possession of the
mob. The first great rush was to the cellars: the Bishop him-

self headed this onset, nor did he rest until he was seated among the prime bins of the noble proprietor. This was not a crisis of corkscrews; the heads of the bottle were knocked off with the same promptitude and dexterity as if they were shelling nuts or decapitating shrimps; the choicest wines of Christendom were poured down the thirsty throats that ale and spirits alone had hitherto stimulated: Tummas was swallowing Burgundy; Master Nixon had got hold of a batch of Tokay; while the Bishop himself, seated on the ground and leaning against an arch, the long perspective of the cellars full of rapacious figures brandishing bottles and torches, alternately quaffed some very old Port and some Madeira of many voyages, and was making up his mind as to their respective and relative merits.

While the cellars and offices were thus occupied, bands were parading the gorgeous saloons and gazing with wonderment on their decorations and furniture. Some grimy ruffians had thrown themselves with disdainful delight on the satin couches and the state beds: others rifled the cabinets with an idea that they must be full of money, and finding little in their way, had strewn their contents, papers and books, and works of art, over the floor of the apartments; sometimes a band who had escaped from below with booty came up to consummate their orgies in the magnificence of the dwelling-rooms. Among these were Nixon and his friends, who stared at the pictures and stood before the tall mirrors with still greater astonishment. Indeed, many of them had never seen an ordinary looking-glass in their lives.

' 'Tis Natur!' said Master Nixon, surveying himself, and turning to Juggins.

Many of these last grew frantic, and finished their debauch by the destruction of everything around them.

But while these scenes of brutal riot were occurring, there was one select but resolute band who shared in none of these excesses. Morley, followed by half a dozen Mowbray lads and two chosen Hell-cats, leaving all the confusion below, had ascended the great staircase, traced his way down a corridor to the winding steps of the Round Tower, and, supplied with the necessary instruments, had forced his entrance into the muniment room of the castle. It was a circular chamber lined with tall fire-proof cases. These might have presented invincible obstacles to any other than the pupils of Bishop Hatton; as it was, in some instances the locks, in others the hinges, yielded in time, though after prolonged efforts, to the resources of their art; and while Dandy Mick and his friends kept watch at the entrance, Morley and Devilsdust proceeded to examine the contents of the cases; piles of parchment deeds, bundles of papers arranged and docketed, many boxes of various size and materials; but the desired object was not visible. A baffled expression came over the face of Morley; he paused for an instant in his labours. The thought of how much he had sacrificed for this, and only to fail, came upon him: upon him, the votary of Moral Power in the midst of havoc which he had organised and stimulated. He cursed Baptist Hatton in his heart.

'The knaves have destroyed them,' said Devilsdust. 'I thought how it would be. They never would run the chance of a son of Labour being lord of all this.'

Some of the cases were very deep, and they had hitherto in general, in order to save time, proved their contents with an iron rod. Now Morley with a desperate air mounting on some steps that were in the room, commenced formally rifling the cases and throwing their contents on the floor; it was soon strewn with deeds and papers and boxes which he and Devilsdust the moment they had glanced at them hurled away. At length, when all hope seemed to have vanished, clearing a case which at first appeared only to contain papers, Morley struck something at its back; he sprang forward with outstretched arm, his body was half hid in the cabinet, and he pulled out with triumphant exultation the box, painted blue and blazoned with the arms of Valence. It was neither large nor heavy; he held it out to Devilsdust without saying a word, and Morley, descending the steps, sat down for a moment on a pile of deeds and folded his arms.

At this juncture the discharge of musketry was heard.

'Hilloa!' said Devilsdust with a queer expression. Morley started from his seat, Dandy Mick rushed into the room. 'Troops, troops! there are troops here!' he exclaimed.

'Let us descend,' said Morley. 'In the confusion we may escape. I will take the box,' and they left the muniment room.

One of their party, whom Mick had sent forward to reconnoitre, fell back upon them. 'They are not troops,' he said; 'they are yeomanry; they are firing away and cutting every one down. They have cleared the groundfloor of the castle, and are in complete possession below. We cannot escape this way.'

'Those accursed locks!' said Morley, clenching the box. 'Time has beat us. Let us see, let us see.' He ran back into the muniment room and examined the egress from the window. It was just possible for any one very lithe and nimble to vault upon the roof of the less elevated part of the castle. Revolving this, another scout rushed in and said, 'Comrades, they are here! they are ascending the stairs.'

Morley stamped on the ground with rage and despair. Then seizing Mick by the hand he said, 'You see this window; can you by any means reach that roof?'

'One may as well lose one's neck that way,' said Mick. 'I'll try.'

'Off! If you land I will throw this box after you. Now mind; take it to the convent at Mowbray, and deliver it yourself from me to Sybil Gerard. It is light; there are only papers in it; but they will give her her own again, and she will not forget you.'

'Never mind that,' said Mick. 'I only wish I may live to see her.'

The tramps of the ascending troopers was heard.

'Good bye, my hearties,' said Mick, and he made the spring. He seemed stunned, but he might recover. Morley watched him and flung the box.

'And now,' he said, drawing a pistol, 'we may fight our way yet. I'll shoot the first man who enters, and then you must rush on with your bludgeons.'

The force that had so unexpectedly arrived at this scene of devastation was a troop of the yeomanry regiment of Lord Marney. The strike in Lancashire and the revolt in the mining districts had so completely drained this county of military, that the Lord Lieutenant had insisted on Lord Marney quitting his agricultural neighbourhood, and quartering himself in the region of factories. Within the last two days he had fixed his head-quarters at a large manufacturing town within

ten miles of Mowbray, and a despatch on Sunday evening
from the mayor of that town having reached him, apprising
him of the invasion of the miners, Egremont had received
orders to march with his troop there on the following morning.

Egremont had not departed more than two hours, when
the horsemen whom Sybil had met arrived at Lord Marney's
head-quarters, bringing a most alarming and exaggerated report of the insurrection and of the havoc that was probably
impending. Lord Marney, being of opinion that Egremont's
forces were by no means equal to the occasion, resolved therefore at once to set out for Mowbray with his own troop.
Crossing Mowbray Moor, he encountered a great multitude,
now headed for purposes of peace by Walter Gerard. His
mind inflamed by the accounts he had received, and hating at
all times any popular demonstration, his lordship resolved
without inquiry or preparation immediately to disperse them.
The Riot Act was read with the rapidity with which grace is
sometimes said at the head of a public table, a ceremony of
which none but the performer and his immediate friends are
conscious. The people were fired on and sabred. The indignant spirit of Gerard resisted; he struck down a trooper to
the earth, and incited those about him not to yield. The father
of Sybil was picked out, the real friend and champion of the
People, and shot dead. Instantly arose a groan which almost
quelled the spirit of Lord Marney, though armed and at the
head of armed men. The people who before this were in
general scared and dispersing, ready indeed to fly in all directions, no sooner saw their beloved leader fall, than a feeling
of frenzy came over them. The defied the troopers, though
themselves armed only with stones and bludgeons; they
rushed at the horsemen and tore them from their saddles,
while a shower of stones rattled on the helmet of Lord Marney
and seemed never to cease. In vain the men around him
charged the infuriated throng; the people returned to their
prey, nor did they rest until Lord Marney fell lifeless on Mowbray Moor, literally stoned to death.

These disastrous events of course occurred at a subsequent
period of the day to that on which half-a-dozen troopers were
ascending the staircase of the Round Tower of Mowbray

Castle. The distracted house-steward of Lord de Mowbray had met and impressed upon them, now that the castle was once more in their possession, the expediency of securing the muniment room, for Mr. Bentley had witnessed the ominous ascent of Morley and his companions to that important chamber.

Morley and his companions had taken up an advantageous position at the head of the staircase.

'Surrender,' said the commander of the yeomanry. 'Resistance is useless.'

Morley presented his pistol, but, before he could pull the trigger, a shot from a trooper in the rear, and who from his position could well observe the intention of Morley, struck Stephen in the breast; still he fired but aimless and without effect. The troopers pushed on; Morley fainting fell back with his friends, who were frightened, except Devilsdust, who had struck hard and well, and who in turn had been slightly sabred. The yeomanry entered the muniment room almost at the same time as their foes, leaving Devilsdust behind them, who had fallen, and who, cursing the Capitalist who had wounded him, managed to escape. Morley fell when he had regained the room. The rest surrendered.

'Morley! Stephen Morley!' exclaimed the commander of the yeomanry. 'You, you here!'

'Yes. I am sped,' he said in a faint voice. 'No, no succour. It is useless, and I desire none. Why I am here is a mystery; let it remain so. The world will misjudge me; the man of peace they will say was a hypocrite. The world will be wrong, as it always is. Death is bitter,' he said, with a deep sigh, and speaking with great difficulty, 'more bitter from you; but just. We have struggled together before, Egremont. I thought I had scotched you then, but you escaped. Our lives have been a struggle since we first met. Your star has controlled mine; and now I feel I have sacrificed life and fame, dying men prophesy, for your profit and honour. O Sybil!' and with this name, half-sighed upon his lips, the votary of Moral Power and the Apostle of Community ceased to exist.

Meanwhile Sybil, separated from her friends, who had made their escape through the grotto, was left with Harold only for her protector, for she had lost even Warner in the crush. She looked around in vain for some Mowbray face that

she could recognise, but after some fruitless research, a loud
shouting in the distance, followed by the firing of musketry,
so terrified all around her, that the mob in her immediate
neighbourhood dispersed as if by magic; and she remained
alone crouching in a corner of the flower-garden, while dreadful shouts and shrieks and yells resounded from the distance,
with occasional firing, the smoke floating to her retreat. She
could see from where she stood the multitude flying about the
park in all directions, and therefore she thought it best to remain in her present position and await the terrible events. She
concluded that some military force had arrived, and hoped
that, if she could maintain her present post, the extreme
danger might pass. But while she indulged in these hopes, a
dark cloud of smoke came descending in the garden. It could
not be produced by musket or carbine; its volume was too
heavy even for ordnance; and in a moment there were sparks
mingled with its black form; and then the shouting and
shrieking which had in some degree subsided, suddenly
broke out again with increased force and wildness. The castle
was on fire.

Whether from heedlessness or from insane intention, for
the deed sealed their own doom, the drunken Hell-cats, brandishing their torches, while they rifled the cellars and examined every closet and corner of the offices, had set fire to
the lower part of the building, and the flames, that had for
some time burnt unseen, had now gained the principal chambers. The Bishop was lying senseless in the main cellar, surrounded by his chief officers in the same state: indeed the
whole of the basement was covered with the recumbent
figures of Hell-cats, as black and as thick as torpid flies during
the last days of their career. The funeral pile of the children
of Woden was a sumptuous one; it was prepared and lighted
by themselves; and the flame that, rising from the keep of
Mowbray, announced to the startled country that in a short
hour the splendid mimickry of Norman rule would cease to
exist, told also the pitiless fate of the ruthless savage, who,
with analogous pretension, had presumed to style himself the
Liberator of the People.

The clouds of smoke, the tongues of flame that now began
to mingle with them, the multitude whom this new incident

and impending catastrophe summoned back to the scene, forced Sybil to leave the garden and enter the park. It was in vain she endeavoured to gain some part less frequented than the rest, and to make her way unobserved. Suddenly a band of drunken ruffians, with shouts and oaths, surrounded her; she shrieked in frantic terror; Harold sprung at the throat of the foremost; another advanced, Harold left his present prey and attacked the new assailant. The brave dog did wonders, but the odds were fearful; and the men had bludgeons, were enraged, and had already wounded him. One ruffian had grasped the arm of Sybil, another had clenched her garments, when an officer, covered with dust and gore, sabre in hand, jumped from the terrace, and hurried to the rescue. He cut down one man, thrust away another, and, placing his left arm round Sybil, he defended her with his sword, while Harold, now become furious, flew from man to man, and protected her on the other side. Her assailants were routed, they made a staggering flight! the officer turned round and pressed Sybil to his heart.

'We will never part again,' said Egremont.

'Never,' murmured Sybil.

CHAPTER 13

It was the spring of last year, and Lady Bardolf was making a morning visit to Lady St. Julians.

'I heard they were to be at Lady Palmerston's last night,' said Lady St. Julians.

'No,' said Lady Bardolf shaking her head, 'they make their first appearance at Deloraine House. We meet there on Thursday, I know.'

'Well, I must say,' said Lady St. Julians, 'that I am curious to see her.'

'Lord Valentine met them last year at Naples.'

'And what does he say of her.'

'Oh! he raves!'

'What a romantic history! And what a fortunate man is Lord Marney. If one could only have foreseen events!' exclaimed Lady St. Julians. 'He was always a favourite of mine, though. But still I thought his brother was the very last person who ever would die. He was so very hard!'

'I fear Lord Marney is entirely lost to us,' said Lady Bardolf looking very solemn.

'Ah! he always had a twist,' said Lady St. Julians, 'and used to breakfast with that horrid Mr. Trenchard, and do those sort of things. But still, with his immense fortune, I should think he would become rational.'

'You may well say immense,' said Lady Bardolf. 'Mr. Ormsby, and there is no better judge of another man's income, says there are not three peers in the kingdom who have so much a year clear.'

'They say the Mowbray estate is forty thousand a year,' said Lady St. Julians. 'Poor Lady de Mowbray! I understand that Mr. Mountchesney has resolved not to appeal against the verdict.'

'You know he has not the shadow of a chance,' said Lady Bardolf. 'Ah! what changes we have seen in that family! They say the writ of right killed poor Lord de Mowbray, but to my mind he never recovered the burning of the castle. We went over to them directly, and I never saw a man so cut up. We wanted them to come to us at Firebrace, but he said he should leave the county immediately I remember Lord Bardolf mentioning to me that he looked like a dying man.'

'Well, I must say,' said Lady St. Julians, rallying as it were from a fit of abstraction, 'that I am most curious to see Lady Marney.'

The reader will infer from this conversation, that Dandy Mick, in spite of his stunning fall, and all dangers which awaited him on his recovery, had contrived in spite of fire and flame, sabre and carbine, trampling troopers, and plundering mobs, to reach the convent of Mowbray with the box of papers. There he inquired for Sybil, in whose hands, and whose hands alone, he was enjoined to deposit them. She was still absent, but, faithful to his instructions, Mick would deliver his charge to none other, and, exhausted by the fatigues of the terrible day, he remained in the courtyard of the convent, lying down with the box for his pillow, until Sybil, under the protection of Egremont, herself returned. Then he fulfilled his mission. Sybil was too agitated at the moment to perceive all its import, but she delivered the box into the custody of Egremont, who desiring Mick to follow him to his hotel, bade farewell to Sybil, who, equally with himself, was then ignorant of the fatal encounter on Mowbray Moor.

We must drop a veil over the anguish which its inevitable and speedy revelation brought to the daughter of Gerard. Her love for her father was one of those profound emotions which seemed to form a constituent part of her existence. She remained for a long period in helpless woe, soothed only by the sacred cares of Ursula. There was another mourner in this season of sorrow who must not be forgotten; and that was Lady Marney. All that tenderness and the most considerate thought could devise to soften sorrow, and reconcile her to a change of life which at the first has in it something depressing, were extended by Egremont to Arabella. He supplied in an instant every arrangement which had been neglected by his brother, but which could secure her convenience, and tend to her happiness. Between Marney Abbey, where he insisted for the present that Arabella should reside, and Mowbray, Egremont passed his life for many months, until, by some management which we need not trace or analyse, Lady Marney came over one day to the convent at Mowbray, and carried back Sybil to Marney Abbey, never again to quit it until on her bridal day, when the Earl and Countess of Marney departed for Italy, where they passed nearly a year, and from which they had just returned at the commencement of this chapter.

During the previous period, however, many important events had occurred. Lord Marney had placed himself in communication with Mr. Hatton, who had soon become acquainted with all that had occurred in the muniment room of Mowbray Castle. The result was not what he had once anticipated; but for him it was not without some compensatory circumstances. True, another and an unexpected rival had stepped on the stage, with whom it was vain to cope; but the idea that he had deprived Sybil of her inheritance, had, ever since he had become acquainted with her, been the plague-spot of Hatton's life, and there was nothing that he desired more ardently than to see her restored to her rights, and to be instrumental in that restoration. How successful he was in pursuing her claim, the reader has already learnt.

Dandy Mick was rewarded for all the dangers he had encountered in the service of Sybil, and what he conceived was
the vindication of popular rights. Lord Marney established
him in business, and Mick took Devilsdust for a partner.
Devilsdust, having thus obtained a position in society, and
become a capitalist, thought it but a due homage to the social
decencies to assume a decorous appellation, and he called
himself by the name of the town where he was born. The firm
of Radley, Mowbray, and Co., is a rising one; and will probably furnish in time a crop of members of Parliament and
peers of the realm. Devilsdust married Caroline, and Mrs.
Mowbray became a great favourite. She was always, perhaps,
a little too fond of junketting, but she had a sweet temper and
a gay spirit, and sustained her husband in the agonies of a
great speculation, or the despair of glutted markets. Julia became Mrs. Radley, and was much esteemed: no one could behave better. She was more orderly than Caroline, and exactly
suited Mick, who wanted a person near him of decision and
method. As for Harriet, she is not yet married. Though
pretty and clever, she is selfish, and a screw. She has saved a
good deal, and has a considerable sum in the savings' bank,
but, like many heiresses, she cannot bring her mind to share
her money with another. The great measures of Sir Robert
Peel, which produced three good harvests, have entirely revived trade at Mowbray. The Temple is again open, newly-
painted, and re-burnished, and Chaffing Jack has of course
'rallied,' while good Mrs. Carey still gossips with her neighbours round her well-stored stall, and tells wonderful stories
of the great stick-out, and riots of '42.

And thus I conclude the last page of a work which though
its form be light and unpretending, would yet aspire to suggest to its readers some considerations of a very opposite
character. A year ago, I presumed to offer to the public some
volumes that aimed at calling their attention to the state of
our political parties; their origin, their history, their present
position. In an age of political infidelity, of mean passions,
and petty thoughts, I would have impressed upon the rising
race not to despair, but to seek in a right understanding of
the history of their country and in the energies of heroic
youth, the elements of national welfare. The present work ad-

vances another step in the same emprise. From the state of Parties it now would draw public thought to the state of the People whom those parties for two centuries have governed. The comprehension and the cure of this greater theme depend upon the same agencies as the first: it is the past alone that can explain the present, and it is youth that alone can mould the remedial future. The written history of our country for the last ten reigns has been a mere phantasma; giving to the origin and consequence of public transactions a character and colour in every respect dissimilar to their natural form and hue. In this mighty mystery all thoughts and things have assumed an aspect and title contrary to their real quality and style: Oligarchy has been called Liberty; an exclusive Priesthood has been christened a National Church; Sovereignty has been the title of something that has had no dominion, while absolute power has been wielded by those who profess themselves the servants of the People. In the selfish strife of factions, two great existences have been blotted out of the history of England, the Monarch and the Multitude; as the power of the Crown has diminished, the privileges of the People have disappeared; till at length the sceptre has become a pageant, and its subject has degenerated again into a serf.

It is nearly fourteen years ago, in the popular frenzy of a mean and selfish revolution which emancipated neither the Crown nor the People, that I first took the occasion to intimate, and then to develop, to the first assembly of my countrymen that I ever had the honour to address, these convictions. They have been misunderstood, as is ever for a season the fate of Truth, and they have obtained for their promulgator much misrepresentation, as must ever be the lot of those who will not follow the beaten track of a fallacious custom. But Time, that brings all things, has brought also to the mind of England some suspicion that the idols they have so long worshipped, and the oracles that have so long deluded them, are not the true ones. There is a whisper rising in this country that Loyalty is not a phrase, Faith not a delusion, and Popular Liberty something more diffusive and substantial than the profane exercise of the sacred rights of sovereignty by political classes.

That we may live to see England once more possess a free

Monarchy, and a privileged and prosperous People, is my prayer; that these great consequences can only be brought about by the energy and devotion of our Youth is my persuasion. We live in an age when to be young and to be indifferent can be no longer synonymous. We must prepare for the coming hour. The claims of the Future are represented by suffering millions; and the Youth of a Nation are the trustees of Posterity.

NOTES

Sybil is full of references, on a great variety of topics. I have tried
to elucidate sufficient of them to make the novel intelligible to the
general reader, but have also included some more detailed notes for
those who would like to take their study of Disraeli's fiction further.

BOOK I

5 *Watteau*. Jean Antoine Watteau (1684–1721), whose decor-
ative paintings often evoke a sense of the transitoriness of
pleasure.

5 *Boucher*. François Boucher (1703–70), the Rococo decorator,
tapestry-designer, and painter.

5 *the marble guest of Juan*. In the old Spanish story Don Juan is a
heartless libertine punished by divine retribution, personified
by a guest of stone. The tragedy *El burlador de Sevilla y convidado
de piedra* (*The Seville Seducer and the Stone Guest*) by Tirso de
Molina (1583–1648) was adapted by Molière, Goldoni, Byron,
and Pushkin, and by Mozart in his opera *Don Giovanni* (1787).
Bernard Shaw uses the legend, ironically, in *Man and Superman*
(1903). The most popular Spanish play on the subject gave it
a happy ending, redeeming Juan by the love of a chaste
woman: José Zorrilla's *Don Juan Tenorio* (1844).

8 *Pompeius before Pharsalia*. Gnaeus Pompeius, Pompey the Great
(106–48 B.C.), Roman senator, consul and military leader, was
finally defeated by Caesar at Pharsalus, a city in Thessaly, in
48 B.C.

10 *Hampden*. John Hampden (1594–1643), the statesman and
Puritan. He opposed Charles I's levying of ship-money, and
attacked the king's evil ministers, but had no aversion to
monarchy in itself and was anxious to establish a permanent
agreement between the king and his parliament. In the Civil
War he mustered men for the Parliament side, and received
his death-wound leading his troops on Chalgrove Field, where
the Parliamentarians were routed by Prince Rupert.

10 *Russell*. William, Lord Russell (1639–83), 'the patriot'. After
the Restoration he was MP for the family borough of Tavi-
stock until 1678. He was driven into the opposition party by
dread of popery, fear of France, and disgust at the Court's
profligacy. Accused of plotting against Charles II, he was exe-

cuted on 21 July 1683. The reference to Hampden and Russell
is an ironic echo of the review of Henry Hallam's *Constitutional
History of England* (1827) by Macaulay, the arch-Whig to
whom Disraeli was diametrically opposed. (See *The Edinburgh
Review*, 48 (1828), 99.) Macaulay, commenting on Hallam's
objectivity and freedom from the vulgar myths in which every
political sect enshrines its heroes, remarks that 'the cause for
which Hampden bled on the field, and Sydney on the scaffold,
is enthusiastically toasted by many an honest radical who
would be puzzled to explain the difference between Ship-
money and the Habeas Corpus Act.' Disraeli repeats the
quotation, more accurately, and has the grace to use quotation
marks – see note on *Sydney*, p. 19, below.

10   *the court of St. Germains*. In exile James II made his home in the
chateau at Saint-Germain-en-Laye, near Paris.

11   *the fall of Mr. Fox*. Charles James Fox (1749–1806), the Whig
statesman and orator. The short-lived coalition government
of Fox and Lord North, with the Duke of Portland as First
Lord of the Treasury, ended in 1783 with George III's opposition to Fox's East India Bill, by which the Commissioners
who were to govern India were to be appointed by Parliament,
not the Crown, which had no power to dismiss them. Portland
was succeeded as First Lord of the Treasury by William Pitt
the Younger.

11   *his grace of Newcastle*. Thomas Pelham-Holles, first Duke of
Newcastle (1693–1768), devoted the whole of his great wealth
and influence to securing the succession of George I and
the triumph of the Whigs. He was Robert Walpole's Secretary
of State for thirty years. He survived Walpole's fall, 1742, and
was First Lord of the Treasury 1754–6; he was then created
Duke of Newcastle-under-Lyme. He was First Lord of the
Treasury again in 1757–62. The central concerns of his life
were the Whig cause, personal ambition, and the political
'game'. Very aware of his own dignity and envious of abler
politicians such as William Pitt the Elder, he was a political
manager rather than a statesman.

11   *a Venetian constitution*. The rule of the country by the great
Whig families, with ironic reference to the oligarchy which
ruled Venice in the days of the Venetian republic. For a good
discussion of Disraeli's Tory theory of history and the 'Venetian constitution' see Robert Blake, *Disraeli*, 1966, pp. 194–8.
Blake points out that Disraeli distorts past history to support
his own theories and that the power of a 'Venetian' aristocracy,

reducing the monarch to a doge, was characteristic of Disraeli's own period, particularly 1832–67, rather than of the eighteenth century. 'Disraeli had no real historical sense; he wrote propaganda, not history' (ibid., p. 273).

13 *Edmund Burke*. Irish-born British statesman, Whig parliamentary orator, and political thinker; a friend of Johnson, Goldsmith, Reynolds, Garrick, and of Fox until Burke's hostility to the French Revolution. In 1765 he became secretary to the Marquess of Rockingham, leader of one of the Whig groups in Parliament, and held this position until Rockingham's death in 1782. He worked to inspire a sense of unity and common principle in the group associated with Rockingham. He was concerned to curtail the power of the Crown, and was author of Fox's India Bill, 1783 (see first note on p. 11 above). When the bill was defeated Burke instigated the impeachment of Warren Hastings (see note on *Hastings*, p. 75 below). His attack on the French Revolution found its fullest expression in *Reflections on the Revolution in France* (1790). He emphasized the dangers of democracy, and majority rule when unrestrained and unguided by the responsible leadership of an hereditary aristocracy; he deplored the devaluation of tradition and inherited values, and appealed to the example and virtues of the English constitution, particularly its respect for traditional wisdom and usage, and its acceptance of a hierarchy of rank and property. All these ideas appealed to Disraeli.

13 *Bolingbroke*. Henry Saint-John, Viscount Bolingbroke (1678–1751), Tory statesman and orator. He was involved in the negotiations for the Treaty of Utrecht (1713) between England and France, ending the war of the Spanish succession (1702–13). The treaty provided for the solemn assent by Louis XIV to the abandonment by Philip V of Spain of the latter's rights to the French throne; prevention of the possible union of the Spanish and French kingdoms had been the basic cause of the war. Also France recognized the Protestant succession in England and abandoned the Stuart cause. The accession to the crown of the elector of Hanover, George I, meant triumph for the Whigs and political defeat for the Jacobite Bolingbroke. In later life he turned his attention to political philosophy (see his *Ideal of a Patriot King* (1749)). He believed the king to be strong enough to override parties and yet derive strength, like Queen Elizabeth, from representing the true rule of the people. He advocated a kind of popular Toryism which anticipates Disraeli's attacks on the Whig aristocracy.

14 *a young and dissolute noble*. Charles James Fox, see note on p. 11 above.

14 *Catiline*. Lucius Sergius Catilina (*c.* 108–62 B.C.), demagogue and conspirator who plotted murder and insurrection in Rome to get himself made consul. He and his followers were eventually defeated by Cicero's decisive action against them.

14 *not even admitted into the Cabinet*. A reference to the coalition of Fox and North in 1783. See first note on p. 11 above.

14 *rent in twain the proud oligarchy*. In 1793 Pitt the Younger was driven into war with France and Burke's attacks on the Revolution became useful government propaganda. Fox refused to serve under Pitt. The Duke of Portland and the group of Whigs associated with him had hitherto remained loyal to Fox. But in 1794 they joined Pitt leaving Fox in opposition with a diminished group of supporters.

14 *Mr. Pitt*. William Pitt the Younger (1759–1806), second son of William Pitt the Elder, Earl of Chatham. Precocious as a boy, he became Prime Minister at the age of twenty-four. Renowned for his leadership of Britain during the French Revolutionary and Napoleonic Wars, his first ministry lasted from 1783 until 1801, his second from 1804 until 1806. His fiscal policy was influenced by Adam Smith and Shelburne (see note on *Lord Shelburne*, p. 15 below). His early support of parliamentary reform faded, and fear of revolution in England on the French pattern led him to suspend the Habeas Corpus Act for the period 1794–1801, and pass the Treasonable Practices and Seditious Meetings Acts, 1795, which practically ended the activities of radical societies at that period. He transformed the character of the House of Lords, increasing its membership by nearly 50 per cent by his lavish creation of peerages to ensure his political influence in both Houses. Hence Disraeli's cutting remarks: 'He made peers of second-rate squires and fat graziers. He caught them in the alleys of Lombard Street, and clutched them from the counting-houses of Cornhill' (see p. 19). Pitt's style of government helped establish the Prime Minister as director of the government's financial policy, the supervisor and co-ordinator of the work of the government's various departments, and the monarch's chief confidant.

15 *Niebuhr*. Barthold Georg Niebuhr (1776–1831), German historian. The first two volumes of his *Römische Geschichte* were published in 1811 and 1812, the third volume after his death, in 1832. The English translation, *The History of Rome*, appeared in 1828–42.

15 *the pages of Gaudentio di Lucca. The Memoirs of Sigr Gaudentio di Lucca* (1737), a romance by Simon Berington, in which the titular hero discovers an imaginary country, Mezzoramia, in the interior of Africa.

15 *the adventures of Peter Wilkins. Peter Wilkins* (1750), a romance by Robert Paltock. Peter is a sailor, shipwrecked on a desert shore. He discovers a country frequented by a race of beautiful winged beings, the glumms and the gawreys. He marries a gawrey, Youwarkee, and goes with her to Nosmnbdsgrsutt, land of semi-darkness, where he remains many years.

15 *Major Wildman.* Sir John Wildman (1621?–93), the republican imprisoned for plotting against Cromwell in 1654 and against Charles II in 1661. Associated with the alleged Rye House Plot to assassinate Charles II and the Duke of York in 1683, and with Monmouth's rising against James II in 1685.

15 *Chatterton.* Thomas Chatterton (1752–70) published poems before the age of twelve. Destitute and despairing because of his lack of recognition as a poet, he committed suicide. Wordsworth described him as 'the marvellous Boy' in 'Resolution and Independence' (1807).

15 *Lord Shelburne.* William Petty, Viscount Fitzmaurice (1737–1805), created Marquess of Lansdowne in 1784. He acknowledged Pitt the Elder as his master in politics. He was First Lord of the Treasury briefly in 1782–3 with Pitt the Younger as Chancellor of the Exchequer. The coalition of North and Fox against his government led to his resignation. He had an independent spirit in party politics, and his manner was supercilious. Yet many of his views were enlightened; he advocated parliamentary and economic reform, Catholic emancipation, religious equality and free trade. He was a patron of literature and the fine arts, to which he devoted much of his later life.

18 *Lansdowne House.* Shelburne's town residence, in Berkeley Square.

18 *the magnetic influence of the descendant of Sir William Petty.* Lord Shelburne was the great-grandson of Sir William Petty (1623–87), mathematician and political economist, one of the founders of the Royal Society. Disraeli was quite capable of intending a pun in 'magnetic'.

19 *Sydney.* Algernon Sydney (1622–83) fought against Charles I in the Civil War and, when Charles II came to the throne, worked for the establishment of a republic. He was executed on 7 December 1683 for plotting insurrection against Charles II. He left a written paper denouncing the injustice of his trial,

and vindicating his political principles. (See note on *Russell*, p. 10 above.)

19 *Dutch finance.* By this Disraeli appears to mean the National Debt, i.e. the accumulated debts of the British Government, whether by borrowing from the British people (either directly or through the Bank of England) or from foreign people or governments. The British National Debt has its origin in economic practices in Charles II's reign, but some historians (Disraeli agrees with them, see p. 20) date its beginning in 1694 during William's reign, on the grounds that the loan of £1·2 million raised with the newly formed Bank of England, for the purpose of financing the war with Louis XIV of France, was the first example of a 'funded debt', i.e. one on which there is no contractual repayment date. However, the bulk of the British National Debt comprises 'unfunded debt' to pay the interest on which the government levies taxes. Hence Disraeli's phrase 'to mortgage industry in order to protect property' (p. 20), implying that the industrialists were taxed to keep the great Whig families in power.

22 *The Duke of Wellington.* Arthur Wellesley, first Duke of Wellington (1769–1852), British soldier and statesman. He was the principal architect of the British victory in the Napoleonic Wars, finally crushing Napoleon at Waterloo in June 1815. He then embarked on a political career motivated by loyalty to the crown rather than a sense of party leadership, although he was always Tory in his opinions. He was Prime Minister from 1828 to 1830. His opposition to parliamentary reform, on the grounds that the British constitution was perfect and needed no change, made him very unpopular at the period when attempts were being made to pass what became the Reform Act, 1832.

22 *Mr. Peel.* English statesman and Tory politician (1788–1850). He was Home Secretary and Leader of the House of Commons in Wellington's ministry (1828–30). In the subsequent Whig ministry he organized a powerful Tory opposition to the Reform Bill. In 1834 he formed a cabinet with Wellington, becoming First Lord of the Treasury and Chancellor of the Exchequer. His 'Tamworth Manifesto' (1834) set out the principles of a new liberal Toryism. He resigned in 1835, but in 1841 became Prime Minister as First Lord of the Treasury. In 1842 his reorganization of finances included a bill for the re-introduction of an income-tax. (See note on *British income-tax*, p. 346 below.) He faced hostility from the protectionists

in his party when he advocated repeal of the corn laws (see note on *Anti-Corn-law League*, p. 361 below) and, although he passed the measure in 1846, the protectionists brought about his defeat, and he resigned. He gave general support to the Whig ministry of Lord John Russell and backed its free trade policy. He died, after a fall from his horse, in 1850.

23 *Bishop Burnet*. Gilbert Burnet (1643–1715), Bishop of Salisbury, theologian and historian.

23 *Lord Shaftesbury*. Anthony Ashley Cooper, first Earl of Shaftesbury (1621–83). Of the king's party at the beginning of the Civil War, but distrusted by the court because he thought that mutual concession was necessary. He went over to Parliament's side and commanded the parliamentary forces in Dorset. He was a member of Cromwell's privy council but subscribed to protestations charging the Protector with arbitrary government. After Richard Cromwell had been deposed Shaftesbury was involved in the plan to restore Charles II to the throne. King Charles made him a privy councillor. In 1661 he was Chancellor of the Exchequer. He supported Charles's Dutch war. In 1672 he became Lord High Chancellor but shortly afterwards he was deprived of the office, probably through the influence of Charles's brother, the Duke of York. Shaftesbury then became one of the most powerful leaders of the opposition, and in his hostility to the Duke of York, who was next in line to the throne, he is supposed to have entered into connection with the Duke of Monmouth, with a view to supporting his claims to the crown. (See the satirical poem 'Absalom and Achitophel' by John Dryden, Shaftesbury's political opponent.) Shaftesbury was sent to the Tower, and tried for high treason. The bill of indictment against him was ignored by the grand jury; he withdrew to Holland, where he died.

23 *Lord Goderich*. Frederick John Robinson, Viscount Goderich, afterwards first Earl of Ripon (1782–1859), the weak and irresolute Tory politician. Cobbett nicknamed him 'Prosperity' Robinson because of the stubbornly sanguine views he expressed while Chancellor of the Exchequer 1823–7. George IV chose Goderich to succeed Canning as Prime Minister in 1827 because he hoped that, as a weak man, he would carry out the king's wishes. The constitution of a Finance Committee forced Goderich to choose between William Huskisson, whom he favoured, and the king's man, John Herries. He tried to evade the difficulty by putting the onus of the decision on the king, who dismissed him.

23 *Mr. Canning.* George Canning (1770–1827), Tory political leader best known for his work as foreign secretary, particularly his opposition of Metternich and his support of the liberation of Greece. He was, however, consistently opposed to parliamentary reform. When the Earl of Liverpool resigned the premiership in 1827, Canning succeeded him but died a few months later.

24 *Lord Liverpool.* Robert Banks Jenkinson, second Earl of Liverpool (1770–1828), Tory politician. His ministry lasted from 1812 until 1827 when he had a stroke and was forced to resign.

24 *Lord Castlereagh.* Robert Stewart, Viscount Castlereagh and second Marquess of Londonderry (1769–1822), Tory politician. He was Foreign Secretary, 1812–22. He managed the Grand Alliance which defeated Napoleon, and represented Britain at the Vienna peace conference in 1815. He was Canning's bitter opponent. He committed suicide in 1822.

24 *in a manner not unworthy of Colonel Joyce.* i.e., in a high-handed manner. George Joyce (born 1618, still alive 1647, but date of death unknown), officer in the Parliamentary army, seized Charles I on 3 June 1647. Joyce's commander, Sir Thomas Fairfax, wanted to court-martial Joyce, who insisted that Cromwell had authorized his action. Cromwell denied this but admitted that he had ordered Joyce to prevent Charles I's removal from Holmby House, where he was seized.

25 *Brennus.* Leader of the Gauls who invaded Italy in 390 or 387 B.C. He captured Rome, accepted ransom from the defenders, and then escaped with his booty.

25 *the tall Gaul sent to murder the rival of Sylla.* The rival of Lucius Cornelius Sylla or Sulla, Roman consul and commander in 88 B.C., was Gaius or Caius Marius, who was compelled to flee Sulla's superior forces. The magistrates of Minturnae, where Marius took shelter, decided to put him to death, but none of the citizens would undertake the task. Whereupon a cavalryman (some versions of the story say he was a Gaul) took a sword and entered the room where Marius was lying in the shadows; his eyes seemed to shoot flame at the soldier, and a loud voice came out of the darkness saying, 'Man, dost thou dare to slay Caius Marius?' The Gaul fled, throwing down his sword and crying, 'I cannot kill Caius Marius.' (See Plutarch's *Lives*, Loeb Classical Library, 11 vols., 1920, ix. 573.)

25 *strawberry-leaves.* An allusion to the row of strawberry-leaves decorating a duke's coronet.

26 *the king*. King William IV (1765–1837), third son of George III. He came to the English throne in June 1830.

31 *The events of 1830*. The defeat of Wellington's government and the formation of the Whig government, led by Lord Grey. The 1830 July Revolution in France had toppled Charles X from his throne. There were fears that a similar revolution might occur in England.

31 *Lord Grey*. Charles Grey, the second Earl Grey (1764–1845), Whig nobleman of the old school, punctiliously honourable and high-minded, and devoted to upholding the constitution and popular liberty as he understood them. He was a man of narrow views and timorous in effecting reform, but he opposed the new corn laws of 1815 whereby corn had to reach the price of 80s a quarter (i.e. eight bushels) before foreign corn could be imported, so raising the price of bread, and he supported parliamentary reform. He was Prime Minister 1830–4.

34 *an East India director*. A director of the East India Company. The English East India Company was incorporated in 1600 to trade with the archipelago of spice islands, known as the East Indies. In about 1624 the English were driven out by the Dutch and began to found settlements on the coast of India. This marks the beginning of the British Indian Empire. The East India Company of Disraeli's reference was formed in 1708 by amalgamating the original company with one of its rivals. Every shareholder who held £500 of the company's stock became a member of the court of proprietors, which annually chose twenty-four to form a court of directors; only those who held not less than £2,000 of stock were eligible for election.

36 *knights of the four orders*. The four orders of knighthood are The Most Noble Order of the Garter, founded by Edward III in *c*. 1348; The Most Ancient and Most Noble Order of the Thistle, instituted by James II in 1687; The Most Honourable Military Order of the Bath, instituted in 1725 by George I, and following a medieval ceremony of knighthood; The Most Illustrious Order of St. Patrick, instituted by George III in 1783.

36 *Grand Cross*. One of the 72 Knights Grand Cross (G.C.B.) of the Order of the Bath.

37 *his majesty, calling for a hackney coach, went down and dissolved parliament in 1831*. William IV's action on 22 April 1831. Lord John Russell's first Reform Bill was under constant attack by the Tories; dissolution meant a general election and popular feeling made it certain that a Whig Parliament would be elected to pass the Bill.

37 *The Thirty at Athens.* The thirty tyrants who took over from the Democrats during the mood of disillusionment at the end of the Peloponnesian War. They ruled Athens from September 404 B.C. until May 403 B.C., when they were themselves overthrown by the Democrats.

37 *a Venetian conclave.* Exclusive government, unrepresentative of the people. Sir Robert Peel's ministry does not embody 'true' Toryism, as Disraeli would define it.

38 *Lord Durham.* John George Lambton, first Earl of Durham (1792–1840), Whig MP for the county of Durham from 1813 until 1828, when he was elevated to a peerage. Together with Lord John Russell, Sir James Graham, and Lord Duncannon he was entrusted by Lord Grey with the preparation of the first Reform Bill. He was present at the interview, on 22 April 1831, when the king was persuaded to dissolve Parliament.

38 *the Carlton.* In the late 1820s and early 1830s political clubs developed as a result of the movement for parliamentary reform. The Reform Club was established by Whig MPs in 1832 to rally support for the Reform Bill. Its rival, the Carlton Club, was founded the same year, centring on the Duke of Wellington and his friends. It became a citadel of Toryism.

39 *Brooks'.* Fashionable gaming-club in Pall Mall bought by Brooks in 1774, and moved to St. James's Street in 1778. It was traditionally associated with the Whig aristocracy.

39 *Crockford's.* Gaming-club opened by William Crockford in St. James's Street in 1828, famous for its excellent food. It was closed in 1844, shortly after Crockford's death.

39 *Swan River.* The Swan River Settlement (1829) was the first colonial settlement in Western Australia.

40 *In a palace in a garden . . .* In the preface to the Collected Edition of his novels 1870–1, Disraeli says that this passage is based on Lord Lyndhurst's description of the scene in Kensington Palace in 1837 when 'the peers and privy councillors and chief personages of the realm pledged their fealty to their new Sovereign'. Disraeli had accompanied Lyndhurst to the Palace and heard his account as they drove home after the ceremony. John Singleton Copley, Baron Lyndhurst (1772–1863), was a brilliant lawyer and Tory leader, and Chancellor of the Exchequer in 1831–4, 1834–5, 1841–6.

43 *Helvetius*. Claude Adrien Helvétius (1715–71), the French philosopher whose hedonistic philosophy included the ideas that all man's faculties may be reduced to physical sensation, and that self-interest, founded on love of pleasure and fear of pain, is the spring of judgement, action, and affection.

44 *Mr. Paget's tales*. The Revd. Francis Paget (1806–82), supporter of the Oxford Movement and so 'high church'; author of improving tales and novels, such as *The Warden of Berkingholt, or Rich and Poor* (1843).

46 *tremendously fierce against allotments*. One of the causes supported by Young England was the provision of allotments which labouring men could rent to grow their own food. On 11 October 1844 Disraeli and Lord John Manners attended a dinner at Bingley, Yorkshire, to celebrate the first allotments there. Several of the great landowners - including the Whig Duke of Norfolk and the Tory Duke of Rutland, Lord John's father - had provided allotments for their tenants, as had also some of the manufacturers. See Sheila M. Smith, *Mr. Disraeli's Readers*, op. cit., pp. 23–4, and note on p. 215 below.

51 *the rural town of Marney*. In creating localities in *Sybil* Disraeli's method generally combines personal experience, often of various places, with facts and scenes taken from Commissions, Reports, sometimes newspapers. Marney might very well owe something to his memories of Ripon, not far from Fountains Abbey, the original of Marney Abbey, but many of the details are taken from Edwin Chadwick's *Report on the Sanitary Condition of the Labouring Population of Great Britain* (1842), and Disraeli's depiction of the rural labourers' plight finds substantial support in *The Assistant Poor Law Commissioners' Reports on the Employment of Women and Children in Agriculture* (1843). See Sheila M. Smith, *The Other Nation*, Oxford, 1980, pp. 117–20; 'Blue Books and Victorian Novelists', *Review of English Studies*, 21 (1970), 23–40; and Martin Fido, ' "From his own Observation": Sources of Working Class Passages in Disraeli's "Sybil" ', *Modern Language Review*, 72 (1977), 267–84, which provides a lot of useful source material despite confusion of the *Reports on Agriculture* with Chadwick's *Report* in the reading of 'Blue Books and Victorian Novelists'.

53 *Synochus*. A continued or unintermitting fever.

53 *merry England*. An ironical use of a phrase much employed in the 'Condition of England' debate of the 1830s and 1840s. See,

for example, Carlyle's 'this once merry England of ours' (*Chartism*, Ch. 10) and Pugin's 'Catholic England was merry England, at least for the humbler classes' (*The True Principles of Pointed or Christian Architecture*, 1841).

53 *the bold British peasant*. An ironic echo of Oliver Goldsmith's 'bold peasantry, their country's pride' in 'The Deserted Village' (1770), deploring the destruction of rural life.

63 *Belvoirs ... Chatsworths ... Wentworths ... Stowes*. Belvoir Castle, Leicestershire, a medieval castle rebuilt 1800–25 by the fifth Duke and Duchess of Rutland, parents of Disraeli's Young England friend Lord John Manners. Chatsworth, the great house in Derbyshire built by the first Duke of Devonshire 1687–1707. Wentworth Woodhouse, Yorkshire, seat of the third Earl Fitzwilliam (1786–1857), a vast structure created by merging two eighteenth-century houses – its east front, begun 1734, is the longest of any English country house. Stowe, Buckinghamshire, another great eighteenth-century house, long a-building; Vanbrugh, 'Capability' Brown, Kent, and Robert Adam worked on it at various periods. It was the seat of the second Duke of Buckingham and Chandos (1797–1861) who succeeded to the estate in 1839. Ironically, in the light of Gerard's eulogy, the Duke ruined himself borrowing money to buy land and by extravagant spending so that he was forced to sell his landed property and all the contents of Stowe in 1848.

63 *the union workhouses ... you have given us a substitute for the monasteries*. The graphic equivalent to this argument can be found in Augustus Welby Northmore Pugin's *Contrasts, or a parallel between the noble edifices of the fourteenth and fifteenth centuries and similar buildings of the present day, showing the present decay of taste*, 1836; 2nd edn. 1841, the illustration 'Contrasted Residences for the Poor' setting a 'Modern Poor House' – a Benthamite Panopticon structure like a prison, with 'The Master' holding a whip and the 'Diet' consisting of bread, gruel, oatmeal and potatoes – against a monastic church where 'The Master' gives alms to the poor and the 'Diet' includes beef, mutton, cheese and ale. Also, for similar arguments against the 'ravage' of the Reformation, see William Cobbett, *A History of the Protestant Reformation* (first published in parts, 1824–6), 2 vols, 1829.

67 *ten-pound days*. The Reform Act 1832 gave the vote to every male householder, in the boroughs, who occupied a house the rental value of which was not less than £10.

73 *Dr. Buckland*. William Buckland (1784–1856), clergyman, geo-

logist, and Fellow of the Royal Society. On Peel's recommendation he became Dean of Westminster in 1845.

73 *Arago*. Dominique François Jean Arago (1786–1853), French scientist and statesman. His achievements were mainly in the fields of astronomy, magnetism, and optics.

75 *Cumberland*. Richard Cumberland (1732–1811), whose work included sentimental comedies, the best of which are *The Brothers* (1769) and *The West Indian* (1771). He is caricatured as Sir Fretful Plagiary in Sheridan's *The Critic* (1779).

75 *Morton*. Thomas Morton (1764?–1838), author of the successful comedies *The Way to get Married* (1796), *A Cure for Heartache* (1797), and *Speed the Plough* (1798) – the latter notable for initiating the idea of Mrs. Grundy, strict upholder of morals, whose disapproval is feared.

75 *Hastings*. Warren Hastings (1732–1818), first Governor-General of Bengal 1774. He went to India in the service of the East India Company when he was seventeen. He retired in 1785; he was impeached in 1788 and charged with extortion and misgovernment. The trial lasted six years. He was acquitted but ruined. The Directors of the East India Company granted him a pension and he retired to live the life of a country gentleman, pursuing his Oriental studies.

77 *Lord North's administration*. Frederick North, second Earl of Guilford (1732–92), accused of being a tool of George III's. He was First Lord of the Treasury 1770–82, during which time the American colonies were lost to Britain.

77 *Mrs. Crewe*. Frances, daughter of Fulke Greville, in 1776 married John Crewe, Whig MP for Stafford 1765–68 and for Cheshire 1768–1802. She was a great favourite with Fox, and in her honour the Prince of Wales proposed the toast 'True Blue and Mrs. Crewe' at a banquet celebrating Fox's re-election for Westminster in 1784. (Blue was originally the Whig colour.) She died in 1818.

80 *with six seats in the House of Commons*. There were six constituencies where his wealth and influence ensured the election of candidates of his choice. See note on *their Richmond or their Malton*, p. 153 below.

80 *Walcheren expeditions*. The Walcheren campaign (1809) was a bungled attempt to divert Napoleon from Austria, which was hard pressed by the French army. It was a fruitless attempt to capture or destroy the French fleet in the Scheldt, and make Antwerp and Flushing useless to the French navy. The landing was made on the island of Walcheren.

80 *Manchester massacres.* On 16 August 1819 cavalrymen and hussars attacked the crowd assembled in St. Peter's Fields, Manchester, to listen to Henry Hunt and proclaim their support for parliamentary reform. Lord Sidmouth, the Home Secretary, had encouraged the magistrates to keep order by means of the yeomanry in areas where large public meetings, of the kind recently held in Birmingham, might occur. Eleven people, including two women, were killed, and several hundred wounded. The radicals immediately dubbed the incident 'Peterloo': as Wellington had formerly defeated the foreigner at Waterloo, Lord Sidmouth had now achieved a victory over his fellow-countrymen at the battle of Peterloo.

80 *Queen's trials.* In 1795 the Prince Regent had been persuaded to marry his cousin, Caroline of Brunswick. She was vulgar and ostentatious, and the royal pair soon parted company, Caroline living abroad for some years. In 1820 George III died and Caroline returned to claim her rights as Queen. George IV determined to have a divorce. On 8 July 1820 a Bill of Pains and Penalties was introduced by Lord Liverpool, the Prime Minister, into the House of Lords to deprive Caroline of her title and to dissolve the marriage. The London crowd had little feeling for her, but they hated George IV and she was escorted by cheering mobs as she drove each day to the Lords for the hearing. The Whigs, who were in opposition, made political capital out of the event and supported her. So many peers withdrew from the Lords because of the temper of the public and the unreliability of the witnesses that the third reading of the Bill was carried by the small majority of nine, and Liverpool announced that the Government would proceed no further with the measure.

80 *the Cottage.* The Prince Regent's country house in Windsor Great Park, built 1812–14, designer John Nash.

80 *they wanted his six votes for Canning.* Canning needed the Whigs' support to maintain his precarious position when, at the king's wish, he became Prime Minister after Lord Liverpool had a stroke and resigned in 1827. In the event, Canning had only a few months in office and died on 8 August 1827.

86 *bate ticket.* A written paper notifying the worker that he was to be fined part of his wages.

86 *small cops.* A 'cop' is the conical ball of newspun yarn on a spindle. 'Small' implies short measure.

86 *bad-bottomed cop.* One in which the yarn is damaged at the beginning of the spinning.

86 *snicks*. Snags, damaged yarn.

86 *snickey*. 'Snick' is to cut. 'Snicking' is the surreptitious obtaining of anything. The manufacturers Shuffle and Screw are as rotten as damaged yarn; there is also the suggestion that they filch a worker's wages on the pretext of bad work. For the source of Disraeli's phrase see M. Fido, op. cit., p. 271.

88 *one 'Northern Star' and two 'Moral Worlds'*. The *Northern Star* was the Chartist newspaper begun by Feargus O'Connor in 1837; *The New Moral World* started publication in 1834, edited by Robert Owen.

90 *'THE TEMPLE OF THE MUSES.'* M. Fido has discovered a description of an entertainment room of the same name, in The Jolly Hatters, Stockport, given in William Dodd's *The Factory System Illustrated in a Series of Letters to Lord Ashley* (1842). See M. Fido, op. cit., pp. 272–3. Besides the name, some of the details are very close to Disraeli's description, but Manchester in the 1840s had many 'music saloons' such as the Apollo in the London Road, certainly not as grand as 'The Temple' but on the same pattern (see the journalist Angus Bethune Reach's description of it in 1849, reprinted C. Aspin, *Manchester and the Textile Districts in 1849*, Helmshore Local History Society, 1972, pp. 57–60). Reach was writing a series of reports for the *Morning Chronicle*'s investigation 'Labour and the Poor', and he visited the Apollo as being 'one of the music saloons, of which I had heard so much'. Evidently there was a vogue for grand classical decorations; another concert room, attended by workers from the Atlas Iron Works, was resplendent 'with oil paintings, one representing the Vale of Tempe' (Aspin, op. cit., p. 61). Disraeli's description might very well be a mixture of reading, hearsay, and, possibly, observation.

91 *Mazeppa*. The eponymous hero of Byron's poem.

92 *Lowell*. A factory town in Massachusetts, U.S.A., described by Dickens in Chapter 4 of *American Notes* (1842).

92 *sherry cobler*. A cobbler is an iced drink of wine or spirits, sugar, and lemon.

96 *rummers*. Large drinking glasses.

97 *Society for the Propagation of the Gospel in Foreign Parts*. Founded in 1698 and incorporated by William III on 16 June 1701.

97 *Juggernaut*. The idol of Krishna at Pūrī in Orissa, annually dragged in procession on an enormous car, under the wheels of which many devotees are said to have thrown themselves, in former times, to be crushed.

97 *Moloch.* Properly Molech, an Ammonite god to whom children were sacrificed by burning.

97 *Godfrey's cordial.* Proprietary mixture of laudanum and treacle used to quieten babies, often with fatal effect.

98 *DEVILSDUST.* Cotton waste, also called 'shoddy'. In the series 'Labour and the Poor' the letter on 'The Cloth Districts of Yorkshire' (the *Morning Chronicle*, 3 December 1849) remarks that 'an essential feature' of the cotton town Oldham 'is the spinning and preparing of waste and refuse cotton', that is, Devilsdust's earliest paid work. He worked in the 'wadding-hole'. Wadding was a loose fibrous material used for padding and made from cotton waste. The letter continues: 'To this stuff the name of shoddy is given, but the real and orthodox shoddy is a production of the woollen districts, and consists of the second-hand wool manufactured by the tearing up, or rather the grinding, of woollen rags by means of coarse willows, called devils; the operation of which sends forth choking clouds of dry pungent dirt and floating fibres – the real and original "devil's dust".'

99 *Truck.* Payment in goods instead of money. In the owner's tommy-shop (see Book III, Chapter 1, and following) the working-people were expected to spend a good proportion of their wages on goods supplied by the owner, often, they complained, expensive and of poor quality.

99 *the ten-hour bill.* The struggle to secure legislation to limit the factory working day to ten hours began in the early 1830s, supported by Chartists, Evangelical philanthropists such as Lord Ashley, and protectionists inspired by hatred of free traders. The Ten-Hours Act, restricting the work of women and of 'young persons' between thirteen and eighteen years old to ten hours, five days in the week, and eight on Saturday, was finally passed in 1847, but proved difficult to enforce in the factories.

100 *The battle of Navarino.* In the Greek War of Independence; the decisive defeat of the Turks by a combined British, French, and Russian fleet on 20 October 1827.

100 *is a – good strike.* In the original manuscript (at Hughenden Manor) from which the text of *Sybil* was printed, this reads 'is – a bloody good strike'. Usually Disraeli's use of slang is stilted and artificial. It is a pity that one example of strong and telling usage of colloquial speech should have been eliminated in the cause of propriety.

105 *the blue ribbon cover.* The best game preserve on the estate. The

phrase derives from the blue silk ribbon worn as a badge of honour, such as the broad dark blue ribbon worn by members of the Order of the Garter.

105 *Christian architecture.* The pointed style in architecture; Gothic. See Augustus Welby Pugin's publications: *The true principles of pointed or Christian architecture* (1841) and *An Apology for the revival of Christian Architecture in England* (1843). For the moral and spiritual qualities associated with the Gothic style, see particularly John Ruskin, 'On the Nature of Gothic', *Stones of Venice,* Vol. II (1853), Chapter 6.

127 *Appropriation clause.* The clause of the Irish Tithe Bill (1835), brought forward by Lord John Russell, whereby any surplus revenue that might accrue by the working of the act was to be appropriated for the education of all classes of Irish Christians. The principle was adopted by the Commons but rejected by the Lords in 1835 and 1836, and was abandoned. The clause in effect laid down that a portion of the endowments of the Irish Church should be applied to secular purposes.

127 *Lord Stanley.* Edward George Geoffrey Smith Stanley, fourteenth Earl of Derby (1799–1869), statesman and scholar, active in Parliament from 1822 until his death. In 1834 Lord John Russell supported Henry Ward's 'Appropriation Resolution' (see note on the *Appropriation clause,* p. 127 above) for the redistribution of the Irish Church revenues, split the Whig Ministry, which was divided on the issue, and caused Stanley to resign as Colonial Secretary. From this point Stanley left the Whigs, and for a time spoke and voted as an independent member but drifted towards the Tories. When Melbourne was dismissed as Prime Minister in November 1834 and Peel was sent for to form a Tory administration after Wellington refused the position of Prime Minister, Stanley was in a commanding position and could have allied himself with Peel by accepting office. This he refused to do, though willing to serve under Peel, whose ministry proved short-lived. Melbourne returned as Prime Minister and Stanley's hopes of leading a 'centre party' faded. He accepted the office of Colonial Secretary in Peel's administration in 1841. In 1844 he moved to the House of Lords, and was leader of the Conservatives in the Lords from 1846 until 1868 when he retired because of ill-health. He was Prime Minister in 1852, in 1858–9 supported by Disraeli, and from 1866 to 1868, when Disraeli himself became Prime Minister.

127 *the proxy.* Written note authorizing a person to vote for another in the House of Lords. The Duke of Fitz-Aquitaine did not bother to record his vote in the House of Lords. The practice of proxy voting in the Lords was discontinued later in the century.

128 *would have gone over with Lord Stanley in 1835.* Lord John Russell, leading the Opposition against Peel, moved a resolution, on 7 April 1835, that no proposal dealing with tithe in Ireland could be considered a final or satisfactory solution which did not accept the principle of 'appropriation' (see note on *Appropriation clause*, p. 127 above). Peel's Government was defeated by 285 votes to 258. This was one in a series of defeats suffered by Peel's Government on the question of Irish titles, so Peel resigned and his brief ministry ended.

BOOK III

140 *Naked to the waist, an iron chain fastened to a belt of leather. The Commissioners' Report on Mines* (Children's Employment Commission, 1842) is illustrated with pictures of girls working like this. Disraeli takes some of the details of his mining scenes from the Report. It created a great stir, especially the pictures. Elizabeth Barrett Browning's poem 'The Cry of the Children' was inspired by the Children's Employment Commission which, in 1843, also reported on Trades and Manufactures.

140 *Society for the Abolition of Negro Slavery.* Irony at the expense of the Whigs of the first Reformed Parliament who passed the Act to abolish slavery in the Crown Colonies, 1833, and of the members of the Society for the Extinction of Slavery, formed in 1840.

140 *that punishment which philosophical philanthropy has invented for the direst criminals.* The Utilitarians, disciples of Bentham, had long urged penal reform. The Reformed Parliament, 1832, established a Royal Commission to revise the whole criminal law; its report was published in May 1837. In this year the Government adopted the so-called 'separate' system as the official penal system, that is, solitary confinement, the prisoners being hooded when they had to move about the prison. Pentonville Prison, London, opened in December 1842, was designed as the new model 'separate' prison, in which convicts were to have a rigorous reformatory period of not more than eighteen months, during which they would be taught useful trades, before being transported to Van Diemen's Land. The Utilitarian philosophy

behind this penal system was that cleanliness, industry, and order were to supplant the dirt and chaos of the old eighteenth-century prisons. The criminal was forced to accept the work ethic of an increasingly earnest society; labour was to be the remedy for his disease (crime), and he was to be kept away from the contamination of other criminals. For Dickens's description of the cruelties of the 'separate' system, see his account of Cherry Hill, the Eastern Penitentiary in Philadelphia, U.S.A., opened in 1830, in *American Notes*, Ch. 7.

141 *Sir Joshua . . . Lady Alice Gordon . . . guardian angels.* A reference to the painting 'Heads of Angels' exhibited in the Royal Academy, 1787: a composite portrait of Miss Frances Isabella Gordon (1782–1831), daughter of Lord and Lady William Gordon, by Sir Joshua Reynolds (1723–92), first President of the Royal Academy. The portrait is in the Tate Gallery, London.

141 *Mr. Landseer.* Sir Edwin Henry Landseer (1802–73), successfull and popular painter much admired by Queen Victoria. Dogs and deer are his best and favourite subjects.

141 *Mr. Etty.* William Etty (1787–1849), the English painter who achieved popularity with pictures of seductive nudes in rich, luscious colours. He also painted cloyingly pretty children's portraits.

142 *young Queen's picture.* The Queen's head on coin of the realm, i.e. he has not yet had his wages paid in money.

142 *bums.* A bum bailiff, or bailiff, or sheriff's officer, who would arrest for debt. The suggested derivation of 'bum bailiff' is that he was so called because he stood close up to the debtor's back.

142 *he do swear at the women . . . a shocking little dog.* Disraeli lifted this, and much of the tommy-shop scene in Book III, Ch. 3, from the *First Report of the Midland Mining Commission*, 1843; see C. R. Fay, *Life and Labour in the Nineteenth Century*, Cambridge, 1947, pp. 193 f.; M. Fido, op. cit., pp. 274–84; and Sheila M. Smith, *The Other Nation*, op. cit., pp. 148–51.

144 *ten-yard coal.* Ten yards was the amount of coal on the coal face of a seam roughly three feet wide apportioned to a miner to be worked in a day. A man who could get this done was a good worker. Hence, Mr. Nixon's words worked well, made their point.

144 *clay.* Clay pipe.

144 *clammed.* Starved.

145 *lushy.* Drunk.

146 *hipped*. Bored, out of sorts, melancholy (from 'hypochondria').

147 *a Screw*. Either someone who forces down prices by haggling, or a man who compels somebody to pay; in either case, a miserly, stingy person. See Shuffle and Screw, p. 86 above.

147 *pricked*. To become sour.

150 *House*. The workhouse. Seven shillings a week was, of course, starvation wages, especially for a man with a family. Lord Marney is one of the best satirical portraits in *Sybil*. His defensive, self-justifying tone is well caught; Disraeli has him damn himself out of his own mouth.

151 *spontaneous combustion*. Taking fire, or burning away, through conditions produced within the substance itself.

151 *Boodle's*. Gaming club, renowned for its cuisine, established in 1763. Originally the Sçavoir Vivre, it was later named after William Boodle, who became manager *c.* 1774. Its beautiful clubhouse in St. James's Street is said to have been designed by the Adam brothers.

153 *their Richmond or their Malton*. Richmond and Malton, both in Yorkshire and both examples of parliamentary seats in the 'pay' of great Whig families, the Dundas family in the case of Richmond, the head of the family being Lawrence, second Baron Dundas of Aske (1766–1839), created Earl of Zetland in 1838; in the case of Malton, Charles William, third Earl Fitz-William (1786–1857), owner of the great house Wentworth Woodhouse (see note to p. 63 above).

156 *stints*. Allotted portions of work, amounts of coal to be hewn. See note on *ten-yard coal*, p. 144 above.

157 *sawney*. Wheedling.

157 *spout*. A pawnbroker. The spout was the pawnbroker's shoot or lift to carry the pledged goods from the shop to the storeroom.

161 *Wodgate*. For Disraeli's creation of this fictional community, see Sheila M. Smith, 'Willenhall and Wodgate: Disraeli's Use of Blue Book Evidence', *Review of English Studies*, 13 (1962), 368–84, and *The Other Nation*, op. cit., pp. 69–73. With typical exaggeration, Disraeli strips the town of all amenities and softening influences to emphasize the barbarousness of its inhabitants, who need guidance from the enlightened aristocrats, like Egremont, yet, ironically, shame the effete aristocracy with their own aristocracy of labour. 'Wodgate' suggests 'Woden', the heathen Saxon god.

163 *Mamlouks*. The members of the military body, originally composed of Caucasian slaves, which seized the throne of Egypt

in 1254 and continued to form the ruling class of that country until the early part of the nineteenth century; more particularly, the Mameluke sultans who ruled Egypt 1254–1517.

178 *prog.* Food.

197 *Information against Thomas Hind . . . 'What a pity', said Morley, 'that Thomas Hind . . .'.* Thom Braun has pointed out that the first edition of *Sybil* prints 'Robert Hind' on both occasions, but that in the one-volume edition of *Sybil* revised by Disraeli as part of the 'collected works', 1853, there was an initial change from 'Robert' to 'Thomas', the second mention of the name being unamended. See Thom Braun, ' "Sybil": A Misprint', *Notes and Queries*, June 1978, pp. 232–3. Most subsequent editions were set from the text of the 1853 revised edition and so they print a 'Thomas' and a 'Robert'.

198 *Bigod and Bohun.* Hugh Bigod (d. 1266), younger son of Hugh Bigod, third Earl of Norfolk. Henry III made him chief ranger of Farndale Forest, Yorkshire. He became chief justiciar in 1258, and had custody of the Tower of London. In 1259–60 he went with two of the principal judges on a circuit to administer justice throughout the kingdom. In 1260 he resigned the office of justiciar, probably because of dissatisfaction with the lawless conduct of the barons. Henry de Bohun, first Earl of Hereford (1176–1220), Constable of England (a position which carried extensive powers of jurisdiction), through whom the hereditary right to the office of constable passed to the family of de Bohun. King John created him Earl of Hereford in 1199. In 1215 he joined the confederate barons who obtained the concession of Magna Charta, and was one of the twenty-five appointed to ensure its observance. He died on pilgrimage to the Holy Land in 1220.

198 *the forest laws.* Laws relating to royal forests, enacted by William I and other Norman kings and were regarded by Disraeli as oppressive.

201 *The dog, invisible, sprang forward and seized upon his assailant.* For the similarities between this melodramatic incident and the contemporary popular dog-melodrama, see Sheila M. Smith, *The Other Nation*, op. cit., pp. 237–8.

BOOK IV

202 *this Jamaica bill.* The Bill suspending for five years the constitution of Jamaica after the colonial Jamaica Assembly had
defied the British Government by proclaiming immediate emancipation of slaves in Jamaica without waiting for the agreed
date 1840 – hoping by so doing to be rid of interference by
emancipationists – and by rejecting the Prison Act giving the
colonial Governor supreme control over the administration of
the prisons and so protecting the negroes against the brutality
of their former masters. The Jamaica Assembly suspended the
exercise of its functions until the Prison Act had been repealed.
Melbourne, the Prime Minister, decided to set up a dictatorship in Jamaica, which was to be ruled by the Governor
assisted by a council appointed by the British Government.
The radicals opposed the Bill because, although they attacked
slavery, they also defended constitutional liberty. Peel attacked
the harsh character of the measures proposed. On 6 May 1839
the Government's majority was reduced to five, and the Cabinet resigned.

203 *these affairs of the Chartists.* In the autumn 1838 there were elec-
tions of Chartist delegates throughout the country to form a
Convention which was to sit as a rival to the House of Commons and to prepare a National Petition, urging acceptance
of the 'six points' (see note on *the Five Points*, p. 373 below),
to be presented to Parliament. The Chartist leadership was
divided on the means by which their aims were to be achieved,
and there developed a running debate between the 'moral
force' Chartists, such as Lovett, and the 'physical force'
Chartists, such as George Harney. This debate is one of the
themes of *Sybil.* Feargus O'Connor, through his propaganda
paper the *Northern Star*, tried to be in both camps with his
slogan 'peaceably if we may, forcibly if we must'. By the end
of 1838 O'Connor had emerged as the dominant Chartist
leader. In February 1839 the Convention met in London, but
there was dissension among the delegates. In May 1839 the
Convention moved to Birmingham where there were riots,
leading to the arrest of the moderate leaders William Lovett
and John Collins. The Convention returned to London where
the Chartists' Petition was rejected by the House of Commons
in July, and provoked the Birmingham riots mentioned at the
beginning of Book V of *Sybil*. The Convention was disbanded.
In November there was conflict between the Chartists and the

military at Newport, Monmouthshire; the leaders of the rising were imprisoned or transported (see note on *John Frost*, p. 324, below) and some Chartist leaders in other parts of the country were arrested and imprisoned. The Chartists realized that they must be better organized to succeed in their aims. In July 1840 the National Charter Association was founded in Manchester, and in 1842 a second National Petition was presented to Parliament and again rejected. Riots and strikes followed in many parts of the country (this period of disturbances is described in Book VI of *Sybil*). The mid 1840s saw a revival of trade and there was less unemployment, partly because of the boom in railway construction, so the Chartist cause lost some of its urgency. This is the period of the conclusion of *Sybil*, when Chartism was losing some of its mass support. The final and third National Petition was organized in 1848 when there was another trade depression and a series of revolutions on the Continent, but again the Petition was rejected by Parliament. Minor strikes followed, but the Chartist leadership was again divided and Chartism as a mass movement collapsed. Feargus O'Connor became insane. The movement lost its working-class impetus, many deciding that social change could be best effected by alliance with the middle class.

203 *a Jacquerie*. From the French 'jaquerie' meaning 'peasants' or 'villeins'; the name given to the revolt of the peasants of Northern France against the nobles in 1357–8, hence any rising of the peasantry.

206 *a Mesmerist*. From the name of F. A. Mesmer, an Austrian physician (1734–1815); one practising his system whereby an hypnotic state, usually accompanied by insensibility to pain and muscular rigidity, can be induced by an influence exercised by the operator over the will and nervous system of the patient.

210 *Cuyp*. Aelbert Cuyp (1620–91), painter from Dordrecht, in the Netherlands. He is most famous for his paintings of landscapes, but he also painted animals, sea-pieces, still-lifes, and portraits.

210 *Allori*. Of the three Florentine painters of this name, Angiolo (1502–72), Alessandro (1535–1607) nephew of Angiolo, and Cristofano (1577–1621) son of Alessandro, Disraeli's painter could be Alessandro but is most likely to be Cristofano; his much-copied and most famous picture is the *Judith* in the Pitti Palace, Florence. Disraeli almost certainly would have known it.

210 *Sir Thomas Lawrence*. The painter (1769–1830) who became

President of the Royal Academy in 1820. He gained a European reputation as a portrait painter, and was commissioned by the Prince Regent to paint portraits of all the great personalities who were engaged in the struggle against Napoleon. He also formed a magnificent collection of drawings by the Old Masters, which in his will he offered to the nation on easy terms. The offer was refused, but fortunately part of the collection was bought later for the Ashmolean Museum, Oxford.

210 *Trenchard's speech.* Trenchard is Thomas Milner Gibson (1806–1884), a school-fellow of Disraeli's who became Tory MP for Ipswich in 1837 but was converted to liberal doctrines and resigned in 1839. He supported free trade and wanted to abolish the corn laws. He failed to regain a seat in Parliament until 1841, when his support of Cobden and his oratory on behalf of the Anti-Corn-Law League (see note on p. 361 below) won him a seat at Manchester. He was a skilful debater.

212 *that Finality speech of Lord John.* See note on p. 128 above.

212 *frondeurs.* Members of the Fronde, the party which rose in rebellion against Mazarin and the Court during the minority of Louis XIV of France; hence 'Fronde' means 'violent political opposition', and 'frondeur' a 'malcontent', an 'irreconcilable'.

214 *hachis.* (French) hash.

215 *the Druid's Altar.* A great rock on the moors above Bingley, in the West Riding of Yorkshire, looking down into the Aire Valley – a favourite subject for 'picturesque' artists. Disraeli, his wife Mary Anne, and Lord John Manners stayed at Bingley in 1844 as the guests of William Busfeild Ferrand (1809–89), a Yorkshire squire very concerned with the future of English agriculture and critical of the effects of increasing industrialization; he was then MP for Knaresborough. They were invited to attend a dinner in the Oddfellows' Hall, Bingley, on 11 October 1844 'for the purpose of celebrating the successful Introduction of Field Gardens into the Parish, as well as the formation of the Bingley Cricket Club', according to the advertisement in *The Bradford Observer*, 3 October 1844. For an account of the dinner, Disraeli's speech, and Young England's support of the allotments scheme, see Sheila M. Smith, *Mr. Disraeli's Readers*, op. cit., pp. 22–4.

223 *Apsley House.* The house at Hyde Park Corner built for Lord Chancellor Apsley in 1771 to his own design, although his initial plans had to be modified as he forgot to include the

staircase! Apsley's son left the house in 1807, and a few years later it became the home of the Duke of Wellington.

224 *pietra dura*. An inlay of coloured, hard stones, such as jasper and agate, set in marble slabs or wood panels. Its chief centre of production was Florence. The art was highly developed by the end of the sixteenth century; the climax of its prestige was the first half of the seventeenth century.

226 *it stood by Simon de Montfort on the field of Evesham*. Simon de Montfort (*c.* 1208–65), brother-in-law to Henry III, attempted to introduce a form of parliamentary government in 1258. With papal support Henry repudiated the parliamentary scheme of government. De Montfort's party for a time had military supremacy, but de Montfort was killed at the battle of Evesham on 4 August 1265.

227 *Paixhans' rockets*. Henri Joseph Paixhans (1783–1854), the French general, invented a howitzer called after him, which carried a hollow shot and cylindrical, conically pointed explosive shells, also of his invention.

228 *I am to represent Richard Cœur de Lion at the Queen's ball*. Manifestation of the Gothic revival can be found in the activities and fashions of high society, witness Maclise's portrait of Sir Francis Sykes, his wife Henrietta (Disraeli's ex-lover), and family in medieval dress (1837); the Eglinton Tournament (1839) swamped by Ayrshire rain and inaccurately described by Disraeli, who was not present, in his novel *Endymion*; and the series of fancy-dress balls given by Queen Victoria and Prince Albert beginning in 1842 when the Queen appeared as Queen Philippa and Albert as Edward III. Landseer's portrait of them is reproduced in colour (Plate 3) in the catalogue to the exhibition *Van Dyck in Check Trousers. Fancy Dress in Art and Life 1700–1900*, Scottish National Portrait Gallery, 1978. This catalogue also reproduces Maclise's portrait (Illustration 105) and discusses the Eglinton Tournament.

230 *a virtuous and able monarch*. Charles I. A typical example of Disraeli's special pleading on Charles's behalf.

230 *customs and excise*. An attack on the Whig method of raising money.

231 *speculating in railway shares*. Disraeli was writing *Sybil* at the height of the 'railway mania', when people scrambled for shares in the numerous companies constructing and running lines. During the period 1844–6 Parliament authorized the construction of over 400 railways.

235 *observed him drop a letter*. A cumbersome device by which

Morley learns Hatton's address. Disraeli was not very adept at devising plots.

237 *the kingdom of Cockaigne*. An imaginary country, a place of luxury and idleness.

242 *the Edict of Nantes*. The Proclamation signed at Nantes on 13 April 1598 by King Henry IV of France, granting a broad measure of religious liberty, civil rights, and security to his Calvinist subjects, known as Huguenots; revoked by Louis XIV.

244 *a Pembroke table*. A table supported on four fixed legs, having two flaps, which can be spread out horizontally and supported on legs connected with the central part by joints.

244 *Bunbury*. Henry William Bunbury (1750–1811), caricaturist and painter of comic pictures. His 'Hints to Bad Horsemen' made him popular and won him the praise of Sir Joshua Reynolds.

244 *Ranelagh*. The house and grounds in Chelsea by the Thames, of Richard, Earl of Ranelagh. In 1742 they were thrown open to the public as a proprietary place of entertainment. The Rotunda was built for concerts, and Ranelagh became the resort of fashionable society. By the end of the eighteenth century its popularity waned; the Rotunda was closed in 1803 and demolished, together with Ranelagh House, in 1805.

252 *the Athenæum*. The famous literary and scientific club founded by Sir Walter Scott and Thomas Moore in 1824.

253 *Dugdale*. Sir William Dugdale (1605–86), antiquarian and historian, created Garter King-of-Arms in 1677. His friendship with Sir Christopher Hatton, comptroller of Charles I's household, might very well have prompted Disraeli's choice of name for his fictional antiquary. Dugdale published *The Baronage of England, or an Historical Account of the Lives and most Memorable Actions of our English Nobility* in three volumes, 1675–6.

253 *Selden*. John Selden, lawyer and antiquary (1584–1654), friend of Ben Jonson.

257 *four stars in India stock*. Asterisks were prefixed to a stockholder's name when his holding exceeded a certain amount. In East India stock each vote to which a stockholder was entitled was denoted by a star; one star meant a holding of over £1,000, two stars over £3,000, three stars over £6,000 and four stars over £10,000.

259 *Watier's*. The dinner club founded at 81 Piccadilly, at the Prince Regent's suggestion, by Watier, the Prince's chef. It was famous for its elaborate cooking, and frequented by men

of fashion, including Beau Brummel. It became a gambling centre. It closed in *c.* 1819.

261 *the Church Commission.* The Royal Commission appointed by Peel in 1835 to examine the question of Church Reform.

261 *Exeter Hall.* A large hall on the north side of the Strand, demolished in 1907. It opened in 1831 and served as a meeting place for religious and philanthropic organizations, for concerts, and for other serious entertainment.

261 *Wilberforce.* William Wilberforce (1759–1833), the friend and supporter of Pitt the Younger. He was a philanthropist and a tireless worker for the abolition of slavery.

261 *Clarkson.* Thomas Clarkson (1760–1846), the persistent and influential anti-slavery agitator.

270 *in petto.* Italian phrase meaning 'in contemplation', 'undisclosed'.

270 *wore – petticoats.* The young Queen's sympathies and friends were Whig, and her trusted adviser was Lord Melbourne. When he resigned the premiership in May 1839 he informed the Queen that she must send for Wellington and persuade him to become Prime Minister or at least to join the Cabinet if Peel were to be the Premier. In the event, it was Peel who had to face the question of the Royal Household. In the past, when the Whigs were in power and the Court was Tory, they had required that those Gentlemen of the Household who were also MPs should be asked to resign their posts. The Tories now faced the difficulty when the Court was Whig, with the added complication that the sovereign was a Queen and her Household, Ladies. In her interview with Peel, the Queen refused to dismiss any of the Ladies of her Household. Wellington failed to resolve the difficulty. Melbourne was recalled, and his colleagues agreed to support the Queen. The Whigs remained in office.

271 *the farce of the 'Invincibles'.* A popular operatic farce by Thomas Morton, see second note on p. 75 above.

271 *the Meal-tub plot.* The plot allegedly against the Duke of York, afterwards James II, contrived by a man called Dangerfield, who hid seditious letters in the lodgings of Colonel Maunsell, and then, on 23 October 1679, informed customs-house officers so that they searched the lodgings for smuggled goods and brought the letters to light. After Dangerfield had been arrested on suspicion of forging the letters, papers were found, concealed in a meal-tub (barrel for storing oatmeal) at the house of a woman with whom he lived, containing the scheme

to be sworn to and accusing of treason eminent Protestants who opposed the Duke of York's succession, particularly the Earls of Shaftesbury, Essex, and Halifax.

273 *William Wyndham.* Sir William Wyndham (1687–1740), politician, Jacobite, and Tory leader, close friend of Henry St. John, Viscount Bolingbroke. After the election in 1715 Wyndham so strongly opposed the terms of George I's proclamation calling the Parliament that he was censured and narrowly escaped being sent to the Tower. Wyndham led the opposition against Robert Walpole, and in the 1730s Wyndham and Bolingbroke supported the Prince of Wales in his quarrels with George I, also attacking Walpole's foreign policy. Wyndham's death was a great blow to the opposition and to the hopes of the Tories.

BOOK V

282 *What does he mean by obtaining the results of the Charter without the intervention of its machinery?* Egremont's speech echoes Disraeli's own when the Petition was debated in the House of Commons. He remarked that 'although they did not approve of the remedy suggested by the Chartists, it did not follow they should not attempt to cure the disease complained of' (Hansard, Third Series, Vol. 49, p. 246).

282 *Sheffield, Duke of Buckingham.* John Sheffield, third Earl of Mulgrave, afterwards first Duke of Buckingham and Normanby (1648–1721), politician, man of letters, and patron of Dryden.

310 *Tom Paine.* English radical (1737–1809) who fought on the American side in the War of Independence. His most famous book is *The Rights of Man* (1791–2) in answer to Edmund Burke's *Reflections on the French Revolution* (1790).

310 *Cobbett.* William Cobbett (1763–1835), English journalist, publisher, political radical, and agriculturist. He is known especially for his *Rural Rides* (1830) and his radical journal, *Cobbett's Weekly Political Register,* which he began in 1802. In 1810 he was charged with sedition for protesting, in the journal, at the flogging of soldiers, and was imprisoned for two years in Newgate. He became MP after the Reform Act, 1832.

310 *Thistlewood.* Arthur Thistlewood (1770–1820), leader of the so-called Cato Street conspiracy, the group who assembled in Cato Street, Edgware Road, and planned the assassination of the ministers at a cabinet dinner. They were betrayed and

arrested on 23 February 1820. Thistlewood and four others were executed as traitors on 1 May 1820.

310 *General Jackson*. American lawyer and soldier (1767–1845), created major-general in 1814. He won fame in the War of 1812 and was the hero of the Battle of New Orleans against the British. A Congressman and member of the Democratic party, he became the seventh President of the United States of America. He was regarded as the symbol and spokesman of the common man.

310 *shrub*. Lemon and spirits, especially rum.

312 *Seven Dials*. A notorious slum, in the parish of St. Giles, through which New Oxford Street was later driven. See Dickens's 'Seven Dials' in *Sketches by Boz*, Second Series, 1837. In Sybil's journey Disraeli, like Dickens, uses the device of 'the unexperienced wayfarer through "the Dials"' to bring his readers in contact with the Other Nation.

314 *a ticket for the Mendicity Society*. Heavily ironical at the expense of the middle classes' obsession with relieving only the 'deserving poor'. The Society was established in Red Lion Square, in 1818. Its aim was to suppress public begging and other impositions. Tickets received from the Society were given by subscribers to beggars, who obtained relief at the Society's house, if 'deserving'.

316 *iarvies*. Hackney coachmen.

316 *link*. The boy employed to carry a link, a torch made of tow and pitch, to light people along the street.

317 *Soult*. Nicholas Jean de Dieu Soult (1769–1851), Duke of Dalmatia, Marshal of France. He was the ardent champion of Napoleon, and commanded the French forces in Spain during the Peninsular War.

317 *Diebitsch*. Hans Karl Anton Friedrich von Diebitsch (1785–1831), German-born Russian field marshal. He distinguished himself at the Battle of Leipzig, 1813; in 1814 he advised Czar Alexander I to occupy Paris and so de-throne Napoleon. When Alexander died he won the favour of Czar Nicholas I. In 1831, during the Polish rebellion against Russia, he defeated the insurgents (of whom Disraeli's 'foreigner' was one), but failed to take Warsaw. He died that year in Poland, of cholera.

318 *prigged*. Stolen.

318 *quid*. A piece of tobacco for chewing.

322 *National Holiday*. National strike.

323 *before their new Police Act is in force*. Lord John Russell established county and district constabularies as a direct result of

rioting in the north of England in 1839. Disraeli violently opposed Russell's statute. Police Bills were passed for Birmingham, Manchester, and Bolton after the riots in July 1839, but the new police Act took some time to come into regular operation.

323 *White Conduit House.* The popular and somewhat disreputable tea-garden, tavern, and ball-room in Pentonville, described in 1833 as 'that paradise of apprentice boys'. It was demolished in 1849; its name derives from an old stone conduit. The Chartists would have met in the field opposite White Conduit House. David Large suggests that Disraeli's reference to the place emphasizes Maclast's militancy in view of the fact that the National Union of the Working Classes projected a similar meeting in the same field in November 1831 to demonstrate for manhood suffrage in resistance to the Whig Reform Bill. But the government prohibited it and, in readiness for violence, called up special constables and maintained extra guards on the prisons. The middle-class press represented the intended meeting as likely to be that of an armed mob. The NUWC sent a deputation of protest at the ban to Melbourne, the Home Secretary, but without success, and the meeting was called off.

323 *Kennington Common.* This was to be the site of the last big Chartist meeting on 10 April 1848, preceding Feargus O'Connor's bungled presentation of the third National Petition to the House of Commons.

324 *broadside.* A large sheet of paper printed on one side only.

324 *John Frost.* The Chartist leader (d. 1877), living in Newport, Monmouthshire; in 1838 he was elected as the Monmouthshire delegate at the National Convention, held in 1839. He was one of the leaders of the Newport Rising in November 1839 and sentenced to be executed. Because of differences of opinion among the judges the sentence was commuted to transportation. He was fifteen years in Van Diemen's Land, but was given a free pardon in 1856 and returned to England.

330 *Dick Curtis and Dutch Sam.* Thom Braun suggests that they are pugilists, and points out that Dutch Sam is mentioned with Tom Molineaux, the boxer (1784–1818) in Thackeray's *Vanity Fair*, Chapter 34: 'the different pugilistic qualities of Molyneux and Dutch Sam'.

330 *slang taverns.* Low taverns.

334 *New Police.* The London police force brought into being by Robert Peel's Act in 1829.

335 *a tick for herrings.* 'Tick' is an abbreviation of 'ticket', that is, a tradesman's bill, written on a slip of paper or card, and so 'credit', 'debt'.

336 *go to my uncle's.* Go to the pawnbroker.

BOOK VI

346 *British income-tax.* First introduced in Britain as a war tax in 1799, reintroduced in 1842, and maintained ever since.

354 *pool of Bethesda.* The pool with the power of healing in Jerusalem, see John 5 : 2–4. 'Bethesda' means 'house of mercy'.

354 *Sun.* The liberal newspaper which began publication in 1792.

354 *the Dispatch.* The *Weekly Dispatch*, the liberal newspaper which began publication in 1801.

354 *Bell's Life. Bell's Life in London*, the sporting daily paper which began publication in 1822.

355 *Mowbray Staty.* The statute fair, where the annual hiring of servants and farm-hands would take place, and the occasion of shows, stalls, and merrymaking.

361 *Anti-Corn-law League.* The corn laws had aroused great controversy. The 1815 Act allowed foreign corn to be imported only when home-grown corn reached the high price of 80s. a quarter (i.e. eight bushels); in 1822 this Act was amended, and in 1828 a sliding scale of import duties was introduced, based on home prices. The Anti-Corn-Law League was founded in Manchester in 1839, and led the crusade to repeal protection. Its leaders, especially Richard Cobden, believed that the industrial depression could be overcome by stimulating international trade, and that the import of foreign corn would increase the ability of corn-exporting countries to purchase British manufactures. Landlords were to lose their special social and political power, and farmers were to learn to behave like business men. The Leaguers offered the hope of cheap bread to the working classes. Peel repealed the corn laws in 1846; the repeal came into full effect in 1849.

366 *Benefit Societies, the Sick and Burial Clubs.* Insurance societies providing money in times of sickness and to defray funeral expenses, thereby avoiding the ignominy of a pauper burial.

368 *the friezecoats.* 'Frieze' is Irish coarse woollen cloth, so Irishmen.

370 *se'nnight.* A week (seven nights).

373 *the Five Points.* The London Working Men's Association, founded by William Lovett in 1836, devised the five points to

secure equal political and social rights: (1) universal male suffrage; (2) equal electoral districts; (3) annual Parliaments; (4) secret ballot; (5) no property qualifications for MPs. When the People's Charter was drafted in London and formally presented at the Birmingham meeting in August 1838, it consisted of these five points plus the stipulation of payment of MPs, so the Charter had six points. Carlyle refers to 'the five points' in *Chartism*, Ch. 6. (All the 'points', except annual parliaments, have since been incorporated into the British parliamentary system.)

374 *the Pilgrimage of Grace*. The name assumed by the religious insurgents in the North of England who opposed the dissolution of the monasteries. After the beginnings of the movement were suppressed in Lincolnshire in 1536, it revived in Yorkshire, and an expedition carrying banners depicting the five wounds of Christ was led by Robert Aske, of an old Yorkshire family, and other gentlemen. It was joined by priests, and 40,000 men largely from Yorkshire, Durham, and Lancashire. They took Hull and York. The Duke of Norfolk marched against them, made terms with them, and dispersed them. Early in 1537 they again took arms, but were suppressed and the leaders executed.

381 *march of mind*. The advance or progress of knowledge. A common catch phrase of the period between 1827, when Henry Brougham published the full prospectus of the Society for the Diffusion of Useful Knowledge, and 1850. The Society began to publish a series of treatises, the Library of Useful Knowledge, in 1827. Many of the Society's committee were Whig MPs; the Vice-President was Lord John Russell. Thomas Love Peacock satirizes the SDUK as the Steam Intellect Society in *Crotchet Castle* (1831), Ch. 2, entitled 'The March of Mind'.

381 *Congo*. A kind of black tea imported from China.

384 *Savings Banks*. The working men's benefit clubs having accumulated stocks of money, a plan was adopted to identify these funds with the public debt of the country, and an extra rate of interest was held out as an inducement; hence savings banks were formed to accept small sums, returnable with interest on demand. The Rt. Hon. George Rose developed the scheme and brought it under parliamentary control in 1816.

384 *the Ancient Shepherds*. Obviously a friendly society, presumably fictitious, on the lines of the Ancient Order of Foresters. See Henry Mayhew: 'There are numerous benefit-clubs made up

of working men of every description, such as Old Friends, Odd Fellows, Foresters' (*London Labour and the London Poor*, 2 (1851), 178).

385 *biggin*. Coffee-pot with a strainer.

393 *younker*. A youngster.

394 *dout*. Put out.

399 *George the Fourth . . . emancipation of the Roman Catholics*. After much havering but finally yielding to persuasion by Wellington and Peel, George IV in 1829 assented to the Catholic Emancipation Act, which repealed all the penal laws subjecting Roman Catholics to civil disabilities.

American Literature

British and Irish Literature

Children's Literature

Classics and Ancient Literature

Colonial Literature

Eastern Literature

European Literature

History

Medieval Literature

Oxford English Drama

Poetry

Philosophy

Politics

Religion

The Oxford Shakespeare

A complete list of Oxford Paperbacks, including Oxford World's Classics, OPUS, Past Masters, Oxford Authors, Oxford Shakespeare, Oxford Drama, and Oxford Paperback Reference, is available in the UK from the Academic Division Publicity Department, Oxford University Press, Great Clarendon Street, Oxford OX2 6DP.

In the USA, complete lists are available from the Paperbacks Marketing Manager, Oxford University Press, 198 Madison Avenue, New York, NY 10016.

Oxford Paperbacks are available from all good bookshops. In case of difficulty, customers in the UK can order direct from Oxford University Press Bookshop, Freepost, 116 High Street, Oxford OX1 4BR, enclosing full payment. Please add 10 per cent of published price for postage and packing.